Getting Your Book Published For Dummies®

Cheat Sheet

Elements of a Great Query Letter

- Runs one page — never longer
- Contains no errors — typing, spelling, punctuation, and grammar
- Gets immediately to the point
- Appears on good quality paper
- Is upbeat in tone and style

Add Value to Your Book

- Obtain celebrity endorsements
- Use a foreword written by a well-known expert or celebrity
- Associate your book with a recognized brand name
- Attach a coupon, a CD-ROM, or another product

Creating a Best-Selling Title

- Keep it brief
- Imply a benefit
- Crystallize a wish
- Promise fulfillment
- Create an "aha" for the reader
- Be provocative

Submission Strategies That Work

- Network to meet editors
- Send your proposal to a well-chosen editor
- Cold-call a highly recommended editor
- Send a great query letter to the editor
- Create a subtle but engaging package for your proposal
- Use a literary agent

What an Agent Can Do for You

- Helps shape your proposal
- Targets the right editor
- Establishes instant credibility
- Helps prepare sample materials
- Uses influence with the publisher
- Generates excitement among publishers
- Sets the appropriate price for your work
- Acts as your advocate throughout

For Dummies: Bestselling Book Series for Beginners

Getting Your Book Published For Dummies®

Elements of a Successful Nonfiction Book Proposal

Cover page: Contains the title, author byline, and contact information

Proposal contents: Gives an overview of the entire proposal

The hook: Offers a brief, tantalizing look at what's unique about the book

The market: Identifies the book's specific audience and how to reach it

About the book: Gives a detailed description of the book including special features and benefits

The competition: Shows how your book fills a void in the market

About the author: Presents yourself in the best possible light

Table of contents: Is the blueprint of your book

Chapter summaries and sample chapter: Highlight important components and showcase your writing

Production specifications: Details the length, format, illustrations, and delivery date

Promotion and marketing: Outlines a plan for selling your book

Attachments: Includes newspaper and magazine clippings on you or your book's topic

Finding the Right Editor for Your Book

- Read acknowledgment pages of books similar to yours — authors often acknowledge their editor's contribution
- Scour press coverage of books you admire for the editor's name
- Go to writers' conferences and/or conventions and network
- Call the company that published a book similar to yours and ask who the editor is

Item 5257-0.
For more information about Wiley Publishing, call 1-800-762-2974.

Praise for Getting Your Book Published For Dummies:

"*Getting Your Book Published For Dummies* is an excellent common sense guide, filled with inspiring anecdotes, that holds your hand all along the sometimes rocky road to publication. Both authoritative and encouraging, it is written by two highly qualified people who have sat on both sides of the editor's desk."

— Vicki Bijur, President, AAR, Association of Authors' Representatives, Inc.

"The authors know their stuff. This book is the clearest map to book publishing you'll find. I've recommended it to a dozen people so far."

— Scott Adams, Creator of Dilbert

"Dig your well before you're thirsty, and before you write your first book, don't just read *Getting Your Book Published For Dummies* . . . study it!"

— Harvey Mackay, Author of *Swim With The Sharks: Without Being Eaten Alive, Dig Your Well Before You're Thirsty,* and *Pushing the Envelope*

"This book is a must-read for any aspiring professional writer."

— Peter Maas, Author of *Underboss* and *The Terrible Hours*

"By writing this excellent book, Sarah and Adrian Zackheim have demystified the process of getting a book published. This is the right book by the right authors, and I recommend it to everyone seriously interested in getting your book published."

— Lawrence P. Ashmead, Vice President and Executive Editor, HarperCollins Publishers

"*Getting Your Book Published For Dummies* is an easy read. It's insightful and pleasantly helpful to those aspiring writers who want their message to be heard."

— Ken Blanchard, Co-author of *The One Minute Manager* and *Leadership by the Book*

"The road to published work is paved with vital questions, some that must be answered before that opening line is typed. This hugely informative book presents all the aspiring author needs to know in one stimulating volume, clearing the barriers to beginning that bestseller!"

— Stephen Horn, Author of *In Her Defense*

Getting Your Book Published FOR DUMMIES®

by Sarah Parsons Zackheim
with Adrian Zackheim

Foreword by Nelson DeMille

Wiley Publishing, Inc.

Getting Your Book Published For Dummies®

Published by
Wiley Publishing, Inc.
909 Third Avenue
New York, NY 10022
www.wiley.com

For general information on our other products and services or to obtain technical support, please contact our Customer Care Department within the U.S. at 800-762-2974, outside the U.S. at 317-572-3993, or fax 317-572-4002.

Wiley also publishes its books in a variety of electronic formats. Some content that appears in print may not be available in electronic books.

Library of Congress Cataloging-in-Publication Data:

Library of Congress Control Number.: 00-103366

ISBN: 0-7645-5257-0

Manufactured in the United States of America

10 9 8 7 6

1B/SS/QY/QS/IN

About the Authors

Sarah Parsons Zackheim worked in book publishing for nearly a decade before becoming a widely published freelance writer. Her tenure at several New York publishing firms, including Doubleday, New York Times Books, and William Morrow, provided invaluable insights as to exactly what publishers look for in submission materials. Ms. Zackheim has written four books as well as numerous articles for such magazines as *Family Fun*, *Family Life*, and *Fairfield County*. Acting as her own literary agent, she placed her third book with Three Rivers Press/Clarkson Potter for a six-figure advance.

Adrian Zackheim is currently Associate Publisher of the General Books Group at HarperCollins Publishers and Editor in Chief of HarperInformation. He began his publishing career in the promotion department at G.P. Putnam's Sons in 1975 and since then has worked as an editor of fiction and nonfiction at St. Martin's Press, Doubleday, William Morrow, and HarperCollins. *Getting Your Book Published For Dummies* is his first book.

The Zackheims live in Westport, Connecticut, with their two sons.

Dedication

To Alex Zackheim and David Parsons Zackheim — two extraordinarily wise and talented young men. Their amazing resilience inspires me to keep writing, keep submitting, and keep getting published.

Thanks, guys! This one's for you.

Author's Acknowledgments

The creation of a book takes more than just one person, and I'd like to thank all of the people who had a part in bringing this book to life: Susan Halligan for the initial recommendation, IMG agent Mark Reiter whose persistence paid off, acquiring editor Tami Booth, project editor extraordinaire Kelly Ewing, acquisitions editor Karen Young, and the talented Betsy Lerner who has faithfully read the entire book for accuracy. Last, but far from least, my partner in more than just the creation of this book, Adrian Zackheim, who has weathered many long days and nights at my side.

While to outsiders the world of book publishing may seem like an insular club of insensitive intellectuals who think nothing of firing off rejection letters, I can assure you that notion couldn't be farther from the truth. From the moment I stepped into my first publishing job as an assistant in the promotion department at Doubleday & Company, I have had the good fortune to work with, meet socially, and get to know some of the kindest, smartest, most interesting people imaginable — and all of them love books! Thank you, all of you!

Nicholas Latimer, Lisa Drew, Alex Hoyt, Susan Knopf, David and Nancy Gernert, Bill Barry, Shaye Arehart, Nancy Tuckerman, Kate Medina, Sally Arteseros, Sam Vaughan, Ken Lang, Hugh and Betsy Howard, John and Judy Coyne, Jack and Karen McKeown, Vicky Bijur and Ed Levine, John Sargeant Jr., Kathleen Maloney and Dominick Abel, Elisabeth Scharlatt, Jonathon Segal, Ruth Fecych, Larry Hughes, Juris Jurjevics, Pam Altschul, Adrienne Ingram, Jody Hotchkiss, Joni Evans, Wayne Kabak, Merrilee Heifetz and Brian DeFiore, Laureen Rowland, Liza Dawson, Roger Cooper, Sandy Dijkstra, Molly Friedrich, Joy Harris, Paul Bresnick, Carol Mann, Jim Fitzgerald, Helen Rees, Rafe Sagalyn, Larry Norton, Kim Witherspoon, Diane Reverand, Frank Albanese, Larry Ashmead, Jim Fox, Richard Cariello, Beverly Crilley, Lisa Herling, Dan Halpern, Cathy Hemming, Jane Friedman, Mark Gompertz, Dan Farley, Roger Scholl, Steve Ross, Jacques de Spoelberch, Pam Krauss, Lorraine Shanley, Connie Sayer, Mary Ellen Curley, Edwin Tan, Lisa Berkowitz, Steven Sorrentino, Susan Weinberg, Marjorie Braman, Janet Dery, Kirsten Sandburg, Michael Morrison, David Steinberger, Megan Will, and my favorite Italian publisher (and dear friend) Marcella Marini.

Publisher's Acknowledgments

We're proud of this book; please send us your comments through our online registration form located at www.dummies.com/register.

Some of the people who helped bring this book to market include the following:

Acquisitions, Editorial, and Media Development

Project Editor: Kelly Ewing

Associate Acquisitions Editor: Karen S. Young

Acquisitions Coordinator: Lisa Roule

General Reviewer: Betsy Lerner

Editorial Director: Kristin A. Cocks

Editorial Coordinator: Michelle Hacker

Production

Project Coordinator: Maridee Ennis

Layout and Graphics: , Amy Adrian, Matt Coleman, Brian Torwelle, Tracy K. Oliver, Jill Piscitelli, Brent Savage, Brandon Yarwood, Erin Zeltner

Proofreaders: Corey Bowen, John Greenough, Susan Moritz, Marianne Santy, Charles Spencer

Indexer: Janet Perlman

Special Help

Amanda M. Foxworth

Publishing and Editorial for Consumer Dummies

Diane Graves Steele, Vice President and Publisher, Consumer Dummies
Joyce Pepple, Acquisitions Director, Consumer Dummies
Kristin A. Cocks, Product Development Director, Consumer Dummies
Michael Spring, Vice President and Publisher, Travel
Brice Gosnell, Publishing Director, Travel
Suzanne Jannetta, Editorial Director, Travel

Publishing for Technology Dummies

Richard Swadley, Vice President and Executive Group Publisher
Andy Cummings, Vice President and Publisher

Composition Services

Gerry Fahey, Vice President of Production Services
Debbie Stailey, Director of Composition Services

Contents at a Glance

Cartoons at a Glance

By Rich Tennant

"I'm not sure 'Stormy Night Publishers' are the right people to handle my cookbook. They're telling me there's not enough dramatic tension between my fish and hors d'oeuvres."

page 115

"Someone want to look at this manuscript I received on e-mail called, 'The Embedded Virus That Destroyed the Publisher's Servers When the Manuscript was Rejected'?"

page 77

"The margins on your book proposal are sooo even, Ms. Holly, and the type so black and crisp. I'm sure whatever the book's about is also good, but with centered headlines and flush left columns like this, we'd be fools not to publish it!"

page 61

page 7

"If you must know, the reason you're not in any of my novels is that you're not a believable character."

page 325

"Your new book, 'Help-My Head's Caught in a Pipe,' has been called by some to be semi-autobiographical. Can you comment on these rumors?"

page 269

"It's an interesting autobiography, Mr. MacDonald. But it needs some editing. For instance — you've got a 'quack quack' here, and a 'quack quack' there, here a 'quack', there a 'quack'..."

page 227

Fax: 978-546-7747
E-mail: richtennant@the5thwave.com
World Wide Web: www.the5thwave.com

Table of Contents

Foreword

As a best-selling author, I get hundreds of letters a year from readers regarding my novels. At least a third of those letter writers ask me to read their manuscripts, help them find an agent or publisher, or simply ask the question: How do I get published?

My own history is no guide to getting published — I was just lucky and talented.

When I first started writing in 1974, there were few "How to Get Published" books on the market, and, in retrospect, the ones I read didn't help much.

Nevertheless, when I get requests for help, I usually answer by saying, "Go to your bookstore or library and find a book on the subject."

There was no specific book I could recommend. Until now. *Getting Your Book Published For Dummies* may be the one totally reader-friendly, comprehensive, and actually useful book on a very difficult and sometimes emotional subject.

I've been in the writing business for over 25 years, yet, as I read this book, I actually learned some new things, especially in the section titled The Part of Tens. Thus, this book can be extremely useful to published authors and could be called *Getting Your Book Published Right For Dummies.*

And if, God forbid, I was starting all over again, this book would be my bible.

I especially enjoyed the clean and open format of the presentation as well as the crisp, concise, and clear writing. Referencing is easy, and the advice is straightforward, without either talking down to the reader, or presupposing any knowledge of publishing jargon.

This is a book that, I suspect, will be bought not only *by* the aspiring writer, but *for* the aspiring writer. If other authors get as many questions as I do from friends and family about how to get published, they can arm themselves with this book and hand it to the friend or relative and say, "Read this."

For less close acquaintances, I would recommend, "Go out and buy *Getting Your Book Published For Dummies*."

Rarely does a book become an instant standard in its field, and rarely does a book say the things you would say about a subject you know well, and more rarely will a book say it all — plus some — in such an engaging way.

After reading *Getting Your Book Published For Dummies*, I felt as though someone had organized my thoughts for me and said what I would say to a good friend who needed my help getting published.

Nelson DeMille

Introduction

In 1999, more than 60,000 new titles were registered for copyright with the Library of Congress. Sixty thousand books by 60,000 authors. Next year, your book could be one of them. Imagine walking into a bookstore and seeing your name emblazoned on the jacket of a published book.

No one is born published. In fact, you have the same chance as the next person at getting your book into print. You just need to know how to make the publishing "system" work in your favor. As you might imagine, publishing has its own terminology, strategies, and conventions. In this book, I tell you what they are and how to work them to your advantage.

About This Book

This book is a tool intended to help previously unpublished authors get their books published. It's aimed at a broad range of writers, from absolute beginners who have only daydreamed about writing a book, to dedicated novelists who have already completed one manuscript or even more. For all of you, and everyone in between, I offer a wealth of advice about how to move toward making your unpublished book a published reality.

Many of the world's most successful writers wish a book like this one had been available when they were starting out. Pat Conroy, for example, would have saved some trouble for himself nearly 30 years ago when, at the age of 24, he sent the manuscript for his first book, *The Water is Wide* (Houghton-Mifflin, 1972), to his literary agent, Julian Bach. Bach sent the manuscript to dozens of publishers, and Conroy had almost given up hope when a call from Bach came out of the blue. "Pat, I have great news for you. It's Houghton-Mifflin for $7,500."

The novelist was thoughtful for a few moments and said, "But Julian, I couldn't possibly afford that."

Today, most writers expect to be paid for their work.

But the market for adult fiction and nonfiction — which is what this book covers — is a competitive place. To thrive, you need to understand how the business works from the inside.

And that's exactly what I provide. I share my personal experience of placing four of my own books with major publishers — two of them without the help of a literary agent. I also enlist the insight of dozens of publishing insiders — agents, authors, editors, and other professionals — to show you how to make all the right moves: from coming up with a salable idea, placing it in front of the right editor, negotiating an advantageous publishing contract, and guaranteeing you the best possible publishing experience.

How to Use This Book

This book is a reference guide for anyone who wants to get published. You don't need to read it from cover to cover. But if you do, it can work as a step-by-step guide to every stage of the publishing process: from the very beginning, when you decide to write a book and brainstorm book ideas, right up to helping your publisher market your book.

However, you can also read the book selectively, focusing only on the material that is helpful to you. The stages of the writing and publishing process are each covered in a part of the book, and each chapter breaks the stages into easy action steps that you can take to move your book from idea to proposal, to publishing deal, and so on. Browse the first few lines of each chapter and decide whether it applies to you. If not, just skip ahead to find the exact information you need. You can also locate answers to specific questions by searching the index at the back of the book.

Instead of relying solely on my own experience, I have assembled a collection of anecdotes and examples that offer several lifetimes worth of insight and wisdom from editors, publishers, and successful writers. The result is a road map through the publishing maze that can make your journey fun and profitable.

How This Book is Organized

This book is organized into seven parts.

Part I: Getting Started

Every book starts with an idea and builds from there. This part gets at your core book idea. What sort of book is inside you? What motivates you to write? How do you capture a vague notion and turn it into a book outline? It tells you how to brainstorm ideas, and, once you've narrowed your choices, it helps you evaluate the potential in your idea, develop a procedure for getting the words on paper, and think strategically about how to launch your idea into the world of publishing.

Part II: Knocking on the Publisher's Door

This part is a crash course on the book publishing industry. How does a publishing house work and, more specifically, how is a publisher likely to view your book idea? With that in mind, I show you how to get your book idea in front of the right person to ensure the best outcome.

Part III: Preparing the Package: Book Proposals and Query Letters That Sell

For authors, your tools to break down the doors of publishing are limited. Whether you are famous and well connected or not, you're going to need a killer query letter and a knockout book proposal in order to grab and hold a publisher's attention. In this chapter, you see how to write an effective query letter when prospecting for a fiction or nonfiction submission. Then, once the door is open a crack, I show you how to write the kind of book proposal that sells. I provide examples of effective letters and proposals to help get your efforts on track. And I show you how to master the art of presenting yourself to the greatest possible advantage in these very special forms of writing.

Part IV: Taking it Public: A Strategic Approach to Placing Your Book

With the query letter and proposal drafted, you're ready to go "live." In this part, I share my battle-tested secrets for actually finding an appropriate editor or agent who is likely to respond to your work. I give you the inside skinny on every kind of publishing house, from the giant corporate publishers in New York, to the tiny firms that have been coming on so strong in the last few years. I also describe a range of literary agents, who they are, and what they're likely to do with your book. I give you pointers on how to represent your work directly to publishers, without an agent. (In fact, this route is the only practical way to go for many first-time writers. It worked for me, and it can work for you!) Finally, I talk about alternate routes for getting published when the standard publishing arrangement doesn't seem to fit — book packagers, subsidy presses, and the exploding world of e-books and online publishing.

Part V: Home at Last! Negotiation and Contract

For some writers, negotiating and signing contracts is the fun part. It feels like you're home free. But beware. Most writers have never seen a publisher's contract before they read their own. In this section, I tell what a publisher's offer actually means and how to negotiate to get the best possible deal from a publisher. I also highlight what's important in a publishing contract and what isn't.

Part VI: After the Deal Is Done

In this part, I get specific about how a book is published today and how an author can improve the outcome. You find out what publishers can do and what they can't, or won't. And I show you how an author can be his or her own best advocate in today's crowded media arena.

Part VII: The Part of Tens

Here, I share more tips and insights that improve your odds for a successful publishing outcome — mistakes to avoid when submitting your work to editors and agents, excuses publishers give when turning down your submission and what they *really* mean, errors authors make once their book is in the publishing pipeline, and even a list of top ten bestsellers of all time.

Icons Used in This Book

If there's a hard way and an easier way, this icon marks the easier way.

Note this common blunder.

A nugget of information from a top professional.

If you remember nothing else in this book, please hold on to these points.

A typically difficult place in the process. I mark these so that you know you have plenty of company if this step seems hard.

Where to Go from Here

In purchasing this book, you have taken an important step toward realizing your goal. Congratulations. You probably already have a few book ideas, and you'd like to start thinking about whether one or more of them can be developed into a book. If so, skip Chapter 1 and move right on to Chapter 2. If you want suggestions on how to brainstorm ideas or fit your thoughts together into a potent book idea, jump right in to Chapter 1. Look within yourself and find the idea that will take your first book from the screen of your computer to the shelf of your nearest Barnes & Noble.

Part I
Getting Started

In this part . . .

A book begins as an idea and builds from there. In this part, you find out where book ideas come from and how to spot a good one when you see it. I clue you in to the important criteria publishers use to evaluate whether your idea has book potential and how best to get your idea on paper.

Chapter 1

The Idea. It's the Heart of Your Book

In This Chapter

- Finding the writer in you
- Opening yourself to inspiration
- Choosing a book idea

There's never been a better time to be an author. Book sales are increasing, and more books, by a broader range of authors than ever before in history, are available. Bookstores are proliferating, from malls, to giant superstores, to the book tables at warehouse clubs and mass merchants. Internet book sales are exploding. And celebrities, like Oprah Winfrey with her televised book club, are making reading the "in thing."

So go ahead. Take the first step to being a published writer. Look inside yourself (or out) for that gem of an idea that sparks a new book. You may already have an idea that's been germinating. If so, skip ahead to Chapter 2. Otherwise, I show you how to spot potential book ideas. The trick is being open to all you read, see, and hear (or overhear). And, it helps to look honestly at what your reasons are for wanting to become a published author.

Three Main Reasons to Get Published

Some first-time authors are instant celebrities and millionaires to boot. You see them interviewed on TV and think, "Hey, I can write a book like that." And you're probably right. The only difference is, they've done it. Now it's your turn.

You need to look at exactly why you want to write a book. Take it from me, writing an entire book is a lot of work. So, what's in it for you?

You have an uncontrollable urge to write

Some people are consumed with an inner need to write. They wake up in the middle of the night compelled to get down thoughts that just can't wait until daylight. Writing is as natural as breathing to these folks. There is simply no stopping it.

While some writers are born with this urge, it can also arise later in life as it did for Stephen King. After marrying Tabitha Spruce, a poet, King began writing at a furious pace. Undeterred by the rejection of three novels and dozens of short stories, King continued to write. Finally, in 1974, Doubleday accepted *Carrie,* a horror novel about a high school girl with frightening telekinetic power. Best-selling books have poured out of him at a prodigious pace ever since.

You have a story to tell

You may have a story inside that's bursting to get out. In fact, it can sometimes feel as if the characters are coming to life on paper and all you're doing is holding the pen! After retiring from his job as a New York City schoolteacher, Frank McCourt sat down to write the harrowing story of his Irish boyhood. Titled *Angela's Ashes* (Scribner, 1996), his book won the National Book Critics Circle Award, The Los Angeles Times Book Award, and the Pulitzer Prize. It also became a #1 New York Times Bestseller, which goes to show that some stories just need to be told.

You're an expert

You may want to help others lead a more successful or fulfilling life by sharing your expertise. Whether it's stress control as prescribed in Richard Carlson's *Don't Sweat the Small Stuff* (Hyperion, 1997) or a list of success skills like those Stephen R. Covey gives us in *The 7 Habits of Highly Effective People,* the market for how-to information is limitless. If your topic has wide enough appeal, you may just hit it big.

As an added bonus, writing a book on your area of expertise might provide that extra boost to your business — making you a household name. It worked for Martha Stewart who started as a caterer in Westport, Connecticut, before writing *Entertaining* (Crown Publishing, 1982). And for John Gray, a monk turned psychologist who used his ideas about resolving the natural differences between men and women in his marital therapy practice. Then he wrote *Men Are From Mars, Women Are From Venus* (HarperCollins, 1992), and the rest is history.

Ideas Are All Around You

So you know you want to write a book — you just don't know what you want to write about. For many people, it's not uncommon to think that you need to write about something exotic or different or strange — that the familiar just could not be appealing to readers. But the opposite is often true. Writing, after all, is a form of understanding; you write best about things you know best. What seems familiar to you might seem very exotic to your reader. Your perception of a familiar truth might trigger insight and pleasure in your readers. And countless books — not to mention countless bestsellers — have been written about the most ordinary details of the most ordinary lives.

Start with what you know

What you know, before you do a minute's research, is the best place to start your idea search. Pay close attention to common, everyday experiences, whether at home or at work. What may seem drab or ordinary on the surface might actually be a book in disguise.

Job experience

Scott Adams, a middle manager for a large phone company in California, discovered that the drab and ordinary wasn't so dull after all. As an aspiring cartoonist, he jotted down notes on the interactions he saw at work during the day and turned them into cartoons at night. Today, Scott's cartoon strip, *Dilbert,* appears in over 2,000 newspapers worldwide and his books, *The Dilbert Principle* (HarperBusiness, 1996), *Dogbert's Top Secret Management Handbook* (HarperBusiness, 1996), and *The Dilbert Future* (HarperBusiness, 1997), which depict the reality of life in the office, have sold millions of copies.

Likewise, Michael Lewis kept his eyes and ears open while working at Solomon Brothers, an investment bank in New York City. While thousands of others enjoyed the same access to the trading floor that Lewis did, it was Lewis who had the vision to see a story in the life of a New York City trader. While the tale played itself out right before his eyes, Lewis wrote it all down in *Liar's Poker* (W. W. Norton, 1989), which became an immediate runaway bestseller. Writing what he saw on the job launched Lewis into a whole new career. He hasn't set foot on the trading floor since.

Hobbies

If it fascinates you, no doubt it interests others, too. So when you're looking for book ideas, think long and hard about your hobby. Whether it's helicopter skiing or collecting first edition books, your prospects are better if you know and care deeply about what you write. Your passion may prove inspirational to readers.

Look inside for inspiration

If you don't know what you want to write about, think about the following questions.

What do you wish you had more time for?

If you could take a year off with full pay, what would you do?

What are you most curious about?

What do you devote the majority of your time and attention to?

What event do you look most forward to?

Do people consistently ask you for advice on a specific topic?

What are your pet issues?

What do you think about when you allow your mind to wander?

Which personal experiences do people often ask you about?

What is your biggest concern?

And whatever aspect of a hobby you find most interesting is the way to slant your book idea. Say, for example, that baseball is your passion. You could write a reference guide (*Baseball by the Rules,* by Glenn Waggoner, Taylor, 1987), a how-to (*The Art of Hitting,* by Tony Gwynn, Good Times Publishing, 1988), a specialized guide (*The Sports Fans Guide to America,* by Mike Tulumello, Longstreet Press, 1999), general information (*Total Baseball,* by John Thorn, et al., Total Sports, 1999), or moneymaking ideas for how to bet on your local team's games (*Baseball Insight Annual* by Phil Erwin, Parrish Publications, 1999). Just make sure that the topic works for you.

Advertising executive Ed Levine toiled with clients by day and shopped for food and drink by night. Among his friends, Ed was the man in the know if you wanted an exotic ingredient or were in search of the best barbecue or croissant or egg cream. Food may not have been Ed's job, but it was his life! Friends repeatedly told Ed that he could write the book on New York food. In 1992, he did just that. *New York Eats* published by St. Martin's Press is the bible of food in New York. Totally updated with 200 new entries in 1997, *New York Eats (More)* was runner-up for the prestigious Julia Child Reference Book Award, further establishing Ed as a fixture in the New York food world. And today, advertising is a distant memory.

Personal experience

Your own personal experience can be a great place to start your search for a book idea. After all, you're the *only* expert on this topic. Your life experience is unique to you; no one else has encountered exactly what you have. Your style, thoughts, opinions, attitudes, and desires are also unique.

Many successful first-time book authors have gone this route. Take Frances Mayes, for example, a professor at San Francisco State University, who along with her husband fell in love with an abandoned old villa in Tuscany. Together, they purchased the place, completely renovated it, and discovered the joys of another culture. All the while, Mayes kept a personal record of the experience. This memoir, titled *Under The Tuscan Sun,* was published in 1996 by Chronicle Books. And even though many other books have been published about buying and remodeling run-down houses in sunny foreign countries, *Under the Tuscan Sun* became a bestseller. The book was very well timed, as it was published shortly after *A Year in Provence* (Knopf, 1990) by Peter Mayle had rocketed to the top of the bestseller lists. Like Mayle's book, *Under the Tuscan Sun* was a voluptuous and witty celebration of food, people, and glorious places — Mayes keen, compelling observations brought Tuscany vividly alive for millions. (See Chapter 2 for more on the importance of timing.)

Before the birth of my two sons, I immersed myself in the research of names, from the most common to the absurdly obscure, including meanings, derivations, connotations, and more. After choosing to name our first son Adrian after my husband and deciding on the classic name David for our second, I realized I had to write a baby name book with all the information I had collected. So was born my first book, *Choose the Perfect Name for Your Baby,* (Walden Books, 1992). Unlike other baby name books, mine included entertaining sidebars. These, alongside the 10,000 names, made the book fun to read as well as thought provoking. By writing it myself, I was able to create the exact baby name book I had looked for, and I was certain others would enjoy it, too.

Indulge a passion

What you care most about, whether it's belly dancing or growing your own herbs, is likely to lead you to a publishable book idea. And what's better than getting paid to revel in the pastime you love?

Andres Martinez, a young journalist, turned his passion for gambling into a book. On the strength of a brilliant proposal, he persuaded Villard Books to advance him $50,000 with the understanding that he would wager all of it in Las Vegas and then write about the experience. The result, after wagering every penny and walking away with only $5,000 in winnings, is a book titled *24/7,* published in November 1999. (See Chapter 8 for more on how to write a proposal.)

Take classes

Taking classes of any kind is always a good idea — it can expose you to new influences, a new outlook, and also potential book ideas. David Denby, a movie critic for *The New Yorker* magazine, was inspired at the age of 48 to re-enroll at his alma mater, Columbia University, and repeat two core curriculum classes: Literature Humanities and Contemporary Civilization. He read what the students read and kept careful notes of his reactions — not only to the classics (he loved them all over again) but to the teachers, the students, the process of education, even the events in his own life while attending school. The result was *Great Books* (Simon & Schuster, 1996) — by no means Denby's first published work, but definitely his first *New York Times* bestseller.

Identify a need

The old business axiom, "find a need and fill it," is alive and well in the world of book publishing. Diet books like *The Carbohydrate Addict's Diet* (Rachel and Richard Heller, NAL, 1993) or exercise books like *Body for Life* (Bill Philips, HarperCollins, 1999) or lifestyle books like *The Art of Happiness* (The Dalai Lama, Riverhead, 1999) are filling a big need as you can tell by their extended stay on the New York Times Bestseller List.

Look around and see what need you can fill. Timeliness is key. Take John Kilcullen, who during the early days of personal computers noticed that computer manuals were almost impossible to understand for a nonengineer. As desktop computers became more and more powerful, he recognized the need for easy-to-read manuals written for the lay person. So came the brilliant idea of writing a comprehensive manual for DOS, a popular computer program, in lay language, aimed at nonengineers and nonexperts (dummies). *DOS For Dummies* by Dan Gookin (IDG Books Worldwide, Inc.) was the beginning of a string of similar bestsellers and eventually the establishment of a huge publishing empire. IDG is also the publisher of this book.

Collect fascinating information and tidbits and create a book

Are your drawers bulging with favorite articles and clippings of references on your hobby or pet subject? If so, you may be on the road to writing a bestselling book. That's what happened to Sarah Ban Breathnach, whose first two books on Victorian family life didn't exactly set the world on fire.

While living the life of a writer and full-time mother in suburban Maryland, her stressed and scattered existence seemed to catch up with Ban Breathnach. "Life had become an out-of-body experience," she recalls. "I was going so fast from one task to another. I always had the feeling there was my spirit trying to catch up with me. On the surface, I had a polished sheen of success, but inside I felt like the hollow chocolate Easter bunny. If I was pressed too hard, I would crumble."

As Ban Breathnach told the *Toronto Star* in 1996, she was coping. But she wasn't happy. So, she did something about it. Wanting to find out what did make her happy, she stepped back and spent five years thinking, writing, and sorting through a mountain of materials she had accumulated on the subject of leading a simpler life.

Idea resource

If you're short on ideas, try these tips:

Watch television news and talk shows.

Read magazines and newspapers.

Notice emerging trends.

Study the bestseller lists.

Listen to people's concerns.

Surf the Web.

Collect publisher's catalogs.

Open your eyes to what goes on around you.

Case the bookstores.

Check out the government printing office's publications.

The result was *Simple Abundance: A Day Book Of Comfort And Joy* (Warner, 1995), written in the form of a diary full of essays, meditations, and homey advice, along with quotes from historical, literary, and philosophical figures. Serving as a source of inspiration to millions of women, *Simple Abundance* stayed at the top of the bestseller lists for years.

Pay attention to what's happening around you

Many a writing career is launched by a writer's ability to observe life. What's in the news? What's popular on television? What's going on in today's schools? What's happening to family structures? What are the people around you saying and doing? By staying open and aware, you'll find lots of books just waiting to be written.

Newsweek describes Scott Turow as "an extraordinarily canny and empathetic observer." Turow, a best-selling author many times over, uses what he observes as a lawyer to create suspense fiction so authentic, it reads like fact. Indeed, Turow may be one of the most observant writers of his generation. Long before he began writing fiction bestsellers, he wrote a book about his experience as a first-year law student at Harvard University titled *One-L* (Putnam, 1977). This book, also uncannily well observed, became a national bestseller, a law school primer, and a classic in its field.

Do you need to be a world-class observer like Scott Turow to succeed as a writer? Of course not! But his example of dogged observation can serve as an inspiration to generations of writers.

Everything you read contains possible book ideas

Nearly every writer is a reader — of the daily newspaper, at least! Hands down, the daily paper is the best source for great fiction and nonfiction ideas. A quick scan of the bestseller list proves the point.

Take, for example, Sebastian Junger, a part-time lumberjack sidelined by an on-the-job injury. Perhaps because he was feeling a bit sorry for himself, Junger walked the shoreline in Gloucester, Massachusetts, watching the waves as a terrific storm pounded the beach. Imagine being on a fishing boat in that! Junger mused.

Inspired by a newspaper account of the fate of a swordfish boat caught in that storm, the *Andrea Gail,* Junger sold a 50-page article to *Outside Magazine.* Based on that article, W. W. Norton offered Junger a contract to write a book about the *Andrea Gail* and that powerful storm.

And so Sebastian Junger wrote his book about swordfishermen trapped in heavy weather. Since then, *The Perfect Storm* (W. W. Norton, 1997) has ridden the bestseller lists for more than three years!

Study the bestseller lists

The best place to find tomorrow's bestsellers is the place where today's are summarized — the New York Times Bestseller List itself. Savvy authors and publishers know that many books, including huge bestsellers, have been inspired by previous bestsellers.

The success of *The Perfect Storm* (see the preceding section), for example, has now inspired other bestsellers. Linda Greenlaw wrote the first one, about a heroic swordfish captain profiled by Junger in his book and described as "one of the best on the East Coast." Nearly two years later, *The Hungry Ocean* (Little Brown, 1997), Greenlaw's own book, debuted on The New York Times Bestseller List.

The same trend applies to fiction, but to an even greater extent. In the years since the best-selling debuts of John Grisham and Scott Turow, I've seen many legal bestsellers by writers such as Lisa Scottoline, Linda Fairstein, Nancy Taylor Rosenberg, Steve Martini, and Richard North Patterson, all of whom emulated Grisham's and Turow's formula for success.

Best-selling success begets best-selling success. It's well worth your time as a writer to study the bestseller list and think carefully about the patterns. Publishers are always looking for original ideas that bear an encouraging similarity to proven bestsellers — and finding an idea that tracks a best-selling trend could greatly improve your chances of landing a contract.

Chapter 2

Evaluating Your Idea

In This Chapter

- Determining whether your great idea is a *book* idea
- Identifying your audience
- Delivering bankable value
- Facing your competition head on
- Being in the right place at the right time

Eureka! Your brainstorming session has kicked out a quality idea. Maybe it's a notion you've been carrying around for a decade, or perhaps you've only slept on it for a night or two. No matter. Before you invest further effort in development, find out whether you have a great *book* idea.

Additionally, your idea must sustain a book-length work, deliver dollar value to a well-defined audience, and face stiff competition from similar books already on the market. If appropriate, you also want to time your book effectively in order to benefit from events taking place in the world.

Is It a Book, a Magazine Article, or an Encyclopedia?

First, think conceptually about what a *book* is — a core idea broken down into subordinate ideas or chapters. A typical book of, say, 200 to 400 double-spaced pages, or 60,000 to 100,000 words, includes approximately 20 chapters of 10 to 20 pages each — roughly the organization of the book you're reading right now, although books can be organized in many different ways.

If your core idea can be fully developed in a single chapter or two, chances are it won't sustain the scope of a whole book. Consider writing an article or a short story. On the other hand, if your idea warrants dozens of chapters, you may be hatching an encyclopedic work, or even a series of books.

Many aspiring writers think they have a book idea in the making, and are disappointed to discover that their idea is really an article. For example, HarperCollins editor Larry Ashmead describes a book proposal he recently received. "The writer proposed traveling through the Louisiana Cajun country in a motorboat, sampling backcountry restaurants. I think it's a great idea for an article in *Southern Living* or *Bon Appétit*. But I didn't see it as a book."

The Cajun motorboat idea might be a successful regional travel book or, in the hands of a humorist, a comic masterpiece. The distinction between article and book depends as much on how the writer shapes what he or she has to say as on the material itself. You have the power to shape what you write. For example, a writer named Henry Petroski wrote an essay on the history of the humble lead pencil that was published in book form and is now considered a classic, titled *The Pencil* (Knopf, 1992).

The overwhelming majority of nonfiction books are sold on the basis of a proposal. One of the first and most basic questions editors ask as they evaluate the hundreds of book proposals that cross their desks each year is, "Is this a book or an article?" How they answer that simple question can determine whether an idea is given an opportunity to become a full, publishable book. If an editor decides the idea is too small for a book, then the writer has a choice — either to move onto another idea or write a great article based on the idea. Who knows? The article may draw so much attention that it warrants later development into a book.

As you think about your idea, be sure to ask yourself, "Is there enough here to fill 200 or more typeset pages?"

Any written work, be it book or article, novel or nonfiction work, must have a logical structure, a beginning, middle, and end. There must be a sense of *closure,* or completion, that casts the core idea in a new and more informative light. Unlike an article, a book needs to introduce and develop a new idea in each chapter, and all the chapters must illuminate the core idea. If your core idea doesn't contain the potential to deliver this much freight — if you find yourself attempting to stretch and pad your text even now, in the planning stages — it's definitely time to consider a new idea.

Writing is much more effective and satisfying when you have plenty to write about. Determining whether your idea has enough scope and substance to fill a book is simple — start building an outline. If you have a book-worthy idea, the outline seems to grow naturally, expanding in every direction. You may even find it necessary to limit the narrative breadth of your work in progress. If, on the other hand, your outline begins to peter out quicker than you anticipated, you are probably better off writing an article or finding a new idea.

While formulating a book idea, you must strike a balance between an idea that is too broad and an idea that is too narrow. For example, you may be inspired by the kings and queens of England. Your first impulse is to write a history of the British Royal Family. However, on sober reflection, you realize that this book could run to several thousand pages! On the other hand, you can write about a tiny aspect of the reign of a single king or queen. In this case, your best solution is either a biography of a single ruler, the history of a single family — the Stuarts or the Plantagenets, for example — or a narrower history of the entire sweep: a brief history, a social history, or a military history of the British Crown.

Who Is Your Audience?

Many aspiring authors make the mistake of thinking their book has a huge potential audience: "every intelligent reader," or "all women," or "all mystery fans." This generalization usually isn't true. Most readers are very discriminating; they know what they like and respond only to a book that is tailored to their exact needs and interests.

In order to reach a substantial audience, you need to target large populations of like-minded individuals — senior citizens, Internet users, courtroom drama fans, and so on — and shape your book with their needs and interests in mind.

While there is no exact rule on how big the potential market needs to be to spark interest from a publisher, generally speaking, most publishers must sell at least 5,000 copies of a single title — and preferably more like 10,000 to 20,000 copies — in order to make it worth their while. Hard experience has taught publishers to expect that a book is unlikely to be purchased by more than 5 percent of its target market, which means that a target market of 100,000 potential readers is needed to generate the absolute minimum sales level of 5,000 copies.

Targeting too narrow an audience can be as unsuccessful as aiming too wide. For example, I remember a book that was sponsored at Doubleday's weekly editorial meeting by Jacqueline Onassis in the early 1980s. Jackie enthusiastically presented a manuscript she had received, written by a security expert. The book was packed full of practical advice to help wealthy people protect themselves and their loved ones from kidnapping.

After Jackie finished her pitch for the book, there was an uncomfortable silence. The editor in chief politely explained that the potential market for the book was extremely limited. Back then, only an international celebrity was likely to need such information — and he or she was hardly going to rely on a book for protection from kidnappers.

Less than 20 years later, a similar book, *The Gift of Fear: Survival Signals that Protect us from Violence,* by security consultant Gavin De Becker (Little Brown, 1997), enjoyed an extended run on the New York Times Bestseller List, which only shows how social changes can affect our taste in books. While kidnapping and random acts of violence were rare when Jackie Onassis first presented that book on protection tactics in the early '80s, they are commonplace today, affecting normal civilians and celebrities alike.

Tailor Your Content

The annals of publishing are full of authors who benefited by targeting a very specific audience — really aimed their book at the preferences of an identifiable group — and then succeeded when word of mouth moved their book out into the mainstream.

For example, *The Millionaire Next Door* by Thomas Stanley, Ph.D., and William Danko, Ph.D, was originally published by a small regional publisher (Longstreet Press, 1996), as a realistic look at the attitudes and mindsets of Americans who have amassed a net worth of $1 million or more. The book was the result of a decade of research and data collection conducted by the authors through first-hand interviews, complete with myriad charts and statistics. It was aimed at readers with a strong interest in finance and marketers interested in reaching the wealthy with products and services. But the potential market for this information was much bigger.

Shortly after publication, word of mouth combined with the publisher's marketing efforts brought the book to the attention of its true audience — anyone interested in increasing his or her net worth. TV show producers caught wind of it and after author appearances on "Sixty Minutes" and other network shows, the book flew right up to the top of national bestseller lists.

Another example of this phenomenon is *Midnight in the Garden of Good and Evil: A Savannah Story* by John Berendt (Random House, 1994), which chronicles a notorious murder in the environs of Savannah, Georgia. Originally, the book was expected to appeal to a local, southeastern audience. It did exactly that.

In fact, Berendt's book became one of the biggest bestsellers of the '90s, demonstrating another critical point: Accurate targeting can result in the paradoxical spread of the book far beyond the original target audience. *Midnight in the Garden of Good and Evil* was exquisitely targeted at a narrowly focused readership. But the audience responded so powerfully, and created such far-reaching word of mouth, that the book began to sell outside of the target area, reaching groups of readers whom the author had never considered. Soon, the book enjoyed a huge national readership, major television exposure, and a run on the bestseller list that continued for years.

Deliver Their Money's Worth

Books cost money, and for many consumers, it's an either/or decision — a book or a CD, a book or a DVD. People don't mind parting with money as long as they're getting good value. Next time you're in a bookstore, watch the customers. You'll see shoppers pick up a book from one of the front tables, read the jacket flap approvingly, and then frown and replace the book when they see the price.

Your challenge, as you shape your idea into a book, is to face this issue head on. What can you offer readers that is worth their hard-earned $15 or $25?

Generally, readers buy a novel — and pay the retail price — when they are offered compelling storytelling, memorable characters, and exotic settings. In a work of nonfiction, readers feel they are getting a good deal if a book delivers in at least one of four important ways, which I cover in the following sections.

Fill a need

If you can find a genuine need and fill it, you deliver value to the reader. For example, diet books fill a need shared by millions — the need to shed excess pounds especially after a season of indulgence (Christmas) or before a season of public exposure (June/July). At these times of year especially, diet books fly off the shelves, proving that while the public may occasionally go off sweets, it will never lose its taste for books packed with new tips to help take off pounds.

Books that deliver useful information of all sorts fit into this category, from medical and parenting manuals, to gardening books, cookbooks, computer guides, and even decorating and hobby manuals.

Martha Stewart, for example, saw an opportunity in the area of imaginative food preparation and entertaining. Having run a gourmet food store along with her own catering business in Westport, Connecticut, Martha saw a trend in the making. A food revolution was underway. Suddenly, steak-and-potato Americans took an interest in fine dining. For the first time, four food magazines prospered instead of one, cooking classes were becoming popular, as was travel focused on exotic cuisine. Soon, people would want to bring this revolution into their own homes — into the way they entertained. How better to capitalize on this revolution than to show them how?

As a successful caterer and the wife of a prominent publisher, Martha masterminded lavish parties, many of them to celebrate the publication of books released by her husband's firm. Executives and editors from other publishing houses attended these parties, and at one of her most spectacular events, Alan Merkin, then publisher of Clarkson Potter, suggested that Martha write a book on entertaining in the high style that had become her trademark.

Entertaining was published by Clarkson Potter in 1982, and the rest is history. In just a few short years, Martha Stewart went from a local caterer in Westport, Connecticut, to America's "Diva of Domesticity" — a national expert on entertaining, decorating, and homemade-gift giving. Martha certainly proved that the public would buy a stylish book on a subject that interests them keenly.

Reveal a secret

People love a secret and are more than willing to pay for the inside skinny on almost any topic of interest. For example, in 1988, a former top British Intelligence agent helped write a book that revealed a long-hidden secret. Specifically, he exposed the fourth Soviet Mole, Anthony Blunt, who, along with Kim Philby, Guy Burgess, and Donald Maclean, fatally compromised Western Intelligence in the early days of the Cold War. The resulting book, *Spy Catcher* by Peter Wright (Viking, 1987), revealed so many classified state secrets that it was actually banned under the National Secrets Act in Britain. The British were unable to prevent publication of the book in the United States, where the book was a huge national bestseller.

The public's fascination with secret details is truly insatiable. One major scandal — Monica Lewinsky's dalliance with President Bill Clinton or OJ Simpson's trial — can spawn several bestsellers and a score or more of other books that reach a large audience.

Reinvent the familiar

The public is fascinated by novelty — books that can capture the latest fad are always in hot demand. But novelty can take many forms: writers known and unknown have found success — and a salable book idea — by reworking a familiar subject in a new way. Some good examples are James Finn Garner and his *Politically Correct Bedtime Stories* (Macmillan, 1994); *The Preppie Handbook* by Lisa Bernbach (Workman, 1980); and *The Biology of Star Trek* (HarperCollins, 1999).

Success has even come to writers who revisit a well-worn topic with fresh insight and energy. For example, Naomi Wolf was unknown and unpublished in 1990. Her first book, *The Beauty Myth* (William Morrow, 1991), explored ground that many feminist writers had already broken. She argued that feminine beauty is a male invention that undermines women's intelligence. Wolf's book found a new, younger audience and presented a set of ideas, albeit familiar ideas, with great energy and clarity. Her reward was a ride on the bestseller list and — years later — a role as advisor to Vice President Al Gore.

In the relatively mundane category of baby name books, one latecomer to the category, *Beyond Jennifer And Jason* (Linda Rosencrantz and Pamela Redmond Satran, Workman, 1994), became a category killer by introducing truly original features, like lists of trendy names, popular names, macho names, cool names, and names you want to avoid.

Deliver the unobtainable

People are willing to pay for information they can't get any other way — either useful information they can look up or secret information that they can only imagine.

For example, the public paid handsomely to read the secret conversations of a mobster. The story began in 1983, when two FBI agents, Joseph O'Brien and Andris Kurins, embarked on a two-year investigation of a prominent New York Mafia family, which ultimately placed Paul Castellano, a Mafia Don, behind bars. In the process, the Feds gathered 600 hours of conversations between Castellano and his inner circle. When informed about these amazing conversations, an enterprising publisher at Simon and Schuster — the legendary editor Michael Korda — immediately recognized a bestseller in the making. He reasoned that while the public had seen Mafia Dons in the movies, they'd never actually heard one talk in real life. Korda offered a generous book contract to the two FBI agents and years later, after Castellano's conviction, their book, titled *Boss Of Bosses* (S&S, 1991), was published and rocketed to the top of the bestseller lists.

Specialized information of all kinds can form a book — it need not be as exotic as the pillow talk of a mobster. Compilations of annual baseball statistics culled from the previous season can justify a new publishing contract, as can the prices of last year's postage stamps, the resale value of last year's cars, even the expected annual rainfall and temperature in farm country — just think of the hundreds of thousands of copies of *The Farmer's Almanac* (*The Old Farmer's Almanac 2000*, Thomas B. Hale (Editor) and Robert Bailey Thomas, Villard, 1999) that are sold each year.

What's Your Competition?

No discussion of potential book ideas would be complete without a serious look at your competition. Every good book idea — including the book you are reading right now — must face the competition squarely or perish!

In the mind of your publisher, the "competition" is any book that could attract the buyer's attention instead of your book. Some popular categories are crowded with formidable competition: *The Joy of Cooking* currently titled *The New Joy of Cooking* by Rombauer, Becker, Becker, la Maestro, Maestro, Guarnaschelli (Intro.), (Scribner, 1997) occupies the same shelf as *The New York Times Cookbook* by Craig Claiborne and Pierre Franey, (Times Books, 1979), *The Good Housekeeping Cookbook* by Mildred Ying (Hearst Books, 1988), *Betty Crocker's New Cookbook* (IDG, 1998), *The New Basics Cookbook* by Sheila Lukins and Julee Rosso (Workman, 1989), *The Way to Cook* by Julia Child (Knopf, 1989), and many others.

Likewise, *Dr. Atkins' New Diet Revolution* by Dr. Robert Atkins (Avon, 1997) glares across the aisle at *The Carbohydrate Addict's Diet* by Rachel and Richard Heller (NAL, 1993) and at *Sugar Busters!* by H. Leighton Steward, Morrison C. Bethea, Sam S. Andrews, Ralph O. Brennan, Luis A. Balart (Ballantine, 1998), *The Zone* by Barry Sears and Bill Lawren (ReganBooks/HarperCollins, 1995), as well as many other diet books.

When you sit down to write a proposal and explain your new book to potential publishers (see Chapter 8), you want to show exactly how your book vanquishes the competition. For now, however, it's enough to size up the competition and know that the book you plan to write offers clear and identifiable advantages over the other books on the shelf — and preferably is superior to them in every way.

To find out about your competition, prowl the shelves of your public library, the listings in Books in Print (at the library or on the Web) and the Web pages of your favorite online bookseller. The online book sites even provide a compilation of competing books. These compilations can be useful, but are not exhaustive. Supplement them with careful bookstore and library research.

If this search turns up a strong direct competitor, study that book carefully to be sure that your book is different from and better than the existing book. Do you have something to add? Is your book new and different? Can you present the information in a more accessible way?

Timing Is Everything

The book you're planning today won't get to the bookstores for 18 months or more. In other words, you're aiming your idea at a moving target, and that moving target is the whim of the public.

Aiming at a moving target may sound tough, but it's not impossible — in fact, hundreds of inspired hunches have paid off magnificently, rocketing writers and publishers to instant bestsellerdom. For example, timing influences all political memoirs. *Faith of My Fathers* by John McCain (Random House, 1999), the political memoir of a senator, was launched in the early days of the presidential primary season and rocketed onto the bestseller lists. If the book had appeared after McCain withdrew from the primary, the sales would certainly have been much lower.

The importance of timing applies even if you're not a politician, pundit, or futurist. Amy Dycyczyn was a housewife in Maine who parlayed her own talent for thrift into a newsletter, The Tightwad Gazette. Eventually the idea of the Gazette was sold to a publisher as a book for the thrifty homemaker: *The Tightwad Gazette*: *Promoting Thrift As a Viable Alternative Lifestyle* (Random House, 1993). That book hit the top of the bestseller list and was followed by other thriftwise titles, including *The Best of the Cheapskate Monthly* by Mary Hunt (St. Martin's Press, 1993), and *Saving Money Any Way You Can* by Mike Yorkey (Vine Books, 1994). When Beanie Babies ruled, books for Beanie Baby collectors ruled the bestseller lists, and by latest count, the Pokémon craze launched 23 titles.

When fad surfing, it's important to spot a fad early and stake your claim. Likewise, it's dangerous to stick with a fad that has run its course. Unless you are very early to the game — or come up with a truly new wrinkle on the subject — chances are that a fad-related book will be hard to place.

Online book search sites

If you love books — and you probably do since you want to write one — then you'll enjoy these Web sites:

Alibris: www.alibris.com

Amazon.com: www.amazon.com

Borders.com: www.borders.com

Barnes & Noble: barnesandnoble.com

Bibliofind: www.bibliofind.com

Books in Print: www.booksinprint.com

Overcoming common publishing objections

When you set out to write your proposal, be mindful in advance of the concerns that a publisher is likely to express about your book idea (see Chapter 22 for a list of more concerns). Build solid answers to their objections into the fabric of your idea. Here are some comments you're likely to get from a publisher and strategies for overcoming them while your book is still in the development stage:

We already have a book like this. Your in-depth survey of the competition tells you which publishers already have competing books. Either don't send your proposal to them or be ready with a good answer as to why your book is different and better.

Too many books are in this category already. Your competition survey is handy here, too. If there's really no meaningful contribution to be added to the category, don't go forward with the book. However, if you still see an unserved need that your book could fulfill, be ready to explain how your book will work while others have not.

This is a magazine article, not a book. If you believe it's a book, demonstrate it with a detailed chapter outline that shows the complete idea developed in each chapter and a riveting sample chapter that makes them want to read more.

The audience and/or idea is too narrow or small. The best way to counter this objection is with hard data: market research, census numbers, and the like, proving that your target audience is large, that enough of them will buy your book, and why.

The audience is not clearly defined. The broader your audience, the more difficult it is to reach. Define your audience as sharply and narrowly as you can. The better you define them, the more effectively a publisher can reach them.

You don't have enough practical application, advice. If your book has a practical aspect, be sure to think through and be ready to state the practical applications you offer.

The story you plan to tell has no clear ending and/or no strong narrative. This problem can mark your book as an article. If the story you plan to tell has no ending, be ready with an explanation as to why this doesn't matter, or how there will be an ending in place before the book is completed.

The characters aren't likable. They don't have to be likable. But if the reader can't root for any of them, you may have a problem. You must find a common thread of humanity that binds your characters to the reader and then tell the publisher how this thread works.

The plot/story/conclusion isn't plausible. Protect yourself from this problem by trying your idea on trusted friends or colleagues. You are the least likely to detect a plausibility problem in your idea, but you certainly want to address this problem before you show your work to an agent or publisher.

There may be legal problems. If you are planning a nonfiction work about living people — or if characters in your novel are identifiable as real people — be aware of the legal issues and, if they're likely to be thorny, consult an attorney before you proceed.

It's too late for this topic. If timing is an issue, alert the publisher to the need for speedy publication. If even a miracle won't get the book to market in time, start working on another idea.

Chapter 3

Refining Your Idea: The Realities of Writing

In This Chapter

- Thinking like a writer
- Considering a collaborator
- Acquiring credibility
- Adding value to your book idea
- Capturing your book idea with a title that sells

The moment your book idea takes shape is one of the most exciting in the whole process. The period of groping and brainstorming is over; now you can begin to test and improve your idea, while you form a strategy for actually getting your book down on paper.

For first-time authors, executing a brilliant idea can entail a great deal more time and work than you ever thought possible. That's why it's a good idea to start fleshing out your idea now with initial research, preliminary outlining, and a work plan for how you intend to get the job done. Can you go it alone, or do you need help? If you need help, what kind of assistance is available, and how can you get it?

The Realities of Writing

Writing a book takes a great deal of commitment. No one stands over you day in and day out with encouragement or enticements. In fact, innumerable distractions, like friends, spouses, children, and jobs, constantly compete for your time and attention. Chances are that in order to write your book, you may have to, at least temporarily, disappoint loved ones and forgo activities you enjoy. If you have the willpower to work no matter what temptations surround you, you're a step ahead of most would-be authors. However, if you foresee a problem, talk to the people around you and set up a plan to make accomplishing your goal a priority. Producing a complete manuscript takes a great deal of discipline.

Are you a self-starter?

Do you get right down to work on a project, or do you tend to talk about a task until it feels as if you've actually accomplished part of it? Do you like to work alone, or are you more comfortable operating in a group or committee? Is it easier for you to perform a task when someone asks you to, or do you tend to work for your own satisfaction?

Because writing is a solitary, entrepreneurial activity, the writer of a book needs to be self-motivated. It is you who must doggedly pursue each line of inquiry in your research. You are the only person who can endlessly refine the outline until it captures the very essence of your original idea. And it is you who must return to the task of writing day after day, bringing the pages into alignment with your outline and, ultimately, your core idea.

No one stands over you, demanding output when none is forthcoming. Even after a publisher buys your book idea, an editor rarely checks your progress. Editors are busy enough working on manuscripts that have been delivered. They trust you to complete your book by the agreed upon due date specified in the contract.

Can you see the project through?

Can you realistically produce the idea you're considering as a finished manuscript? It's not uncommon to get so excited about a book idea that you forget to take into consideration what you may have to spend — in personal sacrifice as well as dollars — to fully execute the idea. For example, Thurston Clarke, a travel writer, faced real financial hardship while writing his classic travel epic, *Equator* (William Morrow, 1988). In the proposal, Clarke described how he intended to chronicle his own travels along the entire Equator, from Brazil, across the Atlantic, across Africa, then out across the Pacific, and back through South America to the Atlantic Coast of Brazil.

As it turned out, he had no way to actually complete this trip because no scheduled flights crossed the Atlantic at equatorial latitude. Instead, the writer was forced to undertake the massive journey in shifts, broken up with returns to his family in New York. Over several years, his 25,000-mile equatorial route burned up hundreds of thousands of miles of air travel, not to mention tramp steamer, car, cart, bus, truck, and foot journeys of thousands of miles more. The cost escalated far beyond the publisher's original advance. Many writers would have given up midway, sacrificing untold dollars and months of work to no particular end. Clarke, however, finished his book, at great personal sacrifice. And lucky for him, *Equator* went on to become a classic in the field.

I recommend, however, that you know before committing to a book idea, exactly what's entailed so that you don't put yourself and your family in this kind of difficult position.

Do You Need a Collaborator?

You may find that transforming your brilliant idea into a polished manuscript all by yourself is just too difficult. Don't let that small impediment stop you from becoming a published author. Find a collaborator — either an expert in the field about which you want to write or an expert writer with the time and ability to produce an eloquent text.

The creation of many, if not most, books involves two parties. First, the source, or expert, provides the key ideas in the book, the story line, or the main content. This person is also usually the spokesperson for the book — the more visible one who speaks about the book to the media after publication.

The second role, that of the writer, is the wordsmith who produces the actual text of the book. In some instances, usually in works of fiction, the same individual fulfills both roles. However, a professional writer can bring a great deal to any book. Aside from actually producing the text — in the expert's voice if desired — the writer can also collect anecdotes, conduct interviews, flesh out characters, smooth out plot lines, and polish the entire text so that it outshines the competition.

You're better off determining early in the process if you want to take on both roles, or if you're better suited to one. No matter what kind of book you have in mind — a coffee-table book, a nonfiction adventure, or a cookbook — a collaborative writing arrangement may help you achieve that goal.

Deciding whether you need a collaborator

The decision to go with a collaborator depends in large part on the time, money, and energy you can devote to creating a book. If, for example, you are the sole proprietor of your own consulting business that occupies 80 hours per week of your time, soliciting the services of a collaborator early in the planning stage makes sense. This collaborator can assist in each step, from refining your core idea to producing a finished manuscript.

If the book is a memoir or a family album or a personal statement, write as much as you can in your own words. If you aren't completely happy with the result, then consider taking on a collaborator or hiring a freelance editor to add luster to what you've already created.

You need a collaborator when:

- You have a book worthy idea, but no writing skills.
- You are an expert with no time to write a book.
- You have no inclination to actually write a book, but you want a published book with your name on it.

Finding a collaborator

Lots of talented people are out fishing for interesting books to work on. Here are a few ways to find the right collaborator for you.

- **Contact a writer or expert whose work you admire or who collaborated on a book similar to the one you plan to write.** They'll be flattered to hear that you value their work. Just write a letter in care of the publisher presenting your credentials along with a brief description of the book you plan to write and ask whether the writer is interested in working with you. This may sound like a long shot, but it's worked before. Alternatively, contact the author's agent who may be more responsive to such a query. The publisher can provide you with the agent's name and contact information.
- **Approach a journalist whose writing you respect, either at your local newspaper or a national newspaper or magazine.** Call them directly at work or send a query letter addressed to them at the newspaper or magazine that they work for.
- **Contact the American Society of Journalists and Authors' Writer Referral Service.** You can reach it by e-mail at `writers@asja.org` or by phone at 212-398-1934.
- **Turn to Literary Market Place.** This directory of the American Book Publishing Industry is updated annually and is available in your library or on the Web at `www.literarymarketplace.com`. LMP includes an Editorial Services index listing agencies as well as individuals that offer complete writing, editorial, and book development services.
- **Study the advertisements in writers' magazines.** Professionals run ads both if they are looking for a collaborator or anxious to be one, in *Writer's Digest, The Writer,* and other writers' and editors' magazines.
- **Find an expert to lend credentials and credibility to your book idea by contacting professional organizations in the specific field.** Consider posting your idea on an Internet bulletin board in that area.
- **Contact your publisher or literary agent.** They set up collaborations all the time. They probably won't get involved, though, unless they have already decided to work with you (see Chapter 9).

Working with a collaborator

In an ideal collaboration, both parties bring unique qualities to the book — an original story, expert knowledge, access to sources, outstanding writing, in-depth research skills, and a tenacious commitment. More than ever before, writers are teaming up, sharing the work, the profits, and, in some cases, the byline of the book.

There are three main types of collaborative writing arrangements, each carrying with it a slightly different role and different amount of credit.

- Collaborator (by expert's name *with* or *as-told-to* writer's name)
- Co-author (by expert's name *and* writer's name)
- Ghostwriter (by expert — no byline for the writer)

In a collaboration, the writer often writes the entire manuscript based on interviews with and tape-recorded dictation from the expert. Or, the writer may do extensive reworking and rewriting of a manuscript already produced by the expert. If you decide to work with a collaborator, be sure to draw up a collaboration agreement between the two of you that clearly defines each person's role, duties, payment, and author credit. *In Search of Excellence* by Tom Peters and Robert Waterman (Harper and Row, 1982) and *How to Talk So Kids Will Listen and Listen So Kids Will Talk* by Adele Faber and Elaine Mazlish (Avon, 1999) are just a few of the thousands of examples of best-selling collaborations.

In a co-author arrangement, you and your partner split the proceeds, in most cases 50/50. You share in the creation of, profit from, and author credit for the book. Be sure to draw up a collaboration agreement stating how you both will participate in all aspects of the book.

A ghostwriter is a collaborator whose name appears nowhere on the book. The ghostwriter writes a book from the perspective of and in the "voice" of the expert author. Generally, the expert has full control over the written text and receives full author credit on the book. In exchange for writing the book, a ghostwriter is paid, either by the expert or the publisher, a pre-agreed upon amount.

While these three types of collaboration arrangements seem quite straightforward, in fact every collaboration is different, and the best intentions of even the clearest collaboration agreement can go awry.

What often happens, for example, is that celebrity "experts" often neglect to read a "collaborative" effort until quite late in the process. For example, the late baseball great Mickey Mantle's book, *The Mick* (Jove, 1986), had been written and delivered to the publisher by Herb Gluck, a professional collaborator, and Mantle himself delivered a rousing speech to his publisher's sales department a few weeks prior to the announced distribution of the book. Privately that evening, Mantle told his editor that he had finally read the book that day and that he *hated* it — not one word in the book had come from his mouth, he claimed, and he would not allow the book to be released under any circumstances. Luckily for the editor, he was able to arrange for Mantle and Gluck to rewrite the offending passages, quickly, and still manage to get the book distributed by the appointed day.

Working with a collaborator or hired writer has both its pros and cons.

Pros:

- A collaborative team can produce the manuscript faster than an individual writer working alone.
- A professional writer can be extremely helpful in shaping the book with an eye to what publishers are looking for.
- The expert is able to continue pursuing his or her career, while the writer takes care of the daily planning, researching, and writing of the book.
- A collaborator can bring to the book experience, expertise, or access to key sources that the expert doesn't have.

Cons:

- Even the most skillful collaborative writer cannot get inside the skin of the other writer, celebrity, or expert.
- The profits must be shared.
- You're entering into a relationship with someone you don't know well; unexpected conflicts may arise from a personality clash or basic work style differences.
- An expert can feel, once the hard work of producing the text is done, that the writer is taking too much credit for the book's content — and vice versa.

Figure 3-1 shows you a sample collaboration agreement.

Collaboration agreements

Collaboration agreements serve to protect the interests of all parties in collaboration: the authors, assuming that there are two or more of them, as well as the publisher. The ideal collaboration agreement is written in clear English and is as brief as possible; however, the collaboration agreement is a legal document that may be tested under very adverse circumstances and needs to be comprehensive enough to serve in a variety of situations.

Collaboration agreements come in different forms, ranging from equal partners, to expert and writer, to work-for-hire agreements where one collaborator is literally hired by the other to work on the book.

The key issues in a typical collaboration agreement are as follows:

Who are the parties? Identify the collaborators.

What is the work? Specify title, if there is one, and provide a brief description of the work.

Who owns the copyright? Both authors, or just one? This usually distinguishes whether it's an equal partnership or not.

How are the authors to be credited on the book jacket? Either the authors receive equal credit (author names on the same line in the same size, separated by "and") or not (different line and type size for each author, or separated by "with," or with one author not on the cover at all)?

How is the money to be divided? Some agreements divide the proceeds down the middle, while others distribute more to one party than to the other. In some cases, the distribution of the author advance is unequal, but the royalty earnings compensate for the difference. For example, the writer, as distinct from the expert, may get 75 percent of the advance and then 25 percent of the royalties, until they have both gotten an equal sum, and thereafter they split the money equally.

What role does each collaborator play in the project? The agreement should say who provides the written words, the research, the sources, and documents. It should also be specific about the number of drafts to be produced and how disputes about the text are to be resolved.

If one collaborator wants to transfer ownership of the book or his share of the proceeds, how is this to be accomplished? The contract should stipulate how one collaborator can buy out the other before or after work is complete. It should also indicate that each collaborator has first refusal to buy out his partner before a third party can buy in to the partnership.

How are expenses going to be paid? The agreement should say how costs are to be shared between the collaborators.

What happens if one party dies or is disabled? The agreement should say exactly what happens in this instance.

How are disputes to be settled? If you and your collaborator disagree, decide in advance whether an arbitrator is to be called in or what other remedy will be sought.

This AGREEMENT between Susan Jones, residing in New York County, City of New York, State of New York (hereafter called Jones), and Michael Stanley, residing in Fairfield County, City of Stamford, State of Connecticut (hereafter called Stanley),

WITNESSETH

The parties will collaborate in the writing of a book:
A GARDENER'S DIARY: A Year in a Gardener's Life, as recounted through the four seasons in Stanley's award-winning garden. A tentative outline of the work is attached.

1. It is the intention of both parties that each chapter is to be drafted by Stanley and then completely revised and rewritten by Jones in consultation with Stanley.

2. The parties agree to work together to produce a detailed proposal for the work and then to engage the services of a literary agent for the purpose of placing the work with a publisher. Selection of agent and commitment to a publisher is by mutual agreement. Any disputes arising from this process are to be resolved as per clause ten.

3. The copyright in the Work shall be obtained and held jointly by both parties.

4. The parties shall receive credit as follows: "By Michael Stanley with Susan Jones," in the same typeface and appearing on the same line on the cover, thev title page, and in all listings of the book except when explicitly agreed by both parties.

5. All earnings derived from the work, including royalty payments and subsidiary rights income, shall be divided equally between the parties.

6. After the completion of the manuscript of the Book, no change shall be made by either party without the consent of the other. Such consent not to be unreasonably withheld.

7. If either party desires to transfer his share in the book to a third person, he shall give written notice of such intention to the other Party. The other party shall have ten days thereafter to exercise his option to purchase the other share in the earnings before said earnings are sold to the third party.

8. All expenses incurred are subject to mutual agreement in advance, and are to be shared equally.

9. If either party dies before completion of the manuscript, the survivor shall have the right to complete it, to change the text, and to negotiate for publication of the rights. However, the decedent shall still appear as co-author, and the decedent's share of all proceeds shall continue to be paid to the decedent's estate.

10. All disputes arising from this agreement or any breach thereof shall be arbitrated in accordance with the American Arbitration Association.

11. This agreement constitutes the entire understanding of the parties.

Confirmed and agreed to

____
Susan Jones Date

____
Michael Stanley Date

Figure 3-1: A sample collaboration agreement.

Platform: Are You Qualified to Write the Book?

In the case of most nonfiction books, and rarely in the case of fiction, an author's qualifications, or *platform,* for writing the proposed book is, to many publishers' eyes, just as important as having a great idea. A publisher wants to know that the author is a notable expert on the book's subject and that his expertise lends credibility, even stature, to the book. For example, a diet book written by a doctor or a nutritionist is more likely to succeed than a diet book written by a housewife. Likewise, a tax guide written by an ex-Internal Revenue Service tax auditor is more likely to sell than a tax guide written by an unknown tax attorney. However, a tax guide co-authored by an IRS tax auditor and a tax attorney is likely to blow away the competition.

An author who has "inside" or specialized knowledge on a subject is the one people are likely to listen to and trust. For example, Peter Lynch was the director of the Magellan fund, a Fidelity Mutual Fund with one of the most enviable records in Wall Street history, when he wrote the blockbuster best-seller, *One Up on Wall Street* with John Rothchild (S&S, 1990), which offered stock-picking advice to ordinary citizens.

Before proceeding down the long, arduous road toward publication, attend to the issue of your platform. What publisher, for example, would invest time, effort, and money in publishing a book on *Raising Morally Superior Children* by a child psychologist whose own child is serving a prison term for armed robbery?

If your credentials aren't all they could be, get to work now on strengthening your platform and enhancing your credibility. It will definitely improve your chances of getting a publisher's attention.

Give talks

Offer to speak at your local library, senior center, school, and community center on the topic you want to write about. Organizing your thoughts for a talk helps focus your book idea. It also gives you the opportunity to present the information in front of an audience whose questions and comments may help you see areas that could benefit from further development.

Get a degree

An advanced degree, in a subject area you plan to write about, is a sure sign of authority. If you're just a few credits away from accreditation in your chosen field, finish the class work before you submit your book proposal. If you don't have time to complete an advanced degree, at least get enrolled so that you can assure publishers that you are on your way to an advanced degree.

Teach a course

Adult education programs, community colleges, even libraries, and senior centers are always looking for resident experts willing to teach a course. Creating a course syllabus is a lot like writing a book outline. As you gather and organize information for the course, keep in mind that you want to entertain as well as inspire.

Gather data

Publishers and publicists love mediagenic data. They are enticed by original research or statistical data that proves your thesis or establishes the size of your audience. If you are in the business of gathering data, you possess a powerful asset. Readers, journalists, and television producers are all impressed by a point demonstrated with fresh, primary research.

Michael Drosnin, a reporter for the *Wall Street Journal*, found an Israeli mathematician who produced impressive new research supporting the existence of a numerical code embedded in the Bible — a code, which, Drosnin claimed, actually predicted many contemporary events. On the basis of this data, Drosnin was able to catch the media's ear, and his book, *The Bible Code* (S&S, 1997), sailed onto the New York Times Bestseller List, propelled by this mathematical data.

Collect testimonials

If you give a speech, teach a course, or show a chapter of your manuscript to influential friends, make sure to take note of your audience's reactions. You definitely want to keep track of all the appreciative notes from enthusiastic students and listeners. Taken together, these comments can amount to testimonials that sway a publisher.

Get press coverage

The sooner you begin getting media coverage, the better. Start with a small piece in your local paper and grow it from there. Think of it as the beginning of an all-important clip file. A tape of TV appearances, even on the local public access channel, will enhance your credibility with a publisher.

Produce a video

If you can't get actual television footage, consider hiring a video professional to make a video tape of you speaking on your area of expertise. Try to hire a professional media coach if you aren't naturally mediagenic.

Look your best

When you look great, you attract attention. Obviously, if you're writing an exercise book, you want to radiate fitness. Likewise, if your subject is reversing the effects of aging, you need to look youthful. If, on the other hand, you're writing an academic treatise, pull out that tweed jacket and put on your horn-rimmed glasses.

Adding Value to Your Book

You can add value to a book project in any number of ways. All of them are intended to help a publisher raise the profile of the book, increase sales, and increase the appeal of the book to readers or buyers.

The most basic and obvious way to add value to a book (and this is often the publisher's province) is to attach it to another product — a CD-ROM glued to the back cover, for example, or another book shrink-wrapped to it, or a discount coupon blown into the book. The author can add value by actually delivering useful information, by pleasing the reader, or by creating a title that attracts readers and promises a real benefit.

You can also add value to a book in more external ways, without changing the title or any of the book's actual content. The following sections cover a few key "value adds" to consider.

Endorsements

Celebrity or expert endorsements can help sell your book at every stage of the publishing process. The gathering of endorsements usually begins in earnest when the book is written. Start compiling a list of potential endorsers and reach out to friends and acquaintances who may help secure a useful endorsement. Be selective — a kind word from your uncle probably won't sway publishers. But if you have any connections to people whose endorsement may help sell your book, now is a good time to make an initial contact and test the water (see Chapter 19).

Celebrity foreword

A foreword by a celebrity or a renowned expert can give your book a leg up. If a public figure — even one you don't know — is out there who might be sympathetic to your book, now is the time to reach out to him or her. Explain that you are writing a book about, say, a cause they support and that you welcome any sort of help they're willing to offer. Suggest that writing a brief foreword would benefit their cause as well as the book (subject of course to their approval of the completed book). You'd be surprised how often this tentative commitment has helped speed a book idea into actuality.

Brand equity

If you can attach a nationally recognized brand to your book, then you have added value that any publisher will cherish. For example, Elizabeth Lawrence is a freelance writer specializing in cooking and home decorating. Several years ago, Lawrence wanted to write a book about place settings and table decoration. She realized that the project would be stronger with the help of a major tableware manufacturer. She canvassed several companies and found a nationally recognized leader, Lenox china, who was interested in cobranding the book with her.

The involvement of a national brand, like Lenox, in a book project signals to publishers that they will enjoy all sorts of marketing benefits when the book is published. In this case, Lawrence had no trouble finding an eager publisher for *The Lenox Book of Home Entertaining and Etiquette* (Crown, 1989).

Your Title Is Your Best Advertisement

A well-designed book jacket is the most important advertisement any book will ever get, and a key feature of any book jacket is the title. Your title is your tag line, the label that people use to talk about your book, the phrase that helps people remember it on the way to the bookstore.

A great title jumps off the page, grabbing people's attention. It can get you noticed faster and more effectively than any other selling tool. So spend some time coming up with a memorable title that communicates the essence of your idea in a compelling, perhaps even beguiling, way.

There are many strategies for creating titles, and publishers brainstorm titles endlessly, often coming up with the "perfect" title only just as a book goes to press. The process is by nature subjective and not very susceptible to the "recipe" approach.

The perfect title for a novel, for example, needs to be evocative, but it need not be terribly informative: Consider the recent best-selling novels such as *The Divine Secrets of the Ya Ya Sisterhood* by Rebecca Wells (HarperCollins, 1997), *Waiting to Exhale* by Terry McMillan (Viking, 1992), and *The Memoirs of a Geisha* by Arthur S. Golden (Knopf, 1997). Readers of novels seem willing to live with a certain amount of mystery when they pick a book up, as if solving the mystery can come in the process of reading the book itself. It's almost as if a title that's too revealing spoils some of the fun.

Nonfiction is different because people usually buy nonfiction out of a sense of perceived need or curiosity about a certain topic. In the world of nonfiction, you need to state your case, clearly, in your title. Beyond that, there are very few hard and fast rules. But a few guidelines apply in most cases.

Brief is better

In order to stick in your memory, a title needs to be brief. Because many computer storage systems (at book wholesalers, for example) tend to have limited space, don't expect your subtitle to be listed with your title in key records of the book. In fact, even a very long title will be cut off in the middle by some database programs. The recent bestseller, *'Tis* by Frank McCourt (Scribner, 1999), proves that even a very short title can lead to success.

Promise a benefit

Memorable titles that explicitly offer a valuable benefit have launched many bestsellers: *Thin Thighs in Thirty Days* by Wendy Stehling (Bantam, 1982), *Getting the Love You Want* by Harville Hendrix, Ph.D. (Henry Holt, 1988), *Body For Life* by Bill Phillips and Michael D'Orso (HarperCollins, 1999), *The Nine Steps to Financial Freedom* by Suze Orman (Crown, 1997), *Nothing Down* by Robert G. Allen (Simon and Schuster, 1984), and *Dr. Dean Ornish's Program for Reversing Heart Disease* (Random House, 1990).

Suggest or imply a benefit

Titles often click with an audience even when the promise of the book is implied below the surface, rather than baldly stated. For example, until a few weeks before the book was first printed, the best-selling business classic *Built to Last* by James Collins and Jerry Porras (HarperBusiness, 1994) was called "Visionary Companies" — a relatively fuzzy title that promised nothing and said very little about the book. The final title, which was added just as the book went to press, conveyed the underlying message of the book — that there is a way to build permanence into the DNA of a large corporation. This message was one that hundreds of thousands of business leaders wanted to hear.

Create an "aha" for the reader

A title can work if a reader sees it and instinctively agrees with it or, even better, feels that the title captures a truth that had been hidden before and is suddenly revealed. *Ten Stupid Things Women Do to Mess Up Their Lives* by Dr. Laura Schlessinger (HarperPerennial, 1998) somehow made women feel understood and held out the promise that the book might offer some help to reverse the process. *Men Are From Mars, Women are from Venus* by John Gray (HarperCollins, 1992) captured perfectly the perception of many embattled couples and suggested the possibility of reconciliation. *Smart Women/Foolish Choices* by Connell Cowan and Melvyn Kinder (Clarkson Potter, 1985) was a bestseller in part because it invited readers to celebrate the difference between their own innate wisdom and the unfortunate mistakes they might have made along the way.

Crystallize a wish

Sometimes, all that's needed in a title is to link the essence of your idea with a widely held belief or wish. For example, John Naisbitt, a consultant and market researcher, studied newspaper headlines for years and plotted the shifting public perception about a wide range of topics. In 1990, he proposed a book summarizing the essence of his findings. While his ideas were powerful, the original title of his book, *High Tech/High Touch*, didn't hit the mark for booksellers. But on the eve of publication, the author and his publisher, Warner Books, changed the book's title to *Megatrends: Ten New Directions Transforming Our Lives*. This title raised Naisbitt's fascinating findings to the level of wish fulfillment — it promised readers deep, meaningful insights into the future of the decade. With this powerful new title, the book sold over five million copies worldwide and launched John Naisbitt as a writer of many bestsellers.

Be provocative

A provocative title creates a reaction, stimulates argument and controversy, or simply jars people into giving it — and the book — a second look. There are many forms of title provocation. A title may allege something that people find inherently infuriating, such as *The Closing of the American Mind* by Allan Bloom (Simon & Schuster, 1987). A title can contain an inherent inconsistency, like *Eat More, Weigh Less* by Dr. Dean Ornish (HarperCollins, 1996) or *First, Break All the Rules* by Marcus Buckingham and Curt Coffman (Simon & Schuster, 1999), or *Die Broke by* Stephen Pollan and Mark Levine (HarperBusiness, 1997). A title can propose something absurd, such as *The Man Who Mistook his Wife for a Hat* by Dr. Oliver Sacks (Summit Books, 1985). A title can even have provocation buried deep within it, as *The Bell Curve* by Richard J. Hernstein and Charles Murray (Free Press, 1994) did, in proposing a radical new interpretation of intelligence testing.

A wonderful title can help position your book in the minds of everyone who encounters it, from editor or agent, to publisher, to bookseller, to customer. Your efforts to marry your book idea to a title that perfectly expresses it gets paid off handsomely all the way down the line.

Putting it all together: The Harvey Mackay story

In 1987, Harvey Mackay, the President of Mackay Envelope Company of Minneapolis, Minnesota, decided that it was high time for him to publish his first book. He had never written a book before and had no credentials as a writer, but he had built his little company from virtually nothing into a prosperous local supplier of specialized envelopes for offices and film development companies. He was active in the Young President's Organization, an association of chief executives under the age of 40. On the lively speaking circuit sponsored by YPO, he honed his considerable skills as a orator. Moreover, Harvey was a tireless booster for the city of Minneapolis/St. Paul, and he was frequently on the front page of the local paper for his activities on behalf of the Twin Cities' many sports franchises.

From these rather modest and regionally based elements, Harvey Mackay built one of the most successful self-help careers of the decade. How did he do it?

First, he networked. Through the YPO, he met Ken Blanchard, co-author of *The One-Minute Manager* (William Morrow, 1982) one of America's best known business speakers. Through that contact, he managed an introduction to a proven publisher of successful business books.

Second, he studied. He learned everything he could about publishing, the publisher he was pitching, and the sort of book he wanted to write. He secured a brief meeting with his target publisher and persuasively described the book that he planned to write.

With the help of a skilled freelance editor, unbeknownst to his publisher, he wrote an excellent manuscript. He then arranged, using his own contacts and money, to meet with many key decision-makers at the booksellers around the country.

Once again, he used his network of contacts in the YPO organization to solicit endorsements of the book from famous opinion makers. These endorsements — 44 of them — appeared in a full page *New York Times* ad that Harvey's publisher was persuaded to run.

He flew himself to the Frankfurt book fair and, using his many international YPO contacts, he managed to place the book with publishers in over a dozen foreign countries.

He persuaded his publisher to allow him to address the publisher's national sales force. He then researched his topic carefully and gave a speech that was laced with astounding insight into little know facts about his editor, his publisher, and the whole publishing process.

He hired a market research firm, at his own expense, to test his title, despite his publisher's reluctance to publish a book with the "awkward title, *Swim With The Sharks: Without Being Eaten Alive* (William Morrow, 1988).

Finally, Harvey achieved what very few writers in his era accomplished. He was invited to appear on the "Oprah Winfrey Show." What Harvey didn't know was that he'd been set up. Harvey was the only guest, the only man in the entire TV studio wearing a business suit that day. The rest of the room was packed with unemployed workers who had been hand-picked to test Harvey's patience and undermine the principles set forth in the book. But Harvey turned the table on Oprah's disgruntled audience. He turned the show into a seminar on bootstrapping yourself from an old job that didn't work into a new job that did. The show ended with a standing ovation for Harvey — and a trip up the bestseller list for his book.

The rest, as they say, is publishing history.

Chapter 4

Categorically Speaking

In This Chapter

- Getting to know the fiction categories
- Getting to know the nonfiction categories

Walk into a bookstore, and you're immediately greeted by both a "new and noteworthy" display and a prominent "bestseller" section. The other books are arranged by category, with travel books in one section, history books in another, cookbooks in yet another, and so on.

Books are organized by category because books are sold by category — even online booksellers systemize their stock this way. So, in order for a customer to find a book — your book, for example — it needs to be located in the correct section of the bookstore, the section where it logically belongs. If it's placed in the wrong section, readers may not find it. And if it falls between two or more categories, it can be so hard to locate that readers either give up the search altogether or settle for someone else's book. Avoid that problem by designing your book to fit comfortably into a clearly recognizable category.

As you're refining your book idea, visit bookstores and online sites to examine the individual categories and take note of the topic areas contained in each. I was surprised to learn, for example, that my last book, *Dress Your House for Success* co-authored with Martha Webb (Three Rivers Press, 1997), is located in the business section. While the book is full of decorating tips, it is really about how to sell your house quickly and profitably — so most booksellers categorized it under "business" rather than "decorating."

Getting Inside the Different Types of Fiction

Fiction is a general term used to describe an imaginative work of prose, either a novel, short story, or novella. Recently, this definition has been modified to include both nonfiction works that contain imaginative elements, like *Midnight in the Garden Of Good and Evil* by John Berendt (Random House,

1994) and *Dutch* by Edmund Morris (Random House, 1999), and novels consisting largely of factual reporting with a patina of fictionalization, such as *Memoirs of a Geisha* by Arthur Golden (Knopf, 1997). However, in the truest sense, a work of fiction is a creation of the writer's imagination.

The two main types of fiction are *literary* and *commercial.*

- **Commercial fiction** attracts a broad audience and may also fall into any *subgenre,* like mystery, romance, legal thriller, western, science fiction, and so on. For example, *The Bridges of Madison County* by Robert James Waller (Warner, 1992) was a hugely successful commercial novel because the book described the fulfillment of a romantic fantasy that is dear to the heart of millions of readers. Written in a short, easy-to-read style, the book was as mesmerizing to 15-year-olds as it was to 100-year-olds. Other blockbuster commercial fiction authors include John Grisham, Sidney Sheldon, Danielle Steele, and Jackie Collins.
- **Literary fiction** tends to appeal to a smaller, more intellectually adventurous audience. A work of literary fiction can fall into any of the subgenres described in the following sections. What sets literary fiction apart, however, is the notable qualities it contains — excellent writing, originality of thought, and style — that raise it above the level of ordinary written works. A recent work of literary fiction that enjoyed wide popularity was *Cold Mountain* by Charles Frazier (Atlantic Monthly Press, 1997). Other popular authors of literary fiction include Toni Morrision, Barbara Kingsolver, John LeCarre, and Saul Bellow.

Mainstream fiction is a general term publishers and booksellers use to describe both commercial and literary works that depict a daily reality familiar to most people. These books, usually set in the 20th or present day 21st century, have at their core a universal theme that attracts a broad audience. Mainstream books deal with such myriad topics as family issues, coming of age initiations, courtroom dramas, career matters, physical and mental disabilities, social pressures, political intrigue, and more. Regardless of original genre or category, most of the novels that appear on the bestseller list are considered mainstream, whether the author is Sue Grafton, Arundhati Roy, Michael Crichton, or David Guterson.

In addition to mainstream fiction, more narrowly defined categories of popular fiction appeal to specific audiences. These different fiction categories, which are described briefly in the sections that follow, are classed as a group as *genre fiction.* Each type of genre fiction has its own set of rules and conventions. So, if you want to try your hand at writing fiction, start with what you like to read. A solid grounding in the conventions of your chosen genre helps a great deal, so the more familiar you are with the books in it, the better.

If, for example, you're a voracious reader of mysteries, look closely at the conventions in the work of Agatha Christie, P.D. James, or whoever your favorite mystery writer is. If you can't get enough of Jennifer Wilde's historical romances, that may be where you start. Likewise, if the thrillers of Le Carre or the westerns of Louis Lamour are on your bedside table, make those your model as you embark on writing your novel.

Mystery

Mystery is a popular genre, boasting a huge established audience. All mysteries focus on a crime, usually murder. The action tends to center on the attempts of a wily detective-type to solve the crime. And the climax usually occurs near the end, in a leisurely setting where all the elements of the mystery are neatly assembled for the reader's convenience. The solution, complete with surprises, is then delivered to the characters and the reader alike.

Mystery subgenres include spy, detective, and crime stories. You can find a vast network of mystery writers associations, conventions, and conferences, as well as publications to help mystery writers pursue their craft. For information, contact Mystery Writers of America, Inc., 17 East 47th Street, 6th Floor, New York, N.Y. 10017, or visit its Web site at www. bookwire.com/mwa/.

Great practitioners in this genre include Arthur Conan Doyle, Raymond Chandler, Dashiell Hammett, and Earle Stanley Gardner, creator of Perry Mason. Present day giants include Carl Hiaason, James Ellroy, Robert Parker, James Lee Burke, and Elmore Leonard.

Romance

Romance is a huge category aimed at diverting and entertaining women. In romance novels, you have elements of fantasy, love, naivete, extravagance, adventure, and always the heroic lover overcoming impossible odds to be with his true love. Many romances, especially the gothic romance, have an easy-to-follow formula — a young, inexperienced girl living a somewhat remote existence is courted or threatened by an evil man and then rescued by a valiant one.

Other subgenres include regency, historical, bodice rippers, and contemporary. If historical detail and settings interest you, try writing a regency or historical romance. If tempestuous relationships are more your cup of tea, bodice rippers are for you. However, if you're interested in more modern stories with sexual candor, then consider writing a contemporary romance.

Certainly, you have lots of opportunity in the field of romance writing, which is the largest, most diverse, and most popular of the commercial genres. And romance writers' organizations can provide exact writing guidelines. To receive a set of guidelines contact Romance Writers of America by phone at 281-440-6885 or visit its Web site at www.rwanational.com.

First-class romance writers include Barbara Cartland, Jude Deveraux, Victoria Holt, Daphne Du Maurier, and Danielle Steele.

Women's fiction

It's common knowledge in the publishing industry that women constitute the biggest book-buying segment. So, it's certainly no accident that most mainstream as well as genre fiction is popular among women. For that reason, publishers and booksellers have identified a category within the mainstream that they classify as Women's Fiction. And its no surprise that virtually all the selections of Oprah's Book Club are in this genre.

From a writer's perspective, some key characteristics of these books include a focus on relationships, one or more strong female protagonists, women triumphing over unbearable circumstances, and the experiences of women unified in some way. The field includes such diverse writers as Barbara Taylor Bradford, Anne Rivers Siddons, Alice McDermott, Judith Krantz, Anne Tyler, Rebecca Wells, and Alice Hoffman.

Science fiction/fantasy

Science fiction/fantasy novels depict distant worlds and futuristic technologies that whirl readers far away from the here and now and yet provoke contemplation of contemporary issues. Imaginative, thoughtful, and other-worldly, this robust category is made even more popular by the *Star Wars* and *Star Trek* series. Leading science fiction and fantasy writers include Ray Bradbury, Arthur Clarke, Isaac Asimov, C.S. Lewis, and J.R.R. Tolkien, as well as the current, multi-best-selling, young adult author J.K. Rowling.

To obtain professional assistance in this genre, contact the Science Fiction and Fantasy Writers of America, Inc., 5 Winding Brook Drive, #1B, Guilderland, NY 12084; 518-869-5361 or visit its Web site at `www.sfwa.org/misc/sfwa_info.htm`.

Suspense/thriller

Suspense novels and thrillers are tense, exciting, often sensational works with ingenious plotting, swift action, and continuous suspense. In this genre, a writer's objective is to deliver a story with sustained tension, surprise, and a constant sense of impending doom that propels the reader forward. Unlike mysteries, thrillers are dominated by action in which physical threat is a constant companion, and a hero (James Bond, for example) is pitted against a nefarious villain.

This genre includes the great espionage writers, including John Le Carre, Len Deighton, Ian Fleming, Clive Cussler, and Frederick Forsythe. It also includes the police procedurals of Patricia Cornwell, Tony Hillerman, and Lawrence Sanders, as well as the courtroom bestsellers of Scott Turow, Richard North Patterson, Steve Martini, and John Grisham, and the military thrillers of Tom Clancy and Stephen Koontz.

Western

Known simply as westerns, these novels about life on America's post Civil War western frontier usually involve conflicts between cowboys and outlaws, cowboys and Native Americans, or Easterners and Westerners. While this category still has a mass-market audience and a thriving regional market, it's not the popular genre it was 25 years ago.

If you're interested in writing a western, contact the Western Writers of America, Inc., 416 Bedford Road, El Paso, TX 79922-1204 or go to its Web site at `www.westernwriters.org`.

Zane Grey and Louis Lamour, both deceased, are still among the popular western writers.

Horror

Filled with gut-wrenching fear, this popular genre keeps readers turning the blood-filled pages. From a writer's perspective, the defining characteristic is the intention to frighten readers by exploiting their fears, both conscious and subconscious: fears of supernatural forces, alien visitations, madness, death, dismemberment, and other terrifying notions.

Tracing its roots back to the classic tales of Edgar Allan Poe, the horror genre today is dominated by Stephen King, whose vast output of bestsellers under his name as well as his alter-ego Richard Bachman has dominated the best-seller lists for nearly 25 years. Other major horror writers include Mary Shelley, Roald Dahl, Clive Barker, Peter Straub, Dean Koontz, and Anne Rice.

While horror isn't science fiction, the SFWA provides a great deal of information and community services aimed at horror writers. To obtain its professional assistance, contact the Science Fiction and Fantasy Writers of America, Inc., 5 Winding Brook Drive, #1B, Guilderland, NY 12084; 518-869-5361, or visit its Web site at `www.sfwa.org/misc/sfwa_info.htm`.

Young adult

This genre includes any type of novel with a protagonist in the 12 to 16 age range that speaks to the concerns of teenagers. Currently, J.K. Rowling and her amazing Harry Potter (Scholastic Press) books are dominating the field. Rowling's accomplishment — a truly universal story, brimming with magic and fantasy as well as likable characters that readers identify with — is an amazing feat. Watch out for all the Harry Potter wannabes in the coming year.

Success stories in this genre share many of the qualities evident in the Harry Potter books: a memorable voice (J.D. Salinger's *Catcher in the Rye,* Little Brown, 1951), believable characters (Golding's *Lord of the Flies*, Perigee, 1959), and a willingness to write about the disturbing subjects that preoccupy teens and preteens (*Are You There God, It's Me, Margaret* by Judy Blume, Dell Yearling, 1972, or *Holes* by Louis Sachar, FSG, 1998).

Breaking Nonfiction into Categories

Nonfiction is the broadest category in the bookstore, comprising everything outside the fiction shelves. These reality-based books rely on research, reporting, and fact-filled content. This huge category occupies most of the space in bookstores, though less than half of total book sales.

Autobiography

Autobiography is a category dominated by the rich and famous. Readers thirst for first-hand accounts and recollections of celebrities. Not surprisingly, best-selling memoirs of the past year include books by presidential advisor George Stephanopoulos (*All Too Human,* Little Brown, 1999) and golf great, Arnold Palmer (*A Golfer's Life,* Ballantine, 1999).

A popular subgenre is the *memoir,* which often attracts first-time writers because it's the one subject in which virtually everyone is an expert: themselves. If you want to write your life's story for posterity, autobiography is the genre. There are few gifts you can give your children and grandchildren that are as valuable or highly cherished. And who knows, you may be paid handsomely by a publisher interested in your life's story.

That's what happened to Jesse Lee Brown Foveaux, a Texas widow in her late '90s who, at the urging of her children, enrolled in a senior citizen writing class. As a gift to her family, she wrote down what she could recall of her life — her childhood, the difficulties she had as a wife, and the experience of raising her eight children. Somehow, word of Foveaux's accomplishment reached a reporter at *The Wall Street Journal* — and a few weeks later, her story was snapped up by a New York publisher for over a million dollars (*Any Given Day*, Warner, 1997).

Frank McCourt, a New York schoolteacher whose recollections of his Irish childhood, *Angela's Ashes* (Scribners, 1996), has been a New York Times Bestseller for nearly two years, is another example. In fact, of the top ten books on Amazon.com's list of best-selling memoirs, almost half are by people whose fame arrived only after they wrote their memoir.

Biography

A *biography* is an account of a person's life written by another person. Success in this category is strongly influenced by the fame or noteriety of the subject. While it is possible for a biographer to bring a relatively obscure subject into the public's awareness, it's easier to sell a biography of a famous person.

Three other essential qualities influence success in this category: the length and depth of the book, the access to the subject achieved by the biographer, and the stature of the biographer.

While length has traditionally been seen as a positive asset in biography, the recent success of the Penguin Lives changes that. These books, all under 200 pages, match prominent writers with fascinating historical figures. The result is a best-selling biography series.

At the other end of the biography spectrum, several exhaustive biographies have recently hit the bestseller lists: *Titan* by Ron Chernow (Random, 1998), *Truman* by David McCullough (Simon & Schuster, 1992), and *Morgan* by Jean Strouse (Random House, 1999). Despite the success of Penguin Lives, richly detailed and deeply researched biographies still appeal to a large, loyal audience.

Biographers are often rewarded for achieving special access to and intimacy with their subjects. Andrew Morton, for example, has scored two immense bestsellers by securing close access to famous women: *Diana: Her True Story* (with Diana, Princess of Wales) (Simon & Schuster, 1992) and *Monica's Story* (with Monica Lewinsky) (St. Martin's Press, 1998).

The third asset that can drive success in biography is the stature of the biographer in his field. For example, esteemed pop-music critic Peter Guralnick was perfectly suited to chronicle the life of America's most influential and beloved pop-music icon. His two-volume biography of Elvis Presley, which required nearly a decade of exhaustive research, has resulted in two major national bestsellers: *Last Train to Memphis* (Little Brown, 1994) and *Careless Love* (Little Brown, 1999).

Still, people like you and me write plenty of biographies that succeed beyond anyone's wildest dreams. Noted journalist Simon Winchester was neither an historian nor a philologist when he decided to write a major biographical work. He was not especially qualified to write an account of the compilation of the original *Oxford English Dictionary*. But Winchester felt there was a good story in the friendship between James Murray and W.C. Minor. Little did he know that the tale he found so fascinating would capture the imagination of two nations. His book, *The Professor and the Madman* (HarperCollins, 1998), was a bestseller for two years in both hardcover and paperback, in America and in Britain.

Business

Business is booming, and so are books on all aspects of business. The subcategories include

- **Business narratives:** In these books, the writer brings a fascinating business story to life. *Barbarians at the Gate* by Bryan Burrough and John Helyar (HarperCollins, 1991) and *Liar's Poker* by Michael Lewis (WW Norton, 1989) are two excellent examples.
- **Investing:** These books offer advice on how to manage your investments. Standouts in this area are the *Motley Fool Investment Guide* by David and Tom Gardner (Simon & Schuster, 1997), *The Beardstown Ladies Commonsense Investment Guide* by the Beardstown Ladies Investment Club (Hyperion, 1995), and *The Wall Street Journal Guide to Understanding Money and Investing* by Kenneth M. Morris (Fireside, 1999).
- **Personal finance:** These books are about acquiring and saving money. The recent runaway bestseller in Personal Finance is *Nine Steps to Financial Freedom* by Suze Orman (Crown, 1997).
- **Management:** These books are about handling, directing, and controlling the affairs of a company or organization. Recent blockbusters in this area include *Reengineering the Corporation* by Michael Hammer and James Champy (HarperBusiness, 1993) and *In Search Of Excellence* by Tom Peters and Robert Waterman (HarperCollins, 1992).
- **Marketing and sales:** These books offer selling information and advice — the more innovative, the better. Included in this subcategory are such classics as *Ogivly on Advertising* by David Ogilvy (Random House, 1987) and *The 22 Immutable Laws of Marketing* by Al Ries and Jack Trout (HarperBusiness, 1994). A notable newcomer is *Selling the Invisible* by Harry Beckwith (Warner, 1997).

- **Memoirs:** When business leaders tell their story, America listens. Consider the bestsellers of Lee Iacocca, Andy Grove, Bill Gates, and Michael Dell; *Iacocca* by Lee Iacocca with William Novak (Bantam, 1985); *Only the Paranoid Survive* by Andy Grove (Doubleday, 1998), *The Road Ahead* by Bill Gates (Viking, 1995), and *Direct from Dell* by Michael Dell (HarperBusiness, 1998).
- **Real estate:** This area is filled with books offering advice on buying, selling, and investing in real estate. Popular examples include my own book, *Dress Your House For Success* by Martha Webb and Sarah Parsons Zackheim (Three Rivers Press, 1997), *How to Sell Your Home in Five Days* by William G. Effros (Workman, 1998), and *Nothing Down for the '90s* by Robert Allen (S&S, 1990).
- **Technology:** This relatively new category of business book sets out to explain the impact of technology on business. Successful examples include *Customers.Com* by Patricia B. Seybold (Times Books, 1998), *Crossing the Chasm* by Geoffrey A. Moore (HarperBusiness, 1991), and *The Innovator's Dilemma* by Clayton M. Christensen (Harvard Business Reviews Press, 1997).

Cookbooks

Americans love cookbooks. Thousands of new cookbooks are produced each year, joining such well-loved classics as the *Joy Of Cooking* by Irma S. Rombauer, Marion Rombauer Becker, Ethan Becker, La Maestro, Laura Hartman Maestro (Illustrator), Maria D. Guarnaschelli (Intro) (Scribners, 1997) and *The Good Housekeeping Illustrated Cookbook* (IDG Books Worldwide, Inc., 1998). Celebrity TV chefs, like Julia Child and Emeril LaGasse, keep writing cookbooks as do well-known restaurateurs, like Alice Watters and Daniel Boulud.

While qualifications and platform (see Chapter 3) are important in the cookbook field, there is always room for a new idea, truly original recipes, or a startling new take on a traditional style of cooking and serving food. If you love to cook, why not start compiling unique recipes for a book?

Computer and Internet

The computer and Internet category is the fastest growing in bookstores. If you have special knowledge in any aspect of this field or can eloquently explain the intricacies of the Internet or computing to a general audience, your talent is needed. The range of possibilities is considerable: from hardware and software manuals, Internet guides, simplified guides (the *For Dummies* series), and graphics guides and books for those seeking professional advancement with computers, certification guides (for professional training). There are also specialized computer book categories for computer scientists, computer network builders, Web developers, and programmers.

Gift books, a.k.a. coffee table books

This category includes *coffee table books* — lavishly illustrated, large format books, usually in color and printed on heavy paper — as well as smaller, impulse gifts intended for birthdays, anniversaries, and holiday gift giving. Coffee table books are complicated and expensive to produce. For that reason, many publishers shy away from even considering them. In order to make it financially worth their while, publishers usually need to print at least 25,000 copies of a full-color book and will not move forward on a gift book unless it has a virtually guaranteed sale of that number or higher. Publishers frequently resort to outside experts, called *book packagers* (see Chapter 13) to produce their gift books.

What this fact means to you, as a writer, is that the road to getting a gift book published can be difficult. Producing this type of book entails marshalling the diverse talents of a writer, illustrator, designer, and a fine arts printer. So, to justify all the cost, it must appeal to a huge audience. And even then, will 25,000 people pay the $45 to $75 price tag? That's the question publishers will ask.

Some recent best-selling examples include *We Interrupt This Broadcast* by Joe Garner, Walter Cronkite, and Bill Kurtis (Sourcebooks, 1998), *Life: Our Century in Pictures* by Richard B. Stolley and Tony Chiu (Bulfinch Press, 1999), and *Women* by Annie Leibovitz and Susan Sontag (Random House, 1999).

In addition to lavish illustrated books, another subgenre is within the larger category of gift books. These include small, elegantly printed books that are intended to be given on certain occasions such as Fathers Day, Mother's Day, Christmas, and so on. Examples include *Harvey Penick's Little Red Book* by Harvey Penick and Bud Shrake (Simon & Schuster, 1992); *Meditations for Women Who Do Too Much* by Anne Wilson Schaef (HarperSanFrancisco, 1990), and *The Art of Worldly Wisdom* by Baltazar Gracian (Doubleday, 1992).

Health

This diverse category is growing, thanks to the aging health-conscious baby boom generation. It includes the following subcategories:

- **General health:** These big, full-service compendiums are offered by the Mayo Clinic, Johns Hopkins, and the American Medical Association.
- **Medical guides:** These more specialized books focus on single ailments, such as diabetes, heart disease, or cancer.
- **Diet:** This explosive category includes several blockbuster bestsellers every season, from *The Zone* by Barry Sears (HarperCollins, 1995) to *Dr. Atkins New Diet Revolution* by Robert C. Atkins (Avon, 1997).
- **Fitness:** This subcategory includes books on exercise, nutrition, and healthy lifestyle. Some recent popular titles include *Body for Life* by Bill Philips (HarperCollins, 1999), *The Fitness Instinct* by Peg Jordan (Rodale, 1999), and *Jane Brody's Nutrition Book* by Jane E. Brody (BDD, 1989).
- **Alternative and holistic health:** This growth area, which sits alongside the more traditional medical books, embraces alternative approaches to health including herbal remedies, meditation, spiritual cleansing, and other unconventional approaches to health, recovery, and fitness. *The People's Pharmacy Guide to Home and Herbal Remedies* by Joe Graedon and Teresa Graedon, Ph.D. (St. Martin's Press, 1999), *The Encyclopedia of Natural Healing* by Gary Null, Ph.D. (Kensington Publishing Corp., 1998), and *The Creation of Health* by Caroline Myss, Ph.D. and C. Norman Shealy, M.D. (Three Rivers Press, 1998) are examples of some top-selling books in this flourishing subcategory.
- **Beauty and fashion:** This subcategory includes traditional beauty and fashion books as well as books on looking and feeling your best. Some favorites include *The World's Best Kept Beauty Secrets* by Diane Irons (Sourcebooks, 1997), *Survival of the Prettiest* by Nancy L. Etcoff (Doubleday, 1999), and *What Should I Wear* by Kim Johnson Gross, Linda Johnson, and Jeff Stone (Knopf, 1998).

History

This traditionally solid category is especially popular with male book buyers. Subcategories include military history, naval history, and ancient history. History bestsellers over the past few year include *A Distant Mirror* by Barbara Tuchman (Knopf, 1986), *No Ordinary Time* by Doris Kearns Goodwin (Simon & Schuster, 1994), *How the Irish Saved Civilization* by Tom Cahill (Talese/ Doubleday, 1995), *The Greatest Generation* by Tom Brokow (Random House, 1998), *The Century* by Peter Jennings and Todd Brewster (Doubleday, 1998), and *The Terrible Hours* by Peter Maas (HarperCollins, 1999).

Home and garden

This growing section includes books on all areas of home and garden decor, design, and repair. Additionally, there are books on antiques, home crafts, flower guides, and flower arranging. This category is dominated by the lavish offerings that resemble the high-priced gift books. (See the section "Gift books," earlier in this chapter.)

Prominent experts in this field tend to have TV exposure, like Martha Stewart and Bob Vila. However, you can always find exceptions, such as homemaker Cheryl Mendelson who wrote a single volume how-to guide on what she does all day — homemaking. The book, *Home Comforts* (Scribners, 1999), was recently No. 1 on Amazon's list of best-selling Home and Garden books.

Humor

The humor section has joke books, cartoon collections, and parodies as well as books that make humorous observations. Not surprisingly, syndicated cartoon columnists and show biz types tend to dominate this area. Books by comedians such as Al Franken, Steve Martin, Bill Murray, Scott Adams, Dave Barry, Paul Reiser, and Chris Rock occupy comfortable spots on the shelf.

But not every humor book is written by a celebrity. Many years ago, a young editorial assistant at St. Martin's Press, known among her colleagues for the endless stream of disgusting jokes she would spring on people, was eventually encouraged by a colleague to send a collection of her "truly tasteless jokes" to a publisher. She did just that using the pen name Blanche Knott. The publisher loved the collection, offered her a contract, and *Blanche Knott's Truly Tasteless Jokes* became a huge bestseller, spawning a whole series of joke books.

Successful humor books can come from unexpected sources. The humor bestseller of 1999, for example, was launched from a popular Web site, The Onion: *Our Dumb Century: The Onion Presents 100 Years of Headlines from America's Finest News Source* by The Onion, T. Herman Zweibel (Introduction), Scott Dikkers (Three Rivers, 1999).

Inspirational and spiritual

This hot category includes "feel good" books like *Chicken Soup for the Soul* by Jack Canfield and Mark Victor Hansen (Health Communications, 1993), motivational books like *Getting The Love You Want* by Harville Hendrix, Ph.D. (HarperPerennial, 1990), spiritual quests such as *Reason for Hope* by Jane Goodall and Phillip Berman (Warner, 1999), or *Conversations With God: An Uncommon Dialogue* by Neale Donald Walsch (Putnam, 1996), and books on living a simpler life such as *Simple Abundance: A Day Book of Comfort and Joy* by Sarah Ban Breathnach (Warner, 1995). It also includes books on astrology, feng shui, psychics, Eastern thought, Buddhism, mysticism, healing and recovery, and life-after-death experiences.

Parenting and family

Parenting books are in demand, no doubt due to the fact that baby boomers treat parenting as serious business. This category includes books on pregnancy, childbirth, and baby names, as well as all aspects of the care and feeding of children, from toilet training and discipline to communication and adolescent issues. Titles in this category can range from encyclopedic works such as *The Baby Book: Everything You Need to Know about Your Child from Birth to Age Two* by William Sears, M.D. and Martha Sears, R.N. (Little Brown, 1993) to smaller, single issue books such as the ever popular *Solve Your Child's Sleep Problems* by Richard Ferber (Simon & Schuster, 1986), and *What to Expect When You're Expecting* by Arlene Eisenberg (Workman, 1984).

Pop culture/entertainment

Readers live in a media-driven society, and they have an insatiable appetite for information about the media and its celebrities. Bookstores set aside plenty of shelf space to serve this category, with books about movies, television, music, theater, radio, and print media, as well as the stars themselves. For example, each year a host of new pop stars emerge, from Brittany Spears and Ricky Martin, to Celine Dion, Brad Pitt, the Three Tenors, and even Pokémon. For each new pop phenomenon, a book is often hastily written and rushed into print in an effort to cash in on the stars' popularity.

This category also includes more serious books of criticism, reference, and analysis, as well as texts of plays and movies and various hard-to-categorize books such as the recent series of wrestling blockbusters: *The Rock Says* by The Rock with Joe Layden (ReganBooks/HarperCollins, 2000) and *Have A Nice Day* by Mick Foley (ReganBooks/HarperCollins, 1999).

Professional

This category of books is intended to assist professionals in their chosen career by helping them achieve mastery in their profession. Professional books are published in such areas as business/management, law, accounting, medicine, computer science engineering, architecture, and education.

Most professional books are published by specialist publishers and sold direct to consumers, though some are sold in bookstores. Typically, these books are higher priced than general books because they have a smaller, very specialized audience. As a prospective writer, if you have a highly specialized professional skill that you can write about, this category is a good one to break into.

Reference

The reference category has the kinds of books you consult for facts, guidelines, and background information. This category is where you look things up and find things out. Amazon.com includes the following subcategories in its reference section: Almanacs & Yearbooks, Atlases & Maps, Business Skills, Careers, Catalogs & Directories, Consumer Guides, Dictionaries & Thesauri, Education, Encyclopedias, Etiquette, Foreign Languages, Fun Facts, Genealogy, Law, Publishing & Books, Quotations, Test Prep, Transportation, and Words & Language, and Writing.

Most reference books present the same challenge to publishers that gift books do — these books are long, complex, and expensive to produce. Often they are produced by expert packagers who hire the writers, illustrators, designers, and fine arts printers. (See the section "Gift books," earlier in this chapter.)

But don't be intimidated. There's plenty of room for a single individual with a distinct passion to produce a wonderful and much-needed reference book. One of the greatest publishing success stories is that of Tim and Nina Zagat. In 1979, the Zagats discovered a large audience with an underserved need. At the time, the only restaurant guides available to New Yorkers were compilations of restaurant reviews culled from the newspapers and written mainly by professional restaurant critics. No guides described the experience of actual restaurant customers. So the Zagats asked their friends to take notes when they ate in restaurants, and they compiled the notes into a small, free newsletter, the Zagat Guide to Restaurants in New York, which evaluated hundreds of restaurants according to a tally of customer surveys. The first guide was such a hit that a year later the Zagat's decided to self-publish their restaurant guide as a slim paperback. Today, more than 100,000 diners contribute their comments to the Zagat series, which rates the restaurants in 40 cities and sells hundreds of thousands of copies annually.

Science and nature

This category includes books about all the natural sciences, from astronomy to zoology, and includes works of exploration, explanation, and research. If your passion is science, then this category is your route to publication. The trick is to find a story that suits your talents, and strikes a responsive chord with readers.

For example, Dava Sobel is a science writer and author of several books on various topics from backache pain to the existence of extra-terrestrial life. One day she attended a symposium on the story of John Harrison and his amazing lifelong search for the right instrument to enable ships to measure their time and position. At the symposium, Sobel realized that Harrison's story contained the seeds of a compelling science adventure story, which combined drama, intricate scientific detail, and a significant outcome. The resulting book, *Longitude* by Dava Sobel (Walker, 1995), was a major best-seller and is destined to be a science classic.

Self-help/how-to

Self-help/how-to is the largest nonfiction category. It encompasses almost every section of the bookstore, from business and health to childcare and home repair. These books tend to be motivational in nature such as *The Seven Habits of Highly Successful People* by Steven Covey (S&S, 1989) and inspirational in spirit such as *The Art of Happiness* by the Dalai Lama (Riverhead, 1998). This category also includes the whole range of parenting books and relationship books such as *You Just Don't Understand* by Deborah Tannen (Morrow, 1990), *The Dance of Anger* by Harriet Lerner (HarperCollins, 1993), *A Child Called It* by Dave Peltzer (Health Communications, 1994), and *My Mother, Myself* by Nancy Friday (Delacorte, 1977).

For writers, this category is fertile ground. You can identify an unmet need (see Chapter 2) and fill it, as Tim and Nina Zagat did with their *Zagat Restaurant Guides* (Zagat, 2000). Or you can add a unique twist to the commonplace as James Finn Garner did in his *Politically Correct Bedtime Stories* (Macmillan, 1994). You can also offer understanding and guidance as John Gray does in his marriage self-help book, *Men are from Mars, Women are from Venus* (HarperCollins, 1992). Or consider delivering what may seem impossible or unobtainable to people as Ken Blanchard and Spencer Johnson did in *The One-Minute Manager.* Whatever tack you take, let your creative juices flow and have fun!

Self-help is such a broad term that most publishers do not view it as a true category — more refinement is needed before a publisher will know what sort of self-help book you have in mind. If you are planning to present a self-help title to a publisher (see Chapter 9), you must be careful to specify which subgenre of self-help the book belongs in. For example, a self-help book about investing should be submitted to a finance editor, whereas a self-help book about diet should go to an editor specializing in nutrition. Many of the broad categories below include self-help titles: there are business self-help titles (in management, finance and sales), there are medical self-help books, diet manuals, spiritual self-help books, and so on.

Sports and outdoors

This popular category includes books, for participants and spectators alike, on such sports as baseball, football, hockey, basketball, tennis, and golf. There are also how-to books on outdoor activities such as camping, hiking, rafting, and so on, as well as sports references, such as *Total Baseball* by John Thorn, et.al., (Total Sports, 1999), and memoirs of famous athletes, coaches, and outdoorsmen.

This category includes many stories about athletes and coaches who overcome adversity. In the process of writing their books, several of the writers in this category also overcome a share of adversity. The most famous is John Feinstein, a little-known reporter who persuaded Coach Bob Knight of the Indiana Hoosiers to accept an unusual request. Knight agreed to let Feinstein virtually live with him and his players through one entire season of college basketball. Feinstein was paid a small advance by a publisher and shadowed Knight's team for months. A year later, the resulting book, *A Season on the Brink* by John Feinstein (S&S, 1989), was an overnight sensation that afforded, as never before, a completely intimate and candid view of one of the most controversial and outrageous figures in sports.

Today, more than a decade later, *A Season on the Brink* is the best-selling sports hardcover of all time. But back in 1989, John Feinstein was an unknown with a clear vision and the chutzpah to ask the impossible.

Travel

The World Wide Web has changed the travel industry: the way people plan their holidays, buy airline tickets, and obtain travel information.

As travel agents are squeezed out of the process, travelers turn to books for their travel information needs. Consequently, a booming market exists for travel books of all kinds: travel series guides, such as Fodor's, the Access Guides, and the Eyewitness Guides, and books of personal travel description, such as *A Year in Provence* by Peter Mayle (Knopf, 1990), and *A Walk in the Woods* by Bill Bryson (Broadway, 1998).

True crime

Works of true crime reconstruct the actual events of a crime, usually a murder. Truman Capote invented this category when his groundbreaking book, *In Cold Blood* (Vintage, 1994), was first published in 1960. In that book, Capote reconstructs the moment-by-moment events surrounding a brutal murder, which took place in Holcomb, Kansas, in 1959. Capote painstakingly interviewed the accused murderers and the survivors, investigators, and everyone else close to the case and produced an intimate portrait of a little-known event. The book was an over-night sensation and pioneered a genre that survives today. Another great classic in this genre is *Executioner's Song* by Norman Mailer (Vintage, 1998).

It's not necessary to be Capote or Mailer to write a best-selling true crime book. What is necessary is the determination to find a suitable case and access to the people involved. Hundreds of true crime books are published every year, and many find a wide readership.

Part II

Knocking on the Publisher's Door

"The margins on your book proposal are sooo even, Ms. Holly, and the type so black and crisp. I'm sure whatever the book's about is also good, but with centered headlines and flush left columns like this, we'd be fools not to publish it!"

In this part . . .

Publishing folks are particular about the way writers approach them. In this part, I alert you to who the key decision-makers are at a publishing company and how best to make your approach.

Chapter 5

How a Book Gets Bought

In This Chapter

- Thinking like a publisher (a little bit)
- Finding the gatekeeper
- Triggering a "buy" decision

To arrive at the right submission strategy for your book (see Chapter 6), it helps to know how the inner workings of a publishing house actually operate and, more specifically, how the decision to purchase a book idea happens. Who are the key players? And what are the key factors involved in the decision to publish a proposed book?

The Players

The core members of any publishing acquisition team are made up of two very different types: the creative, editorial types and the more financially driven sales and marketing types. Generally speaking, the editorial staff is responsible for obtaining a wide range of prospective book ideas and shepherding them through the publication process, while the sales and marketing people are in charge of allocating the publishing house's financial resources.

The editor

The *editor* is your advocate. While an editor's job entails more diverse duties than most people realize, an editor's main concern is to solicit books — hopefully successful ones — for the publishing company to publish. Soliciting books is accomplished in a few different ways: attending lunches and meetings with literary agents and prospective authors, commissioning book ideas, chasing down "hot" literary leads, and wading through the endless stack of query letters, proposals, and manuscripts that arrive daily. Most of the submissions are returned with a polite, albeit brief, rejection letter written by the editor.

The editor presents the more promising submissions at the company's weekly editorial meeting (see the section "The editorial meeting," later in this chapter). If the company decides to publish the book, the editor then works with the author to prepare the manuscript for publication. The editor also supervises the manuscript through the production process, including typesetting and jacket design. And while the book is in production, the editor helps work on the marketing plan and provides the sales team with everything from sample pages to ringing endorsements to help launch the book out into the world.

Through the editor, an author must be prepared to fight for his book during each phase. For example, the author should seek consultation on jacket design and copy at contract time. In addition, the author must insist that his book is marketed and displayed appropriately. However, unless marketing money is promised at contract, an author can do precious little to influence display space provided in bookstores (see Chapter 20). You can sometimes effectively apply pressure to secure additional advertising and/or publicity expenditures on behalf of your book. If the author doesn't ask, the editor usually assumes that the author is content. For that reason, you as an author must be persistent in your requests to your editor. Be kind, but firm.

Remember, the author's interests and the editor's are to a certain extent in alignment: The success or failure of each of the editor's books helps determine the editor's salary (short term) and career success (long term). So editors are looking for books with the likeliest chance of prospering.

The editorial assistant

An *editorial assistant* assists an editor of more senior rank. The assistant performs many secretarial tasks: processing paperwork, filling in forms, endless photocopying, answering the phone, filing, and generally taking care of as many of the day-to-day details for the editor as possible.

In addition, the assistant helps with some of the editorial tasks: writing book descriptions, answering questions from authors, and in some cases acting as a first reader on book proposals and manuscripts submitted to the editor — championing some for the editor's consideration and simply rejecting others, often before the editor even knows they exist. If you're a first-time author, an editorial assistant can play a disproportionately important role in the fate of your book — either guiding it to the attention of a caring editor or killing your chances before you even get to square one.

The Publisher

In publishing parlance, the *Publisher* is the person who oversees the whole process of a publishing company — from which books to purchase and how much to pay for each, all the way through to how the books are sold. In most cases, the Publisher has a fiscal responsibility within the publishing company: responsibility for spending a set amount of money in a given year for the purchase and marketing of books, as well as responsibility for earning a certain profit. A Publisher stays informed about the profitability of each book. If a book doesn't perform up to expectation, the overall revenue and profit targets become difficult to reach, and the Publisher has to make adjustments.

Throughout the book, I use the word *publisher* with a lowercase *p* to describe a publishing company as a whole; I use the word *Publisher* with an uppercase *P* to describe the top executive at a publishing company.

The editorial meeting

Most publishing companies hold a weekly editorial meeting, presided over by the editor in chief (at some houses) or the Publisher. At most firms, the company's editors attend the editorial meeting, as do representatives from other departments such as marketing, sales, or subsidiary rights (see Chapter 17).

The editorial meeting is where projects are discussed and refined. The only absolute decisions being made in this forum are which books to pursue and for what kind of dollar figure. At some companies, more definite acquisition decisions take place at the editorial meeting, especially if the Publisher presides at the editorial meeting. But usually, the editorial meeting provides an opportunity for the editor to confer with other editors about specific book projects — soliciting opinions and expert knowledge from colleagues.

The acquisition process

In all publishing companies, it is the Publisher who has the authority to greenlight a book. In some companies, the Publisher is the sole decision-maker on whether to publish a book. At other firms, the Publisher might solicit the opinion of important department heads such as the sales department, the marketing department, and the subsidiary rights department. The head of sales can provide an estimate of how many copies of the book the company can realistically sell based on previous experience with similar books. The head of marketing can propose a marketing campaign and estimate the probable costs involved in carrying it out. The head of subsidiary rights may be able to estimate income from the sale of such rights as foreign, movie, and book club. This information helps the Publisher make an informed financial decision as to whether to publish a particular book.

The decision to offer a contract to an author is usually based on a profit and loss analysis of the book, known as a P&L. To calculate a P&L, the editor — usually with the assistance of a financial analyst — estimates the number of copies the book is likely to sell, the list price, and the amount of money paid to the author as well as other costs, including manufacturing, distributing, and marketing the book. On the basis of this information, the P&L calculates how much profit (or loss) results if the book is published.

Rarely do publishers move forward on a book that yields a P&L that is not marginally profitable. So, it's important for you, the writer, when submitting your work, to provide the editor with detailed information on the audience and market for the book that translates into a very positive P&L assessment.

The Acquisition Process in Action

Here's how a book project works its way from submission to acquisition in an ideal world. Say that an author sends a proposal for a nonfiction book (see Chapter 8) to an editor whose name she got from the acknowledgment page of a book she admires. The editor's editorial assistant reads it at midnight and is surprised to find it captivating. The assistant strongly recommends it to the editor the next morning. The editor reads it on the train home that night and decides to bring it up at the weekly editorial meeting. She (a vast majority of editors in book publishing are women) sends a copy to two other editors to read before the meeting. At the meeting, the editor sings the project's praises and is seconded by both of the other two editorial readers. The Publisher agrees to read it that night and asks that a copy be sent to the sales director to provide a sales estimate. With a sales estimate in hand, a P&L can be drawn up.

Two days later, the editor is summoned to the Publisher's office. The Publisher relays that the sales director provided a very low sales estimate. Based on the sales director's estimate, the resulting P&L predicted a loss for the book. But the Publisher says that she read the proposal and felt that with a few changes, the book could be much more saleable. The editor and Publisher discuss how the book project can be altered in order to appeal to a larger audience. The editor calls the author, who agrees that the suggested changes are a good idea and may make for a stronger book. The next day, the editor returns to the Publisher with the news that the author is happy to make the suggested changes. The editor produces a new P&L based on these changes. The Publisher then authorizes a contract to be offered to the author for an agreed-upon price.

The editor excitedly calls the author, who is thrilled to learn that her first book will soon be a reality.

Chapter 6

The Right Submission Strategy for You

In This Chapter

- Clarifying your submission goal
- Evaluating strategies for approaching a publisher

How do you get an editor to give serious thought to publishing your book idea? That's the question all aspiring authors ask. And there isn't one simple answer.

In this chapter, I show you seven approaches and identify which ones work best. I walk you through each one, giving examples and tips from my experience and from the experiences of writers who have done it successfully. Additionally, I size up the chances of success for each strategy.

Approaching a Publisher

Like most beginning writers, you probably don't have access to book publishers. After all, not many people count literary agents, editors, or booksellers among their circle of acquaintances. You may not know the names of any editors or literary agents either. Likewise, you may not yet have focused on which publishing companies are proven experts at publishing your sort of book.

All that is about to change, because it's almost time to present your book for consideration, either in the form of a proposal if it's a nonfiction work (see Chapter 8) or as a finished manuscript if it's a work of fiction (see Chapter 8). More than anything else, research is the name of the game. Just as location is critical to real estate success, in-depth, unrelenting research is the way to succeed at getting your book published.

Your goal

Your goal is to get your book idea in front of a key decision-maker who sees the merit of publishing your book. Keep in mind that your goal has two parts: getting your book in the hands of a decision-maker and convincing that person to publish it.

The editor, your advocate

You want the editor of your book to be an unfailing advocate throughout the entire process, from submission all the way to publication and beyond. So, unless you have a personal relationship with a Publisher, plan on enlisting the support of an editor first.

If an editor you approach doesn't see the book's merits, move on. You want an editor to be unswervingly committed to your book. Writers are often amazed by the insightful and powerful suggestions an editor can make to enhance a book. A devoted editor can help make the book a standout in its field. For that reason, it's best to arrive at a publishing house via an editor.

If you come in by way of a relationship with someone else at the firm — a marketing person, the editor in chief, or even the Publisher himself, you are likely to be assigned to an editor. And the editor may not like your book, possibly feeling resentful for having to devote valuable time and energy to it. Take the case of a legendary nightclub act that was signed up several years ago by a very prominent Publisher. Seated at a front row table with the performer's manager, the Publisher decided that this act would serve as the basis for a marvelous book — there and then (well, perhaps after a few drinks) he offered the manager a generous book contract.

A few days later, the Publisher was back in his office and realized that he had no clear idea of what book, exactly, this performer might write or even why he had been so enthusiastic on the night of the performance. He called in one of his top editors and asked that the editor take the project under his wing. With no clear understanding of what the book was or why it had been acquired, the editor did his best. The resulting book was not exactly a work of art, but the editor did manage to create a lavish and praiseworthy book, even though his heart, and the public's interest in the book, was never engaged. Don't let a similar fate befall your book.

The Strategies

You can secure a Publisher's attention in a number of ways. Even the simplest (and least likely to succeed) requires research. The most productive approaches require more research, along with some planning and, often, more daring. Your aim is to plot a submission strategy and craft an approach so persuasive that an editor wants to see your work and reads it with wholehearted interest.

#1: Send your proposal or manuscript

There is simply no situation where sending your material, unsolicited, to a publisher is the best approach or the most likely to succeed.

However, you can use a number of distinct strategies for submitting your work, each one requiring different amounts of background preparation, that improves the reception of your materials once you send them. The first is the simple blind submission to "The Editorial Department" — the least effective of them all.

To the Editorial Department

Sending your proposal in a plain brown envelope addressed to "The Editors" or "The Editorial Department" is pretty much like sending a letter to Santa Claus. It might make you feel better, but it probably won't result in a publishing contract. You can easily locate the addresses of publishing houses on the copyright page of recently published books and then send off your work. Legend has it that authors have succeeded with this method; *Ordinary People* by Judith Quest (Viking Press, 1976) was reportedly discovered in an envelope addressed to the Editorial Department.

More recently, this approach was successful for an unpublished 26-year-old who sent a story to *The New Yorker* magazine addressed "Dear Editor." The story, entitled "The Other Family" by Rob Bingham, was first read by Deb Garrison, a 27-year-old assistant editor who knew as soon as she read it that the writer had a unique voice — a voice that spoke for her generation. She felt confident bringing it to the attention of the senior editors at *The New Yorker.* And sure enough, Bingham's story was published in America's most prestigious literary magazine. But the success rate of "Dear Editor" submissions is too low to be worth your consideration.

Glance inside a publishing house, and you'll be quickly dissuaded from attempting this approach. At one major firm I know, for example, anonymous submissions pile up in a corner near the mail boxes until the stack reaches close to the ceiling and starts to fall over into the hallway. When it can no longer be ignored, the editor in chief orders pizzas for the editorial assistants, who gather in a conference room at lunch time to open up the envelopes, scan the contents, and dispatch them with polite but impersonal rejection letters.

To a specific editor by name

You have a significantly better chance in a publishing house if you address your material to a specific editor. Editors' names are often mentioned on the acknowledgment page of your favorite books and in reference volumes, such as *Literary Market Place* and *Writers Market.* (See the next section on cold calling and Chapter 9). Editors are generally reluctant to take time to read a submission that has arrived unannounced and unrequested — there are plenty of submissions that were requested and are piled up, awaiting a reader. But an editor is more likely to read a letter addressed directly to him or her and might feel some responsibility to at least have your pages looked at by an assistant.

However, as a rule, sending your proposal or manuscript unsolicited is never a good idea. If you do, be prepared to have it returned. If you must send a manuscript unasked, don't include a self-addressed stamped envelope (SASE), as many publishing guidebooks suggest. An SASE marks you as an amateur and invites immediate rejection. Just be sure that you aren't sending your only copy, because the editor's office may not take the time to return it. And make it easy for the publisher to contact you by providing your phone number and e-mail address.

But be aware that you probably won't hear from the editor unless she wants to acquire your book. It's my recommendation that you follow up after a month has passed. If two months pass in silence, just move on. The business of submitting materials to a publisher is hit or miss at best. Whatever you do, be professional: Don't be a pest and don't invite rejection.

#2: Cold call to an editor

This approach entails calling an editor, out of the blue, telling her how much you enjoy the books she edits and letting her know that you have a new book proposal that may be of interest. Describe your book in two or three succinct sentences and ask whether you may send along your proposal.

The key to this approach — and any submission to an editor — is that you do preliminary research. First, you need to find editors that have a track record with the sort of book you have in mind. You can find this out in a couple of ways. One is to comb through the acknowledgment pages of recent books similar to yours. Authors often thank the editor in their acknowledgments. So spend some time at the library as well as a book superstore, looking at the acknowledgments in books similar to the one you plan to write. From these pages alone, you're likely to come up with a substantial list of editors who may welcome your submission.

You can also call the publicity department at various publishing houses and ask them to send you a catalog of upcoming titles. Try to ascertain whether they have a book similar to yours already in the works. If so, they almost certainly won't add another. Also, ask the switchboard operator for the name of the assistant who works for the editor you are going to cold call. Call the assistant first and confirm that the editor is still with the company (editors move around a lot), and whether it's best to call or e-mail the editor. This is a good way to get the editor's direct dial number and e-mail address. If the editorial assistant is friendly, you may feel him or her out for the feasibility of submitting your proposal. Try enlisting the assistant as a preliminary reader. If the assistant likes it, you'll have an advocate to hand-deliver the proposal to the editor. This assistant-as-advocate approach is an extremely effective way of getting the work of first-time writers on to an editor's desk.

Remember, while it's true that editors are always prospecting for new books, they are also constantly pressed for time. So when you call, understand that they may be in the throes of contemplating several potential books. Make your call as brief as possible. Give your name and a word or two of your qualifications. Summarize your book idea in a sentence or two. Then offer to submit it. Don't try to provoke a meeting so that you can sell the book in person (that will come later). Don't launch into a plot synopsis or a description of the outline. Go for the close quickly — "I've written this book, would you be willing to read it?" If the answer is affirmative, great. Get your proposal into the mail as soon as possible. If the answer is negative, accept the verdict and move on. For now.

#3: Query letter by mail to an editor

I occasionally see in conventional how-to-get-published books the recommendation that first-time authors approach a publisher by means of a query letter sent to the editor. (See Chapter 7 for more on query letters.) The theory holds that a good query letter gets across all the important information about a potential book yet isn't as intrusive as a phone call. A good query describes the proposed book in a paragraph or two, followed by a paragraph explaining why you, the author, are qualified to write the proposed book. The third paragraph asks whether the editor is interested in receiving the full proposal or manuscript as a formal submission.

An author can get lucky with this approach and have an editor actually respond. However, the problem with this method is that it leaves a response entirely in the hands of a busy, already overburdened editor. What that means is that you still need to contact the editor by phone to follow up on the query letter. So unless the query letter has the perfect hook to make the editor call you right away, you're hardly better off using this method than if you had made the initial approach by phone. Additionally, this method gives the editor an opportunity to say no without even seeing your well-thought-out proposal. (See Chapter 7 for writing query letters that demand attention.)

Wow them in five minutes

Harvey Mackay, the envelope magnate and author of *Swim with the Sharks: Without Being Eaten Alive* (William Morrow, 1988), used an innovative approach to get the attention of editors. He would call a prospective editor and ask for just two minutes of his or her time. He assured each editor that if he didn't get his point across in two minutes, he would leave immediately. If an editor agreed, Harvey would fly from his home in Minneapolis to wherever the editor was located. (He has pursued two-minute meetings as far away as New York, London, Frankfurt, even Tokyo). Of course, Harvey is a great talker, and it's a rare two-minute meeting with him that lasted only two minutes.

#4: E-mail to an editor

A new option, though somewhat similar to the query letter approach, is to make contact with an editor by e-mail. An e-mail solicitation can be quick and informal as long as it's sure to pique the editor's interest. And e-mail makes it easy for the editor to respond.

Place a quick call to the editor's assistant to make sure that you have the correct e-mail address for the editor. And use an e-mail system that confirms whether an e-mail has been read and/or received.

No matter how tempted you are, don't attach other materials like a full proposal, photographic material, or any video or audio recording to this initial e-mail. That can come later. Software incompatibility and incompetence still abounds, so unless you're invited to e-mail attachments, don't do it. You want to interest the editor, not overwhelm or anger her.

Keep in mind that some people hold e-mail solicitations in contempt as "Spam" and automatically delete them. So if you don't hear anything after a few days, you need to call the editor and introduce yourself. (See strategy #2, earlier in this chapter.)

#5: Gimmicks

The annals of publishing are full of gimmicks that authors and agents use to get a publisher's attention. By far the most extreme case I remember was that of a disgruntled author who felt ignored immediately after the publication of his book. In order to get the Publisher's attention, he chartered a small private plane and flew it several times rather threateningly around the Publisher's

44th floor, Manhattan office. He got their attention all right. The Publisher, outraged by his antics, canceled the author's contract, removed every copy of his book from their warehouse, and sent them to his home via semi trailer.

Many publishers still remember, more than ten years after the fact, the flamboyant presentation by Michigan attorney and literary agent Robert Fenton, of a first novel entitled *Black Tie Only*. The manuscript was written by Fenton himself with a writing partner under the pseudonym Julia Fenton. For good reason, Fenton suspected that a novel written by an unknown and submitted by an unknown (at least in New York publishing circles) was unlikely to be read with much attention by editors in New York. So Fenton packaged it to be noticed.

With the help of his sister, a party planner, he produced an elaborate package to enclose the first 200 pages of the manuscript, placing it in a white satin drawstring bag, enclosed in black and white tissue paper, with an engraved invitation on the outside designed to echo an invitation upon which the plot of the novel hinged. The invitation was personalized to each editor, and each was invited to partake of the first 200 pages. The bottle of fine champagne accompanying each package made the whole submission even more inviting.

Within a few days, six of the editors had offered for the book, and by the end of the week, Fenton had secured an advance of well over $100,000 for his first novel — a handsome sum by today's standards, and even more impressive in 1989, when this all happened.

Fenton went on to sell and publish several more books, but he looks back on this first venture wryly, observing that while the gimmick was fun and probably got his novel on the radar screens of New York publishing, he is certain that his novel would have been published even without all the gimmickry — though probably at a slightly lower advance. And in general, I don't recommend that you resort to a gimmick of this sort. The danger of being viewed as a kook, or worse, is very real.

Authors of romances have sent flowers, candy, engraved invitations, even fur coats, and ballet tickets to prospective editors. Query letters are sent in brightly colored paper, gift boxes, cigar boxes, and many other eye-catching and mind-bending packages, intended to capture the publisher's attention. One author, a squash pro, offered his prospective editor ten free squash lessons by way of introduction to his proposal for a book entitled *Squash: How to Play, How to Win*.

Most editors have, at one time or another, been impressed by a gimmicky approach and given attention to an imaginatively packaged query letter or proposal. So if you know a gifted and imaginative packager — who possesses a sense of appropriateness and decorum — enlist his or her help in coming up with a creative way to package your book idea and get it onto an editor's desk.

Keep in mind, however, that editors are optimists by inclination and skeptics by training. They are likely to be put on their guard by an author or agent who resorts to enticements — or outright bribes — to get a proposal read. Remember that an editor is ultimately judged by the performance of the books she signs on and therefore must evaluate your book's market potential as objectively as possible. If she suspects you're attempting to undermine that objectivity, she's likely to apply tougher standards to your proposal.

#6: Use a literary agent

You're probably wondering why I didn't recommend using an agent in the first place and why I'm encouraging you to research specific editors and their book preferences, if an agent may be more likely to get you into a publishing house?

The answer is simple. For most first-time authors, enlisting the services of a literary agent is as difficult as getting a hearing with an editor directly (see Chapter 11). From experience, I've learned that most first-time authors make their initial contact with a publisher on their own.

However, you can certainly pursue agents and editors simultaneously. The strategies and tips I recommend here for reaching an editor apply just as well for reaching agents. For example, don't show up in person before you have made contact via letter or phone. Publishers and agents alike won't give you a hearing if you act in an unprofessional and disrespectful way.

Bear in mind this crucial difference between editors and agents: A literary agent works for free until a publisher buys your work and then is compensated with a share of your earnings from the book (called a *commission*). An editor is paid by the publisher, who in turn must pay you for the privilege of publishing your work.

#7: Network

Make it your business to be places where editors and agents are likely to be, such as writers' conventions and writers' conferences. Writers' conferences are one of the best places to network because they're so well attended by publishing folk. They also offer an opportunity to have your work read by and discussed with a publishing professional. There's no substitute for actually meeting different editors, sizing them up, and using your instincts to decide which ones may be appropriate for your book.

Also, use the six degrees of separation concept to your advantage. So, okay, you don't know any publishing people, but that doesn't mean your friends don't know anyone in publishing. Ask them — all of them. What do you have to lose? Any sort of introduction is better than a cold call.

LMP: A Writer's Bible — What it is and how to use it

The *Literary Market Place*, known as LMP, is the most useful reference available to writers. It's available in the reference section of most, if not all, public libraries, and it also maintains a Web site, `www.literarymarketplace.com/lmp/us/subscript.asp`, that offers abbreviated LMP information to the general public and enhanced content to subscribers.

LMP contains a complete listing of publishers, agents, book packagers, and all kinds of other publishing professionals. Each entry, for example, provides contact information for the company, as well as a partial list of the staff and an abbreviated summary of the company's subject offerings. LMP's entry on a publishing company won't provide all the background information you need before making your initial approach to an editor. However, it does provide key contact information as well as the types of books the company publishes — it's a good basic guide for eliminating publishers that don't publish the sort of book you have in mind, or for identifying firms that warrant more extensive research.

An LMP literary agency listing is somewhat more comprehensive. It usually includes a complete staff listing and a list of subject categories that the agency handles. Other sources, such as *Writer's Market* (Writer's Digest Books) and *Writer's Guide to Book Editors, Publishers, and Literary Agents* (Prima Publishing), give more specific information on which agents handle which sorts of books. Consulting as many sources as possible before approaching an agent is a good idea. But the phone numbers and contact information listed in LMP helps get you in the door when you're ready to enter.

Part III

Preparing the Package: Book Proposals and Query Letters That Sell

"Someone want to look at this manuscript I received on e-mail called, 'The Embedded Virus That Destroyed the Publisher's Servers When the Manuscript was Rejected'?"

In this part . . .

Getting published is all about preparation — preparing your material for an editor's finely tuned eyes. Editors, agents, and writers communicate book ideas — not over the phone — but in the form of query letters and book proposals. In this part, I show you how to structure query letters and book proposals guaranteed to make an editor stop, take notice, and ask to see more.

Chapter 7

Query Letters That Get Attention

In This Chapter

- Saying it all in one page
- Writing a great nonfiction query letter
- Writing a great fiction query letter
- Tackling online query letters

A good query letter provides editors with a snapshot of your book idea and the market that's clamoring to buy it. It piques their interest and prompts them to ask for more.

Query letters are a universal medium of publishing because editors can't possibly read each and every submission. A great query letter — one page, never longer — breaks through the submission clutter and gets noticed.

In this chapter, I show you exactly what goes into a standout query letter. Once you know the proper format and key elements, it's easy to write effective query letters that get you noticed.

How an Editor Reads Your Query

Bear in mind that your query letter is probably read along with five to ten others that arrive in the same day's mail (20 to 30 if the editor reads queries weekly, as some do), while the phones are ringing, meetings are about to start, authors are on hold, and manuscripts are waiting to be edited. An editor wants to get through the queries quickly in order to move on to the work at hand. So, unless your query letter immediately sparks her interest, she'll scrawl "decline" in the upper-right corner and pass it to her assistant.

Like a resume, a query letter needs to compel attention and respect in every possible way. With this one-page document, you need to convey professionalism, talent, and the passion that drives your work. Make everything about your query letter stand out, starting with the most basic elements of design, layout, format, and tone:

- Query letters are one page, never longer.
- Query letters are typed perfectly, free of any spelling, punctuation, or grammar mistakes in a clear typestyle, large enough — 12 to 14 point size — to be easily read by the naked eye. Print your query on nice quality paper, using a high-quality printer.
- Query letters must get to the point. Ideally, the first sentence communicates your basic idea clearly and somewhat seductively, spurring the editor to read on.
- Direct your query letter to a specific editor or agent and spell her name correctly.
- Query letters are upbeat in tone and broad in scope. Don't, for example, discuss how much you expect to be paid or how long it may take you to write. You want to generate excitement.

Elements of a Great Query Letter

While a query letter for a nonfiction work is slightly different than one for a work of fiction, every query letter must contain the following three essential elements:

- A brief, tantalizing description of the book
- Who and how large the audience is for the book. Be realistic about the potential market for your book. An exaggerated notion about the scope of the market will mark you as a novice in the eyes of many editors.
- A description of the author and why he or she is expertly qualified to write the book

Liza Dawson, literary agent and former executive editor, reveals what she likes to see in a query letter: "What I look for in query letters is previous writing credits, either in books, magazines, or newspapers. I also like lawyers since they write for a living. I'm ridiculously impressed when an author says she has heard about me or likes what I said in one of the agent books, and that she's going to give me a two- or three-week exclusive. I like query letters that are short and clear. If a letter about a novel is too long and bores me, then I figure the novel will too. . . I particularly like it if a writer compares his novel to that of another writer's — for example, 'in the school of *Absolute Power*,' or, 'a novel about an Indian woman with an Amy Tan sensibility.'"

The nonfiction query

A nonfiction query letter usually consists of three paragraphs. The first paragraph describes the book idea. The second paragraph identifies the potential market for the book and details how the book can reach a large portion of that audience. The last paragraph introduces the author and explains why the author is qualified to write the book described in the first paragraph.

Paragraph 1 — The book

This first paragraph carries the heavy freight of your letter — what is this book about. It also contains the "grabber" that persuades your reader to keep reading. Look at these two options:

Dear Editor:

Thanks very much for taking the time to read my query letter. I am a first-time writer, and I am currently thinking about writing a book on home renovation. My brother and I have now renovated both of our homes, and our friends tell us that our renovations look great.

The book that I plan to write is a step-by-step guide to renovating the typical one family home that is in need of repair . . .

Or the alternative

Dear Editor:

In the past year, 2.8 million Americans elected to act as their own home renovation contractor. The book I propose, based on my extensive professional expertise, would be a home renovation bible, from basement to roof, aimed at this huge and growing audience. The book would include step-by-step instructions on every major home renovation task, including materials and tools needed, as well as costs and projected schedules for completion.

See how well the second letter, complete with researched audience figures, commands your attention? In bold, energetic brush strokes, this opening gives a brief overview of the book, what it will include, who the audience is, and even a look at the audience's size.

Agents and editors alike appreciate query letters that get right to the point. And they respond more favorably when the query immediately focuses on the book's idea and establishes a large audience with a need for the book.

The first sample ambles slowly along, actually downplaying the author's qualifications, and waits until the second paragraph to even mention the actual content of the book. Most editors won't bear with you that long.

Paragraph 2 — The market

In most great query letters, the potential market for the book is mentioned in the first paragraph and fully developed — but not overstated! — in the second paragraph. Here's an example from the query letter I wrote for this book.

An estimated 550,000 book proposals were submitted to publishers last year, up from 500,000 five years ago. Why the increase? Writing and researching are easier than ever thanks to the technological advancements that have brought personal computers and the Internet into American homes. In addition, the subscriber base of magazines targeted at aspiring writers has expanded to over 600,000. **Getting Your Book Published For Dummies** *will speak directly to today's more technologically advanced writers about basic strategies, cutting edge publishing trends, and the benefits technology offers today's writers using up-to-the minute examples of what's being published NOW and who's publishing it.*

Note that I identify the overall size of the market in the first line. Additionally, I provide two ways to reach the market — targeted magazines and the Internet. I also explain how the book will be written to specifically address the growth segment of the market. Bear in mind, I sent it to a publishing company that made its name publishing computer manuals *For Dummies*. Keeping the query audience in mind, I made sure to link the national increase in book submissions to the growth in home computers.

It worked.

Paragraph 3 — A few words about me

In a query letter, there's an effective way to write about yourself, and a not-so-effective way. The following are examples of both.

Sarah Parsons Zackheim is a native of Birmingham, Michigan, and a graduate of William Smith College. She attended the International Publishing Symposium at Oxford University in England, before taking a job as a sales promotion associate at Doubleday and Company in 1981. A year later, she moved to the editorial department, where she worked as an editorial assistant to Executive Editor Lisa Drew and then Thomas Guinzburg. Enticed by the high-quality nonfiction, Sarah moved to an editorial position at the New York Times Book Company before relocating to Connecticut with her husband, also a book editor, and her two small children.

As a young mother, Sarah continued to work on a freelance basis for several publishing houses and also launched her career as an author with her first book, **Choose the Perfect Name for Your Baby**, *published by Longmeadow Press in 1992. Her second book,* **365 Ways to Save Money**, *was published by Landmark Press in 1995 and a year later, she began work on* **Dress Your House for Success** *with co-author Martha Webb. Acting as her own agent, Sarah submitted this book to six publishers, conducted an auction, and negotiated the contract.*

The book was published by Three Rivers Press/Clarkson Potter in 1997. In addition, Sarah has written for ***Family Fun*** *magazine,* ***Family Life*** *magazine as well as many local newspapers and is a frequent contributing writer to* ***Fairfield County*** *magazine.*

While this is all true, it isn't very succinct. And it certainly wouldn't fit into a query letter. Query letters call for a tightly focused author description highlighting your achievements that directly enhance the book.

Sarah Parsons Zackheim is a successful publishing professional as well as a widely published freelance writer. After nearly a decade on-staff at several New York publishing firms, she has written three books as well as numerous newspaper and magazine articles. Acting as her own literary agent, she placed her most recent book for a six-figure advance with Crown/Clarkson Potter. The book, **Dress Your House For Success***, was published to wide acclaim in 1997. She and her husband, Publisher at a large New York publishing firm, live in Connecticut.*

As you can see, all that's really necessary is a few facts that establish the writer's credentials to write the book.

Determine which feature of your proposal is the strongest and give prominence to that feature in your query letter. If, for example, your core idea, is strikingly original and addresses a powerful need, then the book description section of the letter may need to be two paragraphs instead of one. If the book is based on some original research conducted by your firm, consider highlighting the research and how you arrived at it. If your credentials and expertise — a special degree, accomplishment, or stint on a national TV show — are the strongest selling points, then emphasize that aspect, perhaps giving it top billing.

The fiction query

Fiction query letters differ from nonfiction. First of all, before writing a fiction query, chances are good that you've already completed your book. If not, finish writing it before you send out a query. Selling a first novel without a complete manuscript is virtually impossible. Also, the author's qualifications alone aren't going to make a work of fiction more saleable — a page-turning plot line, memorable characters, and quality storytelling are what get fiction published.

For that reason, a fiction query letter focuses on a synopsis of the book. Start with a one-paragraph summary of the novel's plot. Your description is critical because it must convey both the plot and the qualities that distinguish the book — specific qualities like "suspense" or "passionate romance," not subjective generalities like "great writing."

Next, write about your experience or expertise that put you in a unique position to write the book. (If your novel is set at a ski resort, mention that you were a ski instructor at a ski resort . . . but only if you were!) If you have previous published works, including short stories, or even articles in the local Pennysaver, mention that here.

Surprisingly, novelists are often the least equipped of all writers to write about their own work briefly and persuasively. If this applies to you, consider enlisting the aid of a professional copywriter to craft your query letter.

If you have any connection to an editor or agent — especially if you met him or her at a writers' conference or similar event — mention it in the letter. This applies even if you've been asked to submit a query letter. Don't assume that the editor or agent remembers asking.

Online Query Letters

Online query letters are becoming more commonplace every day. Most editors are happy to receive query letters online because they can be answered quickly and easily, and the answer, as well as the query, can be easily recorded and recalled.

Ironically, e-mail seems to bring out the wordiness in many writers, and the pattern seems to be for online query letters to go on at excessive length. If anything, the online query letter requires even more precision. Your best bet is to limit your query to the number of words that fit on a single screen in a large font. That way, the editor or agent won't have to scroll down in order to get the gist of your idea.

You're probably fuming at the thought that your query could be spiked because it's longer than a single screen. There's no question that this arrangement isn't very fair. But if you want to take advantage of the speed and efficiency of the new technology, you have to live by the new rules and endure the shortened attention spans that prevail in this new space.

It's tempting to attach your proposal, a photograph, or even a video clip to your e-mail query letter. I recommend resisting the temptation. Wait until they ask for more and you confirm the software compatibility issues. Imagine if your photo or proposal attachment crashed the editor or agent's computer, or worse, their whole network.

Figure 7-1 shows you an online query sent to HarperCollins that resulted in a contract offer. The body of the query fit on a single screen, which made it quick and easy to read. The writer devotes much of the query to his platform — his previous books and all of his other promotional activities. The author called first and secured permission from Adrian's editorial assistant to attach a proposal to the query.

-----------Original Message-----------
From: Peter Cohan [mailto:peter-cohan@email.msn.com]
Sent: Monday, September 27, 1999 9:29 AM
To: adrian.zackheim@harpercollins.com
Subject: The Intelligent Internet Investor

Hi, Adrian:

I hope this finds you well.

I am president of Peter S. Cohan & Associates, a management consulting and venture capital firm in Marlborough, MA (more information is available at the URL below). I am a frequent commentator on CNBC, and my CNBC stock picks made me Bigtipper.com's Top Tipper for 1998. I am also the author of ***Net Profit: How To Invest and Compete in the Real World of Internet Business*** and ***The Technology Leaders: How America's Most Profitable High Tech Companies Innovate Their Way to Success.*** I have been quoted in *Barron's, Dow Jones Newswire, The New York Post,* and *Inc. Magazine* and have spoken at conferences sponsored by *Business Week, Fortune, The Economist,* and *Stanford University*.

I spoke with Devi this morning, and she suggested that it might be worthwhile to submit to you this proposal for ***The Intelligent Internet Investor***. This book will identify the quantitative factors that explain why some Internet stocks outperform the rest and to use this analysis to help investors achieve better Internet investment performance.

I look forward to speaking with you soon.

Best,

Peter

Peter S. Cohan & Associates
Two Turner Ridge Road
Marlborough, MA 01752

Office: 508-460-9348
Fax: 508-485-9627
Car: 508-361-3805
E-mail: peter-cohan@msn.com
WWW: members.theglobe.com/petercohan/

Figure 7-1: An online query letter.

In this successful query, the author:

- Establishes his expertise right away.
- Relays his extensive media experience to show he is "mediagenic."
- Note also, from his reference to Devi (an assistant in the HarperBusiness office), that he had enlisted the aid of an editorial assistant before sending his proposal with the query.
- Explains the book in one, concise sentence that leaves the reader wanting more.

Good e-mail query!

A guide to publishers' e-mail addresses

If you can't wait to start querying via e-mail, here are some publisher's e-mail addresses. Before using this information, carefully read the tips for approaching publishers in Chapters 9 and 10.

BDD/Random House: firstinitiallastname(7 char.)@randomhouse.com

Chronicle Books: 3initials@chronbooks.attmail.com

Disney/Hyperion: firstname_lastname@cp.disney.com

FSG: 2initialslastname@fsgee.com

HB: firstinitiallastname@harcourtbrace.com

HarperCollins/Avon/Morrow: firstname.lastname@harpercollins.com

Holt: firstname_lastname@hholt.com

Little Brown: firstname.lastname@littlebrown.com

Norton: firstinitialilastname@wwnorton.com

Oxford: 3initials@oup-usa.org

Penguin: firstinitiallastname@penguinputnam.com

St. Martin's Press: firstnamelastname@stmartins.com

Simon & Schuster: firstname.lastname@simonandschuster.com

Walker: firstinitiallastname@walkerbooks.com

Warner: firstname_lastname@timeinc.com

Wiley: firstinitiallastname@wiley.com

Chapter 8

Preparing Submission Materials That Sell

- Building a nonfiction proposal
- Creating a dynamite fiction submission
- Knowing exactly what to include
- Mastering the language of sales
- Organizing your materials

The only way to get your entire book idea onto the desk of a publishing professional is in the form of a book proposal. The proposal is a written sales presentation that is used by writers, publishers, and agents to communicate book ideas. In fact, virtually all books published by major publishing houses are bought on the basis of proposals.

In this chapter, I show you how to build a book proposal, section by section. I cover each of the elements publishers want to see presented in a book proposal for a work of nonfiction and fiction. Using the information in this chapter as a blueprint, you can create a book proposal compelling enough that publishers vie for the privilege of publishing it.

The 12 Elements of a Successful Nonfiction Proposal

Think of a nonfiction book proposal as an artfully crafted sales brochure, approximately 10 to 20 pages in length, that shows your idea in its best light and helps a publisher see the market potential for your book. Don't actually write the book. Test market your idea in the form of a proposal. Putting extra effort into the proposal is well worth your time and effort because it forces you to carefully think through the entire book. Certainly, if you're going to ask a publisher to spend between $5,000 and $50,000 to acquire and publish your book, the proposal needs to be a standout — well researched, thorough, and inspiring.

While you can't sell a novel without a finished manuscript, works of nonfiction are almost always sold on the strength of a detailed proposal alone. This means that writing nonfiction is less speculative for you. And, according to agent, author, and former editor Betsy Lerner, "The more work you do upfront in the proposal stage, the better off you'll be."

A nonfiction book proposal has no set format. Just keep in mind that you want to lead off with the information that's most compelling — put your best selling foot forward and then fill in the substantive detail. It's vital that you quickly establish the voice for your book, and the key content that it will convey.

Lerner adds, ". . . establishing an authoritative and substantive voice is the most important first impression an author can make."

Keep in mind that while your book may appeal to a wide audience, your proposal is meant to attract only one reader — the editor or agent. So speak to the editor fairly quickly and credibly about her main concern — who and how large is the audience that's going to purchase this book? What need does it fill that will prompt people to purchase it — in quantity?

Here are 12 important elements of a nonfiction proposal.

- **Cover page:** Contains your title, author byline, and contact information.
- **Proposal contents:** This is a table of contents that provides an itemized list, with page numbers, of the features contained in the entire proposal.
- **Overview:** Summarizes your book with a unique "hook" that generates excitement.

- **The market:** Identifies your book's audience and how best to reach it.
- **About the book:** Describes your book in more detail including special features and benefits.
- **The competition:** Shows how your book fills a void or provides a new slant on the topic.
- **About the author:** Presents yourself in the best possible light.
- **Table of contents:** Functions as the blueprint of your book.
- **Chapter summaries and sample chapter:** Showcases your writing and highlights important components.
- **Production specifications:** Specifies the length, format, illustrations, delivery date, and so on.
- **Promotion and marketing:** Outlines a plan for selling your book.
- **Attachments:** Includes newspaper and magazine clippings about you or your book's topic.

Your proposal may not need all 12 elements. But before discarding any, consider how each one may enhance your book in the eyes of an editor. In the following sections, I discuss each element in depth and provide examples for you to use as a guide in creating your own proposal. A complete book proposal even appears at the end of this chapter so that you can see how all the elements come together.

Employ all 12 elements if you want or as many as are appropriate to your book. Once your proposal is complete, you'll have an impressive sales tool. Keep in mind, though, that a book proposal is a lot easier to write than an entire book. Have fun with it!

Your cover page

Your cover page is the first and the easiest step. Simply type the words "Book Proposal" at the top of the page. Then drop down a few lines to the center of the page and type your book's title in bold lettering. Just underneath the title, in a slightly smaller point size, type the subtitle (if you have one). Below the subtitle, place the *author byline* — your name! Then, in the lower right-hand corner, type your contact information, including address, telephone and fax numbers, and e-mail address. Figure 8-1 shows you an example, although in condensed form to conserve space.

BOOK PROPOSAL
Getting Your Book Published
For Dummies
by Sarah Parsons Zackheim

22 Burr School Road
Westport, CT 06880
203-454-7733
203-227-8833 Fax
e-mail: szackheim@aol.com

Figure 8-1: A sample cover page.

TIP

If you have an interesting (though subtle) graphic that highlights an aspect of the book and enhances the overall presentation, include it on the cover page. If the graphic is too large or detracts in any way from the professional presentation of your proposal, then save it for another purpose. It's more important to convey your book's idea in words than in pictures.

Proposal contents

The proposal contents page confirms for the editor or agent that you have included all the important information in the proposal. It also provides readers with a quick preview of what they are about to read. This small professional touch is well worth the extra effort.

Figure 8-2 shows the proposal contents from the proposal for *Dress Your House For Success* (Three Rivers Press, 1997), a book I co-authored with Martha Webb.

Overview....................3
About the Book....................7
About the *Dress Your House For Success* Video....................8
Program Endorsements....................9
The Authors....................11
Internet Component....................13
The Market....................14
The Competition....................15
Detailed Chapter Outline with Sample Text....................19

Figure 8-2: A sample proposal contents page.

Overview

In one to three pages, communicate your book's main idea in a way that generates interest and hooks the reader. In this section, you want to convey four important points:

- **What is the book's subject and scope:** Think of this section as getting underneath the book idea and explaining why the information is needed and what a notable difference it can make in the lives of a specific, large audience. Write in the third person.
- **Why it's important — for example, what need it fills:** Begin with a dramatic statement of a familiar problem, a shocking reality, or an entertaining anecdote that presents a common predicament or void. Then tell how your book solves this problem, explains the predicament, or fills the need.
- **What benefits it offers readers:** Present specific benefits. *Benefits* are what readers reap from the information.
- **Why you are the best person to write this book:** Touch upon the unique knowledge or credentials you, as the author, bring to the book.

Stay fairly general in this section. Provide just enough information to generate excitement and hurry the editor along to the more detailed sections of the proposal.

Figure 8-3 shows the Overview section from the proposal for this book.

Getting Your Book Published For Dummies

By Sarah Parsons Zackheim

It's no secret that people everywhere dream of seeing their name emblazoned on the front of a published book showcased in bookstores all across the country. And with the media reporting $1 million dollar advances paid to celebrities (Whoopi Goldberg's reported $6 million) and civilians alike (Jesse Foveaux, a 98-year-old Kansas housewife, was paid over $1 million dollars for her memoirs), public interest in "getting published" is higher than ever!

But there's very little reliable information available that penetrates the hype and shows real people how to get published. That is . . . until now. *Getting Your Book Published For Dummies* presents the entire process -- from brainstorming great book ideas, right through to the triumphant publication celebration, and, hopefully, a run up the bestseller lists. Along the way, readers will benefit from knowledge gained deep inside the world of publishing, learning how the pros create irresistible book proposals, how to ensure your query letter gets a publisher's undivided attention, how to negotiate contracts, and much, much more! This book strips away the media-generated mystique of publishing to reveal the nuts and bolts of how the system works and shares practical, battle-tested tactics for breaking in as a first-time author. Each technique is explained in clear, everyday language, using a nonthreatening format that's brimming with practical tips, insights from successful authors, and proven strategies that show readers exactly how to turn their own experiences and talents into salable books.

Figure 8-3: The Overview section of *Getting Your Book Published For Dummies.*

Notice how I begin by boldly stating the problem — "people everywhere dream of getting a book all their own published." Then I show how *Getting Your Book Published For Dummies* solves that problem by guiding readers step-by-step through the entire process. I continue by discussing the main benefit which is "being able to get a book published" and allude to my unique credentials of being able to offer "knowledge gained deep inside the world of publishing."

About the market

The market refers to your book's audience or readers. Who exactly is going to read your book? An editor wants to know not only who the audience for your book is but whether the audience is large enough to justify the time and expense involved in publishing your book.

In this section, you clearly identify your audience, providing as much hard data as possible. For example, if you are proposing a book called *Kite Collecting,* you want to show an editor that there are plenty of kite collectors anxious for such a book. Provide specifics, such as the names of all six weekly kite enthusiast magazines and the two monthly kite magazines, as well as the numerous newsletters and clubs devoted to kite collecting. Include the number of subscribers to these magazines, newsletters, and clubs. Mention that it's worth contacting the 18 national kite manufacturers and over 20,000 kite retailers to see whether they are interested in purchasing a guaranteed quantity of the book or adding onto the print run with their own customized jacket. You may also be able to rent mailing lists of recent kite buyers and target them in a direct mail campaign for the book. Provide as many clear cut ways to identify and target the book's audience as possible.

Figure 8-4 shows you the About the Market section from the proposal for *Getting Your Book Published For Dummies.*

An estimated 550,000 book proposals were submitted to publishers last year, up from 500,000 five years ago. This increasing number of book submissions parallels the growing use of personal computers. Let's face it, PCs make writing easier than ever before. It's no surprise that a larger segment of the population is turning to writing as a hobby, as a career choice, and as entertainment, too. Witness the recent proliferation of magazines for writers. These magazines (list attached) reach an annual subscriber base of over 600,000. Public interest in writing and being published is definitely on the upswing. Over 400,000 Copies Sold is boldly advertised on Judith Appelbaums classic *How To Get Happily Published* originally published in 1978, now in a fourth printing as a $13.00 HarperPerennial trade paperback. *Getting Your Book Published For Dummies* will reflect the changing times, by talking directly to today's more technologically advanced writers about cutting-edge publishing trends and the benefits of technology for today's writers. It also shows today's savvy writers the rules that govern the publishing game and strategies for getting around those rules to ensure that their book proposal will make an editor stand up and take notice. *Getting Your Book Published For Dummies* will reach not only today's 550,000 aspiring authors, but the hundreds of thousands of other writers who are discovering the joys of tinkering with their expanded word-processing power and are beginning to dream of writing a book.

Figure 8-4: The About the Market section of *Getting Your Book Published For Dummies.*

I attached a detailed list of writer's magazines complete with up-to-date subscriber numbers. I also mentioneded the sales figures on the only other complete, insider guide to getting published — written during a very different era in publishing — but still selling because of a continually growing interest in the subject. Because I submitted the proposal to IDG Books Worldwide, Inc., known for their easy-to-understand computer guides *For Dummies,* I didn't go into detail on the computer audience, "the hundreds of thousands of other writers who are discovering the joys of tinkering with their expanded word processing power." IDG Books knows that market better than any other publisher. The mere mention of that audience got their attention.

About the book

As in the Overview section, you're still generating excitement in your description of the book's content and benefits, but in the About the Book section, you go into much more detail. If the Overview is intended to hook the interest of an editor or agent, the About the Book section goes for the close. This is where you answer the editor's main question, "Why should I publish this book?"

Describe your book's unique qualities and the value of the information it contains. Explain its timeliness or the extraordinary contribution it makes to the subject area. Enumerate the special features such as statistics, graphs, checklists, or inside information. Throughout the section, allude to your large audience and the unrivaled benefits your book offers. Give examples, point out startling facts, or describe the solution your book offers to a nagging problem.

Figure 8-5 shows you the About the Book section from my proposal for *Choose the Perfect Name for Your Baby* (Longmeadow Press, 1992).

Four million babies, all in need of a name, were born last year in the United States. Booksellers across the country witness expectant parents purchasing not one, but usually two or more baby name books when faced with the all-important decision of naming their new or soon-to-be born child. Booksellers also find these readers complaining on subsequent visits that the baby name books are all basically the same. And it's true. The baby name books currently on the shelf all have the same dull format -- the list of names, approximately 5,000 to 20,000 of them, preceded by a list of suggestions meant to help readers find an appropriate name for their child.

I bought three baby name books when I was expecting my first child. And like most people, I read the first few paragraphs of each and then, bored with the advice, flipped to the list of names to see whether there were any new or different ones. Often before I was halfway through the girls' names (or boys, whichever came first), I would put down the book, overwhelmed by the choices and exhausted by the interminable lists.

Choose the Perfect Name for Your Baby offers a unique and entertaining solution to the boredom factor. Instead of cramming "introductory" information at the front of the book, I plan to break up the endless lists of names with sidebars throughout the book containing all sorts of useful, humorous, and even fascinating information to make the task of choosing a name diverting, even downright fun. First, last, and always, it will be informative.

I plan to give readers a few pointers about the "name game" that they might not have thought about before. For the astrologically inclined, I'll help them with star sign names. For earth science devotees, a list of birthstones and place names. For movie buffs, I list their favorite celebrities along with their *real* names as well as the cross gender names that are more popular than ever. For sports nuts, I supply a list of all-time greats in several sports -- well, you get the idea. I also plan to offer a checklist that speeds readers to their choice without having to go through the whole list or even part of it.

Figure 8-5: A sample About the Book section.

Waldenbooks made me an offer immediately. The editor called me with a list of additional sidebar ideas that had come up at the editorial meeting where the book proposal was discussed. The editorial committee members obviously liked the proposal enough to suggest ideas of their own for inclusion. That's the kind of reaction you want your proposal to generate in a room full of editors.

The competition

The Competition section answers a question every editor asks. "Aren't plenty of books already published on this topic?" In speaking to this very real concern, you have an opportunity to provide the editor with an important research service.

In this section, brief the editor on what's available in the bookstore on your topic. Be informative, knowledgeable, and upbeat. Show how your book takes a different and much better approach to the subject than anything currently on the market. In fact, discuss how your book goes above and beyond the others to actually reflect the spirit of the times.

Figure 8-6 gives you an example from the proposal for *Getting Rich in America* by Dwight R. Lee and Richard B. McKenzie (HarperCollins, 1999).

Comparable Books

Getting Rich in America will be written to appeal to the markets currently filled by the following books:

- Stephen Covey's *The 7 Habits of Highly Effective People*. *Getting Rich* will rely on the same type of common sense wisdom and will be rule oriented." However, the advice in *Getting Rich* will be far more concrete and to the point.

- Thomas Stanley and William Danko's *The Millionaire Next Door: The Surprising Secrets of Americas Wealthy. Getting Rich* will, from time to time, draw on Stanley and Danko's survey findings of wealthy Americans. However, the Lee/McKenzie book will be much more concise and will be less directed toward exploring the characteristics of existing millionaires and more directed toward explaining how the readers can become millionaires. The Stanley/Danko book is data based; the Lee/McKenzie book will be rule based. The Stanley/Danko book draws up short of offering advice on how to make a million; the Lee/McKenzie book provides the needed advice and shows how the advice can be followed even by people of modest means.

- Steven Landsbert's *Fair Play*, which made *Business Week* magazine's top-selling list of business books for several weeks, seeks to convey economic principles with reference to how children conduct their play in sandboxes. *Getting Rich* will contain many intriguing economic insights that are characteristic of the Landsberg book. For example, in *Getting Rich in America*, the authors use economic theory (without saying so) to explain why a married couple should be expected to accumulate more wealth than an unmarried couple living together, and they also explain why ordinary Americans should not take investment advice from their brokers or the "Beardstown Ladies."

- Charles Schwab's *Guide to Financial Independence*, Larry Swedrow's *Winning Investments Strategy*, and Suze Orman's *The Nine Steps to Financial Freedom* are admiral guides for readers who want instruction on exactly how to invest their savings. These books say little about how people should lead their lives in order to build the requisite savings for investing. *Getting Rich* has a much broader purpose *and* audience, offering a whole-life strategy for achieving a sizable fortune.

Figure 8-6: The Competition section.

Notice how the authors bring up best-selling, brand name books for comparision purposes. This strategy works to link their book to already proven bestsellers. And rather than intimate any negative aspect of the other books, the authors show instead how their book surpasses the bestsellers mentioned. This positive spin works to their advantage. You don't need to knock the competition when you can use it to your benefit!

About the author

Impress agents and editors by presenting your qualifications for writing the book you propose in the best possible light. Unlike a resume, this section allows you to introduce yourself in a more compelling, conversational way. Be sure to highlight the experiences and credentials that pertain specifically to your book. Consider including the following information:

- Topic credentials
- Career credentials
- Writing credentials
- Educational credentials and background
- Awards, honors, and organization memberships
- Media skills for marketing the book
- Personal information

The author bio provides information about you that raises interest in your book. In his one-page bio, novelist Stephen Horn first quickly summarizes his personal story. With a few strokes he creates interest in him and his novel, *In Her Defense*, as shown in Figure 8-7.

Who I Am and How I Came to Write *In Her Defense*

The background and experiences of *In Her Defense* protagonist Francis O'Connell are mine, save for the Irish heritage, which I acquired through marriage. I was born in the Bronx, New York, attended college on a football scholarship, and received an engineering degree and an Army commission. I became an Airborne Ranger, and served as a platoon leader and company commander with the 101st Airborne Division in Vietnam in 1969-70. Francis' recollections of night patrol and the combat assault dream sequences are based on my experiences there.

Law school followed, and in 1973 I joined the Department of Justice as a prosecutor in the Criminal Section of the Civil Rights Division. Our jurisdiction was diverse. The first case I worked on was the killing of four Kent State University students by the Ohio National Guard in May 1970. We investigated and eventually prosecuted several Guardsmen, Shortly thereafter, I was given responsibility for investigating all conspiracy allegations in the assassination of Dr. Martin Luther King Jr., which took me from Memphis to Calgary in pursuit of new theories. In 1976, I was lead prosecutor of an alleged plot to murder an environmentalist by officials of a paper mill in one of America's last true company towns. The story was covered by Harper's magazine and the 60 Minutes TV program, among others.

Late in 1976, I was appointed to a new, five-lawyer task force to investigate the FBI's use of illegal entries ("black bag jobs"), wiretaps, and mail theft in its pursuit of "The Weathermen" and other "New Left" fugitives who claimed responsibility for a series of bombings around the country during the Vietnam era. I prosecuted the first case filed against an FBI agent, which was defended by the late Edward Bennett Williams. When the Attorney General decided that much of what the task force uncovered would not be prosecuted, I and three others quit in protest. It became a national news story, and we, were subpoenaed by a Senate Committee to determine what happened. I was concomitantly profiled in the Washington Post.

After that episode, I left the Justice Department to become a defense lawyer. As did Francis in my book, I spent several years in the cellblocks, taking court-appointed cases for the "immutable hourly rate authorized by law for aiding the indigent." Eventually, my practice grew and I became a partner in a mid-size Washington firm.

In Her Defense is my first manuscript, I wrote it as an entertainment for myself, a change-of-pace from the briefs and memos that are the stuff of litigation. Since it was supposed to represent recreation, I avoided the library to remain within the confines of my own home and, therefore, my own, limited experience. When I began, I knew the first and last lines, as well as the central plot twist, based on my Justice Department experience. I wrote, thought about what should happen next and then wrote some more.

Figure 8-7: The About the author section.

Production specifications

This section is where you present the physical specifications for your book. Include any unusual production details your book may require. The most important elements to include in this section are

- **Book length:** Supply the page or word count for the finished book. Most books range in length from 250 to 350 pages.
- **Size:** Specify whether it's a standard size, like 6 x 9, or any unusual size and shape. Be aware that unusual sizes usually incur higher printing costs and will cause publishers to shy away unless you have a compelling reason for an unusual size book.

- **Binding:** Say whether it's hardcover, trade paperback, or mass-market paperback.
- **Delivery date:** Give the length of time needed to complete the book. Most books take between six and 18 months to write.
- **Artwork details:** List photographs, illustrations, line drawings, or other graphics.

Keep in mind that you are proposing the ideal format you would like to see for your book. This information helps a publisher calculate the production costs involved in actually printing your book. The figures arrived at from your format specifications also help determine the financial viability of publishing the book. So, while you may want color pictures throughout your Gourmet Vegetarian Cookbook, don't be surprised if the publisher insists on only one or two eight-page photo spreads.

Figure 8-8 shows you the production specification section from the proposal for *Dress Your House for Success,* a book I co-authored with Martha Webb.

> Specifications
>
> We envision *Dress Your House For Success* as a 128-page, $9.95 standard trade paperback with approximately 20 to 25 before-and-after photographs of each of the six steps—Cleaning, Uncluttering, Repairing, Neutralizing, Dynamizing, and SHOWTIME! In addition, we'd like to see 35 to 40 line drawings illustrating such critical concepts as where buyers' eyes fall in a room, unique ways to highlight special areas in your home, and more. These visuals will help take the guesswork out of readying a home for the real estate market. The book will also feature an extensive room-by-room checklist with many attention grabbing sidebars and subheads detailing each step in the process and offering the reader an easy-to-follow guide to successful implementation. The book can be delivered within three to six months time.

Figure 8-8: The Specifications section.

Dress Your House For Success ended up being a 192-page, $12 standard trade paperback with 17 black-and-white line-drawing illustrations, innumerable sidebars, charts, and an extensive whole house checklist. Three Rivers Press/Clarkson Potter came up with many creative and inexpensive ways to make important information graphically prominent. Even with only 17 line drawings, the ideas are well illustrated, and the book's checklists stand out in an easy-to-use, inviting way.

While it's important to give your publisher a very clear idea of your intended specifications, it's equally important to bear in mind that the eventual book might differ from that original estimate — you and your publisher will work closely together to determine how the right specifications can best be accomplished.

Table of contents

A *table of contents* is a basic outline of your book. The clearer it is, the easier it is for readers to understand. A brilliant nonfiction book depends in large part upon its organization. You may have a great idea but unless you organize it in a way that makes sense to readers, it won't find an audience.

Look carefully at all your material and decide on an organizational structure that best fits the type of book you're writing.

Here are a few structural types to think about:

- **Chronological order:** Presents information based on the passage of time usually from the beginning to the end, or early in an event/process to later on.
- **Order of importance:** Starts with either the least or most important concepts and moving in increasing or decreasing order.
- **Order of need/step-by-step:** Reveals information methodically, as it is needed.
- **Categorical or thematic order:** Divides your subject up into the parts or themes that comprise the whole.
- **Persuasive order:** Builds an argument that persuades the reader by using an *inductive* (logical) or *deductive* (infer from the information provided) method of reasoning.
- **Literary order/problem-climax-resolution:** Introduces a problem that grows more complicated until it reaches a climax, gets resolved, and teaches an important lesson.

Say, for example, that you want to write a true crime story. Even though you're creating a work of nonfiction — a factual account — the best organizational structure for a true crime story is probably the same structure that's used in novels, which I refer to here as *literary order.* Start with the problem or crime (usually a dead body), which the main character tries to solve. The story revolves around the main character's attempts to find the murderer, becoming more tangled until it reaches a climax. The crime is then solved, and the main character learns a life-changing lesson.

If, on the other hand, you want to write a book that offers readers a new approach to take in a certain area of their lives, you can organize the material in different ways. Map the book out in a couple of different structural ways so that you can see which one presents the material in its best light. As an added bonus, by trying different organizational strategies, you actually look at your material from a number of different angles.

Don't be surprised if the editor who buys your book suggests a totally different structure from the one in your proposal. That's what happened to Stephen Pollan and Mark Levine with their best-selling book, *Die Broke*. At first they organized the book into six parts. The first part introduced the problem. The middle four parts presented specific solutions using a case study approach. The final part pulled together their entire approach. The book's title and table of contents are shown in Figure 8-9.

In this organizational structure, Pollan and Levine present the overall dilemma and then build a convincing case for using their unique approach.

The book, however, ended up being published with an entirely different, two-part organizing structure presenting first their provocative theory and then showing the theory put to work in all areas of the reader's financial life. This approach categorizes the information so that readers can easily flip to areas of major concern. Figure 8-10 shows you the revised title and table of contents.

MAKING LEMONADE
Four Maxims for Thriving in Uncertain Economic Times

Part One: Immigrants In The New Age
Chapter 1: A Time Of Fears & Frustration
Chapter 2: It's Not Your Fault
Chapter 3: New Maxims, Goals & Opportunities
Part Two: It's Just A Job
Chapter 4: The Story of Andrea Dreeson
Chapter 5: The Demise Of Corporate Loyalty
Chapter 6: Forget Climbing The Ladder
Chapter 7: Become A Free Agent
Chapter 8: Andrea Dreeson: Playing Out Her Option
Part Three: Pay Cash
Chapter 9: The Story Of Ken & Mary Schoenfeld
Chapter 10: Stop Reaching Beyond Your Grasp
Chapter 11: A Return To Thrift
Chapter 12: Stop Making Compromises
Chapter 13: Ken & Mary Schoenfeld: Melting The Plastic
Part Four: Don't Retire
Chapter 14: The Story of Rick Darrow
Chapter 15: Between A Rock & A Hard Place
Chapter 16: Retirement = Death
Chapter 17: Become A Ulyssean Adult
Chapter 18: Rick Darrow: A Never Ending Journey
Part Five: Die Broke
Chapter 19: The Story Of John & Wendy Kowalski
Chapter 20: The Estate & Inheritance Obsession
Chapter 21: Every Dollar Left Is A Dollar Wasted
Chapter 22: Live Up To Your Means
Chapter 23: John & Wendy Kowalski: Spending It All
Part Six: The Land Of Milk and Honey
Chapter 24: Choosing Your Own Clothes

Figure 8-9: *Die Broke's* original table of contents.

DIE BROKE

Part I: The Die Broke Philosophy
- Chapter 1: Immigrants In The New Age
- Chapter 2: Quit Today
- Chapter 3: Pay Cash
- Chapter 4: Don't Retire
- Chapter 5: Die Broke
- Chapter 6: Choosing Your Own Clothes
- Chapter 7: Helping Your Parents To Die Broke
- Chapter 8: Helping Your Children To Die Broke
- Chapter 9: The Die Broke Plan

Part II: Putting Theory Into Practice
- Chapter 10: Accountants
- Chapter 11: Annuities
- Chapter 12: Asset Allocation
- Chapter 13: Automated Teller Machines and Cards
- Chapter 14: Automobile Insurance
- Chapter 15: Automobile Loans
- Chapter 16: Banks
- Chapter 17: Bonds
- Chapter 18: Certificates of Deposit
- Chapter 19: Charge Cards
- Chapter 20: Charitable Remainder Trusts
- Chapter 21: Checking Accounts
- Chapter 22: Credit Cards
- Chapter 23: Debt Cards
- Chapter 24: Debt Consolidation Loans
- Chapter 25: Disability Insurance
- Chapter 26: Divorce and Mediation
- Chapter 27: Domestic Partners
- Chapter 28: Durable Powers of Attorney For Health Care

Figure 8-10: The revised partial table of contents.

This is actually a partial table of contents. The book's final table of contents includes more than 72 chapters!

By following a categorical approach, the information is much more accessible to the reader.

Chapter summaries and sample chapter

If the Table of Contents provides the skeleton of your book, the Chapter Summaries show editors how you plan to put flesh on the bones. This section is where you discuss the actual features included in each chapter. The trick is to present just enough information to excite an editor and convey the entire chapter contents in as brief a space as possible.

It's perfectly acceptable to write these summaries in sentence fragments that begin with an active verb. What's key is to let your passion for and detailed knowledge of the topic shine through. Figure 8-11 gives you an example from the proposal for *Consulting Demons* by Lewis Pinault.

> 1. Forward Appended to This Proposal
>
> Introducing management consulting and its weird deep-sea ecology, and by way of personal introduction, how I came to thrive in the high heat, intense pressures, and dark secretive environment of the consulting business. Highlighting briefly the glories and calamities of my dozen years in consulting, and how they tracked key events in the industry. Outlining *Consulting Demon's* organization: a pilgrim's progress from bystander to instigator, with *Checklist* memorials inscribed along the way to mark our journey.
>
> 2. Guide to the Journey: A Consulting Primer
>
> Peeling away layers of revisionist consulting history, exposing key company origins with the incest and blood rivalries intact. Revealing how the business is organized for growth at any cost, and where the money is made. Examining profiles of those who succeed and fail in the business, and how I have seen those profiles evolve with shifts in the scale and focus of the business. *Consulting Demon Checklist: Consulting Companies in Fact and Fiction.* Illuminating the role and influence of consultancies in U.S. and global business by way of choice personal examples.

Figure 8-11: An excerpt from the Specifications section.

Checklist for a successful synopsis

Agents may ask to see a plot synopsis before agreeing to read your entire novel. If they do, don't panic. Plot synopses are easy to write. Just follow the points outlined here.

- Write in present tense.
- Open with the story's conflict and ultimate goal.
- Tell the whole story, in the same sequence as in the novel.
- Focus on the story's main elements.
- Include important character motivations and reactions.
- Weave the story's mechanics — background information, setting, time, character sketches — seamlessly into the synopsis narrative.
- Aim for a length of one to two pages.

Lewis tells his reader a lot about each chapter. He makes the reader an accomplice as he begins "Peeling away," "Exposing," "Revealing how," "Examining," and "Illuminating." He gets specific about such features as checklists, profiles and personal examples. His excitement, his inside knowledge, his slight cynicism are all conveyed. The reader is involved from the start.

If you, like Lewis, have never published a book, include a sample chapter or two. Editors want to make sure that you can write. It doesn't matter whether the chapters are consecutive or which chapters you include. What matters is that they are well written. So, include the chapter(s) that showcase your best writing.

Promotion and marketing

Dazzle an editor with ideas, suggestions, and contacts you have that can help promote, publicize, market, and sell your book. Editors are especially impressed by writers who present a well-conceived, professional marketing plan. After all, editors can't be experts on every subject covered in the myriad books they publish. They look to authors, as experts in the field, to help identify and, ultimately, reach the book's target market through innovative (and usually inexpensive) promotion and marketing techniques. In this section, show

- Your intention and eagerness to promote the book
- Your willingness to use personal connections to generate sales
- Your creative ideas for reaching all segments of the market

The more ways *you* can help sell your book, the more likely an editor is to listen.

Say, for example, that you are submitting a proposal for a book entitled, *Chewing Your Way Through Life: An Inside Look at the Chewing Gum Industry.* The Promotion and marketing section of your proposal may look something like Figure 8-12.

As a frequent lecturer on The History of Chewing Gum, the author plans to step up his speaking engagements, adding workshops on the art of "Walking, Talking, and Chewing Gum at the same time." In addition, the author plans to hold Bubble Gum Bubble Blowing Contests across the country. These events are sure to generate a great deal of publicity including radio and TV appearances. The author is a regular guest on Oprah's Book Club, showing readers how to chew gum and read at the same time.

An active member of the American Association of Chewing Gum Addicts, the author has access to the Association's exclusive mailing list of 450,000 members. These members are proven purchasers of all the latest information in the field.

Because the history of all 24 Chewing Gum manufacturing companies is included in the book, each company may be interested in ordering large quantities of the book as giveaways or promotional sales incentives. The author will make himself available to negotiate quantity purchases with each manufacterer if the publisher desires it.

Figure 8-12: A sample Promotion and marketing section.

If you are committed to promoting and marketing your book and can guarantee selling a substantial quantity, say so in this section. Likewise, if you have professional contacts interested in purchasing and or promoting the book, provide all the specific information here. Or if you have a freelance publicist in your close circle of friends who you plan to pay to help publicize the book, let the editor know that here. All these promotional efforts can make a big difference in the mind of a publisher.

Attachments

Dress up your proposal with any documents that enhance your credibility and the book's timely message. Attachments can include

- Published writing samples such as magazine and newspaper articles
- Published press clippings about you
- Published clippings about your books topic
- Promotional material — flyers, brochures, and advertisements — about you or your business.
- Awards, fellowships, and grant certificates
- Endorsements or testimonials from clients

The complete proposal puts these elements together into one seamless, compelling whole. Figure 8-13 is the proposal for a nonfiction book written by the best-selling team of Demitri and Janice Papolos for their most recent book, which was acquired by Broadway Books for publication in January 2000.

Sample Proposal—The Bipolar Child by: Demitri F. Papolos, M.D. and Janice Papolos

The Bipolar Child

The Definitive and Reassuring Guide to Childhood's Most Misunderstood Disorder

a book proposal

by Demitri F. Papolos, M.D. and Janice Papolos

PROPOSAL TABLE OF CONTENTS

Preface

The telephone rang. It was the assistant principal of the junior high school calling to say that Jason Hunter* was in his office again. This time it was more than just the high jinks that had earned him the reputation of class clown. This time Jason was facing suspension. He had called a bomb threat into the school, and now the police were involved.

Jason's parents, Joan and Greg Hunter* (a pseudonym), knew that they had a lively and rambunctious child from the first year of their son's life: even as an infant he could stay up till all hours of the night and then sleep late into the day. By age six, Jason had become increasingly hyperactive: He'd talk out of turn in class and was distractible and extremely disruptive. The school psychologist recommended the family to a well-known pediatric neurologist and then to a child psychiatrist. Doctor after doctor told them that their son had attention deficit disorder with hyperactivity (ADHD), and that Ritalin was the answer. Even Jason's teacher recommended they do what all the other parents were doing and put him on the medication. After Jason threw a chair through his bedroom window during a temper tantrum one night, his parents finally filled the prescription.

Before starting Ritalin, Jason's explosions of rage happened about once a week. After three weeks on the drug, Jason became enraged on a daily basis. His moods began to shift wildly from extreme irritability to a mean sullenness, all in the space of a few hours.
Sometimes he got a crazed look in his eyes, and he would begin to trash the house. His parents, terrified and desperate, sought yet another medical opinion.

Figure 8-13: A sample proposal.

Unlike the previous doctors, however, the new psychiatrist spent a great deal of time combing through the Hunters' family history (a grandmother suffered from manic-depression). Because of this and Jason's pronounced negative response to Ritalin, the psychiatrist concluded that, rather than attention deficit disorder with hyperactivity, Jason was suffering with childhood-onset manic-depression. The doctor urged the parents to discontinue the Ritalin immediately, and he then prescribed a mood-stabilizer. Within a month, Jason's uncontrollable tantrums and aggressive behavior ebbed, and life began to resume a more normal pace.

BACKGROUND

The Concept

Last year over 12 million prescriptions for Ritalin (a stimulant) and its generic versions were filled for children thought to have attention-deficit disorder with hyperactivity (ADHD). The shelves of the nation's bookstores are crammed with volumes on ADHD—it seems to be the diagnosis du jour.

And in that same year, close to 800,000 children were prescribed one of the newer antidepressants such as Prozac, Zoloft, or Paxil. It is estimated that 20 to 30 percent of American school-age children are taking either a stimulant or antidepressant medication.
But since the mid-1990s—only in the past three years, in fact—psychiatrists in the research vanguard have begun to sound an alarm: What if a large percentage of American children who are presently labeled hyperactive, oppositional, disruptive, or moody actually suffer from a disorder that is not attention–deficit disorder, conduct disorder, oppositional disorder, or major depression? What if, instead, a significant proportion of these children are manifesting some of the first signs of childhood-onset manic-depression—bipolar disorder—a disorder once thought to be rare in childhood?

Since ADHD and bipolar disorder share a number of overlapping features, misdiagnosis is commonplace. In fact, hyperactivity is perhaps the most typical behavioral symptom of mania in children. A recent landmark study by researchers at Harvard Medical School found that 94 percent of the children that they evaluated with current or previous histories of mania *also* met criteria for ADHD.

And, increasingly, clinical research is showing that a significant number of children who first onset with depressive episodes later go on to develop manic-depression. (Retrospective studies of adults with bipolar disorder have consistently found that, for 20 to 40 percent of them, the illness began with episodes of depression in childhood.)

Psychiatrists who treat adults diagnose with the benefit of their patients' histories. Child psychiatrists, on the other hand, are confronted with troubling behavior at an early time in their young patients' lives, with few clues as to the possible future development of bipolar disorder. Moreover, until recently, the training of child psychiatrists placed great emphasis on attention-deficit disorder and tended to overlook manic-depression entirely.
As a result of such diagnostic misperceptions, a potential public-health nightmare is brewing across America.

Medicines such as Ritalin and Prozac are known to induce mania and to increase the severity of manic-depressive illness. The entire course of a childs' illness—and thus the entire course of his or her life—can be devastated by a faulty diagnosis and incorrectly prescribed medications. Reaching a correct diagnosis is not easy, however—not just because of overlapping symptoms, but also because it has only recently come to light that bipolar disorder in children does not look the same as its adult counterpart. For instance, compared to adults, children exhibit considerably more irritability and frequent temper tantrums. In addition, children tend to switch from depressive to manic cycles much more rapidly.

But the situation becomes even more complicated as these children move into early adolescence. If they have been undiagnosed and untreated, it is likely that they have endured years of being viewed as problem children, and the anger that has been directed towards them from frustrated adults—as well as their peers—may have profoundly altered their perception of themselves and markedly diminished their self-esteem. This, combined with a need to quell the agitation, anxiety, and irritability that are symptoms of the illness, predisposes these bipolar children to alcohol and substance abuse.

In fact, a major epidemiological study found that of all major psychiatric disorders, bipolar disorder is the *most likely to occur simultaneously with alcohol and drug abuse*, and evidence is emerging that bipolar patients who abuse alcohol or drugs have a much worse course of illness.

For all of these reasons, it is imperative that people be alerted to and become educated about the symptoms and warning signs of early-onset bipolar disorder.

How Many Children Are Affected?

Epidemiological studies of bipolar disorder in childhood have not yet been published, but because it is such an extremely important public-health issue the National Institute of Mental Health has made determining the prevalence of the illness among children a research priority.

Because bipolar disorder is a heritable condition, the offspring of parents with a mood disorder are at extremely high risk for the development of the illness during childhood and adolescence. Since the prevalence rate in adults is approximately 3.3 million within any one year, it would be conservative to estimate that several million children are at risk each year.

A recent study found that, when care was taken to conduct a thorough diagnostic interview, bipolar disorder was the most common problem diagnosed in adolescents referred to psychiatric inpatient services. Yet there are no books available for the layperson on the subject.

While the conceptual awareness of the commonplace nature of this condition is beginning to be recognized in the psychiatric field, families, educators, and guidance counselors must contend with the puzzling and problematic behaviors of these difficult children without proper understanding and knowledge. Evidence of the desperate need for information, guidance, and support can be found on a new Web site called Parents of Bipolar Children, which received tens of thousands of visits in its first six months.

The Goals of this Book

We propose to write a groundbreaking exploration of a seldom-recognized but common psychiatric disorder among children and teenagers. It will be the first book written expressly for the adults who either live with or spend large parts of their day teaching and dealing with these children, and it will equal our previous book, *Overcoming Depression*—now in its third edition—in its comprehensiveness, clarity, and compassion.

Just as *Overcoming Depression* is the classic resource on the subject of mood disorders in adults, our goal is to write a book that will become the most recommended volume about bipolar disorder in children.

Format and Style

The book will be approximately 280 pages in length, divided into 13 chapters, combining pioneering information with practical coping strategies. In language accessible to the layperson, the book will clarify criteria for the accurate diagnosis of bipolar disorder in children and will note the latest biomedical findings. In fact, the research/biological section will present a wealth of information that has never before been culled and shaped for the layperson.

To broaden the scope of the book, we will conduct comprehensive interviews with a large population, thereby adding the voices of parents and educators who deal with the illness everyday. We are currently working with a leader of a support group of parents with bipolar children, and she has offered to arrange interviews with the 125 families in her group and others across the country. In addition, Demitri has a large data base compiled of families whose children have been rediagnosed early-onset bipolar disorder, after receiving initial diagnoses of ADHD—many of whom have agreed to be interviewed. And, of course, we intend to feature the voices of the children themselves throughout the book.

Many families are torn apart by this illness, and often bear terrible and painfully ambivalent feelings about their ill child, as well as grave concerns about his or her future. Parents have told us: Sometimes we feel so afraid—*of our own child*—and we feel imprisoned in our own home; or, I'm so tired of everyone telling me what's wrong with him, and looking at me as if I'm to blame. I feel so worn down; and, When I saw a very bizarre woman on the street the other day I thought: Will this be my daughter when she grows up? How can I prevent this from happening?'"

We intend to raise these uncomfortable and difficult emotional issues and offer families some relief from their anger, guilt, and sense of inadequacy. We will also provide detailed descriptions of the complete range of treatments (pharmacological as well as therapeutic) so that parents understand that there is help to be had. With early intervention and proper treatment, life can be *infinitely* better for these children and their families.

The tone of the book will be warm, empathic, and authoritative.

Promotion

Just as *The Boy Who Couldn't StopWashing* brought obsessive-compulsive disorder out of the closet and into public discourse, we expect *The Bipolar Child* to provoke the same kind of media stir. Because it will be the first book to cover this topic, and because so many young people are on stimulant and antidepressant medications, there are millions of parents, educators, and mental health professionals who will listen and react to these new findings, which contradict standard pediatric diagnosis and prescription.
Both authors have had extensive media experience, appearing on the nations' major television and radio programs, and can talk convincingly and understandably about the topic.

Targeted Markets

Numerous specialized professionals and grassroot organizations can use, review, and/or sell *The Bipolar Child,* among them:

Mental Health Professionals

Child psychiatrists
Pediatric neurologists
Social workers
School psychologists
Psychiatric nurses
Substance abuse counselors

Educators

Guidance Counselors
Educational consultants
Teachers

All of these professionals read trade journals and newsletters (we have a complete listing of them), and a review or an ad will handily reach these populations.

Grassroot Organizations

*We have had a longstanding relationship with the leaders of the National Alliance for the Mentally Ill (NAMI), which has 144,000 members and is the largest and most influential consumer advocacy organization in the country. Since NAMI already sells *Overcoming Depression* through its national bookstore and its recommended book list, we are quite sure NAMI will add *The Bipolar Child* to its book list, also.
*Dr. Papolos is a former member of the scientific council of The National Depressive and Manic Depressive Association (NDMDA)—the most important patient advocacy group for manic-depressive illness. This organization was the earliest champion of *Overcoming Depression*, and also has a national bookstore.
Both of these organizations have monthly newsletters in which they review books.

Endorsements

We will approach Laurie Flynn, executive director of the National Alliance for the Mentally Ill, as well as Mark Gottlieb, president of the National Association for Depressive and Manic Depressive Illness, for endorsements. Because *Overcoming Depression* is so highly respected, we are optimistic about receiving additional blurbs from Patty Duke, Mike Wallace, and Dick Cavett (all of whom have suffered with mood disorders); Tipper Gore or Rosalyn Carter; and pioneers in the field such as Dr. Hagop Akiskal of the University of California at San Diego, Dr. Joseph Biederman and Dr. Ross Baldessarini, both of Harvard, and Dr. Barbara Geller of Washington University in St. Louis, all noted researchers who know Demitri and his work.

Time Frame

It should take approximately one year to complete the manuscript.

BOOK TABLE OF CONTENTS

ABOUT THE AUTHORS

Demitri Papolos, M.D.

Demitri Papolos is an Associate Professor of Psychiatry at the Albert Einstein College of Medicine in New York City, where he is the Director of the Program in Behavioral Genetics. He is a recipient of an NIMH Physician/ Scientist Award and, most recently, a recipient of the NARSAD Independent Investigator Award.

His primary interest is the genetic basis of manic-depressive illness. For the past several years Dr. Papolos and his collaborators at Einstein have been studying an unusual genetic condition known as Velo-cardio-facial Syndrome (VCFS). Through their research, they have found that almost all (greater than 95 percent) of VCFS individuals over the age of 12 develop some form of bipolar disorder (manic-depressive illness). Since VCFS is associated with a small deletion on chromosome 22, their finding may be the first direct link of manic-depressive illness to a discrete molecular target.

A current focus of the research program has been the clinical observation of a specific developmental sequence of symptoms that precedes the full onset of bipolar disorder in VCFS children: For instance, these children first exhibit symptoms of separation anxiety, followed by attentional difficulties and signs of obsessive compulsive disorder, culminating in rapid-cycling bipolar disorder. This vantage point may provide the first coherent perspective on the course of early-onset bipolar disorder. This recent work was published in the *American Journal of Psychiatry* and the *Journal of Medical Genetics* in 1997.

Dr. Papolos is the co-author of *Overcoming Depression*, Third Edition (HarperCollins, 1997), the most comprehensive book written for the layperson on depression and manic-depression. He is co-editor of the book, *Genetic Studies in Affective Disorders* (Wiley-Interscience, 1994) and was formerly associate editor of the Einstein Publication Series in Experimental and Clinical Psychiatry. He has a private practice in New York and in Westport, Connecticut.

Janice Papolos

Janice Papolos is the author of *The Performing Artists Handbook* and, with her husband, Demitri Papolos, M.D., co-author of *Overcoming Depression,* both recognized as definitive in their fields. Her most recent book, *The Virgin Homeowner,* was published last May by W.W. Norton, and was rated by *The Wall Street Journal* as the most useful book for homeowners in its 1997 selection of outstanding home and garden books. She has been a guest on Good Day NY, Good Morning America, Christina Ferrare's Home and Family Show, and WOR'sThe Joan Hamburg Show in connection with this book.

Janice Papolos has published articles in *Newsweek*, *McCall's*, *Self*, and *Home* magazines. She is a member of The American Society of Journalists and Authors.

SALES HISTORY OF OVERCOMING DEPRESSION

Since its first hardcover edition in 1987, *Overcoming Depression* has become the book most recommended to the lay audience on depression and manic-depression. It is recognized by the public and the psychiatric profession as definitive in its field.

Both the 1988 and revised (1992) editions of the trade paperback returned to press 14 times each, and the third revised edition (published in March 1997) is currently in its seventh printing. To date, over 200,000 copies have been sold worldwide, and it's likely that this figure will soon reach a quarter of a million.

Overcoming Depression (revised edition) was a Quality Paperback Book Club selection (June alternate) and a Book of the Month Club Pick of the Paperbacks. It was also chosen by Prevention Book Club, *Psychology Today* Book Club, Rodale Book Club, Psychotherapy Book Club (April 1992 alternate), Psychotherapy and Social Science Book Club, and Newbridges Behavioral Sciences Book Club (December 1997 alternate).

Both the first and second editions were also published in this country by Consumer Reports. In Italy, Ferro Edizione published the first and second editions, while the third edition is presently being prepared for publication by Longanesi. A Polish edition is published by Rebus.

The Fiction Submission

The selling of fiction is different from nonfiction, requiring different submission materials. The good news is a fiction submission is much easier to prepare than a nonfiction proposal because in order to sell a first novel, you must have a complete manuscript. According to Marjorie Braman, a top fiction editor at HarperCollins, "We very rarely consider novels, especially first novels, unless there is a completed manuscript. And frankly, we almost never consider novels that aren't submitted by a trusted agent. There just isn't enough manpower to screen all of the unsolicited fiction manuscripts that come in every day."

It's much harder to sell a work of fiction because most major publishing houses are reluctant to take a risk — investing time they don't have and money they may not earn back — on an unknown writer. A look at the number of fiction versus nonfiction books published each year is proof enough — approximately 50,000 new nonfiction titles compared to only about 10,000 new fiction titles.

There's no question that the odds against a first novelist are tough — but not at all impossible. Your sales material is first and foremost your manuscript, which you've lavished a great deal of hard work on. So, when you're ready to submit your manuscript to editors and/or agents craft a brief, but compelling cover letter to send along with the first half of your novel. Provide just enough information in this letter to pique the reader's interest and entice them to read on. For example, "I'm enclosing the first half of my novel entitled, *Future Habit.* The story centers on a road trip that takes two unlikely protagonists — a convict on the run and a nun — to a future neither expected." Or, "A father/son drama that turns the Abraham/Isaac story on its head." A great title also helps get your reader's attention.

When selling fiction, it's best to submit the entire manuscript — but only when invited. If you are determined to submit a novel, unsolicited, to a publisher, target a few editors (see Chapter 6), and use a query letter (see Chapter 7) to get in the door. The same submission approach applies with literary agents that you are looking to have represent your novel. An agent won't agree to represent you until she has read a complete manuscript. However, she may ask for a synopsis and sample chapter first to determine whether she's interested in reading the entire manuscript.

What is a plot synopsis?

Your *plot synopsis* is a brief narrative summary — no more than a page or two — of your novel written in the present tense. The purpose of a plot synopsis is to hook an agent's interest enough for them to ask to see the manuscript. Make it as easy and enticing to read as possible.

Make sure that it tells the entire story — don't, for example leave out the story's ending as a gimmick to get the editor to ask for more. You want to get the story essentials across, not the descriptive details or the exact dialogue, so write as clearly and tightly as possible. And create the synopsis as a whole, unified piece. Don't break it up with chapter headings.

To create your synopsis, start with a few sentences containing an action-filled summary of the novel. Introduce the main character and the conflict responsible for moving the story forward. As an example, I have taken the liberty of writing a plot synopsis — of the sort that would be suitable for submission — based on the best-selling novel, *The Pilot's Wife*, by Anita Shreve, shown in Figure 8-14.

Figure 8-14: A synopsis from *The Pilot's Wife.*

Kathryn Lyons is awoken at 3 a.m. by news that the plane of her pilot husband, Jack, with 103 passengers aboard, has exploded off the coast of Ireland. When aircrash investigators indicate they suspect a bomb and Jack is somehow implicated, Kathryn is presented with starting new information about her husband and wonders if she really knows the man she had been happily married to for 16 years.

Then tell how the character plans to resolve this conflict. Also, supply some of the story's essential details up front: Main character's age, occupation, marital status; story setting (place), and time (past, present, future), as shown in Figure 8-15.

Figure 8-15: Include essential details of your story in your synopsis.

The Lyons family—Kathryn, a 38-year old schoolteacher, Jack a 48-year old commercial airplane pilot, and Mattie, their 15-year old daughter—love the ease and simplicity of their life in rural Vermont. Especially since the unusual schedule of Jack's job as a commercial airline pilot with an international route keeps them apart for the better part of each week.

But when Jack's plane explodes and a media frenzy breaks out accusing Jack of responsibility for the bombing, Kathryn, so sure of his innocence, sets out to defend Jack's honor. That was her first mistake. Her second was dialing a phone number she discovers among her husband's papers.

Now, you're ready to tell your story, focusing on what happens. Reread your novel, and as you finish each chapter, summarize the most important events that occur. Remember to focus on what happens in the novel including the character motivation and emotion that propels action and lends a human touch to the storyline.

Imagine that you're telling your story to a group of friends. You won't have their attention for five hours, but you will for a few minutes. So convey the essential storyline complete with tension, pacing and character emotion.

Make your synopsis complete and yet a quick read that stands on its own. The most effective synopsis provides the feeling of having read the entire book.

Of course, it's impossible to tell from a single chapter or even the first few chapters whether an unknown writer can orchestrate the importment elements of fiction — character, plot, dialogue, pacing, setting, and point of view. For this reason, editors find that fiction submissions of a plot synopsis or sample chapters aren't enough to demonstrate that the writer can carry through on what they promise. That's why it's important to write and rewrite your entire novel before submitting it for publication.

Part IV

Taking It Public: A Strategic Approach to Placing Your Book

"I'm not sure 'Stormy Night Publishers' are the right people to handle my cookbook. They're telling me there's not enough dramatic tension between my fish and hors d'oeuvres."

In this part . . .

It's time to submit your work for publication. In this part, I share my battle-tested submission strategies along with all the inside information you need on publishing companies — large, medium-sized, niche, university, and religious — and literary agents, as well as self-publishing options in both print and electronic formats. This part provides you with the knowledge you need to make the book publishing system work for you.

Chapter 9

Battle-Tested Submission Tactics

In This Chapter

- Locating the right editor or agent for your submission
- Ensuring top-quality submission materials
- Understanding submission procedures editors/agents like and don't like

In this chapter, I present tips taken from the experts — writers, editors, and agents — for getting your proposal read by a publishing professional. Read through the entire chapter before sending so much as a query letter to a publisher. Commit the list of submission do's and don'ts to memory.

Treat this chapter like a pilot's final check. Before sending any of your written work off to a publisher, check off the items in this chapter. No matter how many book proposals you've sold, you'll still find a helpful tip or two.

Get the Editor's Name

Submit your query or book proposal to a specific editor or agent by name. Proposals sent to the attention of The Editor or to individuals no longer employed at the publishing house end up on what's called the *slush pile* — the stack of unsolicited manuscripts that are periodically read by a group of young editorial assistants over pizza and sandwiches in a conference room. These submissions are, for the most part, mailed back with a form rejection note attached.

To find the name of an editor or agent who's right for your book:

- **Read acknowledgment pages of books similar to yours.** Writers often acknowledge both their agents and their editors.
- **Scour press coverage of books you admire.** The editor and agent are often mentioned and sometimes even interviewed in a book's press coverage.
- **Go to writers' conferences and conventions, especially if a writer you admire is speaking.** Writers' conferences often hold panel discussions, which include agents, editors, and writers. Additionally, writers attending

the conference often identify their agents and editors. While at the conference, ask around about appropriate agents or editors for your type of book. And make a point of meeting any publishing professionals attending the conference. Engage their interest.

- **Call the publishing company mentioned on the spine of a book similar to the one you're writing and ask who the editor or agent is of that writer.**
- **Once you have the editor's name, call her office to confirm the spelling of her name, address, phone number, and correct title.** A misspelled name or incorrect title can mark you as an amateur — someone who doesn't know his or her way around.
- **Send a fan letter to an author you admire.** You can send it in care of the Publishing House — an editor's assistant forwards all author fan mail directly to the author). Ask who the author's fabulous editor is because you want to send a personal note of congratulations to him or her as well. Be sure to carry through on that promise. You'd be surprised how many authors are happy to oblige.

Use the Industry's Best Sources

Start your search for the right agent or editor at your local library or bookstore using the publishing industries primary research guides: *The Literary Marketplace* (R.R. Bowker); *Writer's Guide to Book Editors, Publishers, and Literary Agents* (Prima Publishing); and *Writer's Market* (Writer's Digest Books). These three core books, when used in tandem, can provide the information you need to get your hunt for an editor (see Chapter 10) or agent (see Chapter 12) underway. Each book provides a slightly different approach to and look at the same body of information.

Industry insiders rely on *Literary Market Place,* referred to as LMP, but officially titled *LMP 2000: The Directory of the American Book Publishing Industry With Industry Yellow Pages* (R.R. Bowker, 2000). The LMP is an expensive, professional reference, used throughout the publishing industry since 1940 as a telephone directory. It's published annually in three volumes and is available in most libraries. It's also available online, although most of the information on the site is fee based. Check your library to see whether it offers the subscriber version of the site — many do.

LMP contains 55 indexed sections providing basic contact information on virtually every publisher and literary agency in the world, as well as electronic publishers, editorial services, book manufacturers, and much more. Publishing professionals rely on *LMP* because of its huge scope. No matter how small or esoteric the need, LMP offers not one, but a number of choices to answer that need.

Once you're ready to home in, you can purchase references that provide more detailed information on a much smaller range of agents and publishers: *Writer's Market* by Kirsten Holm (Editor), (Writer's Digest Books, 2000) and the *Writer's Guide to Book Editors, Publishers, and Literary Agents, 2000–2001* by Jeff Herman (Prima, 2000).

Writer's Market provides information on more than 5,000 editors at 1,150 book publishing companies — providing what they call "quick facts" such as the percentage of first-time authors they publish, number of titles published per year, royalty rate they pay, the time it takes to hear back on submissions, and more. In addition, *Writer's Market* lists the subject preferences, contact information, and recent sales made by 80 extremely reputable literary agencies.

Writer's Guide to Book Editors, Publishers, and Literary Agents, written by literary agent Jeff Herman, describes the cultures inside several hundred publishing companies along with specific editorial contacts. It also includes a gossipy section on literary agents where more than 200 leading agents talk about who they are, what they're looking for, and what they really think. For more information, visit the author's Web site at `www.jeffherman.com`.

Make a Copy

With inexpensive, high-quality copy centers and laser printers readily accessible, you don't need to submit original documents that you want returned. In fact, make plenty of copies of everything you plan to submit to a publisher or agent.

Gone are the days of sending the sole copy of your manuscript to an editor on an exclusive basis and waiting patiently for her response before sending it to another editor. Make plenty of copies on clean, quality bond paper and send the proposal or manuscript to five or more editors and agents who agree to take a look. In the cover letter, say that you are submitting it to others at the same time.

The debate about multiple submissions is a hot one in publishing circles. If you submit exclusively, you are placing yourself at the mercy of the editor or agent with the exclusive. But if you are convinced by your research, interview, or even phone conversation that the agent or editor you're submitting to is right for you, grant him or her a brief exclusive because an exclusive may secure quicker consideration for your work. However, be aware of the privilege that you are extending and don't leave yourself or your work hanging for more than a week or two. On the other hand, if you're not certain about an individual editor or agent, protect your interests by submitting multiples right from the start — just be sure to state that you are submitting to others simultaneously. Publishing professionals are used to competing. But if they think they have your material exclusively and find out once they bid that it's a competitive situation, they may be resentful.

Make Sure That Your Submission Is First Rate

Don't submit anything that is less than your best — intellectually as well as materially. Compromising on the quality of your submission invites rejection. Once the intellectual content of your query letter (see Chapter 7) and proposal (see Chapter 8) are first rate, make sure that the textual materials are, too. Print them on clean white, bond paper, free of stains, creases, or folds.

Don't recycle materials from one submission to another — dog-eared pages or any clearly recycled materials are a turnoff for editors. I've heard editors laugh about submissions they receive with a decline letter from another editor still attached. Avoid any chance of being rejected out of hand by sending only clean, new materials.

Also, when sending multiple submissions, make sure that the submission letter inside each package matches the name on the mailing label. You won't be taken seriously if a submission addressed to one editor finds its way into the possession of another.

If your book proposal contains graphical or photographic elements, be sure these materials are presented in a high-quality, professional way. Enlist the aid of a graphic design professional, if necessary, at one of the better copy centers in your area to ensure good quality.

Skip the SASE

The self-addressed, stamped envelope, or *SASE,* is a holdover from an era gone by, when writers actually submitted their precious, original manuscript or a carbon copy of it to a publisher. Back then, authors were expected to recycle a manuscript through many submissions because a manuscript was difficult and expensive to replace.

However, the days of manuscript recycling and SASEs are over. Writers and agents send out a fresh copy to each editor. Today, the inclusion of a SASE to an editor, like the recycling of submission materials, is the province of amateurs. Realize, however, that you may hear nothing whatsoever back if the editor is not interested in your submission. If you are among the many who want a response whether positive or negative — even only for psychological closure — include your e-mail address and specifically ask for a response. (Agents, on the other hand, insist on SASEs.)

Enclosing a self-addressed, stamped envelope signals to the editor or agent that you'd welcome having your submission returned. There's no reason to suggest to an editor that you're expecting rejection or that you're an amateur. Act like the professional that you are — leave SASEs to the uninformed.

Be Agreeable

When submitting your work, you are, in many respects, auditioning to work with an editor or agent. The most important part of the audition rests on the quality and marketability of the work you submit. But another, significant aspect editors look at is your willingness to participate in the process of focusing, targeting, and marketing your work to its audience.

At some point after you have submitted material, you may hear back from an editor or agent, inquiring about your willingness to revise your material or rethink your approach. Take pains to listen and fully consider any feedback you receive. Be agreeable, accessible, and cooperative. This doesn't mean that you have to agree to every suggested change. But at least listen, think, and offer to "get back to them" after you have digested whatever is proposed.

Be Responsive

Writers often complain that publishers take their own sweet time responding to submissions, and yet they put unbelievable time pressures on writers to rework and deliver their manuscript. Unfortunately, this perception is often true.

What many writers don't know is that editors are subjected to a whole set of financial and list-balancing pressures that sometimes force them to place quite unreasonable deadline pressures on writers. Literary agents can often help you negotiate around such unrealistic deadlines. But in lieu of an agent, you need to respond as quickly and nondefensively as possible. If you can't meet the deadline, speak up and be honest about your reasons. Likewise, if an editor asks for changes to the manuscript that, after careful consideration, you're just not willing to make, tell the editor exactly why those alterations aren't realistic. A compromise may work for both parties. Remain open and encourage constructive communication.

Take the case of a novelist (who asked, understandably, not to be identified) whose first book — published by a major trade publisher and reprinted in mass-market paperback — received enthusiastic reviews and strong sales figures. Her ecstatic publisher immediately commissioned two new books for a great deal of money. The author handed in the first manuscript a year later. And then a problem emerged.

The publisher read and liked this suspense novel, but claimed that several of the secondary characters should actually die rather than be injured. The author felt strongly that killing the characters off was excessive and that the survival of these characters was critical to her conception of the book. The publisher held his ground, and so did the writer. In the end, the publisher refused to accept the manuscript, and the author refused to change it or return the money paid so far which she felt she had earned. As a consequence, the novel was never published, and for contractual reasons (see Chapter 14), the author has had to switch to writing only works of nonfiction.

My advice is to respond quickly and constructively to editorial feedback so that small problems can be addressed before they become insurmountable.

Be Thorough

Visit any writers' conference, and you're sure to hear stories about proposals left on submission for weeks, months, even years without a response. It's true that editors and agents fall behind on their correspondence, and it's also true that first-time writers, with no track record or agent to fight for them, are often relegated to the "back burner" when it comes to reading their submissions.

However, the fact of the matter is that the longer your material sits at the bottom of a pile at a publisher or agent's office, the less likely it is to be read sympathetically. And besides, if you have followed the advice in this book, someone — an editorial assistant, if not the editor herself — is aware that you have sent a proposal or query letter and are entitled to a response.

Always follow through on a submission — notify the editor's office that your submission is on the way. Confirm its arrival a few days later. Follow up after a month for an update on the submission's progress. Don't attempt to sell your book over the phone. If you come across like a high-pressure salesperson — or worse — you'll be dismissed as a kook. Instead, make the follow-up call brief and courteous. Convey your professional interest and attention. If the editor can't or won't decide after two months, assume that you have been declined.

In order to get a book published, you need to develop a thick skin. Thousands of proposals and manuscripts sell only after dozens of rejections. Plan on having your work turned down more than once and sometimes even cruelly. Learn to dust yourself off, print another copy of the proposal, and mail it off to a new editor or two. Experience shows that once you give up is usually when a submission you forgot was out there turns up a contract. Remember, the next submission could be the one to hit pay dirt.

Advice from editors and agents: what they like, and what they don't

Here are some pointers editors and agents have shared with me.

- Don't get on the phone and try to talk me into buying your book.
- Don't get on the phone and deliver a plot summary. The only place for a plot summary is in your proposal, under the heading Plot Summary.
- Don't get personal — don't tell me how badly you need this contract or how many rejections you have already gotten.
- Don't call and ask to meet with me before showing me your proposal. If I'm going to work with you, I'll set up a meeting after I have read and liked your material.
- Unless you're submitting a religious book to a religious house, don't tell me that you are inspired by or speaking on God's behalf.
- If you decide to revise your proposal after I have read it — unless my letter invites a second submission — don't even try to send a revised proposal or manuscript to me. I won't read it.
- If you are referred to me by a colleague of mine or an author whom I have worked with, tell me in your cover letter.
- If you have videotape or actual press clippings, include them with the proposal.
- If you found my name in the acknowledgment page of a book I represented, tell me. Doe Coover, a prominent Boston-area literary agent, says that Cheryl Mendelson, the author of the best-selling *Home Comforts* (Scribner, 1999), "started her letter by saying, 'I found your name in the acknowledgments page of a book by Burton Anderson, one of your clients. He is such a wonderful writer!'" Says Doe, "How could I resist that opening?"

Chapter 10

How to Choose a Publisher

In This Chapter

- Researching your publisher
- Finding the publisher that suits your book

Books are usually identified by their title or author, not by their publisher. In fact, it's the unusual reader who can identify the publisher of even his or her favorite book. That's why most people don't know how one publishing company differs from another.

The truth is, publishing companies are as different from each other as people are. And now that you're ready to communicate with publishers, you need to find out which companies are best suited to your kind of book and, additionally, which editor at that house may be your advocate.

In this chapter, I provide a carefully chosen list of publishers, with detailed information about each, so you can start making your selection. I also cite a few recent publications from each company to show you the kinds of books they are experienced in publishing.

Publishers, Publishers

Today, more than 20,000 U.S. publishers exist, 5,000 of which release a majority of the 60,000 books published annually. At one end of the spectrum are five giant, multinational book publishing conglomerates, like Random House/Bantam-Doubleday-Dell with thousands of employees and several thousand new titles published each year. At the other end of the spectrum are thousands of tiny private labels that release one or two new books each year. In between, you find a huge variety of publishing enterprises: medium-sized independents, university and scholarly publishers, religious and spiritual publishers, political publishers, *subsidy* houses that charge you to publish your own book, and tiny regional firms. Which publishing house you target depends on whether they publish the type of book you plan to write.

Narrowing the Search

Although a lot of publishers are out there, only a few are ideal for your book. Your challenge is to identify the likeliest candidates. Here are a few criteria to help you sort through a list of publishers and identify the ones who are most likely to work for you.

- **Subject matter:** Do they publish books in your genre or subject matter? A Christian publisher, for example, is unlikely to publish a work of rabbinical law. If you are planning a New England cookbook, you may approach a large New York publisher, or a small- or medium-sized publisher based in New England, or both.
- **Format:** Does the publishing company publish in the format that suits your book? If you are planning to write a romance novel, be sure to target the mass-market romance specialists. Rest assured that a mass-market paperback publisher won't consider a scholarly work of history.
- **Size:** Consider large publishers first — they have more money to invest in your book and more clout with booksellers. The drawback is that they're usually less flexible and less willing to take risks on first-time writers. Smaller publishers are quick and nimble and tend to take risks. If the owner of a small press falls in love with your book, he can make it the focus of his universe for months to come.
- **Types of books:** Check out a publisher's Web site and catalogs to get acquainted with its recent and upcoming publications. Find out whether it publishes the sort of book you plan to write. If so, its experience with your type of book can work to your advantage.
- **The editor:** Keeping track of editors is tough in publishing because they move around a lot. The younger an editor — and the more likely to take a risk on a first-time writer — the more she will change companies. Good, young editors are often lured away by competing firms who offer more responsibility and money.

In the following listings, I provide current information on editors' whereabouts and subject interests. However, before you submit any materials, call and verify that the editor you have selected is still in place.

An Inside Look at the Major Publishing Houses

In the following listings, I highlight a few outstanding publishers in each of the most prominent categories: the large New York publishers, the medium-sized houses, the *niche* or small specialized presses, the university presses, and the religious houses. Each entry provides phone and fax numbers, as well as e-mail information when available; identifies the imprints and a few key contacts at the house; gives a sampling of recent publications; and contains an overview of the sorts of books published as well. For in-depth information on a much broader range of editors and publishers, I recommend that you look in *Writers Guide to Book Editors, Publishers, and Literary Agents* by Jeff Herman (Prima, 1999) and *Writer's Market 2000* (Writer's Digest Books, 1999).

The big publishers in New York

These are the big brand names of American publishing. Headquartered in New York, all of them have become divisions of much bigger global media powerhouses that encompass publishing as well as internet ventures, television, film production, magazines, book clubs, and even video chains and non-media activities. They have the deepest pockets, broadest global reach, and some of the highest-powered editorial talent. While each of these firms contain boutique imprints that offer personal attention to authors and have a more narrowly defined brand that is known to booksellers and book reviewers, they are also huge corporations that can simply seem overwhelming and impersonal when you are thinking about submitting your first book.

Random House

1540 Broadway, New York, NY 10036; 212-782-9000; 299 Park Avenue, New York, NY 10171; 280 Park Avenue, New York, NY 10171; 212-751-2600; Web site `www.randomhouse.com`.

The original company called Random House was founded in 1925, when Bennett Cerf and Donald Klopfer purchased The Modern Library, reprinter of classic works of literature, from publisher Horace Liveright. Two years later, in 1927, they decided to broaden their publishing activities, and the Random House colophon made its debut. Under the direction of Cerf, the company prospered for decades, adding over the years many additional distinguished imprints to the original duo of Random House and Modern Library: Alfred A., Knopf, Pantheon Books, Shocken Press, Ballantine Paperbacks, and so on.

In 1998, the Random House group of publishers was acquired by the German-headquartered international publishing giant Bertelsmann, and joined their existing publishing group, Bantam-Doubleday-Dell. The resulting publishing empire, the largest in the English-speaking world, includes children's, reference, as well as adult trade publishers and encompasses publishing offices in London, Toronoto, Sydney, Auckland, Johannesburg, and New York. The many hardcover and paperback imprints, which now comprise Random House, are housed in three Manhattan locations: 280 Park Avenue, 1540 Broadway, and 299 Park Avenue.

Must have an agent to submit a proposal.

The Ballantine Publishing Group

Mass-market, trade paperback, and hardcovers. General fiction and nonfiction. Key recent titles: *Sugar Busters*! by H. Leighton Steward, et.al., *Raising Cain* by Michael Thompson and Dan Kindlon, and *Women Who Run with the Wolves* by Clarissa Pinkola Estés, PhD. Address: 1540 Broadway, New York, NY 10036; 212-782-9000.

Del Rey. Mass-market, trade paperback and hardcover. Science fiction, fantasy and alternative history. Recent publications: novelizations of the three new *Star Wars* films. Key contact: Kuo-Yu Liang.

Fawcett. Mass-market mystery imprint publishing three mystery titles per month, covering a wide spectrum of crime fiction — from tea cozy to hard-boiled — and including such writers as Michelle Spring, Valerie Wolzien, and Steve Womack. Key contact: Leona Nevler.

One World. Hardcover, trade paperback and mass-market. Multi-cultural titles encompassing subjects of African-American, Asian, Latin, and Native American interest across all categories and formats. Key contact: Cheryl Woodruff.

Library of Contemporary Thought. A place for America's best writers, and experts in their fields to write provocative and timely pieces that can spark national debate. Featuring Anna Quindlen on the importance of books in society, Carl Hiassen on Disney and its influence on contemporary culture and more.

The Bantam Dell Publishing Group

Hardcover, trade paperbacks, and mass-market. General fiction and nonfiction. Authors include: Dean Koontz, Tami Hoag, Elizabeth George, and Iris Johansen. Address: 1540 Broadway, New York, NY 10036; 212-782-9000; Web site: `www.bantamdell.com`.

Bantam. Established in 1945 publishes adult fiction and nonfiction. Holds the distinction of being the nation's largest mass-market paperback publisher, in addition to publishing some of the best-selling nonfiction hardcovers of the last decade, including General H. Norman Schwarzkopf's *It Doesn't Take a Hero*; Jerry Seinfeld's *Seinlanguage*; and Daniel Goleman's *Emotional Intelligence*. Best-selling Bantam mass-market and trade paperback backlist authors include Maya Angelou, Jean Auel, Sandra Brown, Pat Conroy, Elizabeth George, Tami Hoag, Dean Koontz, Louis L'Amour, Nora Roberts, Tom Wolfe, and more than 40 original Star Wars fiction titles.

Dell/Delacorte. General fiction and nonfiction. Hardcover, trade paperback, mass-market paperback. Recent titles: *The Horse Whisperer* by Nicholas Evans, is a Dell-Delacorte title, as is his second novel *The Loop*; *Hannibal* by

Thomas Harris and *Summer Sisters* by Judy Blume. House authors: Danielle Steele, John Grisham, Maeve Binchy, Diana Gabaldon, Elmore Leonard, Sara Paretsky, and Belva Plain.

Dial Press. Hardcover and trade paperback. General fiction and nonfiction. Recent publications: *The Running Mate* by Joe Klein. Key contact: Susan Kamil.

The Crown Publishing Group

Founded in 1933, The Crown Publishing Group is recognized for the broad scope of its adult fiction and nonfiction publishing program, from lavishly illustrated books to works of literary and spiritual merit. Address: 299 Park Avenue, New York, NY 10171; 212-751-2600.

Bell Tower. Publishes works from many sacred traditions — books that nourish the soul, illuminate the mind, and speak to the heart. Authors include Stephen Levine, Bernie Glassman, Ram Dass, and Rabbi Joseph Telushkin. Key contact: Toinette Lippe.

Clarkson Potter. Hardcover and trade paperback. Cooking, decorating, and style titles, many beautifully illustrated. Authors include Martha Stewart and Chris Casson Madden. Key contact: Lauren Shakely.

Crown. Hardcover and trade paperback. General fiction and nonfiction. Authors include Jean Auel, Dominick Dunne, Edward Rutherfurd, Sylvia Rimm, Eric Larson, Suzanne Somers, and Kristin Hannah. Key contact: Steve Ross.

Harmony Books. Hardcover and trade paperback. General fiction, literary fiction, general nonfiction, and spirituality. Authors include Stephen Jay Gould, Carolyn Myss, Deepak Chopra, and Chris Bohjalian. Key contact: Linda Loewenthal.

Three Rivers Press. Original trade paperbacks and paperback reprints of books issued initially in hardcover by other Crown imprints. Original titles include *Dress Your House for Success* by Martha Webb and Sarah Parsons Zackheim and *Our Dumb Century* by Scott Dikkers and the Staff of *The Onion*. Reprint successes include *Eat Great Lose Weight* by Suzanne Somers and *Anatomy of the Spirit* by Caroline Myss.

Crown Business

General fiction and nonfiction with an emphasis on business. Hardcover and paperback. Crown Business publishes books about management (Adrian Slywotzky's *The Profit Zone* and Patricia Seybold's *Customers.com*), careers (Robert Kelley's *How to Be a Star at Work*); investment and personal finance (James Glassman's and Kevin Hassett's *Dow 36,000* and Ilyce R. Glink's *100 Questions You Should Ask about Your Personal Finances*), and business narrative (*Losing My Virginity* by Richard Branson and *Built from Scratch* by Arthur Blank and Bernie Marcus). Key contact: Steve Ross.

The Doubleday Broadway Publishing Group

Doubleday began its century of publishing in 1897 when Nelson Doubleday and magazine publisher Samuel McClure, founded the company. Among their first bestsellers was *The Day's Work* by Rudyard Kipling. Address: 1540 Broadway, New York, NY 10036; 212-782-9000. Key contact: Stephen Rubin.

Broadway. Hardcover and trade paperback. General fiction, literary fiction and general nonfiction. Recent best-selling titles include Frances Mayes's *Under the Tuscan Sun*, Bill Bryson's *A Walk in the Woods*, Adeline Yen Man's *Falling Leaves*, Ruth Reichel's *Tender at the Bone*, and Bob Costas's *Fair Ball.* Key contact: Gerald Howard.

Currency. Hardcover and trade paperback. Business and finance. Representative titles include *Six Sigma* by Mikel J. Harry and Richard Schroder and *The Fifth Discipline* by Peter Senge. Key contact: Roger Scholl.

Doubleday. General fiction and nonfiction. Hardcover. Recent titles: *The Brethren* by John Grisham, *The Century* by Peter Jennings and Todd Brewster, and *Tuesdays with Morrie* by Mitch Albom. Key contact: Bill Thomas.

Doubleday Religious. Hardcover and trade paperback. Religion and spirituality. Key contact: Eric Major.

Nan. A Talese. Hardcover and trade paperback. Literary fiction and nonfiction. Her distinguished list of authors include Margaret Atwood, Thomas Kennelley, Thomas Cahill, and Pat Conroy. Key contact: Nan Talese.

The Knopf Publishing Group

Established in 1915, Alfred A. Knopf has long been known as a publisher of distinquished hardcover fiction and nonfiction titles. Address: 299 Park Avenue, New York, NY 10171; 212-751-2600.

Alfred A. Knopf. Hardcover. General fiction and nonfiction, belles lettres. House authors: Toni Morrison, John Updike, Michael Crichton, Anne Rice, Andrew Weil, Anne Tyler, Jane Smiley, and Richard North Patterson, as well as Thomas Mann, Willa Cather, John Hersey, and John Cheever. Key contact: Sonny Mehta.

Pantheon. Hardcover. Quality general fiction and nonfiction. Authors include Anne Morrow Lindbergh, Boris Pasternak, Studs Terkel, Michel Foucault, Julio Cortazar, Marguerite Duras, John Berger, Art Spiegelman, Albert Murray, Italo Calvino, James Gleick, Alan Lightman, Anne Lamott, David Malouf, Madison Smartt Bell, and Jonathan Raban. Key contact: Dan Frank.

Schocken. Hardcover. General fiction and nonfiction, specializing in religious topics, cultural interests, and women's studies. Authors include S. Y. Agnon, Sholem Aleichem, Aharon Appelfeld, Martin Buber, Susanna Heschel, Franz Kafka, Harold S. Kushner, Joan Nathan, Gershom Scholem, Elie Wiesel, and Simon Wiesenthal. Key contact: Susan Ralston.

Vintage Anchor Publishing. General fiction and nonfiction. Trade paperback. Vintage publishes both classic and contemporary writers, from Willa Cather, Dashiell Hammett, Albert Camus, Vladimir Nabokov, and William Faulkner, to Alice Munro, Cormac McCarthy, and Philip Roth. Anchor publishes such authors as Chinua Achebe, Naguib Mahfouz, John Krakauer, and Margaret Atwood. Key contact: Marty Asher.

Random House Information Group

Publishes reference works in both print and electronic formats ranging from dictionaries and thesauruses, to crossword puzzle books, travel guides and foreign language courses. Address: 280 Park Avenue, New York, NY 10017; 212-751-2600. Key contact: Bonnie Ammer.

Random House Reference. Publishes language reference books in hardcover, paperback, and multimedia formats. Titles include Random House Webster's dictionaries, Random House Roget's thesauruses, Random House Webster's Quotationary, and Build Your Power Vocabulary.

Fodors. Trade paperback travel books. Fodor's. Fodor's Travel Publications, the world's largest English-language travel information publisher, has over 300 travel titles in print, which make up over 17 different series. Fodor's is located on the Web at `www.fodors.com`.

Living Language. Foreign and English language instruction in print and audio formats.

The Princeton Review. Publishes books that help students sharpen their academic skills, prepare for standardized tests, and gain entrance into college and graduate school. Titles include *Cracking the SAT, The Best 3331 Colleges,* and *Word Smart.*

Random House Puzzles & Games. Nation's No. 1 publisher of crosswords, including those drawn from the pages of *The New York Times, The Los Angeles Times,* and *The Boston Globe.*

Random House Reference & Information Publishing. Publishes in all types of print and multimedia formats. General and trade reference. Titles include *Random House Webster's Unabridged Dictionary, The Random House Treasury of Best-Loved Poems, The New York Road Runner's Club Complete Book of Running and Fitness,* and *Car Buyer's and Leaser's Negotiating Bible.*

The Random House Trade Publishing Group

Publishes mainstream commerical fiction and nonfiction as well as literary fiction and nonfiction. Address: 299 Park Avenue, New York, NY 10171; 212-751-2600.

Random House Trade Books. Hardcover. General fiction and nonfiction. This is Random House's eponymous imprint known for such bestsellers as *Midnight in the Garden of Good and Evil* by John Berendt, *Dutch* by Edmund Morris, and *The Greatest Generation* by Tom Brokaw. Key contact: Ann Godoff.

Villard. Hardcover and trade paperback. General fiction and nonfiction with an emphasis on popular culture. Authors include John Krakauer, Jesse Ventura, and Aretha Franklin. Key contact: Bruce Tracy.

The Modern Library. Hardcover, trade paperbacks and series of classics in a variety of subject areas including John Krakauer's Exploration Series, Caleb Carr's War Series, Martin Scorsese's *The Movies,* and Steve Martin's Humor Series.

HarperCollins Publishers

Founded in 1817 by the brothers James and John Harper, HarperCollins Publishers as it exists today was formed by the merger of the American firm Harper & Row with the British powerhouse William Collins and Sons, when News Corporation acquired both firms in 1990. With the acquisition in 1999 of William Morrow and Company and Avon Books from the Hearst Corporation, HarperCollins becomes the second largest English Language trade publisher after Random House/BDD, with approximately 1,700 new titles issued each year by all adult imprints in all formats.

HarperCollins is a global publishing enterprise, embracing adult, academic, children's and religious publishing operations with offices in New York; London; San Francisco; Grand Rapids, Michigan, (the home of Zondervan Books, a religious subsidiary); Ontario, Canada; and Sydney, Australia. The General Books Group, under the direction of Publisher and President Cathy Hemming, based in New York, with a small editorial office in San Francisco, accounts for all adult trade titles published by HarperCollins in the United States.

HarperCollins. Hardcovers. General fiction and nonfiction. Recent books: *The Terrible Hours* by Peter Maas, *The Poisonwood Bible* by Barbara Kingsolver, *The Professor and the Madman* by Simon Winchester. Key contact: Cathy Hemming. Address: 10 East 53rd Street, New York, NY 10022; 212-207-7000; `www.harpercollins.com` (applies to all imprints except HarperSanFrancisco).

HarperPerennial. Trade paperback. General fiction and nonfiction. Recent books: *Explaining Hitler* by Ron Rosenbaum, *The Divine Secrets of the Ya Ya Sisterhood* by Rebecca Wells, and *Ophelia Speaks* by Sara Shandler. Key contact: Susan Weinberg.

HarperEntertainment. Trade and mass-market paperback. Celebrity and entertainment related nonfiction. Recent books: *Ally McBeal: The Official Guide* by Tim Appelo, *The Art of the X-Files* by Tim Carter, and *House Broken* by Richard Karn. Key contact: Jennifer Hershey.

HarperBusiness. Hardcover and trade paperback. Business and finance. Recent books: *Now or Never* by Mary Modahl, *What Would Machiavelli Do* by Stanley Bing, and *The Internet Bubble* by Tony and Michael Perkins, *Living on the Faultline* by Geoffrey Moore, and *The Innovator's Dilemma* by Clayton M. Christensen. Key contact: Adrian Zackheim.

HarperResource. Hardcover and trade paperback. General reference and practical nonfiction. Recent books: *HarperCollins Spanish College Dictionary*, *All the Birds of North America* by Jack Griggs, and *Ordinary People, Extraordinary Wealth* by Ric Edelman. Key contact: Megan Newman.

Access Travel Guides. Trade paperback. Travel series. Recent books: *Access New York*, *Access London*, and *Access Florence and Venice*. Key contact: Edwin Tan.

William Morrow. Hardcover. General fiction and nonfiction. Recent books: *Ahab's Wife* by Sena Jeter Naslund, *Stiffed* by Susan Faludi, and *Edward M. Kennedy* by Adam Clymer. Key contact: Lisa Queen.

Morrow Cookbooks. A division of William Morrow. Hardcover and trade paperback. Cookbooks. Recent books: *The Chinese Kitchen* by Eileen Yin Fei Lo, *A Mediterranean Feast* by Clifford A. Wright, and *The Campagna Table* by Mark Strausman. Key contact: Harriet Bell.

Cliff Street Books. Hardcover and trade paperback. General fiction and nonfiction. Recent books: *The Bingo Queens of Paradise* by June Park, *The Most Brilliant Thoughts of All* by John M. Shanahan, and *One of the Guys* by Robert Clark Young. Key contact: Diane Reverend.

ReganBooks. Hardcover and trade paperback. General fiction and nonfiction. Recent books: *I Know This Much is True* by Wally Lamb, *I Refuse to Raise a Brat* by Marilu Henner, and *Have a Nice Day* by Mick Foley. Key contact: Judith Regan.

HarperSanFrancisco. Hardcover. General nonfiction, religion, and spirituality. Recent books: *Legacy of Luna* by Julia Butterfly Hill, *Weaving the Web* by Tim Berners-Lee, and *Mormon America* by Richard Ostling and Joan K. Ostling. Key contact: Steve Hanselman. Address: 353 Sacramento Street, San Francisco, CA 94111-3653; 415-477-4400; 415-477-4444 fax; e-mail hcsanfrancisco@harpercollins.com.

Amistad: Hardcover and trade paperbacks. Specializing in works of African-American interest. Recent books: *The Amistad Pictorial History of the African American Athlete* by Francis C. Harris with Charles F. Harris, Jr., *Skin Deep* by Barbara Summers, and *Dorothy Dandridge*: *A Biography by Donald Bogle*. Key contact: Charles Harris.

Avon Books: Mass-market paperback. Mass-market fiction and nonfiction. Recent books: *Vinegar Hill* by A. M. Ansay, *Dr. Atkins New Diet Revolution* by Robert Atkins, M.D., and *Krondor the Assassins* by Raymond E. Feist. Key contact: Jennifer Hershey.

Ecco Press: Hardcover and trade paperbacks. General fiction and nonfiction, poetry, and belles lettres. Recent books: *Blonde* by Joyce Carol Oates, *Hair Brain, Tortoise Mind* by Guy Klaxton, and *Letters to My Son on the Love of Books* by Robert Cotroneo. Key contact: Dan Halpern.

Simon & Schuster, Inc.

Simon & Schuster, Inc., 1230 Avenue of the Americas, New York, NY 10020; 212-698-7000; 212-698-7007 fax; Web site `www.simonsays.com`.

Parent Company: Viacom.

Simon & Schuster was founded by two young, imaginative entrepreneurs, Richard L. (Dick) Simon and M. Lincoln (Max) Schuster. Their initial project was a crossword puzzle book — the first ever produced — which went on sale April 10, 1924, and became a runaway bestseller. From that simple beginning, the company has grown to become a multifaceted, multiformat global publishing company that publishes more than 2,000 titles per year under 38 well-known imprints.

Simon & Schuster is the company responsible for launching the American paperback industry in 1939 with the founding of Pocket Books. In 1975, Gulf + Western bought Simon & Schuster. Prentice Hall was added in 1984 and Macmillan in 1994. In late 1994, Gulf +Western — renamed Paramount Communications — was itself acquired by Viacom. In 1998, with the sale of the educational, reference, and professional publishing divisions to Pearson, the company once again became wholly focused on consumer publishing, dedicated to publishing the best in books and multimedia products for the general reader.

Simon & Schuster Trade Division:

Simon & Schuster: Editorial contacts: David Rosenthal, Vice President & Publisher; Michael V. Korda, Sr. VP and Editor In Chief; Alice Mayhew, VP & Editorial Director, William Rosen, Charles Adams, Dominick V. Anfuso, Robert Bender, Fred W. Hills, Syndy Miner, Jeff Neuman, Ruth Fecych, Constance Herndon, Roslyn Siegel, Janice Easton, Geoff Kloske, Marysue Rucci, and Denise Roy.

Recent publications: *Before I Say Good-Bye* by Mary Higgins Clark, *When Pride Still Mattered* by David Maraniss, *First Break All The Rules* by Marcus Buckingham and Curt Coffman, *A Heartbreaking Work of Staggering Genius* by Dave Eggers, *The Roaring 2000s Investor* by Harry S. Dent, and *The Harvard Medical School Family Health Guide.*

Simon & Schuster Trade Paperbacks

(Imprints include Fireside, Touchstone, Scribner Paperback Fiction, and S&S Libros en Espanol.)

Editorial contacts: Mark A. Gompertz, Vice President & Publisher; Trish Todd, Vice President & Editor in Chief, Patricia Medved, Caroline E. Sutton, Kris Puopolo, Lisa Considine, and Doris Cooper.

Recent publications: *The Seat of the Soul* by Gary Zukav, *Angelas's Ashes* by Frank McCourt, and *Yesterday, I Cried* by Iyanla Vanzant.

Scribner (formerly Charles Scribner's Sons, Publishers)

(Imprints include Lisa Drew Books, Simple Abundance Press, Scribner Classics.)

Editorial contacts: Susan Moldow, Publisher; Nan Graham, Vice President, Editor in Chief; Lisa Drew, VP & Publisher (Lisa Drew Books); Susanne Kirk, Jane Rosneman, Jake Morrissey, Gillian Blake, and Sarah Ban Breathnach (Simple Abundance Press).

Recent publications: *'Tis* by Frank McCourt, *Hearts In Atlantis* by Stephen King, *Home Comforts* by Cheryl Mendelson, *All The Best, George Bush* by George Bush, and *Close Range* by Annie Proulx.

The Free Press

Publisher of influential and award-winning books in social sciences, psychology, politics, history, the sciences, and business and management.

Editorial contacts; Elizabeth Maguire, VP & Editorial Director, Robert Wallace, Bruce Nichols, Paul Golob, Stephen Morrow, Philip Rappaport, and Chad Conway.

Recent publications: *The Baby Boom* by Elinor Burkett, *Between Silk and Cyanide* by Leo Marks, *Alexander Hamilton,* and *American* by Richard Brookhiser.

Pocket Books

Publishes hardcover, trade paperbacks, and mass-market books with wide ranging, popular appeal to all ages. Adult Imprints include Pocket Books, Pocket Books Hardcover, Pocket Star, Washington Square Press, Sonnet, Star Trek, MTV Books; Young Readers Imprints include Archway Paperbacks, Minstrel Books, Pocket Pulse.

Editorial contacts: Judith Curr, President and Publisher; Kara Welsh, Deputy Publisher, Mass-market; Karen Mender, Deputy Publisher, Hardcover and Trade Paperback. Tracy Behar, Emily Bestler, Linda Marrow (Women's Fiction), Nancy Miller (Washington Square Press), Mitchell Ivers, Tracey Sherrod, Caroline Tolley, Kate Collins, and George Lucas. Nancy Pines, Publisher, Young Readers, Patricia MacDonald, Anne Greenberg, and Lisa Clancy. Star Trek: Scott Shannon.

Recent publications: *The Coming Global Superstorm* by Art Bell and Whitley Streiber, *The Camino* by Shirley Maclaine, *The Millionaire Next Door* by Thomas J. Stanley and William D. Danko, *Night Whispers* by Judith McNaught, *The Green Mile* by Stephen King, and *Fearless* by Francine Pascal.

No unsolicited materials accepted.

St. Martins-Holt-FSG

Parent Company: Holtzbrink

While housed within the large German-based international communications conglomerate Verlagsgruppe, George von Holtzbrink, Henry Holt and Company, St. Martin's Press, and Farrar, Straus & Giroux still maintain their long-standing tradition of editorial independence.

Henry Holt and Company

115 West 18 Street, New York, NY 10011; 212-886-9200; fax 212-633-0748.

Henry Holt & Company, Inc., founded in 1866, publishes approximately 120 books each year, including a wide range of hardcover trade fiction and nonfiction. Holt imprints include Owl Books (its trade paperback division); The College Board; Books for Young Readers; and Metropolitan Books.

Throughout its history, Holt has published such important writers as Robert Frost, A.E. Housman, Frederick Jackson Turner, Norman Mailer, and Kurt Vonnegut. Holt's current authors include Pulitzer Prize winners Tony Horwitz and David Levering Lewis and national best-selling authors Patrick F. McManus, and Thomas Pynchon. Genres and subject areas of particular interest to Holt adult trade editors include: literary fiction, narrative nonfiction, history, science, health, popular culture, biography, women's studies, and parenting.

Adult Trade Editorial Contacts: Sara Bershtel, Associate Publisher and Acquiring Editor for Metropolitan. The following editors acquire for Henry Holt and Owl books: John Sterling Elizabeth Stein, David Sobel, Jennifer Barth, and Jack Macrae.

Recent publications: *The Year of Jubilo* by Howard Bahr, *Virtual Tibet* by Orville Schell, and *Raising A Thinking Preteen* by Myma Shure.

Accepts queries and proposals with three sample chapters. No unsolicited manuscripts.

Farrar, Straus & Giroux, Inc

19 Union Square West, New York, NY 10003; 212-741-6900; fax 212-463-0641; e-mail `acadmkt@fsgee.com`.

Founded in 1946, FS&G emerged in the postwar era as one of a handful of pre-eminnent publishers of belles lettres, as well as serious fiction and nonfiction. FS&G's continued interest in literature and the arts is exemplified in the 120 new titles published each year. Though owned by Holtzbrink, the firm continues to be managed by founder and Publisher Roger Straus. Imprints include Hill & Wang, North Point Press, and Farrar Straus & Giroux Books for Young Readers.

Representative authors: Joseph Brodsky, Carlos Fuentes, Scott Turow, John McPhee, Philip Roth, Aleksandr Solzhenitsyn, Tom Wolfe, Susan Sontag, Alice McDermott, and Jamaica Kincaid.

Editorial contacts: Jonathan Galassi, Elizabeth Dyssegaard, Elisabeth Sifton, John Glusman, Paul Elie, Ethan Nosowsky, and Rebecca Saletan.

Hill & Wang: Traditionally viewed as a publisher of scholarly books, Hill & Wang's publishing program is becoming more commercial in it's reach. Publishes mainly nonfiction encompassing such subject areas as current events, history, politics, as well as a select group of literary and dramatic works.

Editorial contacts: Elisabeth Sifton and Lauren Osborne.

North Point Press: Founded in Berkeley, California, in 1980, North Point Press publishes nonfiction books with an emphasis on nature writing and natural history.

Editorial contact: Ethan Nosowsky and Rebecca Saletan.

St. Martin's Press LLC

175 Fifth Avenue, New York, NY 10010; 212-674-5151; fax 212-420-9314; e-mail `inquiries@stmartins.com`; Web site `www.stmartins.com`; Web site for Minotaur imprint `www.stmartins.com`.

Founded in 1952 as the U.S. outpost of Macmillan/London, St. Martin's Press has grown and thrived under the direction first of Tom McCormack, who ran the company from 1969 until 1997, and currently under the leadership of John Sargent Jr. St. Martin's Paperbacks, one of the few successful launches of the postwar era, was masterminded by Sally Richardson in 1984. Other

St. Martin's Imprints include Picador USA, Stonewall Inn Editions, L.A. Weekly, Minotaur, St. Martin's Griffin, St. Martin's Scholarly and Reference and Thomas Dunne Books. SMP publishes approximately 800 titles per year.

Editorial contacts: Charles Spicer, Kelly Ragland (Crime Fiction), George Witte, Gordon Van Gelder, Heather Jackson, Hope Dellon, Jennifer Enderline, Jennifer Weis, Joe Veltre, Keith Kahla (Gay interest), Marian Lizzi, Matthew Shear, Michael Denneny, Peter Wolverton, Reagan Arthur, Ruth Calvin, Tim Bent, Tom Dunne, and Diane Higgins.

Representative authors and recent titles: *Winter Solstice* by Rosalind Pilcher, *Cuba* by Stephen Coonts, *Hot Six* by Janet Evanovich, *Jackie* by James Spada, *Jacqueline Bouvier Kennedy Onassis* by Donald Spoto, *The People's Pharm*acy by Joe Graedon, and *The Red Tent* by Anita Diamant.

Accepts queries; no unsolicited manuscripts.

Hyperion

77 West 66 Street, 11th Floor, New York, NY 10023-6298; 212 456-0100; fax 212- 456-0112; e-mail `lastname.firstname@abc.com`; Web site `www.hyperionbooks.com`.

Hyperion was founded in 1991 by Robert S. Miller as the trade publishing arm of the Walt Disney Company. Publishing a total of 110 hardcover, trade-paper, and mass-market titles annually, the Hyperion trade division publishes commercial and literary fiction as well as frontlist nonfiction in such areas as pop-culture, health and wellness, current affairs, self-help, humor, business, childcare and parenting, and more. Its Talk/Miramax Books imprint publishes media linked book projects. Hyperion does not accept unsolicitied manuscripts.

Editorial contacts: Martha Levin, Gretchen Young, Peternelle van Arsdale, Leigh Haber, Leslie Wells, Maureen O'Brien, Will Schwalbe, and Jennifer Lang.

Recent titles include *Relationship Rescue* by Phillip C. McGraw, *Mother of Pearl* by Melinda Haynes, and *ESPN Sports Century* edited by Michael MacCambridge.

Putnam-Penguin, Inc.

375 Hudson Street, New York, NY 10014; 212-366-2000: fax 212-366-2666; e-mail `online@penguinputnam.com`; Web site `www.penguinputnam.com`.

Penguin Putnam Inc. is the U.S. affiliate of the internationally renowned Penguin Group, the second-largest English-language trade book publisher in the world. Formed in 1996 as a result of the merger between Penguin Books USA and The Putnam Berkley Group, Penguin Putnam, under the stewardship of President Phyllis Grann, is a leading U.S. adult and children's trade book publisher. The Penguin Group, with primary operations in the United Kingdom, Australia, the United States, and Canada and smaller operations in South Africa and India, is led by its President, David Wan, and is owned by Pearson PLC, an international media group. Pearson has interests in publishing, television, television production, broadcasting, and electronic and multimedia businesses.

Penguin Putnam publishes under a wide range of prominent imprints and trademarks, among them Berkley Books, Dutton, Grosset & Dunlap, New American Library, Penguin, Philomel, G. P. Putnam's Sons, Riverhead Books,Viking and Frederick Warne. The company possesses perhaps the world's most prestigious list of best-selling authors and a backlist of unparalleled breadth, depth, and quality. Penguin Putnam's roster of best-selling authors is a Who's Who of the industry, including among hundreds of others Dorothy Allison, Melissa Bank, Saul Bellow, A. Scott Berg, Harold Bloom, Sylvia Browne, Tom Clancy, Robin Cook, Patricia Cornwell, Catherine Coulter, Clive Cussler, the Dalai Lama, Dick Francis, Sue Grafton, W. E. B. Griffin, Robert Ludlum, James McBride, Terri McMillan, Arthur Miller, Jacqueline Mitchard, Toni Morrison, Kathleen Norris, Joyce Carol Oates, Suze Orman, Robert Parker, Nora Roberts, Nancy Taylor Rosenberg, John Sandford, Carol Shields, Amy Tan, James Van Praagh, Kurt Vonnegut, and Neale Donald Walsch.

Penguin Putnam is a global leader also in children's publishing, through its Books for Young Readers, with preeminent imprints such as Dial Books, Dutton, Grosset & Dunlap, Philomel, Puffin, G. P. Putnam's Sons, Viking, and Frederick Warne. These imprints are home to Ludwig Bemelmans, Jan Brett, Eric Carle, Roald Dahl, Tomie dePaola, Hardie Gramatky, Eric Hill, Brian Jacques, A. A. Milne, Tasha Tudor, and dozens of other popular authors. Grosset & Dunlap issues such perennial favorites as *The Little Engine That Could* and the Nancy Drew and Hardy Boys series. The Young Readers division continues to broaden the worldwide licensing of its renowned Spot and Beatrix Potter brands. More than 200 companies worldwide now license Beatrix Potter merchandise; The World of Beatrix Potter is the largest international literary licensed merchandise program.

Penguin Putnam Imprints

The company publishes under a wide range of imprints and trademarks.

Adult: Ace Books, Avery, Berkley Books, Dutton, G.P. Putnam's Sons, HPBooks, Jove, New American Library, Perigee, Penguin, Plume, Riverhead Books, Jeremy P. Tarcher, and Viking.

Children's: Dial Books for Young Readers, Dutton Children's Books, Frederick Warne, G.P. Putnam's Sons, Grosset & Dunlap, Philomel, Phyllis Fogelman Books, Planet Dexter, Price Stern, Sloan, Puffin Books, and Viking Children's Books.

Adult imprint descriptions:

Ace Books was founded in 1953 and is the oldest continuously operating science fiction publisher in the United States. It is an imprint of The Berkley Publishing Group. Publisher: Susan Allison.

Avery Publishing Group was acquired by Penguin Putnam in 1999. Its publishing program is dedicated primarily to complementary medicine, nutrition, and healthful cooking titles. Publisher: John Duff.

Berkley Books publishes more than 500 titles a year under the Berkley, Jove, and Ace imprints, in mass-market paperback, trade paperback, and hardcover formats. Publisher: Leslie Gelbman.

Dutton currently publishes some 50 hardcover fiction and nonfiction titles per year. Publisher: Carol Baron.

G. P. Putnam's Sons is the leading publisher of both commercial fiction and nonfiction hardcover frontlist titles. In 1999, G. P. Putnam's Sons had more New York Times best-selling hardcover titles than any imprint in the industry. Publisher: Neil Nyren.

HPBooks specializes in cooking and automotive titles, publishing about a dozen books a year. Publisher: John Duff.

Jove is a best-selling paperback imprint of the Berkley Publishing Group. Publisher: Leslie Gelbman.

New American Library offers a wide selection of fiction and nonfiction, aiming at reaching the largest possible number of readers, the true mass-market. The NAL imprints - Signet, Onyx, Signet Classics, and Roc — publish more than 400 titles each year. The majority of titles are original works, supplemented by reprints originating primarily from sister imprints Viking and Dutton. Publisher: Louise Burke.

Perigee Books, originally created as the trade paperback imprint for G. P. Putnam's Sons, features an eclectic range of titles from virtually every category of publishing, both fiction and nonfiction. Publisher: John Duff.

Penguin trade paperbacks carry the most recognized logo of any book publisher in the world, with a list as stimulating and diverse as readers themselves. Covering such subjects as literature, biography, memoir, history, science, business, psychology, popular reference, and self-help, the Penguin list now has more than 3,000 books in print in the United States. Publisher: Kathryn Court.

Throughout its history, **Plume** has been dedicated to giving an opportunity to voices previously neglected by mainstream publishing. The pioneering program in multicultural literature, which began with Toni Morrison and Jamaica Kincaid, has expanded to include ground-breaking works by Latino, African-American, and Asian-American authors. Publisher: Clare Ferraro.

Riverhead Books was formed with the goal of publishing quality books in hardcover and then in trade paperback — both fiction and nonfiction, including significant religious and spiritual titles — that would open readers up to new ideas and points of view. Since its launch in 1994, Riverhead has quickly developed its reputation internationally as a house for up-and-coming young fiction writers. Among the impressive writers whose careers Riverhead has launched so far, and will continue to build, are Pearl Abraham, Junot Díaz, Alex Garland, Nick Hornby, J. Robert Lennon, Thomas Moran, Danzy Senna, and Aryeh Lev Stollman. Publisher: Susan Petersen Kennedy.

Jeremy P. Tarcher was purchased by Putnam in 1991 and currently publishes some 50 books annually on health, politics, creativity, psychology, religion/spirituality, parenting, social issues, gay/lesbian matters, sexuality, business, and others. Publisher: Joel Fotinos.

Viking currently publishes approximately 100 books per year, including titles in its illustrated Viking Studio imprint. The house has earned acclaim and a solid reputation for its ability to issue a broad range of literary titles and for its highly selective and successful list of commercial writers and bestsellers. Viking is recognized for nurturing and increasing the visibility of its established and more prominent authors, while orchestrating the successful launch of new and relatively unknown writers. Publisher: Clare Ferraro.

Time Warner Trade Publishing

1271 Avenue of the Americas, New York NY 10020; 212-522-7200; fax 212-522-7991; Web site `www.twbookmark.com`.

Warner Books — founded in 1960 as the publishing arm of Warner Studio — and Little, Brown and Company — a long established literary powerhouse originally based in Boston — became united under the Times Warner corporate umbrella in 1990. Though merged, the two publishing companies continue to enjoy their own unique editorial independence.

Warner Books publishes frontlist nonfiction and commercial fiction in hardcover, trade paperback and mass-market editions and is recognized for breaking out such blockbuster bestsellers as *Simple Abundance* by Sarah Ban Breathnach and the novels of David Baldacci, Nicholas Sparks, Billie Letts, Sandra Brown and Nelson DeMille. Under its six imprints — Warner Books Hardcover, Warner Business Books, Warner Books Mass-Market, Warner Books Trade paperbacks, Mysterious Press, and Warner Aspect — the company publishes 225 titles per year.

Editorial contacts: Jamie Raab, Les Pockell, Rick Horgan, Amy Einhorn, Maggie Crawford, Rick Wolff, Betsy Mitchell, Caryn Karmatz Rudy, Rob McMahon, Diana Baroni, John Aherne, Sara Ann Freed, and William Malloy.

Recent Warner titles include *The Lion's Game* by Nelson DeMille, *The Switch* by Sandra Brown, *The Biology of Success* by Dr. Robert Arnot, *Jackie, Ethel Joan* by J. Randy Taraborelli, *A Walk to Remember* by Nicholas Sparks, and *Ten Things I Wish I'd Known Before I Went Out in the Real World* by Maria Shriver.

Accepts only agented submissions.

Little, Brown and Company, originally founded in 1837 in Boston, is one of the oldest and most respected names in American publishing. The company releases 100 new hardcover and trade paperback titles annually under several imprints: Back Bay, Bulfinch Press, Little, Brown and Company Books for Children and Young Adults and Little, and Brown and Company.

Editorial contacts: Deborah Baker, Sarah Crichton (Little Brown's publisher), Michael Pietsch, Amanda Murray, Chip Rossetti, Judy Clain, Sarah Burnes, Terry Adams (Director of Back Bak Books, its trade paperback), and Carol Judy Leslie (Bulfinch editorial contact).

Children's Department and Bulfinch Books are located in Boston. 3 Center Plaza, Boston, MA 02108. Main phone 617-227-0730. Children's editorial fax 617-263-2864. Editorial contact Megan Tingley.

212-522-8700; fax 212-522-2067; e-mail `www.twbookmark.com`.

Recent Little, Brown and Company titles include *Fortune's Rock* by Anita Shreve, *Void Moon* by Michael Connelly, *Cradle and All* by James Patterson, and *All Too Human* by George Stephanopoulos.

Accepts only agented submissions.

Smaller publishers and category specialists

This next group includes the "little giants." Every single one of these firms is a clear and defined brand in the minds of reviewers and booksellers. Each has its share of space in the bookstores and its share of bestsellers. But so far, all of these houses have resisted the pull of the conglomerates. Though several of them have grown through acquisition and amalgamation, none has yet been absorbed by one of the big media companies. These companies are smaller and hew more closely to the tradition of personal service from a bygone era. The companies listed here are among the best in this category and were chosen to represent a wide range of publishing styles and interests that can be found at this level of the industry. Each listed company confirmed the information in its listing.

Grove/Atlantic, Inc.

841 Broadway, New York, NY 10003-4793; 212-614-7850; toll-free: 800-521-0178; fax 212-614-7886.

Grove Press, founded in 1952, and Atlantic Monthly Press, founded in 1917, are now united as Grove/Atlantic, Inc., operating as one publishing house but maintaining their editorial individuality as two distinct imprints. Grove/Atlantic is known for publishing first quality literary fiction and nonfiction as well as poetry by such writers as Samuel Beckett, Marguerite Duras, John Kennedy Toole, J. P. Donleavy, Henry Miller, Jerzy Kosinski, Robert Coover, Terry Southern, and Frederick Barthelme. Continuing its committment to publishing significant works of enduring quality, Grove/Atlantic is also focusing on reissuing its backlist of classic works for a new generation of readers to enjoy. The company publishes approximately 70 titles per year covering such subject areas as biography, history, travel, government/political science, literary criticism, poetry, women's studies, and, in fiction, experimental, literary, and translation.

Editorial contacts: Morgan Entrekin at `mentrekin@groveatlantic.com` (Publisher), Joan Bingham at `jbingham@groveatlantic.com` (Executive Editor), Elisabeth Schmitz at `eschmitz@groveatlantic.com` (Senior Editor, Director of Subsidiary rights), and Andrew Miller at `amiller@groveatalantic.com`.

Recently published titles include *In The Fall* by Jeffrey Lent, *The Toughest Indian In the World* by Sherman Alexie, and *Asleep* by Banana Yoshimoto.

Accepts agented submissions only.

Harcourt Inc.

525 B Street, Suite 1900, San Diego CA 92101; 619-231-6616; fax 619-699-5555; Web site `www.harcourtbooks.com`. Also: 15 East 26 Street, New York, NY 10010; 212-592-1000; fax 212-592-1010.

Founded originally in 1919 as Harcourt Brace & Company, Harcourt has evolved through merger, acquisition, and consolidation, into a formidible multinational, multidimensional entity, of which Harcourt Trade Division is one small part. The imprint is headquartered in San Diego, with a small office in New York. The company releases a total of 120 new titles annually in hardcover and trade paperback — through its Harvest Books imprint — with a strong emphasis in literary fiction and serious nonfiction.

Editorial contacts: Dan Farley, David Hough, Jane Isay, Drenka Willen, Walter Bode, and Andre Bernard.

Representative titles: *Father Courage* by Suzanne Braun Levine, *Godfather of the Kremlin* by Boris Berrezovsky, *Spytime* by William F. Buckley, Jr., *The Lost Legends of New Jersey* by Frederick Reiken, *East of the Mountains* by David Guterson, and *Three Miles Down* by James Hamilton-Paterson.

Unagented queries and unsolicited manuscripts not accepted.

Harlequin Books

300 East 42nd Street, New York, NY 10017; 212-682-6080; fax 212-682-4539; Web site `www.eharlequin.com`.

Canadian publishing executive Richard Bonnycastle founded Harlequin in 1949. In its early years, the company published a wide range of American and British paperbacks, including mysteries, westerns, and cookbooks.

It was not until 1957 that Harlequin began buying rights to publish romance novels from Mills & Boon, a British publisher of romance fiction. Mary Bonnycastle, wife of the founder, noticed the enormous popularity of "these nice little books with happy endings" and suggested the company concentrate on them. By 1964, Harlequin was publishing romance fiction exclusively.

Rather than focusing on bookshops, Harlequin took its books to where women shop most — supermarkets, drugstores, and department stores. The strategy worked, and Harlequin boldly crossed the Atlantic in 1971, purchasing Mills & Boon and, with it, the romantic talents of more than 100 British authors.

Since then, the growing popularity of the romance genre, along with Harlequin's effective marketing and promotion techniques, has enabled sales of romance novels to soar from three million in 1970 to the current annual total of more than 160 million worldwide.

Harlequin publishes 58 mass-market titles per month in the following imprints: Harlequin American Romance, Harlequin Duets, Harlequin Historicals, Harlequin Intrigue, Harlequin Presents (Mills & Boon Presents), Harlequin Romance (Mills & Boon Enchanted), Harlequin Superromance, Harlequin Temptation, Mills & Boon Historical Romance, Mills & Boon Medical Romance, Silhouette Desire, Silhouette Intimate Moments, Silhouette Romance, Silhouette Special Edition, and Steeple Hill Love Inspired.

Each of the imprints provides a detailed set of guidelines for writers, which can be found at the Harlequin Web site at `www.eharlequin.com`.

Harlequin. Editorial contacts: Denise O'Sullivan, Margaret O'Neill Marbury, Melissa Jeglinski, Natashya Wilson, Patience Smith, Tracy Farrell, Angela Catalano, and Melissa Endlich.

Silhouette. Editorial contacts: Ann Leslie Tuttle, Debra Robertson, Gail Chasan, Janet Tanke, Jennifer Walsh, Joan Marlow Golan, Karen Kosztolnyik, Karen Taylor Richman, Leslie Wainger, Lynda Curnyn, Mary Theresa Hussey, Tara Gavin, Tina Colombo, and Kim Nadelson.

Accepts queries and unsolicited proposals and manuscripts. See Web site for recently published titles.

Houghton Mifflin Company

222 Berkeley Street, Boston, MA 02116-3764; 617-351-5000; fax 617-351-1202; New York Office: 215 Park Avenue South, New York, NY 10003; e-mail tradwebmaster@hmco.com; Web site www.hmco.com.

Houghton Mifflin founded in 1832, has a formidable reputation for publishing fine literary and educational works. In its early days, the company assembled the most distinguished collection of writers ever associated with one American publishing house — Henry Wadsworth Longfellow, Oliver Wendell Holmes, John Greenleaf Whittier, Ralph Waldo Emerson, Harriet Beecher Stowe, Nathaniel Hawthorne, Henry David Thoreau, and Mark Twain.

Today, Houghton Mifflin publishes general trade fiction and nonfiction in hardcover and paperback as well as general reference titles — releasing 60 new hardcovers and 30 to 40 new trade paperbacks annually.

Editorial contacts: Wendy J Strothman, Janet Silver, Eamon Dolan (nonfiction, business & technology), Pat Strachan (poetry, literary fiction & nonfiction), Eric Chinski (history, biography, Jewish studies), Anton Mueller (narrative non-fiction), Laura Van Dam (science, medicine), Harry Foster (nature, anthropology), Elaine Pfefferblit (literary nonfiction), Heidi Pitlor (literary fiction, short stories), Rux Martin (cooking), Frances Tenenbaum (gardening), Donald Hymans (paperbacks), and Susan Canavan (paperbacks).

Recently published titles: *The Human Stain* by Philip Roth, *Wild Decembers* by Edna O'Brien, and *Hurricane* by James S. Hirsch.

Queries accepted. Unsolicited manuscripts not accepted without query. For submission guidelines, please call 617-351-5914 for more information.

Permissions manager: Theresa Buswell 212-420-5802.

IDG Books Worldwide, Inc.

919 East Hillsdale Boulevard, Suite 400, Foster City, CA 94404; 650-653-7000; 800-434-3422 (catalog requests and book orders); fax 650-653-7500; Web site www.idgbooks.com.

IDG Books Worldwide, Inc. is a leading global knowledge company with a diverse offering of technology, consumer, reference, and general how-to book brands, computer-based learning tools, Web sites and Internet e-services. IDG's best-selling brands include *For Dummies, 3-D Visual, Bible, Unofficial Guides, CliffsNotes, Frommer's, Betty Crocker's, Weight Watchers,* and *Webster's New World.*

IDG Books has well over 600 selections in the popular *For Dummies* series, including titles in computer-related, business and general interest areas, 3-D Visuals accent such areas as Windows, DOS, and network security; Macworld Books concentrates on the universe of Apple users; PC World handbooks are hands-on tutorial reference works. Many IDG books come as packages with bonus software. Technical books are often packaged with useful shareware, freeware, and macros. Some IDG business books are packaged with templates for up-to-date business documents.

IDG Books Worldwide, Inc. (founded in 1990) is a subsidiary of International Data Group. Expanding beyond its original sphere of computer titles, IDG is interested in authors and/or potential projects that are appropriate for single titles and series in all areas of business and general reference. IDG takes pride in issuing books chock full of information and valuable advice the reader is not likely to get anywhere else — brought together with attention to quality, selection, value, and convenience.

Representative computing titles from IDG Books Worldwide, Inc.: *Researching Online For Dummies,* 2nd Edition by Reva Basch and Mary Ellen Bates; *Linux Programming For Dummies* by Francis Litterio; and *Windows 2000 Professional Simplified* by Ruth Marah.

Consumer, business, and how-to hit titles: *Investing For Dummies,* 2nd Edition by Eric Tyson; *Champagne For Dummies* by Ed McCarthy; *The Unofficial Guide to Financial Freedom* by Lisa Iannuci; *Betty Crocker's Cooking For Two*; *How to Cook Everything* by Mark Bittman; *Spanish For Dummies* by Susana Wald & the Language Experts at Berlitz; and *Golf For Dummies* by Gary McCord.

For technical (computer-related) titles, queries, proposals and SASEs should be directed to: Queries & Proposals — Technical Publishing, IDG Books Worldwide, Inc., 919 E. Hillsdale Boulevard, Suite 400, Foster City, CA 94404.

Nontechnical queries and proposals are only accepted for review if they are submitted through a literary agent.

For all business titles: Queries, proposals, and SASEs should be directed to Queries & Proposals — Business Publishing, IDG Books, 645 N. Michigan Avenue, Suite 800, Chicago, IL 60611.

Editorial contacts: Mark Butler, Senior Acquisition Editor (personal finance, taxes, small business, e-commerce); Holly McGuire, Senior Acquisition Editor (management & skills training, business, self-help, technical/how-to); and Karen Hansen, Acquisition Editor (careers).

For education and reference titles: Queries, proposals, and SASEs should be directed to Queries & Proposals — Education and Reference, IDG Books Worldwide, Inc., 10475 Crosspoint Boulevard, Indianapolis, IN 46256.

Editorial contacts: Diane Steele, VP/Publisher (general education, science, foreign language); Joyce Pepple, Senior Acquisition Editor (CliffsNotes – literature, test prep); Kris Fulkerson, Acquisition Editor (CliffsNotes – literature, test prep); and Mike Agnes, Editor In Chief (Webster's New World).

For lifestyle titles: Queries, proposals, and SASEs should be directed to Queries & Proposals — Lifestyles Publishing, IDG Books Worldwide, Inc., 1633 Broadway, New York, NY 10019.

Editorial contacts: Mike Spring, VP/Publisher (travel); Jennifer Feldman, Assistant VP/Publisher (cooking, gardening); Dominique DeVito, Assistant VP/Publisher (pets); and Stacy Collins, Senior Acquisition Editor (sports, self-help, and health and medicine).

Jossey-Bass, A Wiley Company

350 Sansome Street, 5th Floor, San Francisco, CA 94104; 415-433-1740 and 415-433-1767; fax 415-433-0499 and 415-433-4611; e-mail `www.joseybass.com` Web site `www.pfeiffer.com`.

Purchased in 1999 by John Wiley & Sons, this nonfiction publisher of professional and serious trade books specializes in leadership books and periodicals across the nonprofit and business arenas. Founded in 1967 by Allen Jossey-Bass, Jossey-Bass publishes nearly 200 titles per year, including books, journals, periodicals, training materials, videos and audios. Authors include Bennis, Block, Crainer, Hesselbein, O'Toole, Kouzes & Posner and Max de Pree, Parker Palmer, among others. Brand alliances include The Drucker Foundation, The Carnegie Foundation, The Center for Creative Leadership, Booz-Allen & Hamilton, Harvard Medial School, and the American Hospital Association. Ninety percent of the authors are unagented.

Nonfiction subject areas include general education, higher & adult education, management & business, human resources, training, health & health administration, psychology, conflict resolution, mediation & negotiation, religion, nonprofit & public management, and parenting & youth development.

Imprint: Pfeiffer

Editorial contacts: Paul Foster and Cedric Crocker, VP and Publishers; Susan Williams, Acquisitions Editor (Business/Careers); Alan Rinzler, (Psychology); Sarah Polster, Executive Editor (Religion in Practice); Gale Erlandson, Senior Editor (Higher and adult education); Lesley Iura, Senior Editor (Education); Andy Pasternack, Senior Editor (Health); Dorothy Hearst, Associate Editor (Nonprofit and public management); and Matthew Holt, Senior Editor, Pfeiffer.

Representative titles: *Clicks and Mortar* by David S. Pottruck; *Flawless Consulting* by Peter Block (Pfeiffer), *The Courage to Teach* by Parker Palmer, *Fighting for Your Marriage* by Howard Markman et al; *Critical Issues in Global Health* edited by C. Everett Koop et al; and *The Leadership Challenge* by Kouzes & Posner.

Proposal guidelines are posted on the Web site, in the FAQ section. No unsolicited manuscripts accepted.

Kensington Publishing Corp.

850 Third Avenue, 16th floor, New York, NY 10022; 212-407-1500; toll-free 800-221-2647; fax 212-935-0699; Web site `www.kensingtonbooks.com`.

Founded in 1975 by Walter Zacharius, Kensington Publishing Corp. is the only remaining independent publisher in the US that publishes in hardcover, trade paper, and mass-market formats. Known for its aggressive strategies, Kensington has earned its reputation as an astute David-vs-Goliath publisher. Through the following imprints, Kensington publishes over 500 books per year; in addition, in Spring 2000, the company purchased the contractual/ inventory assets of Carol Publishing.

Kensington Books: Alternative health, gay/lesbian fiction and nonfiction, general non-fiction, romance, and mysteries. Special imprints: Dafina Books (African American mainstream fiction and nonfiction), Twin Streams (alternative health), and Brava (erotic historical romance).

Zebra Books: The company's flagship imprint, featuring historical and contemporary romance, and romantic suspense. Zebra's sub-imprints include Bouquet (contemporary romance), Ballad (serial romance), a Regency line, and Precious Gems (contemporary and historical romance).

Pinnacle Books: Commercial fiction, ranging from thrillers, westerns, and horror fiction, to humor and true crime. Encanto, Pinnacle's Spanish and English romance imprint, features heroines and heroes of Latin or Latin-American descent.

Kensington Publishing Corp. is also distributor of BET/Arabesque, a contemporary romance line featuring heroes and heroines of non-Caucasian heritage; and of the Mayo Clinic's health series.

Editorial contacts: Paul Dinas, Editor-in-Chief (true crime, humor, thrillers, special projects); Ann LaFarge, Executive Editor (romance, westerns); Tracy Bernstein, Editorial Director (general nonfiction, parenting, alternative health, inspirational nonfiction); John Scognamiglio, Editorial Director (romance, thrillers, horror, gay/lesbian fiction & nonfiction, mystery); Kate Duffy, Editorial Director (romance); Claire Gerus, Editor (alternative health); Amy Garvey, Editor (historical romance); Hilary Sares, Editor (Precious Gem contemporary romance); Karen Thomas, Editor (BET/Arabesque, Dafina); Diane Stockwell, Editor (romance, Encanto); and Tomasita Ortiz, Editor (romance, Encanto).

Queries are accepted for BET/Arabesque, Encanto, Pinnacle true crime, and Gems *only*; please include SASE. No unsolicited manuscripts, no disks.

See Web site for submission guidelines, or query following editors for these specific guidelines: Kate Duffy (Ballad and contemporary Precious Gems); Amy Garvey (historical Precious Gems); Karen Thomas (BET/Arabesque); Diane Stockwell (Encanto).

W. W. Norton & Company

500 Fifth Avenue, New York, NY 10110; 212-354-5500; fax 212-869-0856; Web site `www.wwnorton.com`.

W. W. Norton & Company, Inc. was founded in 1923 by William Warder Norton and his wife, MD Herter Norton. Norton's early reputation was built on the publication of academics, such as Bertrand Russell, Paul Henry Lang, and Sigmund Freud (as his principal American publisher).

In the 1950s, Norton sealed its place in the memory of millions of college students with the publication of the acclaimed Norton anthologies of literature. Norton's trade department counts among its recent successes, *Guns, Germs and Steel* by Jared Diamond, *The Perfect Storm* by Sebastian Junger, *The New New Thing* and *Liar's Poker* by Michael Lewis, *Voyage of the Narwhal* by Andrea Barrett, *Cowboys are My Weakness* by Pam Houston, and Patrick O'Brian's critically acclaimed naval adventures.

Norton is a full-service hardcover and trade paperback publisher, publishing 125 per year with offerings in literary fiction, biography, history, health, travel, behavior sciences, nature, science, cultural and intellectual history, and illustrated books.

Editorial contacts: Robert Weil, Ed Barber, Jill Bialosky, Amy Cherry, Carol Houck-Smith, Star Lawrence, Angela von der Lippe, Jim Mairs, Alane Mason, and Drake McFeely.

Accepts queries, unsolicited proposals and manuscripts. Submission Guidelines: Submit cover letter, outline, and three sample chapters addressed to "Editorial Department." Must include SASE for response and return of materials.

Prima Publishing

3000 Lava Ridge Ct., Roseville CA 95661; 916-787-7000; fax 916-787-7001; Web site www.primapublishing.com.

Founded in 1984 by Ben and Nancy Dominitz with the publication of *Travel Free,* Prima is now a large California-based trade publishing house. Prima publishes over 400 nonfiction hardcover and trade paperback titles each year in its four divisions.

Prima Lifestyles (www.primalifestyles.com) publishes general trade books in the areas of parenting, business, education, travel, pets, and more. Recent titles include *The New Color of Success* by Niki Butler Mitchell, *Positive Time-Out* by Dr. Jane Nelsen, *The Pre-Paid Legal Story* by Harland C. Stonecipher, and the *Good Gifts from the Home* series by Kelly Reno.

Forum publishes books on current affairs, public policy, leadership, history, and biography. Recent titles include *Let Us Talk of Many Things* by William F. Buckley Jr. and *The Tyranny of Good Intentions* by Paul Craig Roberts and Lawrence M. Stratton.

Prima Health (www.primahealth.com) publishes books on health and natural medicine. Recent titles include *What's Your Menopause Type?* by Dr. Joseph Collins, *The Encyclopedia of Popular Herbs* by Robert S. McCaleb, Evelyn Leigh, and Krista Morien, and *The Laser Vision Breakthrough* by Dr. Stephen Brint, Dr. Dennis Kennedy, and Corinne Kuypers-Denlinger.

The Natural Pharmacy (TNP) publishes books with one purpose in mind: to give consumers responsible, up-to-date, and scientifically accurate information about natural medicine. Some recent TNP titles include the *Natural Health Bible,* edited by Dr. Steven Bratman and Dr. David Kroll, and *Natural Treatments for Diabetes* by Dr. Kathi Head.

Editorial contacts for the above divisions: Ben Dominitz, Alice Feinstein, Steven K. Martin (Forum), Jamie Miller (parenting and education), Susan Silva (health and business).

Prima Games (www.primagames.com) publishes strategy guides for electronic games including PC, PlayStation, Nintendo 64, Game Boy, and Sega Dreamcast. For an update of the titles, see its Web site.

Editorial contact: Debra Kempker

Prima Tech (www.prima-tech.com) 36 South Pennsylvania Ave., Suite 610, Indianapolis IN 46204; 317-488-4300.

Prima Tech division publishes computer software guides and tutorials for laypersons, programmers, and everyone in between. It also publishes up-to-date reference books on operating environments, Web publishing, data management and much more. For proposal guidelines and a complete list of titles visit the Web site.

Editorial contact: Stacy Hiquet.

John Wiley & Sons, Inc.

605 Third Avenue, New York, NY 10158-0012; 212-850-6000; toll-free 800-225-5945; fax 212-850-6088; Web site www.wiley.com.

John Wiley & Sons publishes books, journals and electronic products for consumer, educational, professional, scientific, and technical markets. Founded in 1807 by Charles Wiley, John Wiley & Sons is the oldest publisher in North America. Known in its early years as the publisher of such literary giants as Edgar Allan Poe, Herman Melville, and Nathaniel Hawthorn, the company has since specialized in professional and consumer books, subscription services, textbooks, and educational materials for colleges and universities, as well as scientific and technical works. Today John Wiley & Sons publishes 1,500 titles in a variety of formats each year with operations the U.S., Europe, Canada, Asia and Australia.

The general interest publishing groups publish books in such nonfiction subject areas as: parenting, current affairs, health/medicine, history, military/war, psychology, science, women's isues, African American interest.

Recently published titles: *World of Risk: Next Generation Strategy for a Volatile Era* by Mark Daniell and *BioInquiry: Making Connections in Biology* by Nancy L. Pruitt, Larry S. Underwood, and William Surver.

Editorial contacts: Bob Ipsen (Trade Computer Publishing), Carole Hall (Editor in Chief, Professional and Trade Division), Deborah Englander (Financial subjects), Hana Umlauf Lane (History, biography), Jeanne Glasser (management, business technology), Kelly Franklin (Psychology, counseling), Mike Hamilton (Career development, small business, real estate), Larry Alexander (publisher, investing, business reference), and Tom Mills (Health, how-to, self-help, popular reference).

Queries accepted.

Unsolicited manuscripts are not accepted.

Submission guidelines can be found at www.wiley.com/authors/guidelines.

Workman/Algonquin

Workman Publishing Company

708 Broadway, New York, NY 10003-9555; 212-254-5900; toll-free 800-722-7202; fax 212-254-8098; e-mail mged@workman.com; Web site www.workmanweb.com.

Founded in 1967 by Peter Workman, this pioneering independent forged its unique position in the industry with the publication of such runaway bestsellers as *The Preppie Handbook*, *What to Expect When You're Expecting*, *Brainquest* and *The Silver Palate Cookbook*. Workman is a general trade publisher, producing nonfiction hardcovers and paperbacks, calendars, and children's books, however the house is highly selective and hugely successful, publishing only 40 new titles annually.

Editorial contacts: Sally Kovalchick (gardening, popular reference, humor) Suzanne Rafer (cookbook, child care, parenting, teen interest), Liz Carey (crafts, children, humor), Michaela Muntean (children's), and Ruth Sullivan (fashion, health, humor).

Algonquin Books of Chapel Hill

Box 2225, Chapel Hill, NC 27515; 919-967-0108; fax 919-933-0272; e-mail suzie@algonquin.com; Web site www.algonquin.com.

Algonquin Books was founded as a small independent trade publisher in 1982 by Louis D. Rubin Jr. and Shannon Ravenel, with the help and support of a small group of friends and financial backers. In 1989 the company was acquired by Workman and in 1992, Louis Rubin retired and was succeeded by Elisabeth Scharlatt, who joined the company in 1989. Algonquin specializes in mainstream and literary fiction as well as such nonfiction categories as biography, cooking, gardening, and sports, publishing 20 to 25 new titles each year.

Contacts: Elisabeth Scharlatt and Shannon Ravenel.

Niche publishers

These are the true boutique houses. All of them are full-service publishing houses who can publish bestsellers, and have launched many successful careers. All these publishers truly achieve a personal feel and concentrate their energies in clearly defined areas of the book landscape.

Chronicle Books

85 Second Street, 6th floor, San Francisco, CA 94105; 415-537-3730; fax 415-437-4460, toll-free fax 800-858-7787; e-mail `frontdesk@chroniclebooks.com`; Web site `www.chroniclebooks.com`. The Chronicle Books Web site provides detailed submission guidelines.

Founded in 1966 as a publisher of lavishly illustrated cookbooks, Chronicle Books has grown into a much more diverse house today. The company releases 250 hardcover and trade paperback titles, mainly nonfiction, with a strong emphasis on design and illustration in such subject areas as food, gardening, photography, architecture, nature, pets and some fiction and literary offerings.

Some recently published titles include *Office Yoga* by Darrin Zeer; *Worst Case Scenario* by Joshua Piven and David Borgenicht; and *Olive, The Other Reindeer* by J. Otto Seibold and Vivian Walsh.

Soho Press Inc

853 Broadway, New York, NY 10003; 212-260-1900; fax 212-260-1902; e-mail `sohopress@aol.com`; Web Site `www.sohopress.com`.

Soho Press was founded in 1986 by Laura Hruska and Juris Jurjevics, a veteran publisher with extensive experience at both E.P. Dutton and Dial Press. Soho is a small, tightly focused publisher of hardcover and trade paperback editions of nonfiction (investigative, biography, social sciences, travel and historical) and contemporary fiction, much of it literary. Currently publishes approximately 40 new titles annually. Submission guidelines are available on Soho's Web site.

Imprints: Hera, Soho Crime.

Editorial contacts: Juris Jurjevics, Laura M.C. Hruska, and Melanie Fleishman.

Editors' Areas of specialization: anything but how-to or cooking

Recently published titles: *The Long Firm* by Jake Arnott, *Death of a Red Heroine* by Xiaolong Qiu, and *The Gravity of Sunlight* by Rosa Shand.

Accepts unsolicited queries, proposals, and manuscripts.

Sunset Books

80 Willow Road, Menlo Park, CA 94025; 650-321-3600; fax 650-324-1532; e-mail `doyleb@sunset.com`; Web site `www.sunsetbooks.com`.

Sunset Magazine, founded over 100 years ago, specializes in such topic areas as Western gardening, cooking, travel, and food. The book imprint, Sunset Books, was launched in 1931 with the publication of a cookbook called *The*

Kitchen Cabinet Book. Today, Sunset publishes more than 200 food, garden, and home repair books. Titles include the now-famous *Western Garden Book* and its companions, *Western Landscaping* and *Western Garden Problem Solver*. Sunset's broader range of gardening books address all areas of North America, as do their home improvement and decorating titles. Sunset Publishing was acquired by Time Warner in 1990, but is still run as a completely independent subsidiary.

Editorial contacts, send query letter and SASE: Bob Doyle (gardening and landscaping); Marianne Lipanovich (building and home improvement); and Linda Selden (home decorating).

Recently published titles include *Complete Home Wiring*, Scott Atkinson and the Editors of Sunset Books, *Ideas for Great Kitchens* by the Editors of Sunset Books, *Western Garden Book* by The Editors of Sunset Books and Magazine, *Roses* by Philip Edinger and the Editors of Sunset Books, and *Trellises & Arbors* by Scott Atkinson, Philip Edinger and the Editors of Sunset Books.

Accepts queries; no unsolicited manuscripts.

Ten Speed Press/Celestrial Arts

P.O. Box 7123, Berkeley, CA 94707; 510-559-1600; fax 510-559-1629; e-mail `orders@tenspeed.com`; Web site `www.tenspeedpress.com`. The Web site provides detailed submission instructions.

Based in Berkeley, CA, Ten Speed Press was founded in 1971 by Philip Wood, a former sales rep for Penguin Books, who launched his company with the best-selling *Anybody's Bike Book* by Tom Cuthbertson. His success continued to explode with the publication of *What Color is Your Parachute* by Richard Bolles, which has topped the career category for nearly three decades. Ten Speed also publishes notable cookbooks, including Charlie Trotter's, *White Trash Cooking,* and the *Moosewood Cookbook* by Mollie Katzen. Known for its individualistic and unconventional approach to Amercian cultural interests, Ten Speed Press/Celestial Arts currently releases 125 titles per year.

Ten Speed Press Editorial contacts: Philip Wood, Kirsty Melville, and Lorena Jones.

Celestial Arts founded in 1966 as an independent publisher specializing in hardcover and trade paperback titles as well as posters and journals. Acquired in 1983 by Ten Speed Press, the Celestial Arts list includes titles on popular psychology, relationships, pregnancy and parenting, self discovery as well as the many kitchen arts. Recent titles include *Uncommon Sense for Parents with Teenagers* by Dr. Michael Riera, *Tap Dancing in Zen* by Geri Larkin, and *Shortcuts to God* by Gerald Jampolsky.

Celestial Arts Editorial contact: Veronica Randall.

Walker and Company

435 Hudson Street, New York, NY 10014; 212-727-8300; toll-free 800-AT-WALKER; fax 212-727-0984; e-mail georgegibson@walkerbooks.com; jjohnson@walkerbooks.com; mseidman@walkerbooks.com; Web site www.walkerbooks.com.

Walker and Company was founded in 1959 by Sam Walker with the firm belief that there can never be too many good books. This committment to quality editorial content combined with a hard hitting approach to marketing makes Walker and Company a concentrated powerhouse. Currently under the leadership of Publisher George Gibson, Walker publishes 70 trade nonfiction and mystery fiction titles per year in both hardcover and tradepaper. Subject areas include History, Popular Science, Health, Nutrition, Natural History, Mathematics, Sociology, Juvenile fiction and picture books, and Mysteries.

Editorial contacts: George Gibson (Nonfiction); Jacqueline Johnson (Nonfiction); Michael Seidman, (Mysteries); and Emily Easton (Juvenile).

Recently published titles include *Galileo's Daughter* by Dava Sobel; *The Basque History of the World* by Mark Kurlansky, *Morrie: In His Own Words* by Morrie Schwartz, and in mystery: *Nothing But the Night* by Bill Pronzini, *Lady Vanishes: A Rachel Alexander and Dash Mystery* by Carol Lea Benjamin.

Recently published children's titles include *The Adventures of Marco Polo* by Dieter Wiesmuller and *Bud* by Kevin O'Malley.

Accepts queries. Query before sending in unsolicited materials. For complete submission guidelines and a current catalog send a 9 x 12 SASE.

University Presses

University Presses are all affiliated with universities and all enjoy nonprofit status. However, university presses can be very formidible publishers, with access to the trade market as well as the academic world. Especially if you have a book with scholarly content or that might appeal to university course adoptions, you should consider a university press for your submission.

Oxford University Press

198 Madison Avenue, New York, NY 10016-4314; 212-726-6000; Web site www.oup-usa.org.

Oxford University Press, the world's largest university press and most prolific academic publisher, produces more than 4,000 new titles each year, reflecting the diverse offerings of the University itself. The U.S. office of the press, founded in 1896, is located in New York, and produces 600 titles annually. The Press is organized into four major publishing divisions: Academic; College and Medical; Scholarly and Professional Reference; and Trade, including Trade Reference, Young Adult, Trade Lexical Reference and Paperbacks. Oxford does not publish fiction.

Editorial contacts: Sonke Adlung (physics — trade); Paul Banks (astronomy, chemistry, life sciences, physics — college); Joyce Berry (archeology, art and architecture, earth sciences, geography); Joan Bossert (Psychology, social work); Jeffrey Broesche (Psychology, sociology — college); Paul Donnelly (Business and economics); Lauren Enck (Medicine — trade); Toni English (English language and literature — college); Dedi Felman (political science, sociology — trade); Susan Ferber (American history, world history); Peter Ginna (history — trade); Peter Gordon (computer sciences, engineering and technology); Jeffrey House (medicine — trade); Kirk Jensen (Life sciences); Susan Lee (chemistry); Ken MacLeod (Business and economics — college); Robert Miller (Classical literature and languages, philosophy, theology — college); Elissa Morris (African-American, American and women's studies; classical and English literature and languages); Peter Ohlin (philosophy); Maribeth Payne (music); Cynthia Read (religion); and Nancy Toff (children, young adult).

Recently published titles: *Gotham: A History of New York City to 1898* by Edwin G. Burrows, Mike Wallace (Winner of 1999 Pulitzer Prize for History); *Freedom from Fear: The United States, 1929–1945* by David M. Kennedy (Winner of 2000 Pulitzer Prize for History); *Microelectric Circuits* by Adel S. Sedra, Kenneth C. Smith; and *American National Biography* edited by John Arthur Garraty et al (24 vols.).

Submission guidelines are listed on the Web site by publishing unit; accepts queries and unsolicited manuscripts.

Harvard University Press

79 Garden Street, Cambridge, MA 02138-1499; 617-495-2600; fax 617-495-5898; e-mail `firstname_lastname@harvard.edu`; Web site `www.hup.harvard.edu`.

Founded in 1913 as the publishing arm of this distinguished university, Harvard publishes 190 hardcover and trade paperback titles in a wide variety of scholarly disciplines; each year, a handful of the Press's offerings reach a significant general readership. Subject areas of particular interest include: Behavioral science, biological science, classics, economics, history, literature, literary criticism, essays, philosophy, psychology, psychiatry, science, social sciences, and sociology.

Editorial contacts: Joyce Seltzer (history, contemporary affairs); Michael Fisher (medicine, neuroscience, science); Lindsay Waters (literary criticism, philosophy, multicultural studies); Michael Aronson (social sciences, economics, law, political science); Margaretta Fulton (classics, religion, music, art, women's studies, Jewish studies); Elizabeth Knoll (behavioral sciences, neuroscience, education); and Elizabeth Suttell (history, East Asian studies).

Accepts queries and proposals; no unsolicited manuscripts.

Submission guidelines: Submit your proposal by mail or fax — not e-mail — along with a cover letter, a curriculum vitae, an outline or table of contents, a preface or introductory chapter, and another sample chapter — but not the complete manuscript to Harvard University Press, Editorial Department, 79 Garden Street, Cambridge, MA 02138.

The Press does not publish original poetry, fiction, festschriften, memoirs, symposium volumes, or unrevised doctoral dissertations.

Harvard Business School Press

60 Harvard Way, Boston, MA 02163; 617-783-7400; fax 617-783-7489; e-mail bookpublisher@hbsp.harvard.edu; Web site www.hbsp.harvard.edu.

Harvard Business School Press is a business unit of Harvard Business School Publishing, a wholly-owned, not-for-profit subsidiary of the Harvard Business School headquartered in Boston, Massachusetts. Established in 1984, HBS Press currently has more than 300 titles in print. Other business units of Harvard Business School Publishing include: *Harvard Business Review*, Academic Cases & Reprints, the Interactive Multimedia group, Harvard Business School Publishing Videos, the newsletters *Harvard Management Update* and *Harvard Management Communications Letter*, and *The Balanced Scorecard Collaborative*.

Harvard Business School Press publishes trade and professional books for the business and academic communities that take a broad look at the questions business people face every day and provide answers that will have a profound impact on their work and lives. Areas of publishing interest encompass strategy, general management, marketing, in finance, the digital economy, technology and innovation, and human resources.

Editorial contacts: Hollis Heimbouch, Kirsten Sandberg, Marjorie Williams, Melinda Adams Merino, and Nikki Sabin.

Recent titles: *The Innovator's Dilemma* (1997) by Clay Christensen, *Digital Capital* (2000) by Don Tapscott, David Ticoll, and Alex Lowy, *Blown to Bits* (1999) by Philip Evans and Thomas Wurster, and *The Social Life of Information* (2000) by John Seeley Brown and Paul Duguid.

Unsolicited queries, proposals and manuscripts accepted; no e-mail submissions. Complete submission guidelines are on the Web site.

Johns Hopkins University Press

2715 North Charles Street, Baltimore, MD 21218-4319; 410-516-6900; fax 410-516-6968; Web site www.press.jhu.edu.

Founded in 1878, the Johns Hopkins University Press is a full service scholarly publishing operation, releasing 180 hardcover and trade paperback titles per year. Much of the the press's output is academic in intent, but many titles are of interest to the general public. The press publishes in a wide range of subject areas including ancient studies, developing trends in medicine, science and technology, literary criticism, drama, religious studies, political science, history, women's studies and more.

Editorial contacts: Jacqueline Wehmueller (medicine, higher education, history of medicine); Henry Tom (political science, European history); Ginger Berman (science); Robert J. Brugger (history, including history of science & technology); Wendy Harris (medicine); George Thompson (geography, environmental studies, urban planning); James Jordan (science), and Maura E. Burnett (humanities).

Recently published titles: *Secret Yankees: The Union Circle in Confederate Atlanta* by Thomas G. Dyer, *Fast Food: Roadside Restaurants in the Automobile Age* by John A. Jakle and Keith A. Sculle; *The Bees of the World*, by Charles D. Michener; *The Democratic Invention*, edited by Marc F. Plattner and Joao Carlos Espada; and *The Invention of Literature: From Greek Intoxication to the Latin Book*, by Florence Dupont, translated by Janet Lloyd.

Unsolicited queries, proposals and manuscripts are accepted, but the Press will not consider unsolicited poetry or fiction. No e-mail submissions.

Submission guidelines: Submit a resume, description of project, sample of text, and descriptive table of contents.

University of California Press

2120 Berkeley Way, Berkeley, CA 94720; 510-642-4247; fax 510-643-7127, e-mail `ucpress@ucop.edu`; Web site `www.ucpress.edu`. Complete submission guidelines are available on the Web site.

Founded in 1893, the nonprofit publishing arm of the University of California publishes a full spectrum of distinguished works, from inventive first books by young academics to volumes of research results and creative thinking from many of the world's foremost scholars. The press is especially well known for its books on critical issues, collected writings of great authors, special editions of classics, art books, major historical studies and monumental works of research. The press's mandate is to serve the University and the people of California as well as scholars and university communities around the world by giving voice to great ideas. Publishes approximately 200 of titles per year in both hardcover and paperback.

Editorial contacts: Howard Boyer (Environmental sciences, neuroscience, medicine, public health); Stephanie Fay (art, art history); Doris Kretschmer (natural history, biology, natural sciences, physical anthropology); Mary Lamprech/Kate Toll (classical studies); Sheila Levine (Asian studies, European history); Reed Malcolm (religious studies, politics); Monica McCormick (American studies, African studies); Linda Norton (literary studies, American studies, gender studies, cultural studies, belles lettres, world literature, and linguistics); Naomi Schneider (sociology, politics, gender studies, women's studies, law, cultural studies, Latin American studies); Eric Smoodin (film, media studies, philosophy); Lynne Withey (music, Middle Eastern studies); and Charlene Woodcock (architecture).

Recently published titles: *Dame Edna Everage and the Rise of Western Civilization* by John Lahr; *In Search of England* by Michael Wood, *The Lost Chronicles of the Maya Kings* by David Drew, and *Renaissance* by Andrew Graham-Dixon.

Yale University Press

302 Temple Street, P.O. Box 209040, New Haven, CT 06520-9040; 203-432-0960; fax 203-432-0948; e-mail `custservice.press@yale.edu`; Web site `www.yale.edu/yup`.

Yale University Press, 23 Pond St., Hampstead, London NW32PN, U.K.

Founded in 1908, to publish both scholarly and general interest books, the press now publishes 150 new hardcover and trade titles each year. Having Pulitzer prize and national book award winners in its backlist, the Press continues as one of the nation's largest and most distinguished university presses.

Editorial contacts: Jonathan Brent (Classics, literature, philosophy, poetry); Susan Arellano (psychology, education, child development, psychiatry, sociology, anthropology); Jean E. Thomson Black (science, medicine); John S. Covell (economics, law, political science); Judy Metro (art, art history, architecture, history of architecture, landscape, geography), Henning Guttman (business), and Mary Jane Peluso (languages and ESL). In London: John Nicoll, Robert Baldock, and Gillian Malpass.

Recent titles include *Piano Roles* by James Parakilas, *How to Increase Your Child's Verbal Intelligence* by Carmen McGuiness and Geoffrey McGuiness, *Marcel Proust: A Life* by William C. Carter, and *Perseus 2.0: Interactive Sources and Studies on Ancient Greece* by the Perseus Project.

Queries and unsolicited manuscrips accepted. See guidelines at Web site.

Spiritual and religious presses

These are publishers, some nonprofit some for profit, which specialize in the spiritual side of things. A few of these firms include the service of god or of the spiritual side at the top of their mission statement. Especially if your book will appeal to a particular religious denomination, you should be aware of the special interests at these expert firms.

Abingdon Press

P.O. Box 801, Nashville, TN 37202-0801; 615-749-6290; fax 615-749-6056; Web site www.abingdon.com opening 2/2001.

Founded in 1789 as the publishing arm of the United Methodist Church, Abingdon is America's oldest theological publisher with approximately 120 nonfiction titles published annually in hardcover, trade and mass-market paperback. Aimed at both the religious professional and lay person, the Abingdon list consists of reference, academic, gift, and children's books.

Editorial contacts: Harriett Jane Olson (Senior Vice-President of Publishing), Mary Catherine Dean (Adult General Interest Director), Bob Ratcliff (Academic/Professional editor), Bob Shell (Youth Director), and Peg Augustine (Children's editor).

Recently published titles: *Passion, Power and Praise* by James Harnish; *The Empowerment Church* by Carlyle Fiedling Stewart III; *Mission Mania: A Can-do Guide for Youth* by Mark Bushor; and *Read with Me: Bible Stories for Early Readers* compiled by Peg Augustine.

Accepts queries; no unsolicited manuscripts.

Harvest House

1075 Arrowsmith, Eugene, OR 97402; 541-343-0123; fax 541-302-0731; e-mail mathisp@harvesthousepubl.com.

Founded in 1974, as a nondenominational religious and spiritual publisher, Harvest House publishes books from an Evangelical Christian perspective, on topics of current interest such as the media, technology, parenting, family, relationships, politics and more. Its mission statement is evident in all its publications: "Helping people grow spiritually strong." The firm publishes 120 hardcover, trade, and massmarket paperbacks annually.

Editorial contact: Pat Mathis.

No queries or unsolicited manuscripts accepted.

Health Communications, Inc

3201 SW 15 Street, Deerfield Beach, FL 33442-8190; 954-360-0909; fax 954-360-0034.

Founded in 1976, Health Communications publishes 25 trade paper and hardcover titles per year in the areas of self-help, health, wellness, spirituality, relationships, teen topics and other life issues. Most HCI authors have been published before, but will accept material from first-time authors who are experts in their field or have an established platform for speaking or publicity. Editorial contacts: Christine Belleris, Allison Janse, Lisa Drucker, and Susan Tobias.

Recently published titles: *Chicken Soup for the Christian Family Soul* by Canfield, Hansen, Aubery & Autio; *Teen Love* by Kimberly Kirberger, *Taste Berries for Teens* by Jennifer Leigh Youngs; and *Remembering Mother, Finding Myself* by Patricia Commins.

Submission guidelines are available on its Web site or by calling extension 404. No unagented material accepted. Do not call to see whether they received or have reviewed your material.

The Jewish Publication Society

2100 Arch Street, 2nd Floor, Philadelphia, PA 19103; 215-832-0600; fax 215-568-2017; e-mail `jewishbook@aol.com`; Web site `www.jewishpub.org`.

First founded in 1888 to provide the children of Jewish immigrants books on their heritage in the language of the New World, JPS is the oldest, continuous publisher of Jewish titles in the English language. The Jewish Publication Society publishes 12 new nonfiction titles each year in the subject areas of history, religion, women's issues, language, and literature.

Recently published titles include *The JPS Hebrew-English Tanakh*, *The Jewish Moral Virtues*, by Eugene B. Borowitz, Frances Weinman Schwartz, and Francine Schwartz; *Trees, Earth, and Torah: A Tu B'Shvat Anthology* by Ari Elon (Editor), Naomi Hyman (Editor), Arthur Waskow (Editor).

Editorial contacts: Ellen Frankel and Carol Hupping.

Submit a query with proposal that includes; an outline, description of the book, table of contents and an SASE.

Nelson Word Publishing Group

501 Nelson Place, P.O. Box 141000, Nashville, TN 37214-1000; 615-889-9000; fax 615-391-5225; Web site `www.thomasnelson.com`.

Nelson Word Publishing Group is the corporate banner under which Thomas Nelson, with its numerous imprints and Word Publishing operate — though the two remain editorially independent.

Thomas Nelson Inc

Founded in 1961, Thomas Nelson is "the largest publisher of bibles and inspirational books in the English language." Specializing in Christian lifestyle nonfiction and fiction, Thomas Nelson publishes hardcovers as well as trade and mass-market paperbacks. The imprint releases 150 to 200 new titles annually.

Editorial contacts: Mark Roberts, Janet Thoma, and Victor Oliver.

Word Publishing

Web site: www.wordpublishing.com.

This nondemoninational, Christian publisher specializes in best-selling Christian authors, fiction, marriage and family, self-help, current issues, Christian living, devotional, and general trade crossover titles. Acquired by Thomas Nelson, Inc. in 1992, Word Publishing continues to enjoy editorial independence.

Editorial contact: Mark Sweeney.

Recently published titles: *When Christ Comes* by Max Lucado, *The Visitation* by Frank Peretti, *The Mystery of God's Will* by Charles Swindoll, and *Leaking Laffs Between Pampers and Depends* by Barbara Johnson.

Shambhala Publications

P.O. Box 308, Boston MA 02117; 617-424-0030; fax 617-236-1563; e-mail firstinitiallastname@shambhala.com; Web site shambhala.com.

Shambhala was founded first as a bookstore in 1969 by two friends, Sam Bercholz and Michael Fagan, who were looking to establish a place where people could exchange ideas. From the bookstore, they published their first book, *Meditation in Action* by Chögyam Trungpa, a Tibetan Buddhist teacher, which set the tone for all the publications that have followed. Shambhala specializes in books that present creative and conscious ways of transforming the individual, the society, and the planet. Today the company releases 65 new titles annually in hardcover and trade paperback.

Contacts: Samuel Bercholz, Peter Turner, Jonathan Green, Joel Segal, and Eden Steinberg.

Editors' areas of specialization: Philosophy, religion, art, literature, psychology, and health

Recently published titles: *When Things Fall Apart: Heart Advice for Difficult Times* (1997) by Pema Chodron, *A Mapmaker's Dream: A Nove*l, (1996) by James Cowan, *Toward a Psychology of Awakening: Buddhism, Psychotherapy, and the Path of Personal and Spiritual Transformation* by John Welwood (2000), and *A Brief History of Everything* (1996) by Ken Wilber.

Accepts unsolicited queries, proposals and manuscripts.

Submission guidelines are available on request.

Zondervan Publishing House

5300 Patterson Avenue, S.E., Grand Rapids, MI 49530; 616-698-6900; fax 616-698-3439; e-mail zphonline@zph.com; Web site www.zondervan.com. For a recording offering submission guidelines call 616-698-3500, ext. 3447.

Founded in 1931 by Pat and Bernie Zondervan who recognized, especially during the Great Depression, the need for spiritual resource materials. Zondervan's commitment to its original mission statement remains constant: "to be the leading Christian communications company meeting the needs of people with resources that glorify Jesus Christ and promote biblical principles." Today, the firm releases 150 titles in hardcover trade and mass-market paperback per year.

Editorial contacts: David Lambert (fiction), Lyn Cryderman (General), Paul Engle (Academic), and Mary McNeil (Children's).

Recently published titles: *The Case for Christ* by Lee Strobel (1998), *Fresh Wind, Fresh Fire* by Jim Cymbala (1997), and *What's So Amazing About Grace* by Philip Yancey (1997).

Direct query letters to the attention of Diane Bloem.

Chapter 11

Acting as Your Own Agent

In This Chapter

- Thinking like an agent
- Perfecting the pitch
- Conducting an auction

Finding an agent for your book is often more difficult than securing a publisher. For that reason, I recommend approaching publishers and agents at the same time. If a publisher shows interest before an agent, you can either negotiate for yourself or find an agent at this point, which is considerably easier when you have an offer in hand.

In this chapter, I walk you through exactly what you need to know about exclusive or multiple submissions, pitch meetings, and, should it become necessary, book auctions.

It's a well-known irony that the easiest time to get an agent is when you already have a publisher's offer in hand. Many first-time writers do opt to involve a literary agent once they have an offer — and pay the 15 percent commission — and, probably, you should to. Going it alone can be risky.

You Can Be Your Own Agent

You can choose to be your own agent right from the start, pocketing the 15 percent commission that traditionally goes to the literary agent, or end up acting as your own agent by default. If, for example, you submit your proposal to agents and editors simultaneously and a publisher responds before an agent, you may want to reel in the offer yourself. But if you're not sure that you can navigate the entire negotiation, then bring in an agent or literary lawyer (see Chapter 12) to actually land the deal.

Having sold two of my own books without the help of an agent, I know exactly what's entailed. *Dress Your House for Success*, which I cowrote with Martha Webb a few years ago, is the most recent. Admittedly, I have an advantage over most first-time writers because I worked in book publishing for many years, I'm married to a publisher, and I have a good idea of what editors are looking for in a proposal. As a result, I knew exactly how to create upbeat, thorough proposals.

Over the years, I have befriended many publishing people. And when it's time for me to sell a new book, I consult with these friends about which editors are most likely to be interested in the book. The advice they offer is extremely helpful.

A few years ago, I met Martha Webb while vacationing at a spa in Mexico. It didn't take long to discover that we shared a common interest in preparing and dressing up homes for rental and resale profit. We decided to team up and write a book based on a video program that Martha had created for real estate professionals. Her excellent video showed homeowners how to prepare a home to be sold, how to literally "stage" a house in order to increase its value on the real estate market. Most real estate agents feel they can't deliver fix-up information without the possibility of alienating clients. But if they can give clients a book that details a step-by-step program for preparing a home for resale, it makes them look even more thorough and professional. Based on her *Dress Your House for Success* video sales, Martha knew there was a big market for such a book.

While preparing the proposal, I shared early drafts with a few agents, but none of them showed much enthusiasm for the project. Martha and I, certain of its value, were frustrated by our attempts to find an agent who shared our vision. So finally, I decided to try selling the book myself. After all, we had an excellent video to show, Martha is a persuasive speaker, and I felt certain that if we could get a polished proposal in front of the right editor, we'd be able to make a sale.

But which editor would be right? I didn't know anyone who specialized in books about selling real estate. I asked around among my agent friends — none of who wanted to represent my book! — and got a few names. Also, I had heard that an editor instrumental in supervising the publication of my first book had recently moved to Crown, a publishing house known for doing stylebooks. I called to ask her if she might be willing to direct my book to the right person at Crown. She was more than happy to help.

After several months of writing and revision, I had a polished proposal ready to go, several copies of Martha's video, and a list of viable editors on my desk. I called each of the six editors on the list, said they had come highly recommended to me, and that I'd like to send them my proposal for a book entitled *Dress Your House for Success*. They all agreed to look at it — some reluctantly — and so I sent the material out to all six editors at once (a *multiple submission*) and followed up a few days later with a phone call. I mentioned that my co-author and I were happy to meet with them in person to answer any questions. This type of face-to-face meeting is called a *pitch meeting*.

As it turned out, two houses were interested in meeting with us. Martha flew in for the meetings, and, dressed in our crispest, most impressive meeting attire, we set out for our first meeting with a senior editor at Little Brown. She was quite excited about our book and seemed to want to make a bid right then and there. This would have been a *pre-emptive bid*, trying to take it off the market before anyone else has a chance to offer. Thanking her for her interest, I said we had another meeting scheduled and would touch base with her the next day. (Sometimes it's best to allow editors to stew in their enthusiasm for a day or so.)

The meeting at Crown was with a young associate editor, who quite clearly loved the project. After a fruitful meeting, the editor confessed that she hoped to come up with a formal offer in the next few days. I mentioned that Little Brown was also interested in making an offer, and she asked that we not accept any offers until she had a chance to talk to her superiors.

Later that day, I called the editor at Little Brown to tell her how much we had enjoyed meeting with her and let her know there was serious interest in the proposal — so serious in fact that I planned to hold an auction the following week and would call her back Friday with the details. She seemed nervous to hear this news and made her offer right there and then. "We'd like to offer $50,000." *Eureka,* I thought. *We've got $50,000 — $50,000 more than we had a few minutes ago*. But I kept my cool and said, "Thanks for the offer. I'm delighted to hear you're interested. Martha and I will think about the offer." I wanted to buy some time to contact the editors I hadn't yet heard from. Chuckling to myself, I remembered that one agent we had briefly worked with in the early proposal stage had said, "You'll be lucky to get a $25,000 offer."

While $50,000 wasn't going to be enough to take the book off the market, it was enough to cover our costs so we now knew that we could afford to write the book.

Next, I called the editor at Crown. I told her that we had a generous offer in hand and would be scheduling an auction for the following week. She blurted that she'd very much like to own the book. I told her I'd call with the auction details on Friday.

On Friday, I called the Little Brown editor to discuss the auction, saying that her $50,000 offer could be a *floor,* which meant that I was proposing that she guarantee a minimum bid in my auction. If there were no higher bids, she would take the book for that amount; if there were higher bids, she could top by a set percentage and win the book with her topping bid. "But that's as high as I'm cleared to go. $50,000 is our top offer," she said. I told her I doubted that offer would win the book. I called the editor at Crown, and she still seemed quite determined to get the book. "How much do you need to sell the book to us today?" she inquired. I hesitated for a minute, knowing what that figure was. "$100,000," I said.

"That shouldn't be a problem," she said. "Let me call you back."

And an hour later, she did just that — our book was acquired by Crown/Three Rivers for $100,000. We were walking on air!

Every detail of this story is true, and it's a fact that nonprofessionals are able to sell their book in a publishing auction, though usually not without at least informal help from insiders, as I did. Certainly, this is not commonplace, and it's highly unlikely that your first submission will stimulate an auction. I do, however, want you to be prepared in case it does.

What You Need to Know

If you have no agent and a publisher makes an offer, call the agents who have your proposal and alert them. Unless you've made a thorough study of what's involved in a publishing negotiation — as you can by reading this book — it's best to be represented by a pro.

But if you can't find an agent that you like, or if no agent is banging down your door, don't let that stop you from submitting your query and/or book proposal to a few editors. Here are some expressions, used by publishers and agents, to familiarize yourself with before acting as a self-representing literary agent.

Exclusives

An *exclusive submission* guarantees that you are allowing only one publisher the opportunity to consider your book for a set length of time. While publishers love exclusive submissions, it is not in your best interest to submit your material exclusively.

In fact, I recommend that you steer away from exclusive submissions to publishers — the reason publishers don't like to compete for projects is because competition drives up the price. You want to get as high a price as the market can bear for your book.

Multiple submissions

A *multiple* or *simultaneous* submission is a submission of the same material to more than one publisher at the same time. A selective multiple submission targeting editors who have agreed to read your proposal or manuscript is the best way to rouse healthy competition for your book. Just be sure to send the same material to each target editor at the same time and mention in your cover letter that it is being submitted to other editors simultaneously. You don't need to ruffle feathers by giving one editor an advantage over another.

If you have targeted several editors in a large, multidivisional publisher, beware. Many of these firms have ground rules about multiple submissions to editors at more than one division simultaneously. For example, if you submit to Doubleday and Crown and Random House, you may have a problem because they are all part of the same company. Many of these large firms (see Chapter 10) won't allow their imprints to compete for the same book projects — especially for books in the $1 million range.

Pitch meeting

Your book proposal — a sales pitch on paper — worked to get an editor's attention and now that editor wants to meet you in person. This face-to-face meeting, or *pitch meeting,* is your opportunity to sell your book in person. Be prepared and enthusiastic.

If travel is involved, assume that you are paying. Publishers only pay for pitch meeting travel if the author has a strong track record and/or a close pre-existing working relationship with the editor.

The editor's purpose in asking or agreeing to meet with you is to assess your professionalism and ability to produce and help market the book you propose. She wants assurance that you're as good in person as you appear on paper.

Here are a few pointers on how to prepare and execute a first-rate pitch meeting.

- **Submission:** A prepitch meeting submission has got to be letter perfect. It should also be structured to stimulate an invitation.
- **Staging:** Bring only those people who take center stage with you in the book's creation. If you have a co-author, bring him or her. Don't show up with your entire supporting staff. The fewer people involved, the easier and more efficiently you can get your idea across.

- **Appearance:** Make sure that you look great — as neat, crisp, and professional as possible. It's never casual Friday at a pitch meeting.
- **Materials:** Make sure that you have duplicates of the material you sent and bring new material — preferably no more than a page — that summarizes recent developments or crystallizes your proposition. Avoid handing out a lot of material — it may distract listeners from your presentation.
- **Arrival:** Arrive on time.
- **Agenda:** Prepare a clear agenda of items that you want to get across in the meeting. For example:
  - Cover who you are and what your platform is
  - Talk about what the book is, how it will get written, and what structure or outline is planned
  - Define and discuss your book's audience or market
  - Summarize your vision of how to reach the market
  - Give reasons why the publishing company you're pitching is a good fit for your book, but let them sell you, too

  Get these points across in 45 minutes, maximum, and then take questions.
- **Audio/visuals:** Keep any audio/visual material short and simple. If your supporting material is a 30-minute video, screen no more than a minute or two to give the flavor of the piece.
- **Time/length:** Plan on a one-hour meeting and not a minute longer. It's best to wow them in an hour or less — don't hold them hostage for two.

- **Money:** Don't talk money during this meeting unless the editor brings it up. Call later to discuss the actual deal specifics.
- **Questions:** Be sure to ask questions of your own about the publishing house, its experience with your sort of book, and its vision of how to publish your book. Encourage the editor to ask direct questions of you; practice fielding questions in advance so that you won't be taken off guard. If you don't know the answer to an editor's question, don't lie. Say you'll find out and be sure to get back to her with an answer quickly.

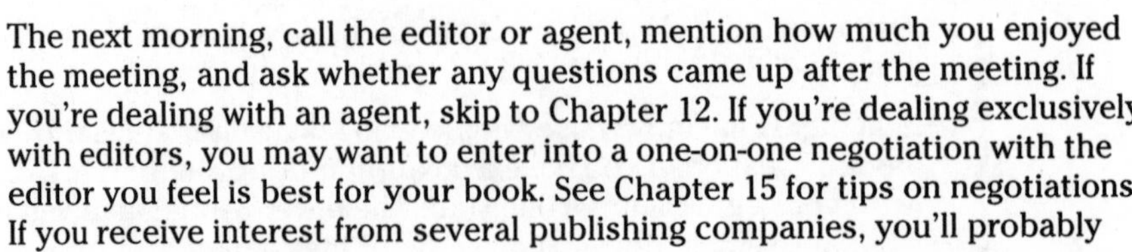

The next morning, call the editor or agent, mention how much you enjoyed the meeting, and ask whether any questions came up after the meeting. If you're dealing with an agent, skip to Chapter 12. If you're dealing exclusively with editors, you may want to enter into a one-on-one negotiation with the editor you feel is best for your book. See Chapter 15 for tips on negotiations. If you receive interest from several publishing companies, you'll probably want to stage an auction.

An Auction

A *publishing auction* is a method of selling books when you have interest from more than one publishing house. The auction allows multiple editors to bid — usually confidentially — on the rights to publish a book. Conducted on the telephone, an auction takes a day or two to conclude. The bidders (editors) sit in their offices going about their usual daily business, while the auctioneer (you or your agent) spends the day calling the bidders, collecting bids, and updating participants on how to proceed.

If you want to conduct an auction, set a date for the auction, making sure that it's no more than a week ahead and preferably within the next day or so. Inform each editor of the date and promise to send a sheet of auction ground rules in advance.

Because an auction seems to play one publisher against another, you may be wondering how publishers feel about bidding in an auction. Do they resent the process? Will you get a fairer hearing if you submit your book to one publisher at a time? Even at large publishing firms, some editors resent auctions and try not to participate. They feel, with some justification, that an auction can place a book with the wrong editor or at the wrong house. Smaller publishers must be selective about auctions, because in general the auction process inflates the price of a book. On the other hand, most experienced editors and publishers are entirely accustomed to auctions; they participate in an auction several times a week. And most publishers agree that an auction is often the only equitable way to match publisher with book and to assure that the writer is fairly compensated according to the price the market can bear.

Setting ground rules

Write up a set of ground rules for the auction. These ground rules should detail exactly what is being auctioned and how the auction is conducted.

- **The rights:** Unless you are working with an agent or lawyer who can sell subsidiary rights such as audio or foreign, I recommend that you retain only movie and performance rights (which include theatrical production, tv, and video rights). The publisher is better equipped to sell the rest, such as book club, audio, foreign, electronic, and serialization (magazine excerpts), than you are. Contact a movie agent to sell movie rights if it's appropriate. The auction notice should say, "Rights available: book, first and second serial, reprint and book club, audio, verbatim electronic and permission. All other performance rights retained."

- **Splits:** In the contract, every form of income derived from the book is itemized, and for each item, the author's share of the income is stipulated. For example, if the book club split is 50/50 (which is standard), then a $5,000 book club payment will be divided $2,500 to the author and $2,500 to the publisher. Splits are not usually addressed in the auction notice, but if one of the bidders proposes a nonstandard split arrangement, don't be taken by surprise and do read the explanation of splits in Chapter 16.
- **The territory:** Publishing contracts always stipulate the territory governed by the contract. In the case of agented contracts, the publisher usually has the right to publish the book in North America, and the author, through his or her agent, places the rights in all foreign countries. If you don't have an agent, you're better off letting your publisher sell the rights overseas. What you say in the auction notice is "Territory: World Rights." (See Chapter 14 for an in-depth look at foreign rights.)
- **The rounds:** A *round* is a turn in which each bidder is invited to bid once, usually in a set order. In the auction notice, it's customary to say "after the first round of bids, the auction will be conducted in rounds, going from lowest to highest bidder."
- **A floor and topping privileges:** A *floor* is a guaranteed minimum bid, which is usually determined before the auction begins. The floor holder guarantees to bid a certain amount, say $10,000. If no other bids occur, the floor holder wins the auction for that amount. If bids above $10,000 occur, the floor holder can win the auction at the end by bidding above the final bid by a set percentage — usually 5 percent or 10 percent of the highest received bid. This right to win with a final bid is called a *topping privilege*. If the best bid in the auction is $20,000 and the topping percentage is 10 percent, the floor holder can win by bidding $22,000. If you accept a floor bid, say so in your auction notice. For example: "There is a floor of $10,000 with 10 percent topping privileges." When many publishers are vying to bid in an auction, sometimes a preliminary auction is held for the right to bid for the floor. This is called a *floor auction*.

  What is the lowest floor bid you should accept? The best way to determine the right floor bid is to take the first bid you receive and see whether that bidder is willing to have his offer be a floor. Don't accept a floor bid unless it's enough to cover your costs in writing the book. Remember, if you accept a floor, you are bound to accept that amount as your advance unless there is another, higher bid.
- **House floor:** If you have not received a floor bid, you can set a *house floor*, which stipulates that no bids will be accepted below a certain level.

The problem with house floors is that if no bidder meets the house floor, then the auction cannot proceed. You'll never know whether a bidder would have paid slightly less than your house floor. I don't recommend a house floor because it can sabotage an auction before it starts.

- **Right not to accept the highest offer:** Be sure to reserve the right to accept an offer that is not necessarily the highest. This condition allows you to sell to the company you like best, the editor you clicked with, or the team that has the most appealing vision of how your book will be marketed. Your auction notice should say, "The winning bid will be determined on the basis of all factors, including guaranteed advance, marketing plan, and the publisher's vision of the book. The author reserves the right to accept an offer below the highest dollar offer."
- **Get it in writing:** To ensure clarity, ask that each publisher's first offer be put in writing, stipulating the financial terms of the offer, the publisher's editorial vision for the book, the marketing plan, and the *marketing commitment,* which is a promise of what they plan to spend in order to market your book. The auction notice should say, "Please put all first bids in writing, including all terms: financial guarantee, territories, rights, splits, marketing plans, bonus provisions, and marketing commitments." Some agents and authors also ask that best or final bids be put in writing, too, but this need not be mentioned in the auction notice.
- **The deadline:** Set a deadline when first bids must be received. I recommend a weekday morning at 10 a.m., which leaves plenty of time in the day for bidding.

Variations on a standard auction

Agents often use two auction strategies when they sense that publishers are interested in a project but not motivated to start bidding at a high enough level. You may want to consider using one of these two slightly unusual strategies in order to provoke a bid that is higher than the rest. If you have a lot of interest from publishers, it's worth a try.

- **Qualification round:** If editors are trying to jump the gun and bid before the auction, you can save time and secure a higher level of bids by waiting until the day of the auction, or the night before, and announcing a *qualification round.* Say that five publishers have expressed interest in your book. You can announce that only the top three bidders in the qualification round will be invited to bid after the first round.
- **Blind bid:** Invite bidders to participate in a one-round auction in which each bidder will offer his or her best bid without knowing what the others have bid. The book goes to the highest bidder. There is no second round — at least that's how to present it. In reality, if the bidders want to keep bidding and raising the price, who are you to stop them?!

Conducting the auction

On the eve of the appointed day, call each potential participant and find out which editors want to bid. If you don't have any interested parties, don't go forward with your auction. Submit your materials to publishers you haven't tried yet. Then decide whether an auction is really the best way to go.

If you have firm interest from at least two editors, you're in business! Get a good night's sleep in preparation for auction day.

- **The starting point:** Call in your first bids. If you haven't accepted a floor, contact each interested editor about an hour before the first-round deadline and remind them that the deadline is approaching. Once the deadline passes, you cannot accept any additional first round bids.
- **Rounds:** With first round bids in hand, contact each bidder, from lowest to highest, and tell each one what the first round bids were. For example, "There were five bids in the first round, from $10,000 to $30,000. You were lowest in the first round, so you can now open the second round. You must bid above $30,000." All bidders then place their second round bids, and again you inform the bidders where they fall, from lowest to highest. Bidding in rounds continues until no higher bids are offered. At this point, ask each remaining bidder to make one final best bid. With your best bids in hand, determine which offer is most appealing. Congratulations!

When conducting an auction, it is common practice not to reveal the identity of any of the bidders to each other.

At the auction's end, make sure that you have received an offer high enough to make writing your book financially viable. If not, it's acceptable to withdraw your project, informing all of the publishers that the book has not been sold. See Chapter 14 for an in-depth look at getting what you need in order to write the book.

Once the auction is over and all major financial terms are determined, you need to negotiate your contract. Refer to Chapter 15 for tips on contract negotiation.

Chapter 12

Going the Agent Route

In This Chapter

- Finding an agent
- Choosing the right agent for you
- Facilitating a partnership
- The trouble with agents

A literary agent brings writers and publishers together. The agent submits your work, helps formulate your deal, acts as your advocate throughout the book's life, scrutinizes your flow of earnings and, in exchange, takes as payment a percentage of your total earnings — usually 15 percent.

Many authors think of their agent as a member of the family. And in these days of publishing company consolidations, the relationship between agent and author has become more important than ever. Agent-client bonds often endure throughout your entire career while editors can change with each book.

In this chapter, I show you what a literary agent can and should do for you, and I offer some pointers on how to find a literary agent. I also provide guidelines for structuring a successful working relationship with your agent.

How an Agent Works

You can certainly get published without the help of a literary agent. But having an agent represent you greatly increases your chances. Editors know that if an agent chooses to represent your book, it's worth looking at quickly. After all, agents only receive payment if and/or when a project they represent sells. They simply don't take on books they don't feel confident they can sell.

Agents nurture relationships with writers and publishers alike. They stay on top of all the fluctuations and movements in the publishing industry as well as scouting new, talented writers. So, when an agent sees material from a writer that she thinks a publisher may buy, she takes on the writer as a client, usually signing a formal contract. The agent then works with the writer to increase the sales potential of the submission material and submits it to a few handpicked editors.

When an agented submission arrives in an editor's office, the editor takes notice because he knows the agent screens out material that is not first rate. If the editor makes a formal offer to publish the material submitted, the agent negotiates a deal for the writer. The agent also acts as the writer's advocate in all dealings with the publisher, mediating when a problem arises — and problems usually do surface at some point. While the agent clearly understands the wants and needs of both parties, the agent works for, and is paid by, the writer.

What an Agent Can Do For You

Agents come in all sizes and shapes with different interests and areas of specialty. While their main job is to act as your business agent, some do much more than that. Think about what you would like an agent to do for you and take a look at some of the ways I list that agents can help advance both your next book and your whole career.

Act as an editorial sounding board

An agent can read your query letter or proposal with deep understanding, perhaps even comprehending what you are trying to accomplish more clearly than you can. With her understanding of the book market and of your particular book, your agent is likely to provide specific advice on how to make your book better, and how to position it so that publishers can see its potential.

Help shape the idea

Beyond pure advice, an agent can actually provide very specific instructions on how to shape or change your book in order to make it stronger and more salable to a publisher. Some agents provide light editing. If you need a full-time writer to help write your proposal and your book, an agent can recommend qualified writers or collaborators to work with you in creating the book. If your manuscript is complete but needs some sharpening, your agent knows good book doctors who can provide last minute fine-tuning before submission.

Agents are often aware of specific features and subject areas that attract certain editors. The agent may suggest you make modifications in order to attract the attention of a particular editor.

Help prepare sample materials

Agents can provide expert guidance on supplementary materials that add heft and persuasiveness to a submission. For a work of nonfiction, this assistance can include helping you solicit endorsements. It may also entail helping you assemble a portfolio of press clippings. And to show how mediagenic you are, some agents arrange for the creation of a sample video reel.

Choose the right publisher and editor

Literary agents spend several hours every day cultivating publisher relationships via phone calls, office meetings, lunch meetings, dinners, and industry events. Most literary agents count publishers and editors among their friends and nurture ongoing professional friendships with publishers that last their whole career.

Agents know when editors move from one publisher to another. They study the output of every publishing house and scrutinize the performance of successful books. They track the activities of a wide range of editors, and can identify the specific editors who are actively buying or are *due* to start buying after a period of inactivity.

Agents make a study of trends in the publishing industry. They have strongly held opinions about fluctuations of public taste and can offer valuable insights into what categories are likely to enjoy a surge in popularity during the coming months. Likewise, their many publisher contacts give them insight into the trends that publishers anticipate.

Agents are shrewd judges of literary talent: They can evaluate a writer's work and offer advice on the best application for a writer's talent. An agent knows which editors and publishers are hot, and which are not. It's his or her job to understand the book that you want to write — or the manuscript that you have already written — and link you with the publisher that's best equipped to bring your book out into the world.

Establish instant credibility

Agents enjoy a high level of credibility with editors. After years of nurturing a relationship with an editor, agents can virtually assure that a particular proposal is read attentively, quickly, and usually with the result of an offer. At the very top level of the industry, certain agents can elicit offers on just about every submission they tender — they pick their properties with exceptional care, and they submit books selectively to editors they have cultivated over many years.

Use influence with publishers

An agent is likely to have many relationships at a particular publishing company. It's not unusual for an agent to submit a proposal to an editor and call that editor's publisher or editor in chief just to make sure that the proposal is being treated respectfully. The agent may call other editors at the same company, in order to raise awareness of the book, and influence the reception the book receives at the company's editorial meeting. The agent wields power, in large part, by representing other important clients whom the publisher hopes to publish.

Generate excitement among publishers

It's the agent's job to submit a project so as to create as much buzz, excitement, and urgency as possible. For example, an agent can submit a proposal for a first-time author or manuscript for a first novel to several editors one day and then set a closing date for one or two days later. One of the editors may try to obtain clearance to bid before the deadline. Then the agent calls all the other editors, telling them that a bid is imminent. They then scramble to secure an offer from their own companies. Before long, several editors have committed many hours, and a great deal of anxiety, in pursuing the project. If the agent plays them skillfully, they are all determined to buy the project, and are motivated — by the spirit of urgency and competitiveness — to bid more than they first intended. This process is repeated every week and explains why such astronomical advances are paid for books that, when finally written and published, fail to spark the same excitement in bookstores that they stirred in publishing offices around New York.

Set the appropriate price for your work

An agent knows the approximate value of your book on the open market. She can stir excitement that compels publishers to offer as much as they dare, and more. And once all the bids are in, she can identify the one publisher — not necessarily the highest bidder — who is most likely to share your vision of success and deliver it. If it means accepting a slightly lower advance payment, so be it. What you lose in the short term may just pay off over the lifetime of the book.

Act as your advocate throughout the entire publishing process

Once your book is placed and the terms of the deal are settled, the agent remains your advocate throughout the publishing process.

- An agent negotiates the minute terms of your publishing contract. The contract can include hundreds of clauses and over a dozen pages. While the law requires these documents to be written in plain English, a non-professional reader still won't understand many provisions. An agent makes sure that your interests are represented in resolving these issues.
- An agent supervises the editing of your book and stays abreast of the general communications that pass between you and your editor. The agent makes sure that your editor is not placing unreasonable demands on you during the writing and revision of the book and looks over your editor's editorial judgments. An agent can protect you, for example, from an editorial mistake or an extreme case of editorial neglect.
- A contract includes author payment provisions that are triggered when portions of your manuscript are delivered and accepted by your publisher. Your agent makes sure that these payments are made on time.
- Your agent supervises your publisher's marketing efforts, provoking assurances and updates.
- As publication day nears, your agent confirms that the publisher's marketing promises, if any, are being kept, and that the publisher is working hard to market and distribute the book.
- Your agent scrutinizes all financial reports from your publisher and supervises the payments of money due after the publication of your book.
- Your agent begins to sell your next book.

Help with career planning

An agent works with you to look beyond the book you are currently working on. With the expert help of your agent, you can look at your writing career more clearly and plan for the kind of growth that increases your income along with your skills.

How to Get an Agent

It's common knowledge that the easiest way to find an agent is to already have a published book or an offer from a reputable publishing company. If you're a first-time writer, you may not have either of these. Don't despair. My many agent friends recommend the following ways for first-time writers to hook up with a good literary agent:

- **Query letter:** Agents especially like query letters (see Chapter 7) that are short, clear, and that compare your work to another writer (a novel about a Mexican woman with an Amy Tan sensibility). Across the board, literary agents say that they prefer to be approached by first-time writers via query letter with SASE.

- **Referrals:** Agents love referrals because they count interesting individuals and talented writers among their friends and acquaintances. Before sending a referral query to an agent, look into whether the agent is a good fit for your type of book — keep in mind that the agent/client relationship has to work for both parties. If you don't know an agent, I bet one of your friends or acquaintances does. Ask around. Network.
- **Writers' conferences and conventions:** Be where agents, editors and writers abound — at writers' conferences and conventions. Ask other writers for agent advice and listen carefully to the agents who offer workshops or give talks. Ask questions. Collect a list of agents who represent the kind of book you want to write.

  At some writers' conferences, agents and editors meet with attending writers and critique their work. Take advantage of this service and take notes on the advice they offer. Don't get defensive and argumentative. Show your appreciation and ask what agent may be a good fit for you and your work.
- **Industry associations.** Contact the Association of Author's Representative's (AAR) for a list of their member agents — all members abide by a strict code of ethics and have passed a rigorous application and screening process. Check out its Web site at `www.bookworm.com/aar` for a list of member agents. The site also offers helpful hints on finding an agent and more.
- **Publishing industry source books.** *Writer's Market* and *Writer's guide to Book Editors, Publishers, and Literary Agents, 2000–2001* provide a great deal of information on agents. *Writer's Market* cross-references agents by subject area in order to help narrow your search for the right agent. *Writer's Guide* provides the most in-depth information on agents, offering a glimpse into the agent's personalities, hobbies, likes, dislikes, and more. Refer to both guides before actually contacting an agent. You may just discover that you both attended the same college.

The Problems with Agents

Agents are known to reject over 90 percent of the projects they receive for consideration. Because most agents are self-employed and they work strictly on a commission basis — receiving money only after they sell a book — they are often more interested in the salability of your book than the quality of your writing. So be sure to impress upon each agent how marketable you and your book are. And don't despair when agents don't want to take you on as a client. Just remember, the agent that's right for you is the one who can see the value in your work. Remember, you're the paying client. Make sure that you get your money's worth.

Memorandum of agreement

This sample letter of agreement between agent and author features the key terms that you can expect to encounter in such a document.

1. This letter will confirm our agreement under which you ______ (Author) appoint American Literacy Agency, Inc., as your literary representative, and we (ALA) agree to use our best effort to place your next Work, and subsequent books, for publication with a publisher acceptable to you and to exploit and turn to account such other publication, subsidiary and television and film rights in and to the Works as may be appropriate under the circumstances. We may use and/or employ subagents and corresponding agents at your suggestion and/or with your approval for such purposes. We shall make no agreements on your behalf without your approval.

2. In return for services rendered and to be rendered by agent in connection with the Work, the Author agrees to pay, and irrevocably authorizes Agent to receive in Agents name, all moneys due or to become due to Author and to retain as its commission fifteen percent (15 percent) of all gross moneys payable to Author under each agreement relating to the Work except that commission on the sale of British publication rights shall be twenty percent (20 percent) and commission on the sale-of foreign language publication rights shall be twenty percent (20 percent).

3. In addition to the aforementioned commissions, ALA shall be reimbursed for the expenses incurred on behalf of the Work (not to exceed a total of $150.00 without written permission), including photocopying, messengers, cables, and overseas postage in connection with submissions for sales both foreign and domestic, long distance telephone calls, copies of the published book when purchased by the Agency for subsidiary rights submissions, and other similar and related charges. Agency shall bill Author periodically for such expenses, or deduct same from funds received by the Agency for the Author's account.

4. This agreement is effective from the date of your acceptance and shall continue until canceled by either of us by the giving to the other of at least seventy-five (75) days written notice. In the event of such cancellation, you are to continue to act as Agents and to collect all the sums due me under contracts negotiated during the term of this agreement, and to deduct your commissions and the above specified expenses from such sums.

5. If any controversy, claim or dispute arising out of, or in connection with this Agreement, exist in or the breach thereof between Agency and Author, cannot be resolved, then Author and Agency agree to arbitrate their differences in [Agents's state] in accordance with the rules of the American Arbitration Association, and judgment confirming the Arbitrator's award rights may be entered in any court of competent jurisdiction.

6. Any written notice called for by this Agreement must be sent by registered U.S. mail, return receipt requested to the addresses set forth in this Agreement.

7. This Agreement represents the complete understanding between the Author and the Agency, supersedes any prior oral understandings and may not be amended except in a writing signed by the Author and the Agency.

8 If the foregoing is acceptable to you, please so indicate by signing your name below.

Sincerely,

ACCEPTED AND AGREED TO______________s

SOCIAL SECURITY NUMBER______________

A 15 percent commission

With the exception of a few large agencies like ICM and William Morris, which collect a 10 percent commission, most agents collect 15 percent of all income generated by a book — 15 percent of your money! A 15 percent commission is the acceptable industry standard. It may seem like a big percentage but experience shows that established agents often get publishing companies to pay more for your book than you do acting on your own. Keep in mind that literary agents sell book projects for a living — you don't. And the higher the purchase price, the higher the agent's commission or income. It is definitely in your agent's best interest, and yours, to get top dollar. If, however, you don't feel that you're getting your 15 percent worth, then consider looking for an agent who provides more of the type of services you want.

Make sure that you read agent agreements carefully and are aware of the following:

- **Fifteen percent is a fair commission.** Don't pay more.
- **Don't sign an agreement with an agent that extends indefinitely.** The duration of the agreement should be stipulated as this single project or a distinct period of time — perhaps one to three years.
- **Don't pay readers' fees.** It's okay for an agent to charge you for reasonable expenses such as postage, messengers, and photocopying, but reading your work is part of an agent's job.

An agent's influence may change your project

Your agent is likely to suggest changes to your book — changes that may significantly alter the shape and scope of your book. If you're comfortable making these kinds of alterations and think it will increase the salability of the book, go ahead.

Don't assume that you have to take your agent's advice, no matter what. Listen to the logic and, if the agent is willing, brainstorm solutions together. If you find that you and your agent just don't share the same vision for your book, it may be time to part company.

Finding an agent can be harder than finding a publisher

An agent definitely makes the job of selling your first book easier. But chances are good that you'll find a publisher before you find an agent.

Choosing the 'right' agent for you

You may be so excited when an agent wants to represent you that you don't think to ask a few key questions about how he or she operates. It's worth taking the time to find out up front, before you sign any kind of binding agreement to work exclusively with this particular agent. Here are some issues to think about and questions to ask an agent before signing an Author/Agent Letter of Agreement.

What commission do you charge? Don't proceed if it's more than 15 percent.

How many books do you sell each year? An active agent sells at least ten books per year.

Who are your current clients? What recent books have you sold? If you've never heard of them or if they are quite different from the book you plan to write, beware.

Do you require a written agreement with me? If so, may I look over the contract's wording? It's okay to sign a contract that entitles your agent to receive a commission for this book only. Don't sign an agreement to share all of your income, whether from this book or any other activities. And don't commit to representation on future books.

What fees do you charge, if any, over and above your commission? Don't pay a reader's fee. Many agents do charge for photocopies of your manuscript or proposal and postage.

Which publishers do you work with? Are most of your clients with one publisher? If your agent sells mainly to one publisher, your agent is probably working as hard for your publisher as he is for you — and chances are that you'll get the short end of the stick.

How do you keep me informed of the activities you perform on my behalf? Will you notify me of any and all offers? Your agent should outline a submission strategy and explain what he will do if his first strategy doesn't work. Make sure that the agent keeps you informed and in the loop on all matters affecting your book. Find out whether the agent has the capacity to handle first serial sales, magazine assignments for you, foreign rights, film rights, tv, performance, and audio rights. Remember, you're the one paying for these services, you should know what they are.

I recommend pursuing agents and editors at the same time. Be persistent. Even if you are accumulating a huge collection of rejection letters, don't give up. Most first-time authors — including many of the most famous writers — receive dozens of rejection letters before they break through. Make the most of the feedback you get along the way and stick with it!

Choosing an Agent Who's Right for You

There is no right or wrong way to choose a literary agent. Every literary agent is a person, with a distinct personality. Because literary agents and their clients work together closely, through good times and bad, over many years, it's vital that you select a literary agent you feel comfortable with. If you are considering signing an agreement with a literary agent, I offer a few suggestions about how to test the relationship.

Before your first meeting, I recommend that you check your prospective agent carefully in the published industry sources. An agent who is not even mentioned in any of these guides — especially the *Literary Market Place,* which is comprehensive — may not be a safe bet.

While you want your relationship with your agent to be friendly, keep in mind this is about business. So apply the same criteria that you use when hiring a lawyer or accountant. Is this a person you feel comfortable sharing private information about your income, your working habits, and your living situation? And is this a person you can talk to honestly about your work? If not, your agent won't be able to fully represent your interests.

To ensure a comfortable, personal fit, you need to meet the agent in person. Don't hire a literary agent you've never met or at least talked to at length. Spend enough time talking to the agent so that you get a basic feeling about them. Are your direct questions being answered? Are you at ease with this person, or intimidated?

If you find yourself feeling comfortable with the prospective agent, then discuss your career goals and find out whether this agent is willing to work with you to help achieve them. Make sure that the agent is experienced at representing the sort of books you plan to write. And, if possible, push the agent for feedback on your current work to determine whether this is an editorial voice you find helpful and you feel you can trust.

Always ask to see the agent's letter of agreement or contract (see sidebar). Determine whether the financial terms at the agency are acceptable. Ask whether they require you to sign an exclusivity agreement and, if so, look at the terms carefully.

Successful literary agents are clustered in New York and Los Angeles, with easy access to customers on both coasts: publishers, movie and television studios, and national magazines. However, many excellent literary agents are located in other parts of the country. The location of your agent is much less significant than her proven ability to sell the work of writers like you.

A Survey of Literary Agents

The following listing is intended to be a representative sample — by no means exhaustive — of the hundreds of literary agents active today. This is not a complete list by any means, and only includes agents we contacted who confirmed the information about them. You can find comprehensive listings of literary agents in other reference works such as *Literary Market Place* and

Writer's Guide to Editors, Publishers, and Literary Agents. But the following listings serve as a handy sampling of some of the better-known and established agencies, large and small.

Large agencies

These large, established powerhouse agencies include some of the most powerful and connected literary agents in the business. The advantage of working with one of these powerhouses is that the clout of the whole agency's client list is behind you and can influence the behavior of a publisher. Some of the agents that work at these large international powerhouses are without question among the most able in the business. Also, these agents provide (and often insist upon) one-stop shopping. They maintain offices in New York, Los Angeles, and in many foreign countries, so they will do an expert job of placing performance and foreign rights for you.

The downside is that it's very easy for even a prominent writer to get somewhat lost on one of these giant lists, and you may find yourself waiting an awfully long time to get your call returned or your agent's undivided attention.

That being said, bear in mind that several hundred professional writers, including some of the most famous names on the bookshelf, are successfully represented by one of the following marquee agencies.

Curtis Brown, Ltd.

New York office: 10 Astor Place New York, NY 10003; 212-473-5400. Contact: Tim Knowlton. *San Francisco office:* 1750 Montgomery Street, San Francisco, CA 94111; 415-954-8566. Contact: Peter L Ginsberg. *Toronto office:* 457A Danforth Avenue, Toronto, ON, M4K 1P1 Canada; 416-406-3389. Contact: Dean Cooke.

Founded in 1914, Curtis Brown, Ltd. is known as one of the most distinguished, well-established literary agencies in the country. With the opening of the San Francisco office in 1992 by Peter Ginsberg, the company has continued to flourish.

Member of AAR; Query letters with SASE; represents general adult and children's fiction and nonfiction; Accepts queries and brief unsolicited proposals both with SASE; no unsolicited manuscripts or lengthy proposals; additional charges for photocopying and Express Mail.

Recently published works include *Genome* by Matt Ridley (Harper Collins, 2000) and *Built to Last* by Jerry Porras and Jim Collins (HarperBusiness, 1995).

Advice for first-time writers: Strong, pointed, and brief query letters that capture the essence of the book and the author's credentials receive the most serious attention. Potential authors should do their homework and learn about both the potential market for their book and the agent to whom they're submitting.

International Creative Management, Inc. (ICM)

40 West 57 Street, New York, NY 10019; 212-556-5600; fax 212-556-5665.

ICM was originally formed half a century ago, when Lew Wasserman, a Hollywood mogul, added a talent agency to go with his movie studio, MCA/Universal. The government only allowed him to keep the studio, and so the talent agency was spun off as a separate business. That business prospered, with major film and literary clients around the world.

Today, the company has a West Coast office, headed by the legendary Jeff Berg, and a New York office, under the direction of two other legends, Esther Newberg and Amanda "Binky" Urban. According to *The New York Post,* these two are "among the most powerful literary brokers in the city." Newberg handles John Stanford, Thomas J. Friedman, Tom Peters, Carl Hiassen, Pete Hamill, Patricia Cornwell, the I-Man-radio personality Don Imus, and sportswriter Mike Lupica. Urban handles Chris Buckley, Toni Morrison, Suze Orman, Anna Quindlen, Richard Ford, Cormac McCarthy, and E.L. Doctorow. ICM is one of the most distinguished agencies in the business, with hundreds of household name clients and many more soon to be discovered stars on their roster.

Agents: Richard Abate, Lisa Bankoff, Kristine Dahl, Mitch Douglas, Suzanne Gluck, Sloan Harris, Esther Newberg, Heather Schroder, Denise Shannon, and Binky Urban.

Member AAR; 10 percent commission; represents up-market fiction and narrative nonfiction; accepts unsolicited proposals and manuscripts but prefers a query letter sent with sample chapters; requires an author/agent contract; no additional fees charged.

Recently published works represented by ICM: *Black Notice* by Patricia Cornwell (Putnam, 1999); *Blind Man's Bluff* by Sherry Sontag, Christopher Drew, and Annette Lawrence Drew (HarperPerennial Library, 1999); *As Nature Made Him* by John Colapinto (HarperCollins, 2000); and *Sick Puppy* by Carl Hiaasen (Knopf, 2000).

IMG Literary

825 Seventh Avenue, New York, NY 10019; 212-489-5400; fax 212-246-1118; e-mail firstinitiallastname@imgworld.com.

International Management Group was founded in the early 1960s by attorney Mark McCormack as a sports agency, boasting both Arnold Palmer and Jack Nicklaus as its original clients. Today, IMG is a worldwide sports marketing colossus, which includes a large literary department. In fact, *Getting Your Book Published For Dummies* was sold to IDG Books Worldwide, Inc., by IMG agent Mark Reiter.

Agents: Mark Reiter, Carolyn Krupp, David McCormick, and Sarah Wooldrige (U.K.).

Member of AAR; 15 percent commission; represents fiction, self-help, sports, biography, history, and narrative nonfiction; accepts query letters; no unsolicited proposals or manuscripts; author/agent contract required.

Recently published works represented by IMG Literary: *Winning Every Day* by Lou Holtz (HarperBusiness, 1999); *Fair Ball* by Bob Costas (Broadway Books, 2000); *The Greedy Hand* by Amity Shlaes (Random House, 1999; Harvest Books, 2000); and *The Entertainment Economy* by Michael J. Wolf (Times Books, 2000).

Advice for first-time writers: Write what you know better than anyone in the world and only submit your finest, most polished material.

Janklow & Nesbit Associates

445 Park Avenue, New York, NY 10022-2606; 212- 421-1700; fax 212- 980-3671; e-mail Postmaster@Janklow.com.

Janklow/Nesbit was a small boutique agency, founded by two of the most established and powerful forces in the literary world in 1989. At that time, literary lawyer and agent Mort Janklow merged his commercial fiction powerhouse with the office of Lynn Nesbit, who had been the lead agent at ICM for over a decade. Together, they now command the attention of every publisher in the business and count among their clients many of the world's best-selling writers including Tom Wolfe, Richard Price, Danielle Steele, and Sidney Sheldon.

Agents: Morton Janklow, Lynn Nesbit, Tina Bennett, Anne Sibbald, Eric Simonoff, and Cullen Stanley.

Represents fiction and narrative nonfiction; accepts query letters; no unsolicited proposals or manuscripts; author/agent contract required; no additional fees.

Recently published works represented by Janklow & Nesbit Associates: *A Man in Full* by Tom Wolfe (Farrar, Straus & Giroux, 1998: Bantam Books, 1999); *Accident* by Danielle Steele (Dell, 1995); *The Best Laid Plans* by Sidney Sheldon (Warner Books, 1998).

Advice for first-time writers: Keep trying.

Sterling Lord Literistic, Inc.

65 Bleecker Street, New York, NY 10012; 212-780-6050; fax 212-780-6095.

Sterling Lord-Literistic was formed by the merger in 1988 of two prominent agenting traditions. Sterling Lord formed his powerhouse agency uptown, in the early '50s, and counted such luminaries as Jack Kerouac and Ken Kesey among his early clients. Peter Matson, a descendent of one of New York's earliest and most successful agents, Harold Matson, formed his firm, Literistic, in 1979. Together, they opened a new cutting edge office in Noho, and have represented some of the hottest bestsellers of the late 1990s.

Agents: Sterling Lord, Peter Matson, Philippa Brophy, Chris Calhoun, Jody Hotchkiss (film & TV), Neeti Madan, and George Nicholson (children's books).

Member AAR; 15 percent commission; represents popular and literary nonfiction, popular and literary fiction, and children's books; accepts unsolicited proposals and manuscripts but prefers a query letter sent to an individual agent first; no author/agent contract required.

Recently published works represented by Sterling Lord Literistic: *Faith of My Fathers* by Senator John McCain (Random House, 1999); *Seeing Through Places* by Mary Gordon (Scribner, 2000); *High Fidelity* by Nick Hornby (Riverhead, 1996); *Dr. Atkin's New Diet Revolution* by Dr. Robert Atkins (National Book Network, 1999); *Professor and the Madman* by Simon Winchester (HarperCollins, 1998; HarperPerennial, 1999); *The Color of Water* by James McBride (Riverhead Books, 1996) as well as all of Dick Francis's books, the most recent being *Second Wind* (Putnam, 1999).

Advice for first-time writers: Submit your work to literary agencies that represent the kind of book you're writing.

Writers House

21 West 26th Street, New York, NY 10010; 212-685-2400; fax 212-685-1781.

Al Zuckerman, originally a playwright, founded this firm in 1973 to represent "a few clients," mostly authors of plays, movies, and television scripts. However, the agency has built its superior reputation through representing books. Housed in a magnificent Manhattan townhouse that was built as the Astor family's private bank, the large staff at Writers House now represents over 500 clients, embracing a full line of literary properties, including novels, children's books, cookbooks, and adult nonfiction. Clients include Barbara Delinsky, Ken Follett, Stephen Hawking, Nora Roberts, Michael Lewis, Jane Feather, Joan Johnston, Neal Gaiman, F. Paul Wilson, Ann Martin, Francine Pascal, Bruce Sterling, and Ridley Pearson.

Agents: Albert Zuckerman, Amy Berkower, Susan Cohen, Susan Ginsburg Merrilee Heifetz, John Hodgman, Simon Lipskar, Jennifer Lyons, Steven Malk, Michelle Rubin, Robin Rue, and Karen Solem.

Member of AAR; 15 percent commission; represents all types of major fiction and nonfiction, including children's and young adult. Accepts query letters — no unsolicited proposals or manuscripts; charges for photocopies and overseas mailing of books; author/agent contract required. The agency sold approximately 400 titles in 1999.

Recently published works represented by Writers House: *Carolina Moon* by Nora Roberts (Putnam, 2000); *The New New Thing* by Michael Lewis (W.W. Norton & Company, 1999); and *The Hammer of Edge* by Ken Follett (Crown 1998; Fawcett 1999).

Advice for first-time writers: Write an irresistible, one-page letter that includes what's wonderful about your book, what the book is about, and why you're the perfect author to write it.

Small Agencies/Solo Practitioners

Don't select an agent until you read about the smaller agencies. These independent practitioners are just as skillful and well connected as the agents at the powerhouse giants. They represent many of the great and most commercially successful writers of this time. And they are structured to provide the highest level of personal attention and service to their clients.

Most of these agents use subagents to represent their clients on the West Coast and overseas. But owing to the size and scope of their stable of clients, many agents on this list possess just as much clout as the some of the senior agents at the powerhouse firms.

Virginia Barber Literary Agency

Now called The Writers Shop; see listing later in this section.

Black Inc.

156 Fifth Avenue, Suite 608, New York, NY, 10010; 212-242-5080; fax 212-924-6609.

Founded in 1989 by David Black, the son of Hillel Black, a publishing veteran and former long-time editor in chief of William Morrow. Black Inc., is one of the hottest agencies in the chic Flatiron District, with such blockbuster clients at Mitch Albom, Bill Phillips, and Ken Davis.

Agents: David Black, Gary Morris, Susan Raihofer, Laureen Rowland, and Joy Tutela.

Member AAR; 15 percent commission, domestic, 20 percent foreign; represents literary and commercial fiction and nonfiction, especially sports, politics, social and women's issues and business. No poetry, plays, or screenplays; Query letters with SASE, no unsolicited proposals or manuscripts; no author/agent contract required.

Recent published works: *Tuesdays with Morrie* by Mitch Albom (Doubleday, 1997); *Isaac's Storm* by Erik Larson (Crown, 1999); and *Body For Life* by Bill Phillips with Mike D'Orso (HarperCollins, 1999).

Vicky Bijur Literary Agency, Inc.

333 West End Avenue, Suite 5B, New York, NY 10023.

Formerly an editor at Oxford University Press, Bijur is a specialist in the mystery and thriller genres. Her clients tend to be award winners. As current president of the Association of Authors' Representatives, Inc., Bijur is extremely dedicated to making sure that the agent/client relationship is the best it can be. Bijur currently represents approximately 45 clients including

Julie Smith, James Sallis, Margaret Maron, Larry Gonick, Alice Outwater, Robert Kanigel, Ed Levine, Laura Lippman, and Mickey Pearlman.

Agents: Vicky Bijur.

President of AAR; 15 percent commission; represents narrative nonfiction, thrillers, and health-related topics; accepts query letters — preferably one page — and unsolicited proposals with an SASE; no unsolicited manuscripts; charges clients for photocopies, postage, and so on.

Recent published works: *Storm Track* by Margaret Maron (Mysterious Press, 2000); *The Sugar House* by Laura Lippman (Avon Books, 2000); *The Body Clock Guide to Better Health: How to Use Your Body's Natural Clock to Fight Illness and Achieve Maximum Health* by Michael Smolensky, Ph.D., and Lynne Lamberg (Henry Holt, June 2000); *Chester Himes: A Life* by James Sallis (Walker Publishing, 2000); *Don't Drink the Water* by Susan Rogers Cooper (Avon Books, 2000); and *The Wedding Game* by Susan Holtzer (St. Martin's Press, 2000).

Advice for first-time writers: Research agents and try to find out which ones represent books that are similar in some way to your book. Mention these books in your query letter to the respective agents. Keep your query letter short — one page is best. If you're writing nonfiction, put together a strong proposal. If you're writing fiction and you want to send some chapters, send the first chapter or two, not chapters from the middle of the novel. Don't send a detailed synopsis unless you're also sending chapters — many agents find synopses alone unhelpful. And most agents won't respond if you don't include an SASE.

The Doe Coover Agency

P.O. Box 668, Winchester, MA 01890; phone 781-721-6000; fax 781-721-6727.

After previous editorial positions at Scribner and Addison-Wesley, Doe Coover started The Doe Coover Agency in 1986. Among her earliest clients were Henry Hampton and the producers of the landmark PBS series "Eyes on the Prize," financial guru Peter Lynch, and best-selling cookbook authors Chris Schlesinger and John Willoughby. The agency expanded in 1991 when Colleen Mohyde, formerly an editor at Little, Brown & Co., joined as a partner and added her talents with fiction to the business. The agency now represents a wide range of fiction and nonfiction including a formidable cookbook list.

Query with SASE. Proposal for nonfiction; synopsis and sample chapters for fiction. Every submission receives a reply. Agent/author contract not required. Standard 15 percent commission.

Agents: Doe Coover, Colleen Mohyde, and Amanda Lewis.

Recent published works represented by The Doe Coover Agency: *Home Comforts* by Cheryl Mendelson (Scribner, 1999), *Pack of Two* by Caroline Knapp (The Dial Press, 1999), *Vegetarian Cooking for Everyone* by Deborah Madison (Broadway, 1997), *American Home Cooking* by Cheryl Alters Janison and Bill Jamison (Broadway, 1999); and *The Realm of Secondhand Souls* by Sandra Shea (Houghton Mifflin, 2000).

Advice for first-time writers: Write what you love and be ready to listen to the opinion of others.

DeFiore and Company, Author Services

853 Broadway, Suite 1715, New York, NY 10003; 212-505-7979; fax 212-505-7779; e-mail submissions@defioreandco.com.

Brian DeFiore brings nearly 20 years of book publishing experience — at Dell, St. Martin's, Morrow, Hyperion, and Villard — to his new role as literary agent. Having opened the agency in 1999, he knows — from the inside — what publishers look for and how to create effective, lucrative submission packages. DeFiore's expertise is in popular fiction and commercial nonfiction. Mark Roy joined the company in March, bringing with him past agency and international experience.

Agent: Brian DeFiore.

Fifteen percent commission; represents fiction, commercial and suspense, and nonfiction, biography, business, cooking, entertainment, health, inspiration, sports, and psychology. Associate: Mark Roy represents fiction (literary and suspense) and nonfiction (business, cooking, entertainment, fitness, gay and lesbian, health, inspiration, pop culture, psychology, religion, and spirituality). No reader's fees. Contact by query letter or e-mail — no e-mail attachments, please. In your query, describe the book and the author's credentials including educational, employment and/or life experience that figures into the writing of the book; author/agent contract preferred.

Recent deals: *The Mailroom: Big Dreams and Raw Ambition in Hollywood's Boot Camp* by David Rensin (Ballantine); *Life is More than Just Your Cell Phone* by Loretta LaRoche (Broadway Books); *Parenting the Extreme Teenager* by Scott Sells, Ph.D. (St. Martin's); and *Us Vs. Them: An Oral History of the Ryder Cup* by Robin McMillan (HarperCollins).

Advice to first-time writers: Do your homework. Make sure to submit your material only when it's in the best shape you are capable of and then make sure to submit it to people whose experience indicates they're interested and skilled in handling material in your subject are. The cover letter/query letter is critical. Keep in mind that the introductory letter is the first chance you have to demonstrate your persuasiveness as a writer, and the agent is looking at it that way. Craft the letter to prove your highest level of sophistication, professionalism, and creativity.

Sandra Dijkstra Literary Agency

1155 Camino del Mar, Suite 515-C, Del Mar, CA, 92014; 858-755-3115; fax 858-794-2822.

Sandra Dijkstra is a Bronx native who followed her academic inclinations out West to the University of San Diego, where she received a Ph.D. in French literature and later taught. Her career as an agent started in 1978 as an informal effort to help her fellow professors place their work with publishers. Her agency was formally established in 1983 and since then, Sandy, as she is known in the business, has emerged as a major literary presence, with high-profile clients such as Amy Tan and Lisa See.

Agents: Sandra Dijkstra.

Member of AAR; 15 percent commission, domestic and 20 percent foreign; represents literary and commercial fiction and nonfiction; no westerns, romances or poetry; accepts query letters, proposals, and partial manuscript with synopsis and SASE; fees charged for photocoping and postage; author/agent contract required.

Recently published titles represented by the Sandra Dijkstra Literary Agency: *Sister of My Heart* by Chitra Divakaruni (Doubleday, 1999); *Stiffed: The Betrayal of the American Man* by Susan Faludi (Morrow, 1999); *Unwanted Company* by Barbara Seranella (HarperCollins, 2000); and *Tough Cookie* by Diane Mott Davidson (Bantam, 2000).

Joy Harris Literary Agency

156 Fifth Ave., Suite 617, New York, NY 10010; 212-924-6269; fax 212-924-6609; e-mail `jhlitagent@aol.com` or `gem.office@jhlitagent.com`.

Formerly known as the Lantz-Harris Agency, Joy Harris took over the business in 1993, when the beloved Robby Lantz retired from author representation. Boasting an eclectic list, weighted to the literary side, the agency currently represents approximately 100 clients including Jeffrey Kluger, Judy Mercer, Whitney Otto, Mark Singer, and Lawrence Leamer.

Agents: Joy Harris and Leslie Daniels.

Member of the AAR; represents general nonfiction — everything from serious biography to popular culture — and fiction, both literary and commercial;

query first with SASE; does not accept unsolicited proposals or manuscripts; charges for photocopies and overseas mailings; standard 15 percent commission.

Recently published works represented by the Joy Harris Literary Agency: *Ahab's Wife* by Sena Jeter Naslund (William Morrow, 1999; HarperPerenial, 2000); and *Remembering Blue* by Connie May Fowler (Doubleday, 2000).

Advice for first-time writers: Be serious about your work and have fun at it.

Jeff Herman Agency, Inc.

332 Bleecker St., New York, NY 10014; 212-941-0540; fax 212-941-0614; e-mail jeff@jeffjerman.com; Web site www.jeffherman.com.

In 1987, while still in his twenties, Jeff Herman founded The Jeff Herman Agency, Inc. With its emphasis on nonfiction, the agency has expanded rapidly since its beginning and currently represents approximately 100 clients including Dave Pelzer, Mark Victor Hansen, and Jack Canfield.

In addition to agenting, Jeff Herman is also the author of several books of special interest to writers. His annual publication, *Writer's Guide to Book Editors, Publishers, and Literary Agents* (Prima, 2000), is one of the most useful writers' resources on the market.

Agents: Jeff Herman, Deborah Levine Herman, and Amanda White.

AAR Member; 15 percent commission; accepts query letters and proposals; unsolicited manuscripts are not appreciated; prefers to work with an author/agent contract; represents all areas of adult nonfiction.

Recently published works represented by the Jeff Herman Literary Agency: *A Man Named Dave* by Dave Pelzer (Dutton, 1999) and *A Setback is a Setup for a Comeback* by Willie Jolley (St. Martin's Press, 1999).

Advice for first-time writers: Always assume that you will get published.

Ellen Levine Literary Agency, Inc.

15 East 26th Street, Suite 1801, New York, NY 10010-1505; 212-889-0620; fax 212-725-4501.

Ellen Levine worked her way up the publishing ladder, editing literary writers before becoming a literary agent. As an agent, she worked at two agencies — Paul Reynolds and Curtis Brown — before founding her own agency in 1980.

Strong in literary and commercial fiction, commercial and narrative nonfiction, and politics, the agency's stellar client list includes Christopher Andersen, Michael Gross, Garrison Keillor, Russell Banks, Cristina Garcia, Mary Morris, Todd Gitlin, Carolyn Heilbrun (Amanda Cross), Colette Dowling, Michael Ondaatje, and Alex Shoumatoff.

Agents: Ellen Levine, Diana Finch, Elizabeth Kaplan, and Louise Quayle.

Member AAR; 15 percent commission; queries accepted; no unsolicited proposals or manuscripts; no author/agent contract required; charges for photocopying, galleys, and books for foreign submissions; represents mainstream fiction and nonfiction.

Recently published titles represented by the Ellen Levine Literacy Agency: *Anil's Ghost* by Michael Ondaatje (Knopf, 2000); *The Angel on the Roof* by Russell Banks (HarperCollins, 2000); *The Frailty Myth* by Colette Dowling (Random House, 2000); *The Day John Died* by Christopher Andersen (Morrow, 2000); and *Losing Julia* by Jonathan Hull (Delacorte, 2000).

Advice for first-time writers: Write, don't phone, and always include an SASE.

James Levine Communications, Inc.

307 Seventh Avenue, Suite 1906, New York, NY 10001; 212-337-0934; fax 212-337-0948; e-mail `jlevine@jameslevine.com`. Web site `www.jameslevine.com`.

Jim Levine loves putting people, ideas, and money together. He's been doing it his entire adult life in both the not-for-profit and academic sectors before opening his literary agency in 1989. Jim's agency specializes in a wide range of nonfiction topics with approximately 150 clients including Geoff Moore, CNBC, Larry Dossey, The Onion, and Patricia Seybold.

Agents: James A Levine, Arielle Eckstut, and Daniel Greenberg.

Member AAR; 15 percent commission; represents such nonfiction topics as business, psychology, parenting, narrative nonfiction, fiction, technology, medical, how-to, cookbooks, and spirituality; query letters only accepted by electronic submission on Web site at `www.jameslevine.com`; no unsolicited proposals or manuscripts accepted; fees charged for photocopies and postage; author/agent contract required.

Recent published works represented by James Levine Communications: *Living on the Faultline* by Geoffrey Moore (HarperBusiness, 2000); *The Onion's Finest News Reporting, Vol 1* by Scott Dikkers and the Staff at The Onion (Three Rivers Press, 2000); *The Complete Cancer Survival Guide* by Peter Teeley and Philip Bashe (Main Street Books, 2000); *Lipshtick* by

Gwen Macsai (HarperCollins, 2000); and *Power Plays: Shakespeare's Guide to Leadership and Management* by John Whitney and Tina Packer (Simon & Schuster, 2000).

Advice for first-time writers: It's a good idea to be published in a magazine, journal, or newspaper or else to have some sort of platform. This adds a great deal of support in taking you on and presenting your manuscript, be it fiction or nonfiction, to a potential publishing house. Also, it helps to be a good speaker, someone who is comfortable giving lectures, workshops, or readings on your particular work/manuscript.

Lowenstein Associates, Inc.

121 West 27 Street, Suite 601, New York, NY 10001; 212-206-1630; fax 212-727-0280.

Barbara Lowenstein is a notoriously hard-edged negotiator and one of the most admired nonfiction experts in the business. She is also known as one of the most physically fit agents in the business. Barbara got her start as a secretary at the Sterling Lord Agency and also served a stint at the marketing powerhouse of Walter Zacharias (CEO of Kensington Publishing) before founding her own literary agency in 1976. Lowenstein Associates specializes in major health and spirituality books as well as other kinds of high-quality nonfiction and both commercial and literary fiction. It currently represents approximately 125 clients including Perri O'Shaughnessy, Gina Nahai, Deborah Crombie, Jan Burke, Leslie Glass, and award-winning journalist Melinda Blau.

Agents: Barbara Lowenstein, Eileen Cope, Dorian Karchmar, and Nancy Yost.

Member of AAR; 15 percent commission; represents fiction — literary and commercial — and many nonfiction areas including relationships, pop-culture, self-help, spiritual, business, travel adventure and travel narrative, ethnic, historical, suspense, biography, current affairs, narrative nonfiction, gay and lesbian, health, history, and social issues. No children's or young adult. Query with SASE for nonfiction. For fiction, include outline and first chapter with SASE. No SASE, no response. The agency charges for photocopies and international postage. Author/agent contract required.

Recently published works represented by Lowenstein Associates: *Moonlight on the Avenue of Faith* by Gina Nahai (Harcourt Brace, 1999; Washington Square Press, 2000); *Move to Strike* by Perri O'Shaughnessy (Delacorte, 2000); *Smart vs. Pretty* by Valerie Frankel (Avon, 2000); *Getting Everything You Can Out of All You've Got* by Jay Abraham (St. Martin's Press, 2000); *Is Your Thyroid Making You Fat* by Sanford Siegal, M.D. (Warner Books, 2000); *Emotional Alchemy* by Tara Bennett-Goleman (Harmony Books, 2000); and *The Mozart Effect for Children* by Dan Campbell (William Morrow, 2000).

Advice for first-time writers: Do your homework and know the market you are writing for before sending material to agents.

Margret McBride Literary Agency

San Diego office: 7744 Fay Avenue, Suite 201, La Jolla, CA 92037; 858-454-1550; fax 858-454-2156; e-mail `staff@mcbridelit.com`. *New York office:* 255 East 49 Street, New York, NY 10017. Mail all submissions with SASE to La Jolla office; submissions are not accepted via e-mail or fax.

Margret McBride began her publishing career in the publicity department of Warner Books. She then relocated to the San Diego area, and in 1980, established her literary agency. A year later, she burst back on the New York scene with a new book by two San Diego writers, *The One Minute Manager,* by Ken Blanchard and Spencer Johnson, (Morrow, 1982), one of the best-selling books of the decade. She now represents approximately 50 clients.

Agents: Margret McBride.

Member AAR; standard 15 percent commission; represents commercial fiction and nonfiction and business; query letters and proposals accepted; no unsolicited manuscripts; no author/agent contract required; fees charged for overnight delivery and photocopying of projects for submission to publishers, if not provided by clients.

Recently published works represented by the Margret McBride Literary Agency: *Special Circumstances* by Sheldon Siegel (Bantam, Doubleday, Dell, 2000); *Instant Emotional Healing* by Dr. Peter Lambrou and Dr. George Pratt (Broadway Books, 2000); *Eat Fat, Be Healthy* by Matthew Bayan (Scribner, 2000); *Winning Ways* by Dick Lyles (Putnam, 2000); *Fish! A Remarkable Way to Boost Morale and Improve Results* by Stephen C. Lundin Ph D, Harry Paul and John Chriestensen (Hyperion, 2000); and *Leadership By The Book* by Ken Blanchard, Bill Hybels and Phil Hodges (William Morrow, 1999).

Advice for first-time writers: Continue sending your query letter to agents until you find the right one for the project.

Carol Mann Agency

55 Fifth Ave., New York, NY 10003; 212-206-5635; fax 212-675-4809; e-mail `cmla55@aol.com` (no queries by e-mail).

Carol Mann got her start in publishing in the mid-'70s at Avon Books — at that time a hotbed of literary creativity. She founded her own literary agency in 1977 and has built a distinguished list of literary fiction and literary and commercial nonfiction. It currently represents approximately 100 clients including Paul Auster, Judith Wallerstein, Shelby Steele, Fox Butterfield, Lorraine Johnson-Coleman, and James Tobin.

Agents: Carol Mann, Gareth Esersky, and Jim Fitzgerald.

Member AAR; standard 15 percent commission; best way to contact is by query letter with SASE; no unsolicited manuscripts accepted; represents general nonfiction and literary fiction. No genre fiction, please.

Recent published works represented by the Carol Mann Agency: *Timbuktu* by Paul Auster (Henry Holt, 1999; Picador USA, 2000); *Mastering the Zone* by Barry Sears (HarperCollins, 1996); *Protein Power* by Drs. Michael and Mary Dan Eades (Warner Books, 2000); *A General Theory of Love* by Drs. Thomas Lewis, Fari Amini, and Richard Lannon (Random House, 2000).

Jean V. Naggar Literary Agency

216 East 75 Street, Suite 1-E, New York, NY 10021; 212-794-1082

Jean Naggar pursued a brief editorial career before striking off in 1975 as an agent and establishing her own agency in 1978. The meteoric success of client Jean Auel with *Clan of the Cave Bear* (Crown, 1980) sealed the success of her agency. The agency has subsequently launched many notable writers including Karleen Koen, Mary McGarry Morris, and Phillip Margolin.

Agents: Jean Naggar, Frances Kuffel, and Alice Tasman.

Member and past president of the AAR; member of Women's Media Group and Women's Forum; 15 percent commission, domestic, 20 percent foreign; represents literary and mainstream fiction, biography, science and psychology; query first with SASE. No unsolicited proposals or manuscripts. Author/agent contract required.

Recently published works represented by the Jean V. Naggar Literary Agency: *The Missing Moment* by Robert Pollack (Houghton Mifflin, 1999); *Hotel Alleluia* by Lucinda Roy (HarperCollins, 2000); *Wild Justice* by Phillip Margolin (HarperCollins, 2000); *Fiona Range* by Mary McGarry Morris (Viking-Penguin, 2000); and *Conversations With Fear* by Mermer Blakeslee (Viking-Penquin, 2000).

Advice for first-time writers: Present as polished and self-edited a manuscript as possible because you will have one chance only to make it to a particular agent's list. Research agents carefully and do not ask them to sell themselves to you.

The Palmer and Dodge Agency

One Beacon Street, Boston, MA 02108; 617-573-0609; fax 617-227-4420; e-mail swilson@palmerdodge.com.

Palmer and Dodge LLP is one of Boston's older law firms founded in 1887. John Taylor "Ike" Williams joined the firm in 1983 as cochair of its Publishing and Entertainment Group and in 1990 formed its adjunct literary and dramatic rights agency. In the almost ten years since its establishment, under Ike and its managing director Jill Kneerim, the agency has grown substantially to include such major authors as Dr. Susan Love, Howard Gardner, Brad Meltzer, Elizabeth Marshall Thomas, Norris Church Mailer, Reverend Peter J. Gomes, Dr. Edward Hallowell, Edward O. Wilson, Michael Dertouzos, and Lawrence Schiller and a number of leading screenplay writers such as Ernest Thompson, Robert Brustein, Michael Mailer, and Charles Marowitz. It remains the only literary and dramatic rights agency within a major U.S. law firm. Its agency clients receive both agency and relevant legal services for the traditional agents fee of 15 percent.

Literary agents: Ike Williams, Jill Kneerim, and Lindsey Shaw.

Dramatic agents: Ike Williams and Elaine Rogers.

15 percent commission, which includes legal services; fees can vary on dramatic rights projects; represents adult nonfiction and fiction; query letters accepted; unsolicited proposals and manuscripts only accepted with references or prior query letter; author/agent contract required.

Recently published works represented by The Palmer and Dodge Agency: *All Souls* by Michael Patrick MacDonald (Beacon Press 1999; Ballantine Books 2000); *Chinese Cinderella* by Adeline Yen Mah (Dell, 1999); *The Windchill Summer* by Norris Church Mailer (Random House, 2000); *Social Life of Dogs: The Grace of Canine Company* by Marshall Thomas (Simon & Schuster 2000); and *Some Things That Stay* by Sarah Willis (Farrar, Straus & Giroux, 2000).

Aaron Priest Literary Agency, Inc.

708 Third Avenue, 23rd Floor, New York, NY 10017; 212-818-0344; fax 212-573-9417.

Aaron Priest founded his agency in 1974 after 14 years as a Doubleday sales rep first in upstate New York and then in Dallas. His agency quickly rose to prominence with the success of several early clients, notably Erma Bombeck.

Molly Friedrich, whom Priest remembered as an energetic publicist at Doubleday, came on board in 1978 to help Priest manage his growing agency. Before long, Friedrich, daughter of author Otto Friedrich, had a huge clientele of her own. Both Priest and Friedrich, with their enviable eye for fiction, have built one of the most formidable client lists in the industry including but by no means limited to Jane Smiley, Sue Grafton, Terry McMillan, Robert James Waller, David Baldacci, Melissa Bank, and Frank McCourt.

Member of the AAR; represents mainstream fiction and nonfiction; query with SASE; no unsolicited proposals or manuscripts — they are returned unread. 15 percent commission; Charges for photocopying and foreign postage; No author/agent contract required.

Agents: Aaron M. Priest, Molly Friedrich, and Lisa Erbach Vance.

Recently published works represented by the Aaron Priest Literary Agency: *'Tis* by Frank McCourt (Scribner, 1999); *O is for Outlaw* by Sue Grafton (Henry Holt, 1999); *Saving Faith* by David Baldacci (Warner Books, 1999); *LA Reqieum* by Robert Crais (Doubleday, 1999; Ballantine Books, 2000); and *Moment of Truth* by Lisa Scottoline (HarperCollins, 2000).

Advice for first-time writers: Don't be put off by the people who criticize your work.

Helen Rees Literary Agency

123 North Washington Street, 5th Floor, Boston, MA 02114; 617-723-5232 ext. 233; fax 617-723-5211.

Helen Rees founded her Boston agency in 1981. Since then she has handled a number of bestsellers, including *Chutzpah* by Alan M. Dershowitz (Little Brown, 1991), *Reengineering the Corporation* by Michael Hammer and Jim Champy (HarperBusiness, 1993), and *The Discipline of Market Leaders* by Michael Treacy and Fredrik Wiersma (Addison-Wesley, 1995). She is ideally located to attract clients from the distinguished universities in the Boston area. Currently representing about 50 clients, her office is located in an attractively renovated loft space on Washington Street near the docks in Boston.

Agents: Helen Rees and Barbara Rifkind.

Member of AAR and PEN; 15 percent commission; represents mainstream fiction, nonfiction, and business; accepts query letters and unsolicited proposals; no unsolicited manuscripts; no author/agent contract required.

Recently published works represented by the Helen Rees Literary Agency: *The Arc of Ambition* by James Champy and Nitin Nohria (Perseus Books,

2000); *Just Revenge* by Alan M. Dershowitz (Warner Books, 1999); and *The Autobiography of Joseph Stalin* by Richard Lourie (Counterpoint, 1999).

Advice for first-time writers: One of the most difficult tasks an agent has is offering advice to first-time writers. This is true because an agent knows how difficult the path can be and because an agent appreciates the talent and skill involved in the writing process. Having said this, my advice falls into two buckets. One — be persistent and organized in your writing. Two — learn how to listen to a few select critics who are qualified readers, because they can guide you . . . and you will profit from their insights.

Sagalyn Literary Agency

4825 Bethesda Ave., Suite 302, Bethesda, MD, 20814; 301-718-6440; fax 301-718-6444.

Founded in 1981 by Raphael Sagalyn, a Massachusetts native who had already worked in book publishing at Pocket Books and Little Brown before deciding to try his luck in Washington, D.C., a news media center with surprisingly light literary representation. Sagalyn's client list is strong on first-rate journalists and political writers, as well as business writers and academics. His first major hit, *Megatrends*, was also a mega-bestseller and quickly launched the Sagalyn Agency on the high road to success.

Agents: Raphael Sagalyn.

Member AAR; represents adult fiction and nonfiction, especially science, business, social and political history; send query letter to `agency@sagalyn.com`.

Recently published works represented by the Sagalyn Agency: *When Pride Still Mattered* by David Maraniss (Simon & Schuster, 1999, Touchstone Books, 2000); *NonZero* by Robert Wright (Pantheon Books, 1999); *Future Wealth* by Stan Davis and Chris Meyer (Harvard Business School Press, 2000); and *The Visionary's Handbook* by Watts Wacker and Jim Taylor (HarperCollins, 1999)

Advice for first-time writers: Write the perfect cover letter.

Witherspoon Associates, Inc.

235 East 31st Street, New York, NY 10016; 212-889-8626; fax 212-696-0650.

In 1991, after several years as an agent at the John Brockman Agency, Kim Witherspoon opened her own literary agency. While her client list is truly eclectic, ranging from novelist Robert Olen Butler to ex-Spice Girl Geri Halliwell, she is perhaps best known for her work with serious writers of fiction; in the last year she placed novels by zine writer Pagan Kennedy, first novelist Jeffrey Lent, and many others.

Agents: Kim Witherspoon.

15 percent commission, domestic, 20 percent foreign; accepts query letter by mail with SASE; no unsolicited proposals or manuscripts; charges for photocopying, postage, and so on; author/agent contract required.

Recently published works represented by Witherspoon Associates: *Mr. Spaceman* by Robert Olen Butler (Grove, 2000); *The Best Thing I Ever Tasted* by Sallie Tisdale (Riverhead, 2000); *Lying: A Metaphorical Memoir* by Lauren Slater (Random House, 2000); and *In the Fall* by Jeffrey Lent (Grove, 2000).

Writers' Representatives, Inc.

116 West 14th Street, 11th Floor, New York, NY 10011-7305; 212-620-9009; fax 212-620-0023; e-mail `transom@writersreps.com`; Web site `www.writersreps.com`.

This thriving downtown agency was founded in 1985 by Glen Hartley, a seasoned marketing veteran from Harper & Row, and his attorney wife, Lynn Chu. Writers' Representatives handles a broad range of high-quality clients, including bestselling polymath Harold Bloom, the medical National Book Award winner-writer Sherwin Nuland, and the Pulitzer Prize-winning journalist Manuela Hoelterhoff. They have also represented many politicians, notably Newt Gingrich, and political commentators like Laura Ingraham.

Agents: Glen Hartley and Lynn Chu.

Fifteen percent commission; no reader's fees; accepts query letters with SASE; prefers manuscript submissions to synopses; charges for photocopying, postage, and so on.

Recently published works represented by Writers' Representatives: *Bobos in Paradise: The New Upper Class and How They Got That Way* by David Brooks, (Simon & Schuster, 2000); *From Dawn to Decadence* by Jacques Barzun (HarperCollins, 2000); *Why We Buy: The Science of Shopping* by Paco Underhill (Simon & Schuster, 1999, Touchstone 2000); and *How to Read and Why* by Harold Bloom (Scribner, 2000).

The Writers Shop

101 Fifth Avenue, New York, NY 10003; 212-255-6515; fax 212-691-9418; e-mail virginia@thewritersshssop.com jennifer@thewritersshop.com jay@thewritershop.com.

What for 30 years was The Virginia Barber Literary Agency has entered the new millennium as The Writers Shop headed by partners Virginia Barber and Jennifer Rudolph Walsh. Already a hotbed of literary success, the addition of Jennifer Rudolph Walsh as partner and copresident ensures the agency of long standing success.

Established in 1970, the agency currently represents 107 clients including Rosellen Brown, Alice Munro, Anne Rivers Siddons, Anita Shreve, Peter Mayle, Kathy Reichs, and Ethan Hawke.

Member of AAR; 15 percent commission; Represents general fiction and nonfiction. No horror, fantasy, children's, young adult, or poetry;accepts query letters with SASE or via e-mail to query@thewritersshop.com and unsolicited proposals though no more than 20 pages; No unsolicited manuscripts; Author/agent contract required.

Agents: Virginia Barber, Jennifer Rudolph Walsh, and Jay Mandel.

Wylie Agency, Inc.

250 West 57 Street, Suite 2114, New York, NY 10107; 212-246-0069; fax 212-586-8953; e-mail mail@wylieagency.com.

The Wylie Agency, one of the few smaller agencies with an active office in London as well as New York, is run by Andrew Wylie. The son of a distinguished editor at Houghton Mifflin and a poet in his own right, Wylie joined the now disbanded literary agency of the late John Cushman in the early '80s. When Wylie opened his own agency in the late '80s, many of the most established literary writers on both sides of the Atlantic flocked to his stable. His star-studded client list ranges from distinguished novelists (Salman Rushdie and Philip Roth) to photographers (Richard Avedon), biographers (Edmund Morris), and journalists (James Atlas and Bryan Burrough).

Agents: Andrew Wylie, Sarah Chalfant, and Jeffrey Posternack.

Fifteen percent commission; no readers fees; no unsolicited proposals or manuscripts accepted; new clients mainly on a referral basis; no author/agent contract required.

Recently published works represented by the Wylie Agency: *The Human Stain* by Philip Roth (Houghton Mifflin, 2000); *The Ground Beneath Her Feet* by Salmon Rushdie (Picador USA, 2000); and *Bellow: A Biography* by James Atlas (Random House, 2000).

Chapter 13

Publishing Outside of the Box

In This Chapter

- Understanding the self-publishing options
- Mastering online publishing: e-books, print on demand services, and bookselling sites
- Working with a packager
- Using a vanity press

Today, you have several attractive alternatives to the traditional publishing route. Publishing a book on your own, either online or in print form, is easier and more profitable than ever. You can work with a book packager who hires all kinds of experts to orchestrate the creation of a book and also sells it to a publishing firm, or you can self-publish in print or electronically. Online publishing is booming, with online booksellers, e-book publishers, and traditional publishers vying for position in a constantly expanding world of downloadable books.

In this chapter, I introduce you to the whole universe of unconventional publishing options, from the traditional packagers, printers, and vanity houses, to the attractive innovations of publishing on the Internet.

Commercial Publishing Isn't the Only Way

Commercial publishing isn't right for everyone. Just to get your foot in the door, you need to learn a new skill that's quite different from writing a book — the art of book proposal writing. For many writers, it's much more practical to skip this step — along with the time-consuming task of approaching agents and publishers — and get the book published on your own. In fact, for certain books, it's completely unnecessary to go through a commercial publishing company. For example, if you're writing a family history, or the story of your life, or a collection of family or regional recipes, a commercial publisher probably won't be interested. You're much better off writing and distributing the book yourself and perhaps later finding a publisher.

The One-Minute story

In 1981, two very talented San Diego authors named Ken Blanchard and Spencer Johnson decided to work together on a book. They had developed an exciting set of ideas about how managers could achieve much better results. And they hit on an innovative new format for presenting their ideas. Instead of the conventional dry exposition of instructions, they decided to convey their ideas in the form of a short story or parable.

At the time, Ken Blanchard was a popular business lecturer, offering management seminars that taught communication and leadership skills to business people. Spencer Johnson had also written several published books. Together they decided to hire a local printer to produce a limited quantity of their book to sell at the seminars or distribute to seminar attendees. They arranged to print several thousand copies of their new book, which they titled *The One Minute Manager.*

Over the coming months, they conducted several seminars with their new book as the text. They asked readers for feedback on the book, and they incorporated many of these comments to make their story more powerful. When they ran out of books, they produced a second edition and again solicited feedback from seminar attendees who read the book.

After six months and several small print runs, the authors had sold nearly 20,000 copies of this "workshop" edition of *The One-Minute Manager.* They had also accumulated many enthusiastic comments from readers who benefited from the book's simple, yet innovative message.

Armed with these endorsements and copies of the self-published edition, Spencer Johnson and their agent, Margret McBride, met with publishers in New York because Ken Blanchard was occupied with his busy speaking schedule. The publishers not only liked the book, the number of copies Johnson and Blanchard had sold on their own impressed them. They were also impressed by the endorsements the authors had received, including comments from several key business leaders. As a result, there was a spirited auction, and in 1981 William Morrow acquired the book for a six-figure advance.

Today, nearly 20 years and over 12 million copies later, *The One-Minute Manager* (Morrow, 1982) is one of the best-selling management books of all time. Both Blanchard and Johnson have each written several new best-sellers, alone and together. Each time, they have produced test versions of their books, in order to get feedback and make refinements, before approaching publishers.

That's what happened to Ken Blanchard and Spencer Johnson with their first collaboration, *The One-Minute Manager* (see sidebar). Every year, hundreds of cookbooks, local travel and restaurant guides, highly targeted reference books, poetry collections, literary novels, and business manuals are printed and distributed privately. Of these, a surprisingly large number gradually find a big enough audience to attract the attention of book publishers. Many of these wonderful books, like Richard Bolles' *What Color is Your Parachute* or J. Jackson Brown's *Life's Little Instruction Book,* would never have seen the light of day if the authors had waited for a publishing company to offer them a contract. Instead they self-published, and gained such a large audience that publishing companies sought them out. *Life's Little Instruction Book* (Rutledge Hill Press, 1991) has sold over five million copies, and *What Color is Your Parachute* (Ten Speed Press, 1970) has sold well over ten million copies.

Whether you choose to self-publish in printed form, or on the Web, the story of *The One-Minute Manager* illustrates several benefits of self-publishing. First, it's important to get your book in front of readers, especially readers who care about or can benefit from the content. Then, you can solicit constructive feedback from these readers and use that information to improve the book in subsequent printings. Additionally, by self-publishing, you can distribute copies to friends, customers, business associates, and start developing an audience for your ideas.

The Advantages of Self-Publishing

If you choose to self-publish your book, you are in excellent company. William Blake, Virginia Woolf, Mark Twain, and many other literary giants — as well as plenty of today's best-selling writers — have opted to self-publish. Self-publishers enjoy two particularly powerful advantages.

Money

The financial benefits of self-publishing can be compelling. A commercial publishing company pays you a set standard royalty that works on a sliding scale: for hardcovers, it's from 10 percent to 15 percent, and on trade paperbacks it's a flat 7.5 percent (see Chapter 16). What this means is that your share of a $20 hardcover is 10 percent for the first 5,000 copies sold; 12.5 percent for the next 5,000; and 15 percent on all copies sold thereafter. If you sell 10,000 hardcovers, your royalty earning is $22,500. On a trade paperback book priced at say $15, your royalty earning is $1.13 per copy or $11,300 if you sell 10,000 copies.

Say that you self-publish the same book — your revenue picture improves dramatically. Assuming that your book is a standard size and format containing no illustrations, you should be able to find a printer who can produce a run of 10,000 hardcover copies for between $2 and $3 per copy in hardcover and trade paperbacks for between $1.50 and $2.50. If you sell the same 10,000 copies through booksellers and wholesalers such as Ingram or Baker and Taylor, Barnes and Noble, or Amazon.com, your total revenue on hardcovers is approximately half of the list price or $100,000, and on trade paperbacks it's about $75,000. If you sell the book directly to consumers, your revenue increases to approximately $200,000 on hardcovers and $150,000 on trade paperbacks. What this means is that after the cost of goods is deducted from your revenues, the net income is still very high. Ten thousand hardcovers sold via bookstores puts $70,000 into your pocket ($100,000 minus $30,000); ten thousand paperbacks nets you $50,000 ($75,000 minus $25,000).

In other words, if you're able to successfully sell your self-published book, you stand to earn twice as much as you can earn via a book publisher.

Control

Another great feature of self-publishing is that you have complete control over each aspect of your book's creation. If you work with a commercial publisher, you are ceding a great deal of control to them. The publisher edits and copy edits your manuscript, asking for changes and revisions. Most publishers retain control over the final title of your book, the jacket design, and the book's overall design. They dictate the book's production schedule and overall production specifications for the book. They also decide on the format and retail price for your book, as well as the quantity they'll print and where the book is distributed.

By contrast, if you self-publish your book, you are the final arbiter of every publishing question, including title and cover design, type design, production specifications, and schedule. You determine the format of your book, the price, and the size of each printing. You plan the marketing strategy and make arrangements with retailers to display your book.

The Disadvantages of Self-Publishing

If there were no disadvantages, everyone would self-publish. Before deciding to self-publish, consider these two potential drawbacks.

Money

In order to self-publish, even utilizing the print on demand (see the "Print on Demand" section, later in this chapter) capacities of the new e-publishers, you need cash. It costs at least $15,000 to produce 5,000 hardcover copies of a book. You'll also have to pay for shipping and fulfillment, in addition to the cost of designing and typesetting the book, as well as marketing (see "Self-Publishing, Step by Step" for all that is entailed in these items). Design, production, fulfillment, and marketing charges can increase that $15,000 initial investment by $5,000 or more. On top of all this, a self-published author does not receive an advance for expenses while writing and publishing the book.

Print on demand and e-book publication is much less capital intensive — as low as $100 to post an e-book at some sites (see "Print on demand" section) — and for most first-timers, it's a much more sensible way to get your feet wet in the sea of self-publishing.

Celestine Prophesy

The story of the *Celestine Prophesy* is one of the most famous in the annals of self-publishing. The author, James Redfield, wrote the book and arranged to produce a small printing through a local printer. He distributed the book to local booksellers out of the trunk of his own car. Gradually, word of mouth about the book began to build and, over several years and many print runs, he managed to sell 80,000 copies. As word of this amazing feat began to spread via bookseller gossip, New York publishers took notice, and eventually Warner Books purchased the rights to publish a new edition of *The Celestine Prophesy* in 1993. The book became a national bestseller, selling over five million copies.

Time and hard work

If you self-publish, you are responsible for each and every facet of your book's creation: from writing, to layout and design, to marketing, to distribution — which includes pitching your book to booksellers, packing books in jiffy bags or boxes, and even clearing credit-card orders. These varied functions take time to learn and perform successfully. They also require a great deal of hard work.

You may be the type of person who enjoys learning and accomplishing a lot of different tasks. But if you don't want to put in the time and effort required to perform such varied functions as order fulfillment, customer service, accounting, designing, packaging, and so on, then self-publishing probably isn't for you.

Self-Publishing, Step by Step

The steps involved in self-publishing are similar to those carried out by the various departments at a commercial publishing company (see Chapter 17). The major difference is that you are in charge of each step. At first, the process may seem complex and daunting, but once you produce your own book, you'll feel an exhilarating sense of accomplishment.

Study the overview I present here to get a sense for what's involved. If you decide to self-publish, consult one of the excellent, in-depth manuals on self-publication such as *How to Get Happily Published* written, and originally self-published by Judith Appelbaum (HarperPerennial, 1998), *The Complete Self-Publishing Handbook* by David M. Brownstone and Irene M. Franck (Plume, 1999), or *The Self-Publishing Manual,* written and self-published by Dan Poynter (Poynter, 1999). At each step along the way, you have a choice — engage the services of a freelancer to help or do it yourself.

Write the book

If you have a complete manuscript of the book you want to publish, skip to the next step. If not, the first step is to write your book. If you don't have the time or ability to write the manuscript yourself, explore the options for hiring a collaborator, co-author, or ghostwriter (see Chapter 3). If you intend to proceed on your own, start with a detailed working outline and then produce a complete draft of the highest possible quality.

Edit the book

Do you have great editorial skills? Can you look objectively at the manuscript you've created? If you have any doubts, consider hiring a freelance editor to help strengthen and improve the manuscript. A professional editor can help with overall structure, content, and market knowledge, providing information on how your book is likely to be perceived by booksellers as well as its target audience of readers.

The best way to find a freelance editor is to look for the editor's name on the acknowledgment page of books similar to yours — most authors thank their editors in the acknowledgements. Often these editors — though they are employed by a publishing firm — are willing to work on outside editing jobs for a fee. And if not — because some editors are prohibited to take on freelance assignments — they may be able to recommend a good freelance editor. Additionally, you can consult the *Literary Market Place* under the "freelance editor" section. Be sure to obtain references from each freelance editor and check them thoroughly.

The current market rate for qualified book editors is between $50 and $150 per hour. Depending on the state of your manuscript, assume that most editors work at the rate of five to ten pages per hour, making the overall cost of editing a 300-page manuscript run about $3,000.

Produce the book

Producing your own book used to be incredibly expensive because of the astronomical costs involved in manual typesetting — requiring highly trained and skilled typesetters. Today, typesetting and book design are done on desktop computers, bringing book production costs way down. What used to run $20,000 to produce a print run of 5,000 hardcover copies now runs a little more than half that, or $10,000 to $12,000. Included in these costs are typesetting and design, paper, printing, and binding.

Once your manuscript has been written and stored on a disk, you're ready to begin the production process. For each of these services, *Literary Market Place* lists qualified professionals. I recommend that you get references and prices from at least three freelancers in each category.

Copy edit

It's a good idea to engage the skills of a professional copy editor who can correct the grammar, punctuation, and spelling in your manuscript. Copy editors charge about $20 per hour, adding another $800 or so to your total cost. Most copy editors can also proofread, which is the next step in the process.

Typeset

Once your manuscript is copy edited, turn the corrected disk over to a desktop publishing professional who can convert your manuscript into book pages. These first-pass pages should be read carefully to confirm that no new errors were added during the transfer from manuscript to book pages.

Design

Before printing, you need to design a cover for your book. While your own computer can turn out display type, only a professional designer can produce a high-quality, eye-catching jacket design. The going rate for a book jacket design, using a professional designer in New York City, is $1,000 to $3,000, but you're likely to find a high-quality local designer who's willing to undertake the assignment for less.

Print

Printing is the single most expensive item on this list and has the biggest potential for problems. Here are a few tips on how to shop for print:

- **Solicit competing bids:** Get bids from at least three printers — large and small operations — because printing costs can vary widely. The way to solicit bids is with a "request for quotation." Keep in mind that printers each have their own specialty. For example, some printers are expert at printing illustrated books, while others are better at large reference works, or small volumes of poetry. Ask each printer you contact what kinds of jobs they prefer to take on.
- **Ask for feedback:** Because every printer has different equipment, expect the bids to vary. But don't decide on a printer without going back to each one you have a bid from and asking them to recommend a "most economical approach." They may offer suggestions for minor adjustments that could make the job much, much cheaper on their equipment. Ask to see samples of their work and get references.

List your book

In order for booksellers, librarians, and consumers to find your book, it must be registered and listed correctly. Here's a run-down of the critical listings:

- **Obtain an ISBN:** Register your book for an International Standard Book Number by contacting the International Standard Book Numbering Agency, R.R. Bowker, 121 Chanlon Road, New Providence, NJ 07474; 908-665-6770 or have your credit card ready and order an ISBN on R.R. Bowker's Web site at `www.bowker.com/standards/home/isbn`. The fee is $195 per publisher, *not* per book.
- **Obtain a bar code:** To find out about bar codes, which enable most retailers to handle your book, order a copy of *Machine-Readable Coding Guidelines for the Book Industry* ($7.50) from The Book Industry Study Group, 160 Fifth Ave., #625, New York, NY 10010; 212-929-1393. To order online visit their Web site at `www.bisg.org`.
- **Get a Books in Print listing:** To get your book listed in *Books in Print,* the major reference guide of the book industry, contact the ABI (Advanced Book Information) Department, R.R. Bowker, 121 Chanlon Road, New Providence, NJ 07974; or visit their Web site at `www.booksinprint.com`.
- **Register your book with the Library of Congress and obtain Cataloging in Publication data:** The *Cataloging in Publication,* or CIP, information is given by the Library of Congress to books that are deemed, "likely to be widely acquired by the nation's libraries." This information is printed on the copyright page of a book, below the copyright line, and on the book's library catalog card (or control number) used by libraries throughout the country. In order to obtain CIP information, send a copy of your manuscript to the Library of Congress in advance of publication: The Library of Congress, Washington, DC 20540. For further information call 202-707-6345, or check the Web site `www.lcweb.loc.gov`.
- **Register for copyright protection:** To register your book for copyright send a completed application form, a $30 filing fee, and a nonreturnable deposit of the work being registered to The Library of Congress, Register of Copyrights, 101 Independence Avenue, S.E., Washington, DC 20559-600; 202-707-3000. For detailed copyright information check out `www.loc.gov/copyright`.

Set your price

The right price for your book is a balance between what generates the best possible return to you and still presents an attractive value to your customers. You can arrive at the right retail price for your book in two ways. First, you can deduct the price from your cost. Large publishers generally price books at five times cost, with cost being production expenses plus royalty.

Because the royalty is a payment to the author, you may think as a self-publisher that you can afford to price the book slightly lower. But in reality you can't because you don't enjoy any of the benefits of scale that large publishers get: quantity discounts on paper and printing; easier access to national media; a pre-established co-op display fund at all the major booksellers. Instead, you have to invest a great deal to market each copy of each title you publish. And so most self-publishers plan a seven or eight times markup over production costs. If your book costs $3 to manufacture (including editorial and preparation costs as well as paper, printing, and binding), the book should be priced at no less than $21 and possibly as much as $24.

In addition to this cost-based pricing formula, it's a good idea to check out the price of recently published books that are similar in format and content to yours. If most of them are priced far above or below the cost-based price you arrived at, adjust the price to bring it in line with the competition.

Calculate the retail price as soon as you receive production bids. Once your book is designed, printed, and bound, you don't want to discover that in order to turn a reasonable profit, you have to price your book 25 percent above the competition. You'll be crushed. So do your competition survey during the planning stages, and if necessary adjust your production specifications to ensure a book that's competitive at the "seven times cost" principle.

Distribution

Distribution is critical to a book's success. If you have an active mailing list of customers you do business with or fellow members of an organization you belong to, that list could serve as the basis for an effective direct mail sales effort. If you are a speaker or lecturer, sell books at your speaking engagements. If you don't have any opportunity for direct selling, you'll want to develop some of the following channels of distribution:

- **Booksellers:** By latest count, 10,000 independent booksellers are in America, in addition to another 3,000 other bookstore accounts, including national chains such as Barnes and Noble, Borders, and Crown, and regional chains and wholesalers. Independent booksellers are often happy to stock books by local or regional authors, as are some of the major chains — often you can persuade the central buying office to place a few copies in the store located near your home. But for the most part, booksellers prefer to buy books from wholesalers and distributors because booksellers operate on a return system. If they purchase books from you that don't sell, they'll want to be able to return the books for full credit. When dealing directly with distributors, major publishers, and wholesalers, booksellers know they'll be fully credited for returns. They may not be certain about you. While the tradition of returns may seem unreasonable to the self-publisher, there are no exceptions — you must be prepared to accept returns.

- **Mass merchants and warehouse clubs:** These huge institutions account for massive book sales. However, they're extremely selective about their suppliers. The only way to get your book into one of these venues is via a distributor (see next section).
- **Distributors:** Distributors buy books direct from publishers and resell them to wholesalers, retailers, and individuals. Small- and medium-sized publishers who don't have their own sales force rely on distributors to get national visibility for their books — the distributor provides sales reps, a catalog, and a credit rating to facilitate the sales process. In return, the distributor takes a percentage of the revenue received from the bookseller, usually 25 percent to 32 percent of net received. In round numbers, this means that for each copy of your $20 book the distributor sells, the bookseller pays the distributor $10, and the distributor pays you about $7.50.

  To find a reputable distributor ask for recommendations from your local booksellers and other small publishers in your area. Be sure to examine each distributor's catalog carefully, so that you can determine whether your book is a good fit.
- **Wholesalers:** Wholesalers like Baker & Taylor and Ingram buy books in bulk from you at a high discount, 50 percent to 60 percent, and extend a reduced discount to booksellers and libraries, often 40 percent, keeping 10 percent or more as their fee. In exchange for the 10 percent that they keep, they offer fast delivery, wide selection and allow customers to mix and match titles in order to qualify for deeper discounts on bulk orders.

Marketing

When it comes to book marketing, all publishers — including you — start out in the same situation. Except for some direct sales, almost all book sales are driven by word of mouth — people have to say good things about your book to other people, who then go to a bookstore, Web site, or coupon ad and buy the book. In order to build word of mouth, you need to create awareness of the book and find ways to keep putting the book and author in front of people's eyes. This process requires a great deal of hard work, imagination, and money. One great source of low cost/high output marketing ideas is Jay Levinson's *Guerilla Marketing* (Houghton Mifflin, 1998).

Marketing is expensive — large publishers who enjoy the benefits of scale described in the pricing section — allocate $1 per copy sold. Self-publishers, in order to achieve the same effect, need to spend more. If you hope to sell 5,000 copies of your book, a marketing fund of $10,000 is necessary, though I explain ways to reduce this sum in "Advertising" and "Publicity" sections later in this chapter.

If you have $2 per copy or more to invest, consider hiring one of the professional book marketing services listed in *Literary Market Place*. A seasoned publishing pro can guide you to marketing solutions that deliver the most bang for the buck. Solicit quotes from several of these services, compare the cost of each relative to the promised outcome, and take into account the personalities of the people who would be working with you from each service.

Promotion

Promotion is the part of the book's marketing mix that you don't actually pay for, like reviews, radio, and TV interviews, and more.

The book's jacket

The jacket is the single most important piece in any book's marketing plan; sometimes it's the only piece. The most crucial element of the jacket is the title — devote attention and talent to coming up with exactly the right title and then concentrate on a jacket design that highlights this title. Books with a great title and eye-catching jacket start selling from the day they arrive in stores, long before any other marketing has a chance to spur sales.

Other key elements of a book jacket are the flap copy, the *back ad,* which is what insiders call the back of the book's jacket, and the author bio, which usually appears at the bottom of the back flap.

The purpose of your book's jacket and title is to entice customers into picking up your book; the purpose of the flaps is to persuade the customer to buy the book or at least to open and read some of it. Endorsements from celebrities that appear on the jacket expedite this process. In fact, commercial publishers spend a great deal of time and energy securing celebrity endorsements for books. I urge you to do the same.

If you know a celebrity and feel comfortable asking whether he or she would be willing to provide an endorsement, by all means ask. If you don't know the celebrity you hope to get an endorsement from, then call the celebrity's TV station, movie studio, or book publisher to obtain a contact person to send a copy of the book to — either a bound galley of the book or a bound manuscript copy — to along with a persuasive cover letter asking for an endorsement (see Chapter 19 for a sample letter).

Reviews

Review coverage is vital in the marketing of any book; good reviews build terrific word of mouth for a book. And it's important that these reviews appear as close to publication date as possible. So start planning your publication schedule as soon as you have a production schedule from your printer. Pub date is usually set for eight weeks after books are printed and bound, which allows enough time for books to be shipped to bookstores, and reviewers to read and review the book.

To solicit reviews, you need to write a press release, which is a one-page sales description of the book, including an author bio as well as basic information such as the book's price, the publication date, and any endearments or advance reviews you've received on the book. A well-written press release is often used by newspapers and magazines as the basis for their review of your book. So it's worth devoting time to crafting this one-page press release. At many publishers, the press release for first novels is printed in the form of a postcard, including endorsements, as shown in Figure 13-1.

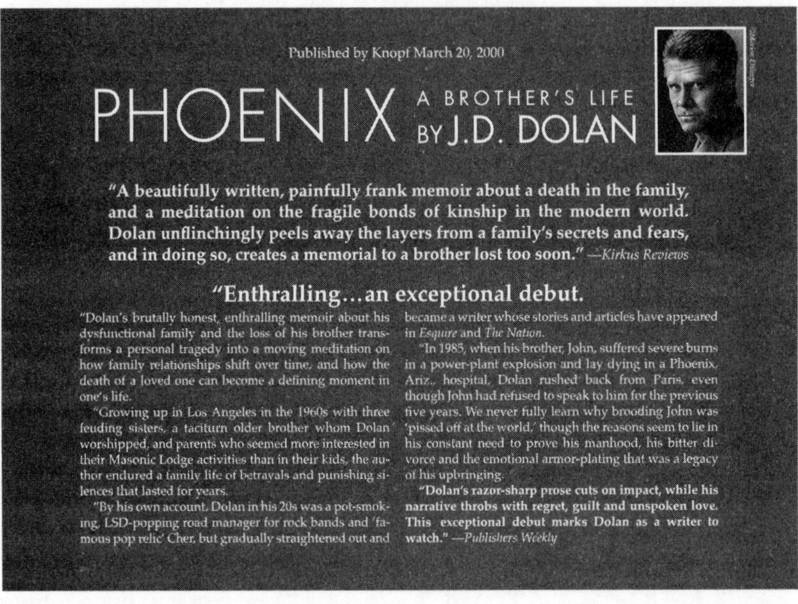

Published by Knopf March 20, 2000

PHOENIX A BROTHER'S LIFE BY J.D. DOLAN

"A beautifully written, painfully frank memoir about a death in the family, and a meditation on the fragile bonds of kinship in the modern world. Dolan unflinchingly peels away the layers from a family's secrets and fears, and in doing so, creates a memorial to a brother lost too soon." —*Kirkus Reviews*

"Enthralling...an exceptional debut.

"Dolan's brutally honest, enthralling memoir about his dysfunctional family and the loss of his brother transforms a personal tragedy into a moving meditation on how family relationships shift over time, and how the death of a loved one can become a defining moment in one's life.

"Growing up in Los Angeles in the 1960s with three feuding sisters, a taciturn older brother whom Dolan worshipped, and parents who seemed more interested in their Masonic Lodge activities than in their kids, the author endured a family life of betrayals and punishing silences that lasted for years.

"By his own account, Dolan in his 20s was a pot-smoking, LSD-popping road manager for rock bands and 'famous pop relic' Cher, but gradually straightened out and became a writer whose stories and articles have appeared in *Esquire* and *The Nation*.

"In 1985, when his brother, John, suffered severe burns in a power-plant explosion and lay dying in a Phoenix, Ariz., hospital, Dolan rushed back from Paris, even though John had refused to speak to him for the previous five years. We never fully learn why brooding John was 'pissed off at the world,' though the reasons seem to lie in his constant need to prove his manhood, his bitter divorce and the emotional armor-plating that was a legacy of his upbringing.

"Dolan's razor-sharp prose cuts on impact, while his narrative throbs with regret, guilt and unspoken love. This exceptional debut marks Dolan as a writer to watch." —*Publishers Weekly*

"An aching testament
to the often unmappable terrain
of the human heart."
—Rick Bass

PHOENIX
A BROTHER'S LIFE
J.D. DOLAN

"This book rises from the ashes
and takes the reader with it."
—Mary Karr

ISBN 0-375-40342-6 • $22
knopfpublicity@randomhouse.com

For author interview, contact:
Francesco Sedita (212) 572-2195 fsedita@randomhouse.com

KNOPF PUBLICITY 299 PARK AVENUNE NEW YORK NY 10171 (212) 572-2104

Figure 13-1: A good press release can help your book receive reviews.

Use *Literary Market Place* and *The Standard Periodical Directory*, both of which are in your libraries reference section, to compile a list of reviewers to send your press release and review copy to. The first wave of review mailings — done with bound galleys or manuscripts — should be sent out three to four months prior to publication. Although it may seem early, a full three-month lead time is customary for many national magazines, including *publishing magazines,* which alert libraries and booksellers to your book in advance of pub date. These publishing magazines include *Publishers Weekly*, *Library Journal*, *Kirkus Reviews*, and *ALA Booklist.* Send each reviewer a copy of the book, a press release, and a note from you expressing your excitement about the book.

The second wave of review mailings is done when printed copies of your book are available, about six to eight weeks before pub date. This mailing should be targeted to a general list of national and local publications and also to a more focused list of publications that are likely to be interested in your book — food magazines if you are writing a cookbook, gun magazines if you are writing a guide to rifles, and so on.

Radio and television interviews

A successful radio or television interview can build powerful word-of-mouth for your book. To test your media skills, start by contacting local radio and TV producers in your area. Send them a copy of the book along with your press release and an enthusiastic cover letter. Local media (radio and TV stations, newspapers, and magazines) love to feature local authors. Ask for a tape of each appearance, duplicate the tape and send it to other stations to solicit interviews.

You may want to consider hiring a professional media coach to prepare you to discuss the most appealing aspects of your book. And as you build upon your media experience, you can even hope for a shot at one of the big national shows like *Good Morning America* or *Oprah.*

Whatever happens, remember that national TV exposure is not a requirement for success with a self-published book. Many of the most successful self-published books have received national media attention only after they achieve a huge sales volume via other means of word-of-mouth.

A cost-effective way to get you and your book out to radio and TV producers is to pay for a listing in one of the periodicals that are read by these producers, like Radio-TV Interview Report. Contact Bradley Communications, 1135 East Plumstead Ave., Landsdowne, PA 19050-8206; 610-259-1070. This way, when producers are putting together shows on specific topics, they'll come across your listing, and if it's right for their show, they'll contact you directly.

Advertising

Advertising is the most expensive and least effective form of book marketing. To place an ad for your book in general interest newspapers or magazines or on television, you're competing for space with national consumer products companies like Procter & Gamble or Microsoft, national media companies such as Universal, Disney, Fox, or Warner Brothers, and major commercial publishing companies — who pay approximately $40,000 for a full-page ad in a major daily newspaper. I highly recommend that you concentrate on other ways to market your book.

In some instances, spending that kind of money on an ad is cost-effective — mainly when the ad does more than just sell books. For example, if you're a consultant, attorney, salesperson, or accountant and your book lends credibility to your business, a large ad may provide visibility to your business, increase your client base, and sell books.

Also, if you book has a very specific target audience, advertising in publications aimed right at these targeted readers can be extremely effective. Always try for review coverage first. And then consider following the review with an ad.

Direct mail

Direct mail marketing is often responsible for self-publishing sales success. Once your press release is written, converting it into an effective direct mail solicitation is easy. Just add a response coupon that itemizes the cost of the book plus shipping and handling. Then compile your own mailing list of the book's target audience or rent a list from an industry publication that reaches your specific audience. If your first mailing is effective, after the additional costs of mailing, handling, and fulfillment, consider renting other lists from direct mail list houses.

Personal selling

Selling copies yourself is the most efficient sales channel for the self-publisher — it accounts for most of the self-published bestsellers in history. Copies of the book that you sell directly, either at full price or at a discount, are clean, reliable cash transactions with no hidden costs. If you're an effective speaker and lecturer, then you can personally sell copies of your book better than almost any major publishing company because you interact with your book's audience on a regular basis. As you sell more copies, it fuels the word-of-mouth that will eventually drive sales through other channels as well.

Fulfillment

Most self-publishers handle their own *fulfillment services* — processing orders, packing and shipping books, collecting payment, and then processing returns if necessary. It's easy, but can be time consuming.

First, set up a billing procedure with your accountant and talk to your bank about opening up a merchant account so that you can accept credit cards. Credit card purchases are more expensive for you, but impulse purchases made with credit cards constitute huge sales so it's worth your while. But check out the rates at two or three banks in your area. Expect to pay a percentage of sales, usually between 3 to 5 percent, along with a small transaction fee of about 50 cents per transaction and a monthly charge of approximately $15.

Purchase a supply of padded shipping envelopes and a home accounting software program such as QuickBooks that offers invoicing, address labeling, and postage through your computer and printer. For shipping, many self-publishers rely on the services of a commercial carrier like UPS, Federal Express, or DHL. Any service with order tracking and two-day delivery will do.

When fulfilling to bookstore accounts, keep in mind that you have to accept returns 90 days after the stores receive your books. Booksellers are entitled to full credit for the price of the book, but not for the shipping cost involved in returning the books to you.

Consider contacting your bookseller accounts every month to check on their stock of your book — booksellers often lose track of stock levels and forget to reorder when they've sold out of a title.

When your book's sales start to really take off, you may want to consider delegating the fulfillment operation to a fulfillment house. *Literary Market Place* has an extensive list of book fulfillment services. Be sure to get price quotes from a number of these operations and discuss your specific needs since charges can vary considerably.

Subsidy or Vanity Publishers

If dealing with all the steps in the self-publication process is more than you had in mind, consider using a subsidy or vanity publisher. Subsidy presses claim to offer the same services provided by commercial publishers — editing, printing, distributing, and marketing your book. However, they charge a fee to perform these services, and the fee usually includes a substantial profit for the publisher.

Nonetheless, if you want to get a book in print quickly, with minimal work, a subsidy publisher may be a good alternative. There's no question that the services they offer can reduce an otherwise overwhelming task to a very simple transaction. But realize that you are probably paying top dollar for the job. If price is an issue and you want to self-publish at a more competitive price, look into the burgeoning alternatives available in electronic publishing, especially *print on demand* or POD books (see the section later in this chapter).

Book advertisement do's

There's no reason not to try your hand at creating an ad for your book. If you plan to spend more than $500 for the ad space, consider soliciting professional help with the copy and layout. Here are some pointers on producing effective book ads:

Show the book's cover in the ad. Jacket art almost always stays in readers' minds — even when the title and author name don't.

Include a response coupon in the ad. An order coupon makes it easy for the customer to order the book directly from you.

Make the message simple. It's usually best to convey how the book benefits readers. Use review excerpts or powerful endorsements, too.

Book Packagers

Book packagers create, present, and sell books to publishers — they often dream up a book idea, assemble the talent necessary to produce it, and oversee the production process from start to finish. For all this work, the packager takes a significant portion of the revenue from the books they package — as much as 50 percent or more. Most book packagers employ writers and illustrators on a *work-for-hire* basis, which means they pay a flat, one-time fee for services rendered.

If a book packager approaches you to write a book, understand that you probably won't get paid as much as if you had a contract directly with a publishing firm. However, it may be an interesting project and if you have the time, why not do it? Who knows? The book may be incredibly successful and raise your author profile.

Publishers like to work with book packagers for a number of reasons: they can save the publisher time and manpower by overseeing the myriad details involved in producing a complicated book; they can save the publisher money by obtaining inexpensive color separations and/or printing through their many production connections; they come up with interesting projects; and they're experts at producing unusual die-cut books that most publisher's simply can't produce.

Many packagers, like Callaway Editions, for example, produce lavishly illustrated, high-quality books that exceed the in-house facilities of most publishers. Another standout, Stonesong Press, generates complex reference works, such as the *Harvard Medical School Health Reference* or *The New York Public Library Desk Reference* (IDG Books, 1998).

And then there are the packagers of incredibly successful book ideas like Bill Adler and John Boswell. These guys have come up with some of the funniest and most interesting books as well as many bestsellers. Adler's productions include *Who Killed The Robbins Family* (Morrow, 1983), a contest mystery written by Tom Chastain, the *I Love New York Diet* (Warner, 1983) written by Bess Myerson, and *Outwitting Squirrels* by Bill Adler himself (Chicago Review Press, 1996). Boswell's successes include *365 Ways to Cook Chicken* (HarperCollins, 1996), *The First Family Paperdoll and Cutout Book* (Dell, 1981), and *What They Don't Teach You at Harvard Business School* (Bantam, 1983).

Electronic Publishing: The Wave of the Future

Opportunities for writers to publish in cyberspace abound. E-publishing is expanding as quickly as documents can be electronically transmitted. And that's exactly what *e-publishing* is — storing and transmitting the text of a book, electronically.

E-books can be delivered in a number of different formats — downloaded from the Internet and printed on a printer; downloaded into an electronic reading device; on a CD-ROM; or as a POD, which is a copy of the text printed on demand, bound, and shipped.

Few people realize that e-publishers fall into the same basic categories as print publishers: commercial, subsidy, and individual self-publishers. Here's a quick look at each.

Commercial e-publishers

Commercial e-publishers operate much like commercial print publishers. They publish, sell, and distribute e-books. Authors submit their text — electronically — to an editor who decides whether it's marketable and/or appropriate for the e-publisher's list. If it's accepted, the work is — in theory, at least — edited, copy edited, proofread, and published. Once published, the e-book is promoted and hopefully advertised online by the publisher.

The major difference between print and e-publishing is in the way authors are paid for their work. Rather than paying a lump sum of money up front as an advance against the anticipated sales of the book, commercial e-publishers share in the actual royalties received with the author — anywhere from 20 percent to 70 percent. Because royalty rates vary considerably from one e-publisher to another, read each contract carefully for payment specs, length of contract, and the exact rights being purchased by the e-publisher. Don't submit your work to an e-publisher who demands exclusive electronic rights. You want to be able to post and sell your book on as many sites as possible.

Here are three good e-publishers to try.

- **BookLocker.com:** BookLocker.com, located at `www.booklocker.com`, is a selective online book publisher, posting both fiction and nonfiction titles daily. Its A-list titles — selected by an editorial board — receive editorial and marketing services for free. Non-A-list title authors pay for each service they request: e-book formatting and design runs $25 per 100 pages; ISBN registration costs $149, pdf conversion is $15. Booklocker pays 70 percent royalties; they accept non-exclusive rights, meaning authors are free to list and sell their books anywhere else they choose. For submission information, send an e-mail query to `publisher@booklocker.com`.
- **Ematter/Fatbrain:** This e-publisher, located at `www.mightywords.com`, pays 50 percent royalties, charges a $1 hosting fee per month, per book, publishes every submission, and accepts non-exclusive rights. It also offers lively author promotion suggestions.
- **PC Books, Inc.:** PC Books, located at `www.pc-books.net/publish.htm`, pays 50 percent royalties (payments are made quarterly), publishes every submission, charges a $25 setup fee, and accepts non-exclusive rights. PC Books offers no editorial services and requires no revisions. No pornography, please.

Many e-publishers demand exclusive electronic rights — though the three provided here do not. Read all e-publisher's contract carefully and be aware that these contracts can change daily. So if you read through a sample contract last week, still reread the specifics one last time before signing.

Subsidy e-publishers

Subsidy e-publishers happily publish anyone's work electronically or as a print on demand book (see POD) for a fee ranging from $99 to $500 or more. This initial payment covers the production of and distribution of your e-book. They also offer a number of services à la carte, such as editing, copy editing, proofreading, and so on. If you request any of these services, expect to pay an additional fee. Authors receive royalty payments, though substantially less than if you publish on your own or through a commercial e-publisher because the royalties are calculated on the book's net price which is the book's selling price minus all publisher expenses. Because subsidy publishers make money in up-front payments from the author, they aren't always as interested as commercial e-publishers in putting energy into the promotion of your book.

Here are two good subsidy e-publishers to check out:

- **Iuniverse:** This large Internet publisher, located at `www.iuniverse.com`, has allied itself with Barnes and Noble to offer increased exposure for a few select authors. Iuniverse features several programs. The barebones e-book service requires an up-front payment of $99 and pays a 50 percent royalty. The POD plan requires an up-front payment of $299, but pays 20 percent royalties on all copies sold and offers discounts on author purchases, see the "Print on demand" section later in this chapter. Iuniverse also offers editorial and marketing services for an additional fee. The Iuniverse contract is exclusive.

- **Xlibris:** Located at `www.xlibris.com`, Xlibris describes itself as an "on demand publishing services provider." An alliance with Random House brings select authors to the attention of the Random House editors. The site provides a range of publishing plans, from a free bare bones "core service," up through more elaborate plans priced at $300, $600, and $1,200, depending on the quality of the design, and the other publishing services desired. Xlibris pays a 25 percent royalty, offers a 25 percent author discount on purchases of POD copies, and has non-exclusive rights.

Print on demand

Print on demand, or POD, is a technology that allows for the printing of small quantities of paperback books. Many e-publishers can provide POD service. POD is attractive because it allows you to print the exact number of copies you need. Design and graphics services are offered for an additional fee to give an eye-catching, professional look to the book.

The problem is, POD is quite expensive. For example, Iuniverse sells books to authors at a modest discount from the retail price: a 25 percent discount on purchases of 1 to 20 copies; a 30 percent discount on 21 to 99 copies, and a 35 percent discount on purchases of 100-plus copies. You'll do better with a major publisher, who charges much less for author copies — usually 40 percent off retail. However, there is not a more quick or economical way to produce high quality copies of your book in small quantities.

Self e-publishing

Just like the self-published author of a printed book, the self-published e-book author creates, produces, distributes, and markets his or her work. The author pays all expenses, retains all rights to the work, and receives all proceeds from the book's sales.

Selling your self-published e- or POD book

There are wonderful opportunities for writers to not only self-publish on the Web, but to sell their self-published works as well — and they're changing almost daily. The following sections outline two current options.

Sell your book via an online bookseller

Releasing your book through an online bookseller allows you to bypass the hurdles of traditional book distribution. Amazon.com is the pioneering leader in this field, but Barnes & Noble.com and Borders.com are also offering programs for the self-publisher. Their sites are, respectively,

```
www.amazon.com/exec/obidos/subst/partners/direct/advantage-
          for-books.html/ref=b_bh_b_ad/103-2393681-3390251
www.barnesandnoble.com/help/b_faq.asp?userid=6H713C7CUH&serer
          =;
```

```
contact Borders by email: corrections@Borders.com
```

Check out Amazon.com's Advantage program for authors. Just fill out a simple form, provide a sample copy of your book, and you're part of the program. Once in, Amazon buys copies of your book at a 45 percent discount and produces a display page for your book on its site, just like they do for any of the blockbuster books by Stephen King or John Grisham. This page features an image of your book's jacket, a description of your book, reader comments, and reviews. You also receive listings in all the amazon subject and category summaries making it easy for customers to find your book.

With your book featured on Amazon, there's no need to worry about distributing and filling book orders. Just send customers to Amazon.com by setting up a link from your Web site. Rest easy knowing that sales from amazon.com are reported to all the national bestseller lists. Never before has there been a book selling initiative that levels the playing field for self-published authors like the Amazon Advantage program

Build your own Web site

Many authors have their own Web sites. Certainly having a Web site can provide worldwide exposure for your book and makes communication with your audience easier. The fact is writers rely on the Web to carry out daily research, so they understand better than most people the importance of having a dedicated place on the Web where you can reach your audience. Here are a few good reasons to consider building your own Web site if you're a published author:

- You're planning a direct sales campaign, and you'd rather not share the proceeds with an online retailer or e-book publisher. Keep in mind that you'll need to open a merchant account through your bank and fulfill orders yourself.
- You want to continually update information in your book and make the updated information available to your readers.
- You have other goods or services you'd like to advertise or sell in connection with your book.

Take note of the costs and/or steps involved in creating and maintaining your own Web site.

- You pay $100 to register your domain name and $35 annually thereafter.
- You pay an Internet service provider a monthly fee to host your site.
- If you're not conversant in HTML code writing, you may need to hire a Web site designer, which can run as high as $2,000 or more. Alternatively, purchase a copy of *Creating Web Pages For Dummies* by Bud E. Smith and Arthur Bebak (IDG Books Worldwide, Inc.) and do it yourself.
- Become an associate of Amazon, Yahoo!, Fatbrain, Iuniverse, and other portals. As an associate, you can participate in the sales referred to these sites from your site.

The field of e-books exploded in March 2000 when Stephen King arranged for his 66-page novella, *Riding the Bullet*, to be distributed electronically through a cartel of Web sites who offered to download the story in a format that was encrypted so that the story could be read on screen, but neither copied nor printed. Within days, over half a million copies had been downloaded by Kings fans many for free, but many more for a fee of $2.50. Suddenly, e-books were legitimized as a source of huge revenues for authors and publishers. King's entrance into the field has shaken many bystanders out of their stupor, and dozens of publishers, large and small, are rushing to get their books online and to seize control of all available e-book publication rights.

For more information about e-publishers, e-books, and Web-based publishing services, consult the sites of The Midwest Book Review (`www.execpc.com/~mbr/bookwatch`), Bookzone (`www.bookzone.com`), Booklocker.com (`www.booklocker.com`), and Aeonix.com (`www.aeonix.com`).

If electronic publishing intrigues you, a good in depth source is *The Secrets of Our Success*, by M J Rose and Angela Adair-Hoy, which they self-published on CD-ROM and is recently available in print form from St. Martin's Press.

Self-Publishers Hall of Fame

The Self Publishers Hall of Fame is a nifty Web site dedicated to the amazing accomplishments of self publishers through the ages. Here's a sampling from John Kremer's fascinating compendium (excerpted from the Self-Publishing Hall of Fame, established by John Kremer, author of *1,001 Ways to Market Your Books*). For the complete, up-to-date list, see `www.bookmarket.com/selfpublish.html`.

H. Jackson Brown originally self-published his *Life's Little Instruction Book*. Soon thereafter, the book was bought by Rutledge Hill, a local publisher, who went on to sell more than five million copies. The book made the bestseller lists in both hardcover and softcover.

John Cassidy self-published *Juggling for the Complete Klutz*. The book went on to sell more than two million copies and led to the establishment of Klutz Press, which has published more than 50 books. Nine of those books have won Parents' Choice Awards, and 12 have made the *Publishers Weekly* children's bestseller list.

Laura Corn self-published *101 Nights of Grrreat Sex* and several other books. She sold 100,000 copies of *237 Intimate Questions Every Woman Should Ask a Man* from the trunk of her car. Total sales for *101 Nights* was 525,000 copies as of March 1999. Check out her Web site at `www.grrreatsex.com`.

Les and Sue Fox self-published *The Beanie Baby Handbook* in 1997. By July 1998, they had gone back to press eight more times for an in-print total of three million copies while the book established itself in the #2 spot on the *New York Times* bestseller list (under advice, how-to, and miscellaneous). Later in 1998, they published *the Beanie Baby Cookbook*. Here's an example where a self-publisher took a hot topic and ran with it long before any larger publishers could get a book out. Congrats! Check out their Web site at `www.bookazon.com`.

John Javna self-published *50 Simple Things You Can Do to Save the Earth* just in time to catch the environmental awareness wave of the 1980s — and months before the major publishers came out with other ecology titles. His book got all the press and sold over 4.5 million copies, half of those as premiums.

John Kremer, author of *1001 Ways to Market Your Books* and developer of this hall of fame, is not above promoting himself, even in this hall of fame. He has helped thousands of authors and publishes to get their books on or near the bestseller lists. Indirectly, at the very least, he has inspired the sales of half a billion books.

Irma Rombauer used $3,000 from her husband's estate to self-publish *The Joy of Cooking* in 1931. Since then, this cookbook has sold millions of copies. Sixty-six years later, it still sells more than 100,000 copies per year. In November 1997, Scribners published a completely revised fifth edition, the first new edition in 20 years. By early December, the book had already made the bestseller lists with more than 750,000 copies in print.

H. Leighton Steward, Morrison Bethea, Samuel Andrews, and **Luis Balart** originally self-published and sold 165,000 copies of *Sugar Busters! Cut Sugar to Cut Fat* in 18 months. The book went on to become a national bestseller when published by Ballantine.

In 1918, **William Strunk** self-published *The Elements of Style* for his college classes at Cornell University. The book was later revised by **E.B. White** and continues to sell many thousands of copies every year.

Henry David Thoreau originally self-published *Walden*, an American classic that sells many thousands of copies every year — more than 100 years after his death!

Walt Whitman self-published many editions of his collected poems, *Leaves of Grass*. While he didn't get wealthy from self-publishing, he did become known as America's poet. His *Leaves of Grass* continues to sell thousands of copies every year — 100 years after his death!

Part V

Home at Last! Negotiation and Contract

"It's an interesting autobiography, Mr. MacDonald. But it needs some editing. For instance — you've got a 'quack quack' here, and a 'quack quack' there, here a 'quack', there a 'quack'..."

In this part . . .

Find out how to decipher a publishing offer and negotiate the best possible deal from a publisher. In this part, I show you what a publishing contract looks like and how it works. The better you understand a contract, the more effective it can be in protecting your — rather than just your publisher's — interests.

Chapter 14

The Offer

In This Chapter

- Deciphering a publisher's offer
- Understanding what the words mean
- Knowing what to ask for

Nothing can match the excitement of your first publishing offer. In a single moment, you're transformed from an amateur dabbler to a professional writer. A publishing house is offering to pay you to write a book! In the midst of your excitement, stay calm and focus on exactly what the publishing offer includes.

Even if an agent represents you — and especially if one doesn't — you need to understand the terms of the offer. No doubt you'll have questions: What, exactly, do the terms of the offer really mean? Are these terms advantageous to you or not? Are the terms fair? Is this the best deal you can get? And if not, what's realistic?

In this chapter, I share my own disastrous first offer experience along with tips to avoid a similar experience. Then I explore in detail the features of a typical publishing offer so that you know what to expect and how to evaluate the offer you receive.

What's an Offer?

When a publishing company offers to "buy" your book, what exactly is the company buying? And what exactly are you "selling"? In legal terms, most publishing contracts are actually licensing agreements, in which the author licenses certain rights to a publishing company. These licensed rights always include the right to print and distribute the author's book in hardcover and/or softcover in the United States. And in most contracts, other rights are granted as well — the right to license the book to book clubs, for example, the right to sell excerpts from the book to magazines, and sometimes the right to license foreign translations of the book overseas.

My work-for-hire experience

I wrote my first book, *Choose the Perfect Name for Your Baby* (Longmeadow/Walden, 1992) on a work-for-hire basis. At that time, Waldenbooks — a huge bookstore chain — was publishing its own books to profit from its market knowledge of which categories enjoyed consistently strong sales. In each high-performance category, Walden wanted to have a book of its own to recommend to buyers. Because I had no track record on which to base my desire for a higher advance or a royalty arrangement (see the section on royalties, later in this chapter) and because the publisher had come to me with the basic book idea, I agreed to a one-time payment of $2,500 in 1991 for a baby name book consisting of 10,000 names — complete with meanings, derivations, and famous examples of each name — and dozens of sidebars filled with exciting and unusual name facts and fancies.

Choose the Perfect Name for Your Baby, a $4.95 paperback, ended up selling 25,000 copies. In a standard paperback royalty arrangement, I would have earned $9,250 over the life of the book. Instead, the meager $2,500 one-time payment was spent long before the book even hit stores. Don't make the mistake I did — make sure that your offer includes a royalty arrangement.

Advance against royalties

In exchange for the right to print and distribute the book, the publisher pays the author a sum of money, called an *advance.* The advance is literally an interestfree loan, paid to the author in installments and collateralized by the revenue that the publisher anticipates receiving from sales of the book once it is published. If the author fulfills his or her obligation and delivers a manuscript acceptable to the publisher, then the author keeps all the advance money whether the book's sales actually earn the amount advanced or not. Once the book is published and starts selling, the author receives a portion of the book's earnings, called *royalties,* but only after the publisher has recovered the initial amount advanced to the author.

An exception to this is known as a *work-for-hire* arrangement. Under a work-for-hire contract, the author is paid a flat, one-time fee for delivering the manuscript, but receives no share of the book's earnings. While magazine articles are almost always written on a work-for-hire basis, books are not. Beware of any book publisher that offers you a work-for-hire arrangement — it's usually much more beneficial to the publisher than the writer. (See sidebar.)

Royalties

Royalties are commissions paid to the author based on sales of the book. In most contracts, royalties are calculated on the basis of the publisher's list price for the book or on the net amount received by the publisher from the bookseller. If, for example, the royalty rate is set at 10 percent of list price then, on a $20 hardcover, the author's royalty share is $2 per book. If the royalty is 15 percent of the amount received from the bookseller, then the same $20 hardcover will generate a royalty of 15 percent of $12 (the amount received by the publisher) or $1.80.

The industry standard for hardcover royalties is 10 percent of list price for the first 5,000 copies sold, 12.5 percent on 5,000 to 10,000 copies sold, and 15 percent on all sales above 10,000 copies. Publishers pay a lower royalty rate for paperbacks: the standard trade paperback royalty is 7.5 percent, and the standard mass-market royalty is 8 percent.

Payout

A royalty advance is generally paid to the author in installments, starting with a payment when the contract is signed, another payment when the manuscript is accepted by the publisher, and often a final payment upon publication of the book. The publisher may ask that the advance be doled out even more slowly, with payments due after publication, on paperback publication and even after paperback publication.

There is no question that it's in the publisher's interest to delay full payment of the advance as long as possible. It's in the author's interest to get paid in full once the manuscript is complete and accepted by the publisher. Keep this in mind when listening to your offer.

Delivery schedule and materials requirement

When a publisher offers a contract to an author, the offer usually includes a specific delivery and publication schedule. A typical offer calls for a final delivery date for the manuscript, including illustrations or other artwork and permissions cleared. Some contracts require interim manuscript deliveries, when a certain number of pages or chapters are due, and the publisher makes a partial payment upon acceptance of these pages.

Most publishers stipulate the length of manuscript required, in page count or word count, and exactly what other materials the author is expected to produce — permissions, illustrations, and so on. These details are itemized in the offer.

How advances and royalities work

Here's how a typical advance/royalty arrangement works. Say that the publisher agrees to pay an advance of $30,000 payable in thirds— on signing, completion of the manuscript, and hardcover publication. When the contract is signed, the publisher releases a check for $10,000 to the agent, who deducts 15 percent or $1,500 dollars and pays the author $8,500. The author then writes the manuscript. When the publisher accepts the manuscript, a check for $10,000 goes to the agent who deducts $1,500 dollars and sends a check for $8,500 to the author. A final payment of $10,000 occurs when the book is published in hardcover.

Say that the book sells quite well. In the first three months after publication, 20,000 copies are sold. The book is priced at $20, and the author has a standard royalty rate. The royalty payments are calculated as follows: On the first 5,000 copies, the rate is 10 percent or $2 per copy, for a total of $10,000. On the next 5,000 copies, the rate is 12.5 percent or $2.50, for a total of $12,500. On the remaining 10,000 copies sold, the rate is 15 percent or $3 per copy, for a total of $30,000 — adding up to a total of $52,500. This means that the author's royalty account now shows earnings of $52,500 minus the $30,000 initial advance, leaving a balance owed to the author of $22,500. Money earned in this way is paid on a semiannual basis in the form of royalty payments (see Chapter 20). Of course, the agent takes his commission from whatever the author is paid.

Items You Should Ask About

In most cases, a publisher's initial offer for a book includes very little detail; usually only the advance guarantee, the payout, and the delivery date are specified. However, you should address a few other issues before agreeing to a deal.

In the sections that follow, I mention contract provisions stipulating that money earned from sales and licenses is to be divided between the author and the publisher. In each instance, it is understood that every payment made by the publisher to the author is subject to the agent's commission. Only production grants and permission fees covered by the publisher are exempt from commission deduction.

Territory

If a literary agent represents you, the standard arrangement is that the U.S. publisher is limited to North America, which means the publisher has the right to publish and distribute the book in the U.S. and Canada. Because many U.S. publishers have U.K. affiliates or try to coordinate publication of a book in every English language country, many agents sell publishers *World English rights.* This means that the publisher is granted the right to sell the book in every English-speaking country or to license the rights in every English-speaking country where that publisher elects not to distribute the book directly.

If you are not represented by an agent, consider accepting an offer for *world rights,* which means that the publisher has the right to distribute the book, or license the distribution rights, in every country throughout the world. In practical terms, this means you are granting the right to license translations in every country where English is not the national language.

In general, the proceeds from foreign licenses are shared between the author and the publisher. On translations, the author generally receives 75 percent of the proceeds, and the publisher 25 percent. On English language licenses, the author receives 80 percent and the publisher 20 percent.

Subsidiary rights and splits

The contract entitles your publisher to distribute editions of your book in the specified territory. Any arrangement with a third party to distribute or sell material derived from your book is described as a *subsidiary right* and refers to a wide range of activities, from book club editions of your book, to serial excerpts purchased by newspapers or magazines, to audio books, to electronic and online versions of your book, to film, TV, and multimedia adaptations of your book.

In a typical publishing contract, the publisher retains hardcover and paperback rights in the territory, whether North America, World English, or World. The publisher also retains the right to license book club editions, magazine or newspaper serializations that appear after the book is published, known as *second serial rights,* paperback editions that are licensed to other publishers, and use of the verbatim text in an electronic media. The proceeds from all these license sales are divided 50/50 between the author and the publisher.

The publisher may negotiate to purchase the right to license other rights, including serial adaptations published before book publication, known as first serial rights. First serial rights are divided 90 percent to the author and 10 percent to the publisher. Other rights up for negotiation are audio editions (divided 50/50), and multimedia adaptations.

Agents like to hold onto your performance rights, which include television or movie adaptations of the book (divided 85 percent to author and 15 percent to agent). However, if you don't have an agent, allowing the publisher to license performance rights is a good idea. Most publishers maintain relationships with movie agencies in Los Angeles who specialize in the licensing of these rights, and chances are very good that these agents know their way around the movie and TV business better than you do.

Accounting and flow through

You may not think accounting has much to do with you and your book, but actually, it can be very important when it's time to collect the earnings from your book.

To show you what I mean, I'll work out the accounting in a foreign rights sale: one where the publisher holds foreign rights and one where the author and agent retain foreign rights. Surprisingly, this simple distinction can have a profound impact on how money changes hands once the book is published.

When the publisher retains the right to license foreign rights, the income from foreign publishers is, "accounted against the author's advance," meaning that foreign rights income is not paid to the author until the original advance is recouped by the publisher.

If the agent and/or author hold the foreign rights, then the income from foreign publishers flows directly to the author, or *flows through* — around the advance in publishing parlance.

Here's how it works. Say that you write a novel for Acme Publishing and receive an advance of $50,000, all of which has been paid, and Acme retained the foreign rights. Acme sends your manuscript to a publisher in Estonia, who loves the book and offers to pay $20,000 for the Estonian translation rights. The Estonian publisher agrees to pay $10,000 on signing. Its check for $10,000 arrives at Acme, amd Acme deducts its 25 percent, or $2,500, and places the remaining $7,500 in your royalty account. This reduces your unearned Acme advance from $50,000 to $32,500. But your publisher does not have to pay you anything from the foreign sale until sales of the book (or other rights income) earn back the rest of your advance. When the advance is finally earned out, whatever sum is owed to you is then sent to your agent, who deducts 15 percent (meaning that on the portion of the earnings that come from foreign sales, you pay a 25 percent commission to the publisher and a further 15 percent commission to your agent!).

If, on the other hand, you retain the foreign rights, then your agent sends the manuscript to Estonia. The Estonian check for $10,000 is then sent to your agent, who deducts his commission (usually 20 percent on foreign sales, or $2,000), and hands over the remaining $8,000 to you immediately. As you can see, it is definitely to your advantage for your agent to retain the foreign rights.

The only reason for an author to allow a publisher to retain these rights is if you don't have an agent to sell them for you, or if a publisher is willing to pay you a significantly increased advance for the rights. Agents — who tend to work as independent operators and do not have access to funding as publishers do— generally don't advance money to authors as a speculation against foreign rights income (or any other kind of income). Additionally, you should know that income from foreign publishers (after the initial payment on signing) is slow to be paid, because the work has to be translated and then printed and distributed before further payments are made.

Editions

Most large publishers possess the capability to publish a book in hardcover, trade paperback, or mass-market paperback. Publishers are usually quite specific about their format intentions. If it isn't spelled out in the offer, now is the time to clarify whether the publisher intends to release the first edition of your book as a hardcover or a paperback. Every format has its pros and cons. You may, for example, have your heart set on a hardcover edition. Certainly, hardcovers are more likely to be reviewed; they also cost more and earn a higher royalty. On the other hand, some books are better suited to trade paperback or mass-market distribution, and may languish in hardcover. Work closely with your publisher and agent to determine the best format strategy for your book.

Approvals

Once the publishing process is underway, your publisher acts on your behalf in a number of ways — writing descriptions of your book that appear in catalogs, advertisements, and brochures, approving contracts with licensees, designing the book jacket, selling second serial excerpts, and controlling many other decisions that powerfully impact the success of your book in the marketplace.

Now is the time to establish the ground rules for how these decisions are to be handled. The highest level of author control is called *approval,* meaning that the publisher must secure written or verbal approval from the author before making a final decision. *Consultation* is a milder level of author control, meaning that while the publisher will consult with the author before taking certain steps, the final power over the decision resides with the publisher.

For example, it is all but universally understood that not a single word can be changed in the text of the book without the author's approval, though informally the creation of the text is often a team effort, with both sides contributing a great deal to the choice of words, style, and syntax. (See Chapter 18 for more on this topic.)

However, most publishing contracts stipulate that the final title of the book and the book's jacket are the sole discretion of the publisher — only the most powerful best-selling authors are able to exert approval over jacket and title. That being said, most publishers are willing to consult with authors about the jacket and title. By contrast, publishers are almost all willing to grant any author the right to approve the licensing of paperback rights to a third party, the right to consult regarding the type design of the book, and the right to approve the wording that appears on the jacket flaps of the final book.

Options

When a publisher signs a contract with a new writer, he is wagering on the author's future success — not only the success of this first book, but the success of future books as well. For this reason, most publishers insist that first-time authors agree to some sort of option provision.

An *option* is a clause in a publishing contract that spells out the publisher's claim to the author's next book. I talk about options at greater length in Chapter 16. In this section, you just need to know that option clauses serve the interests of the publisher, not the author. If you can avoid any option language in the offer, so much the better. It may not come up during the offer, but if it does, try to hold out for a simple first refusal option to be based on sample pages, not a manuscript, and to be exercised "upon acceptance," not "upon publication," of your current manuscript. Otherwise, your publisher will have the right to delay a decision to publish your next book until as much as a year or more after you have finished writing your first.

Number of free copies of your book

Make sure that the publisher agrees to provide a substantial quantity of free copies of your book. Most publishing contracts provide the author with 10 to 20 copies of the book gratis and then sell additional copies at a 40 percent discount from the retail price.

You definitely want more than 20 copies, and most publishers can be persuaded to part with 50 to100 free copies. Keep in mind that printed copies of your book are very inexpensive for the publisher.

Promotional commitments from your publisher

Especially if you are in the fortunate position of having a few offers to compare, ask about promotional commitments. Before you sign a contract, it's perfectly fair to ask how much the publisher plans to spend on marketing your book. You can even request an itemized scheme of promotional and marketing efforts the publisher plans to expend on behalf of your book. To get a clear idea of the kinds of efforts that can and should be used in the marketing of your book, see Chapter 19.

Electronic rights

Electronic rights (see Chapter 13) are generally described as the right to earnings derived from sales of the book, or part of the book, in digital form. Electronic rights are booming — there are new and exciting developments in the evolution of digital products derived from books every year. Currently, a great deal of attention is focused on print on demand products and electronic books. In terms of electronic rights, the trend is for authors to retain all electronic rights to their books except for the right to verbatim electronic reproduction. This means that the publisher and the author, together, share in the revenue from every use of the actual text of the book in an electronic format, including e-books, digital databases, serializations on the Web, print on demand editions, and so on.

What an actual offer sounds like

Most publishers make their offers informally, over the phone. Here's what a typical conversation might sound like, between an agent and an editor, as an offer is made, and the key elements of the deal are clarified:

"We'd like to offer $30,000, payable in thirds, for world rights," the editor might say, after dispensing with the pleasantries.

["The advance will be $30,000, payable $10,000 on signing, $10,000 on acceptance, and $10,000 on publication. The territory will be world."]

"Is that for standard royalties?" asks the agent.

["Does that mean 10 percent of list for the first 5,000 copies, 12.5 percent for the next 5,000, and 15 percent thereafter?"]

"Right," continues the editor. "Also straight 7.5 percent for trade paperback, and 8 percent for rack size. We'll split 80/20 for U.K. and 75/25 for translation."

[The editor confirms standard royalties for the hardcover, 7.5 percent of retail royalty for the trade paperback edition, and 8 percent for the mass-market edition. If the book is licensed in Britain, the proceeds will be divided 80 percent to the author and 20 percent to the publisher. Translation or foreign rights revenue will be divided 75 percent to the author and 25 percent to the publisher.]

"We'd really like approval on the hardcover jacket. And how about a royalty escalator on the mass market at 100,000?" asks the agent.

[By this, the agent is asking for approval on the appearance of the hardcover edition's book jacket. He's also asking whether the royalty on a mass-market edition — if there is to be a mass market edition — can increase from 8 percent to 10 percent of the retail price after 100,000 copies are sold.]

"I can't do the jacket approval, but I'll get back to you on the escalation."

[Most publishing houses have guidelines on royalty escalations. The editor will have to secure his bosses' approval for such a change.]

"Okay. While you're at it, we want no option clause."

[Many agents try to dispense with option clauses.]

"We're adamant about the option. But we'll settle for first refusal."

[Publishers are pretty determined about option clauses. At the very least, they usually want a first refusal arrangement whereby they see sample material for the next book before any other publisher. They are then allowed 30 days to arrive at a deal for the new book. If no deal is in place after 30 days, the agent can send the material out to other publishers on the 31st day.]

"Okay, but only based on an outline, and we want to submit 30 days after acceptance. Also, will you give us a marketing commitment?"

[This means that the agent will be able to submit an outline for the author's next book a mere 30 days after the manuscript for the present book is accepted. He's also asking that the publisher commit to spending a specific dollar amount to market the book.]

"How about 120 days after acceptance? Best I can do on marketing is a plan. How about I fax one to you this afternoon?"

(continued)

(continued)

[By delaying the decision by 120 days, the publisher buys more time to collect feedback on the first book and determine how well it's faring in the publishing process. This enables the publisher to form a more intelligent opinion of the value of the author's next book. Also, he's not willing to commit money to marketing before he has read the book. For now, he'll itemize a few marketing steps that will probably be taken, but which won't be binding on him or his company.]

"Okay, we'll wait on the marketing, but let's compromise on 60 days after acceptance."

[It's very unusual to make a marketing guarantee for a first book, so this outcome is pretty normal. An option clause good for 60 days after acceptance of the first manuscript is fairly typical for a first book.]

"Can we get 100 author copies?"

[The author is a lecturer and wants to use the book to solicit new business.]

"You can have 100 paperbacks but only 25 hardcovers. I'll get back to you on those other points."

[Free books are a good investment; there will be more sales generated if the author's lectures are successful. But hardcovers cost more than paperbacks. Besides, the author's business will buy many hardcover copies to promote his lecture activities.]

This offer is going well. The agent will soon relay it to the author, and a real negotiation can begin.

Chapter 15

The Negotiation

In This Chapter

- Knowing what you need
- Bargaining for the necessities

It's tempting when you hear that first offer from a book publisher to feel a surge of elation and just say "yes" without fully evaluating whether the specific terms of the offer work for you.

In this chapter, I look at the three factors most important to you in writing a good book: time, money, and available sources. In order to intelligently assess an offer, you want to make sure that the offer includes enough time to write the book based on the demands in your life; enough money to live on while you write the book; and access to enough reliable sources and reference material to complete the necessary research. I help you make an informed and practical assessment of these factors before you negotiate the final deal — that way, you can ask for exactly what you need. When your needs are properly addressed, the actual experience of writing your book is easier and much more fulfilling.

Be Alert

Listen carefully to each offer you receive. If it's helpful, ask for the offer in writing so that you can study it. If you have any question or confusion about the offer, ask the editor for clarification. Be sure to thank the editor for her support and belief in your book. But don't feel that you need to give an immediate yes or no answer.

In fact, the better negotiating strategy is to simply tell the editor that you'd like to think about the offer and promise to get back to her as quickly as possible. Now the editor, who has invested a great deal of time and effort in securing an offer for your book, is in the uncomfortable position of waiting for your response. You've demonstrated that you're no amateur. In fact, you're mentally preparing the editor to improve her offer if necessary.

Know What You Need to Write the Book

Writing a book takes a great deal of time, focus, and effort. Many new authors think that the sense of accomplishment they'll feel when their book is boldly displayed on a bookstore shelf will make up for the many hardships they endure during the writing process. I want you to know that this notion is not only unrealistic, it's ridiculous!

The fact is, if the publisher doesn't pay you enough or give you enough time, or if you can't get access to important source material, writing your book can turn into a horrible experience. Chances are good you'll be angry with the publisher — you may even feel abused. And yet the publisher won't understand your anger and frustration. In fact, the editor may wonder why you didn't ask for what you needed before you agreed to the offer. That's why it's important for *you* to discern — before you sign a contract — exactly what you need in terms of time, money, and support to write the best possible book.

Time

The mythology of literature is full of legendary achievements, of great novels and plays written in a few weeks or months. Fact is, no two writers work at the same pace. And because writing a book can be arduous and time-consuming — even if you're lucky enough to avoid writer's block — it's important to be realistic in the assessment of your own writing speed.

Because all writers work differently, it's difficult for a publishing professional to evaluate the amount of time you need to complete your book. For that reason, it's important for *you* to look realistically at your work style, and the time at your disposal, when you contemplate a contract offer.

Say, for example, that you find yourself in the situation I faced when IDG Books offered me a contract to write *Getting Your Book Published For Dummies*. I submitted a proposal and discussed the project many times with my agent and the publisher over the course of nearly two years. But as sometimes happens, decisions get waylaid inside a publishing house. Twenty-two months after I submitted the proposal for *Getting Your Book Published For Dummies*, IDG made me an offer. That was in November, and the offer stipulated that the complete manuscript was due no later than April 15. This meant that I had only from Thanksgiving to tax day to produce a 400-page manuscript. I did a quick calculation — 18 weeks to write 400 pages. This worked out to 22 pages each week, or about three pages of finished text every day of every week.

I realized that this schedule didn't allow for a single day off, and, given my family obligations, I knew that I'd be lucky to get five full working days each week. Also, I hadn't calculated in any additional time for research. I knew perfectly well that I'd have to do at least two weeks of library research and probably another two weeks of interviewing. This allocation cut my actual writing schedule down from 18 weeks to 14, meaning that I'd have to produce 29 pages of final text in each five-day work week, or roughly six pages of finished text every working day. I did make the deadline — though there were plenty of late nights and early starts along the way. In this case, I was intimately familiar with my subject matter. I had access to plenty of research sources. And I knew enough about my writing pace to anticipate that I could do it.

Nevertheless, the process was, at times, torturous. A more complex project on a less familiar topic would have been completely out of reach.

The publishing industry does have a standard writing schedule. For books of average length — 250 to 300 pages — whether fiction or nonfiction, most publishers allow the writer a year to 18 months in order to produce a finished manuscript.

Creating a writing timetable

The writing of a nonfiction book falls into fairly predictable stages: Creating the outline; conducting preliminary research; writing the first draft; follow-up research to fill in gaps along with fact checking; and a full revision and polish of the manuscript. You need to calculate the time needed for each of these important steps.

The outline: For a detailed working outline of the book, you want time to create a detailed list of the topics you want to cover, in the correct order, for each chapter and every subsection within the chapter.

Preliminary research: Scope out your research needs and determine where your sources are located, how much interviewing time and library work to allow for, as well as any travel time that's required to complete the research.

First draft: Construct a realistic writing schedule that allows enough time for you to produce top-quality pages. Most writers have a daily time limit for this sort of quality work — often four to five hours. An output of two to three quality pages per day is considered an average pace. This means that to write 300 pages of quality text, you should allow at least 175 working days or 35 weeks.

Secondary research and fact-checking: Once the first draft is complete, you'll see where you have gaps that need to be filled in with more in-depth research and/or additional interviews. Allow time for follow-up research as well as for double-checking your facts and data.

Revised draft: Allow time to put your manuscript aside for a week or more before returning to it for a final polish. After some time away from the manuscript, you will return refreshed and able to see errors and omissions that you may have missed when you were immersed in the process of creating your book. This revision process is where you incorporate all of the follow-up research and make the manuscript as reader friendly as possible.

For fiction, an offer is generally made only on a complete manuscript, so your time calculation is formulated on necessary revisions. Listen carefully to the kinds of changes the editor asks for in your novel. Does she want you to more fully develop certain characters or restructure the entire novel? Based on the length of time it took to create the novel in the first place, you can probably calculate the length of time needed to make the requested revisions.

Money

There is no standard dollar figure that authors are paid to write a book. In fact, the same writer is paid different amounts for different books. That's because from a publisher's perspective, the money paid to a writer is based on a calculation of the anticipated earning from the book's sales (see Chapter 14). If, for example, the publisher anticipates that your book will be a best-seller, the dollar figure it offers will be much higher — close to a million — than for a short-story collection with only a small sales potential, for which it may offer only $5,000.

The best-case scenario is to be paid a fair market price. The way to arrive at this price is to solicit competing bids — either on your own or with the help of a literary agent. When a number of publishers are competing to publish your book, you quickly ascertain the top price the market can bear to pay for the book.

But even market data may not provide an accurate measure of the value of your time. If you already have a full-time job, you need to figure out how much your spare time is worth. If you have to turn away other kinds of paying work to write the book, how much income are you sacrificing? If you are a parent or caregiver, what will it cost to hire a substitute to care for your children or aged parents? If you can't possibly work at home and must pay for outside office space, your advance must cover this cost. Consider all these issues when contemplating an offer so that you can receive exactly what you need.

Sources

A writer's greatest source is inspiration, and that comes from within yourself. But even a novel that is entirely the product of your lively imagination requires some research — and many novels require a surprisingly large amount of detailed background information. In order to secure the information you need to infuse your book with the necessary authority and authenticity, you want access to a wide range of research material available in a well-stocked library and bookstore; you also may need access to newspaper back issues and firsthand eyewitness subjects who can provide the substance of your narrative. Before accepting any offer, you need to identify the sources of your book and confirm that you'll have sufficient access to these sources to gather your information in the time allotted.

If any of the sources for your book are alive, secure their cooperation before you sign a contract. While it sometimes happens that sources cooperate once a contract is signed — rather like bowing to the inevitable — it's my recommendation that you settle this detail up front.

Support

To write a book — even if you're doing it alone — you need support from family, friends, and loved ones. Writing a book is a job, and yet it's somehow more than a job. No matter what, your family will be affected. Believe me, it's in your interest to plan for your book to change the flow of life around your home.

If you have caregiving responsibilities, find a qualified substitute. You can't write effectively if you're worried about what's going on in the next room.

If, once you evaluate your sourcing needs, your monetary needs, and your time needs, you arrive at the conclusion that you need more help in the form of a research assistant, clerical assistant, or collaborator, address that need before you accept an offer. Keep in mind that support of this type has financial implications that you'll want to consider in your contract negotiation.

Use an Intermediary to Negotiate

Once you know what you need, hold out for terms that permit you to do your best work. Securing these terms is where the help of an intermediary — a lawyer or a literary agent — is indispensable. Remaining cool and objective when negotiating for yourself is difficult — especially when it's a conversation upon which your entire literary future hinges. For this reason, you want an intermediary who is experienced at negotiating — with publishers in particular. A professional can help ensure that you don't settle for any offer that places you in an impossible situation, no matter how much you want to get your book published. A skilled intermediary can not only secure a higher advance guarantee from your publisher, but she can also help persuade a publisher to assist you in other ways — for example, by granting a separate budget for permissions or photographs or some other costs that would otherwise be your responsibility.

Negotiating on Your Own Behalf

Here are a few pointers to bear in mind if you are negotiating on your own behalf:

- **Negotiate when it's convenient for you.** If the editor calls and says, "We're ready to make an offer," make certain that you're ready to *receive* an offer. It's probably best to say, "That's great. Do you mind if I call you back in a few minutes?" (or whenever you have some uninterrupted time to commit to this important process). Then, make sure that you are seated comfortably, with no distractions. Have a notepad in front of you. Read through this chapter carefully, especially this section, as well as Chapter 16. Then initiate the call.
- **Get it in writing.** Ideally, ask the editor to send the whole offer in writing. If that isn't feasible, don't be rushed or impulsive. Ask questions and write down the answers. Don't accept any feature of the offer until you can study all of it. Have several conversations if necessary, but be sure that you have every piece of relevant information in front of you.
- **Identify the key problem areas.** Study the offer and decide which features are acceptable to you and which are not. Try to prioritize. If the money is almost sufficient, will a larger payment on signing help make the book feasible? If the advance is too low, will a grant for photographs make the difference? Start the negotiation on a positive note, agreeing with the items that are acceptable to you. From that positive note, indicate that you see only a few minor problem areas that you are certain can be ironed out. Presenting the unacceptable items in an upbeat, agreeable way generally results in a positive outcome.
- **Don't agree until everything is settled.** Once the negotiation starts to move along, be deliberate. Don't act like the negotiation is done until you truly are satisfied with every point in the deal. Once you feel that most of your major issues are settled, ask for more time to study the deal. Be sure that enough time has passed for you to re-examine the key points carefully before calling back to signify that the deal is done.
- **Get it in writing again.** Be sure to create a written description of the deal points and send it to your editor. Ask for a countersigned copy via fax as soon as possible.

Chapter 16

The Contract

In This Chapter

- Looking inside a publishing contract
- Deciphering what the terms mean
- Getting your fair share

A contract is an unwieldy document that seals the deal between you and your publisher. It's written in formal, technical publishing language that many writers find off-putting. But remember, if negotiated properly, this document can protect the interests of you and your book.

In order to familiarize you with a publishing contract, I include a sample contract at the end of this chapter. Be sure to consult it for exact language as I explain what the clauses really mean and what's important about each one. I also let you know which clauses you have a good chance of amending or changing and which ones are carved in stone. Keep in mind that this guide is not a substitute for an experienced literary agent or publishing lawyer. But it does cut through the legal chatter and set you up as a knowledgeable and informed first reader of your own contract.

What Is a Contract?

A *publishing contract* is a written agreement in which the author licenses certain rights to a publishing company. These licensed rights always include the right to print and distribute the author's book in hardcover and/or softcover in the United States. Other rights are usually licensed as well. (See the section "Subsidiary rights splits," later in this chapter.)

Contracts have a time limit — usually the term of copyright of the work (see the "Copyright" sidebar in this section), but sometimes it's an actual period of years. The typical publishing contract includes a stipulation that the book be registered for copyright by the publisher on behalf of the author, and that the contract survives in force for as long as the work remains in print with the publisher, or until the copyright expires, whichever is sooner.

Copyright

Copyright is "a form of protection provided by the laws of the United States to the authors of 'original works of authorship.' This protection is available to both published and unpublished works." You own the copyright to an original work that is written by you as soon as you write it. In other words, if you are the original author of a written work, then you are the copyright holder. The fact that copyright is bequeathed automatically, by the act of writing an original work, explains why individuals own the copyright to letters they write, and why letters cannot be reproduced anywhere without the author's written consent.

According the U.S. Copyright Office, "A work that is created (fixed in tangible form for the first time) on or after January 1, 1978" is automatically protected from the moment of its creation and is ordinarily given a term enduring for the author's life plus an additional 70 years after the author's death. In the case of "a joint work prepared by two or more authors who did not work for hire," the term lasts for 70 years after the last surviving author's death. For works made for hire, and for anonymous and pseudonymous works (unless the author's identity is revealed in Copyright Office records), the duration of copyright will be 95 years from publication or 120 years from creation, whichever is shorter."

Quite simply, the copyright is yours by virtue of the act of writing the work. Beware of contract language that asks you to assign your copyright to anyone else. It is not in your best interest.

(The information in this sidebar is taken from the Web site of the United States Copyright Office. For much fuller information about copyright protection and how it works, visit its Web site at `www.loc.gov/copyright` or call 202-707-3000.)

A contract is important because it defines your relationship with your publisher for as long as your book remains in print — from the day the contract is signed until the book goes out of print. Bear in mind that contracts are generally written with the "worst case" in mind. What that means is that your contract becomes most important to you when things go wrong, and probably won't have much bearing as long as relations with your publisher go smoothly.

The Clauses in a Contract

If you sell your own book to a publisher, you should work out the broad contract points yourself. If a literary agent is representing you, definitely let that experienced professional negotiate the contract. However, if no agent is acting on your behalf, I strongly urge that you engage the services of a professional to negotiate the myriad details of your contract — either a literary agent or an attorney with experience in publishing or entertainment law. Lawyers who do not have publishing experience lack the publishing expertise to be of much help in negotiating a publishing contract (see Chapter 15).

Even if a professional represents you, it's a good idea to read your contract and get to know what the important clauses mean. In the old days, publishing contracts were written in impenetrable legalese. But today, publishers are obliged by law to write their contracts in modern, everyday English. And while this is the case — as you'll see if you examine the sample contract at the back of this chapter — you still need to be aware of a few booby traps to lurking behind the most benign sounding phrases.

The following sections describe the essential clauses in a typical publishing contract.

Author name

This clause is pretty straightforward if you are a single author writing under your own name. The author line becomes more complicated if you are planning to register the copyright in the name of your company or if you are working with a collaborator. If you are writing in the name of your company, the publisher may require you to sign a *performance letter,* in which you, as an individual, agree to perform the duties (writing and promoting the book) ascribed to your company in the "author name" line of the contract.

If you are collaborating with someone else, now is the time to work out how the collaboration is going to work. Are you going to get equal billing, meaning that your names appear in the same size on the book, in alphabetical order? Or is one collaborator going to get more prominence? Are your names going to be separated by an "and" or a "with"? Is only one collaborator's name going to appear on the cover of the book? These issues, as well as the key issue of how the money is going to be divided between you, should be resolved before the contract is finalized (see Chapter 3).

The work

Most contracts require a sentence or two describing the book. This description provides recourse for the publisher if the finished manuscript bears no resemblance to the book the publisher contracted for you to write. In the event that your finished book departs significantly from your outline, particularly if this departure comes as an unwelcome surprise to your editor, the publisher can either refuse to publish the book or ask you to revise the manuscript so that it conforms to the contractual description.

If you read the fine print, you'll note that the boilerplate of most publishing contracts grants to the publisher final control over all publication details, including the title of your book, the design of the jacket, and the price tag it carries. In some instances, you can whittle down the publisher's control of these details somewhat so that you can retain a role in deciding the title, and so that you are at least consulted before a jacket design is approved. Keep in mind, however, that the publisher does not have final control over the actual words in your book and cannot make changes without your consent.

Territory

In most cases, the territory is negotiated before the contract is issued. Make sure that the territory as described in this contract clause matches the terms of your negotiation (see Chapter 14).

Manuscript delivery

This clause stipulates the length of the manuscript, usually stated in number of book pages or number of words, and the due date. Because most writers work with a word processor, finding out the length of the manuscript before you deliver it is easy. Most contracts allow a variance of 10 percent (either higher or lower) from the stipulated length.

Editors tell me that they receive about ten late manuscripts for every one that is delivered on time. The contract requires the publisher to notify the author when the manuscript is late. Once notified, the author must then deliver within 90 days. Once the 90 days are up, the publisher can demand repayment of any money advanced to the author so far. While publishers don't always exercise this option, they are well within their rights to do so.

I advise you to read the language in your contract about late delivery very carefully — not every contract is alike in this respect — because this issue could come back to haunt you at a time when you have a great deal on your mind and won't want to think about returning your advance.

In most contracts, a phrase in the delivery clause requires that the manuscript be delivered in the form of printed pages as well as a computer disk or e-mail copy.

Note that the manuscript delivery clause requires you to deliver a manuscript "acceptable in form and content to the publisher." This means that the publisher can find your manuscript unacceptable and refuse to publish it and even, in the case of some publishers, demand repayment of the advance.

The law sides with the author on this point, at least in New York State where most publishing contracts originate. The publisher can't reject your manuscript without supplying good faith editorial guidance to you in a timely manner. Only after a demonstrated effort at helping you revise your manuscript can a publisher cancel. This explicit protection is often written into publishing contracts. For contracts originating in New York, it is understood. There should also be a stipulation requiring that your publisher respond to your manuscript within a limited period of time after it is delivered — ideally within 60 days.

Permissions, index, and artwork: Who pays?

Most contracts require the author to secure and pay for textual or illustrative materials in the book, including any indexing costs. If you know that any of these costs are going to be exceptionally high, try to persuade your publisher to pay them outright, split them with you, or at least pay them as an additional advance that can be earned back in the form of royalties.

Next work

Most publishers want assurance that the book referred to in the contract is in fact your next book and that you won't write another book for a different publisher before you deliver the book specified in this contract. If you plan to complete another book first, either alone or with a collaborator, get this fact out in the open before you sign the contract. Publishers are usually accommodating if they know in advance and are less accommodating if the news comes as a surprise later on.

Editing

Language in the contract should confirm that as the copyright holder, only you are entitled to approve changes in the text of the book. This doesn't necessarily hold true in a work-for-hire agreement (see Chapter 14).

Proofs

When your book is ready to go to the printer (see Chapter 18), the publisher will ask you to read through a typeset copy of your book so that you can make last minute corrections and approve the text for printing. Make sure that the contract allows enough time for this process to be carried out correctly; I recommend at least two weeks.

Publication

Most authors are eager to see their book in published form as soon as possible. The publisher, by contrast, wants the flexibility to release each book so that it accommodates their overall publishing program — to rush publication if an opportunity presents itself or to delay if a backup of books occurs in the production department.

Your publisher will want the flexibility to publish your book up to 18 months after your editor accepts it. I recommend that your publisher be required by contract to publish within 12 months after acceptance.

Author copies

Publishers usually provide complimentary copies of the book for the author's use. The standard number is 10 to 20 copies of each edition. These copies are for your own use — perhaps to give to family and friends. Publishers, when specifically asked, are often willing to increase this quantity to 50 or 100 gratis copies, depending on the cost of producing the book. It's always worth asking.

Royalties

Royalties come in two different types: standard royalties and net royalties. *Standard royalties* are calculated on the full retail price of the book, while *net royalties* are calculated on the amount actually received by the publisher, after discounts are deducted. Net royalty rates tend to be higher than standard royalty rates, but they general put less money in the author's pocket. For example, a standard hardcover royalty is 15 percent at the highest sales level. If your book costs $20, the royalty payable would be $3 per book. On a net basis, say that the author's royalty rate is 20 percent of net (which is typical), and the publisher receives $10 from the bookseller on a $20 book. In that case, the author collects only $2 per copy.

When your contract arrives, you will have already settled on the royalty rates (see Chapter 14). Verify that the rates you negotiated are in fact in your royalty clauses. Scrutinize these clauses carefully. Here's what's typical.

- **Hardcover:** The standard industry royalty rate paid to authors is 10 percent on the first 5,000 copies; 12.5 percent on 5,001 to 10,000 copies, and then 15 percent on all copies sold over 10,000. These percentage rates are based on the full retail price listed on the book's jacket. Some authors are able to negotiate a full 15 percent royalty rate on all copies sold — though that is the exception, not the rule.

- **Trade paperback:** The standard trade paperback royalty rate is 7.5 percent of list price. Why is it so low? Because with the lower retail price on trade paperbacks, the profit margin for publishers is lower than on hardcovers. This lower profit margin is passed along to the author in the form of a lower royalty rate — sometimes as low as 5 percent or 6 percent of list price, especially on color illustrated books — and rarely above 7.5 percent (see Chapter 14).

  Publishers rarely increase a trade paperback royalty unless it's a brutally competitive bidding situation. And even then, publishers can only be persuaded to offer a slightly higher royalty rate until the advance is earned, and then they revert back to the standard 7.5 percent. But even this small increase means the author earns out the advance quicker, making royalties payable sooner.

- **Mass market:** The industry standard royalty rate on mass-market paperbacks is 8 percent of the book's retail price. In some cases, you can negotiate for a royalty escalation to 10 percent on copies sold over 150,000. If you can sell 150,000 copies of your book, most publishers are happy to increase your share in the profits.

- **Deep discount:** Publishers sell books to booksellers at a discount. Each publisher has a slightly different discount scale, but the industry standard ranges from a 40 percent discount for retailers who order small quantities, to a 55 percent discount to wholesalers who order in huge volume. Many publishers, in order to protect their bottom line, reduce the author's royalty rate on deeply discounted orders of 48 percent or higher.

  I recommend that you try to control this kind of royalty reduction. The fact is, a lot of books are sold at deep discounts, especially with the rise of wholesale clubs, and if you agree to a reduced royalty, your share becomes wafer thin.

- **Special sale:** *Special sales* are the sales of books that occur through channels other than bookstores or book sections in retail establishments. This category can be big because it consists of sales through catalogs and nonbookstore retail channels, such as gift shops, hardware stores, wedding supply stores, drugstores, and much more. In most publishing contracts, these sorts of special sales, along with *premium sales*, where the book is bought in quantity to be given away as a promotion, are assigned a royalty rate of 10 percent of the amount received by the publisher.

  Unless the author takes an active role in facilitating the sales through these special channels, publishers usually don't increase this rate. You are more likely to get a slight royalty increase — perhaps a point or two — if you demonstrate how instrumental you can be in landing large special or premium sales.

Subsidiary rights splits

Subsidiary rights are the rights that your publisher licenses to third parties. The proceeds from these sales are split between you and your publisher on a prearranged basis.

If a right — for example, first serial, book club, performance, and so on — is listed and the split between author and publisher itemized in the contract, that means that the publisher has retained this right. In other words you have appointed the publisher your agent in selling this right, and the money advanced to you by the publisher is advanced against earnings, of which earnings from sales of this right are a part. If the right, like first serial, does not appear in the contract, then you have retained that right, and your agent is entitled to sell it without any compensation going to the publisher.

- **First serial:** When an excerpt from your book is sold to a newspaper or magazine and appears in that publication prior to the book being published, it is known as a *first serial sale.* The author generally retains control of first serial, especially if represented by a literary agent. However, some large publishers want to sell first serial rights because they, too, have excellent connections with the larger magazines.

  If your agent has a strong track record of placing first serial, you're better served by holding this right back from the publisher. The standard publishing contract split on first serial is 90 percent of the proceeds go to the author and 10 percent to the publisher (90/10). If the publisher retains the first serial, ask for approval of the sale and of the excerpt.

- **Second serial:** When an excerpt from your book is sold to a newspaper or magazine and appears in that publication after the book has been published, it is known as a *second serial sale.* The publisher generally holds second serial rights, and the proceeds from these sales are divided half to the author, half to the publisher (50/50). Again, get approval over the excerpt and what periodical it will appear in.

  The author's share of second serial and all other rights retained by the publisher is accounted against the advance and, once the advance is earned back, earnings start to flow to you, the author. Your agent, of course, receives his or her commission on all such earnings.

- **Permission:** This right refers to the right to grant permission to a third party who requests to print excerpts of your book in another publication — especially anthologies. The standard split for a permission sale is half to the author, half to the publisher (50/50).

- **Condensation and abridgments:** If a publisher that issues condensed versions of books, such as *Readers Digest* condensed books, wants to print a shortened version of your book, they purchase the right to do so from your publisher. The proceeds from that sale are split half to the author, half to the publisher (50/50).

- **Book club:** Book clubs, such as Literary Guild, History Book Club, Quality Paperback Book Club, and the Book of the Month Club, purchase the right to sell books via their club membership. Once they decide to purchase the right to sell a particular book, the book clubs then have a choice between buying copies of the book from the publisher or printing their own "book club edition" copies. In either case, the proceeds from book club sales are divided equally between the author and the publisher (50/50). The publisher always retains book club rights.

Book clubs generally pay an advance and a very low royalty, often 5 percent of net received. The text of the book club edition is identical to the publishers original edition, but in some instances the book clubs arrange to print their own copies of the book, and use different — often cheaper — materials.

Premium or special

These are bulk sales of the book to customers who will use the book as part of their businesses. For example, special sales often take the form of copies of your publisher's edition of the book sold to mail-order catalogs, like Williams Sonoma or The Common Reader, or to a training company who will use the book as part of a seminar program.

Premium use entails buying copies in bulk to be given away for use in a customer incentive program, such as a bank or brokerage firm giving a free copy of a financial advice book to every customer who opens a new account.

Direct marketing is the business of offering copies of the book directly, usually with a mailed brochure. Many publishers (Rodale, Wiley, and Jossey Bass, for example) specialize in cultivating sales through the direct channel — they cultivate lists of customers, produce lavish brochures, and seek out books that are suited to this sales channel. In some unusual instances the right to sell the book through direct distribution, such as via mail order, are sold to a third party, usually a direct marketing expert. Two well-known experts in this field are Time Life and *Readers Digest,* which both specialize in direct distribution. When direct distribution rights are licensed to a third-party distributor, the proceeds are divided equally between the author and the publisher (50/50).

- **Foreign and U.K.:** If you are represented by a literary agent, the agent usually retains foreign rights and sells these licensing rights to publishers in as many countries as are interested in translating your book for their market. When a literary agent sells foreign rights, the proceeds are split, 80 percent to the author, 20 percent to the agent.

When a publisher retains the right to sell foreign rights, which require a translation, the proceeds are split, 75 percent to the author, 25 percent to the publisher. English language foreign rights have a slightly different split — 80 percent to the author, 20 percent to the publisher. Keep in mind that when a publisher sells the foreign rights, the proceeds are not paid to the author until the full amount of the money advanced to the author to write the book is earned back. Only then does the author receive any portion of the 75 percent from the foreign sale.

- **Paperback reprint:** Publishing companies often license paperback rights to another publishing company. Many authors wonder why the original publisher doesn't simply issue the paperback. Puzzling as it may seem, the only explanation is that the purchasing paperback publisher believes he can sell more copies of the book than the hardcover publisher. Because of the paperback publisher's confidence in the book, it's a worthwhile transaction for both buyer and seller. When paperback rights are licensed, the proceeds from the sale are then divided equally between the hardcover publisher and the author (50/50).
- **Hardcover reprint:** I know — this term is confusing. But there are instances when a publisher buys the right to reprint an existing book in hardcover. The original book may be either out of print, or hard to find, or in print only in paperback, or even in print in an existing hardcover edition. The most common reason to produce a hardcover reprint is that the licensee specializes in selling to a particular market. For example, some hardcover reprinters are especially good at library distribution, and put out special editions of books in library bindings. Other companies print special high quality collector's editions of existing books, and sell them to customers at a premium above the normal retail price. Generally these rights are licensed on an advance/royalty basis, and the proceeds are divided equally between the author and the publisher (50/50).
- **Performance:** *Performance rights* include movie, TV, and dramatic rights. If you have a literary agent, the agent typically controls these rights, and this clause does not appear in your publishing contract. If you don't have an agent and the publisher sells the performance rights to your book, you receive 90 percent of the proceeds, the publisher 10 percent.

You should know that most publishers are not well equipped to sell performance rights. If you do grant these rights to your publisher, I recommend that you amend this clause in the contract with a line that reverts performance rights back to you in the event that the publisher is unable to place them within a fixed period of time — say, one or two years.

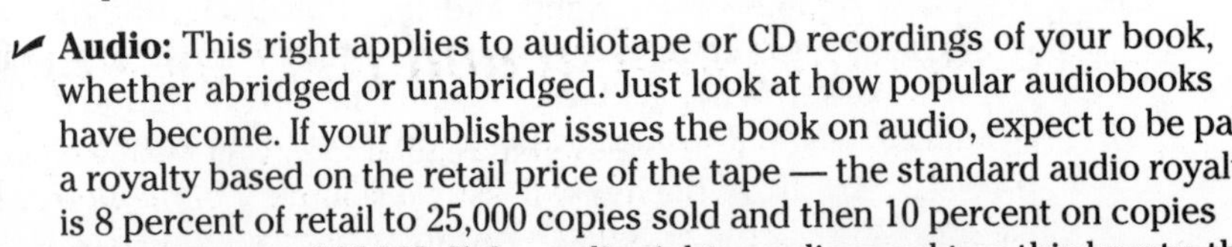

- **Audio:** This right applies to audiotape or CD recordings of your book, whether abridged or unabridged. Just look at how popular audiobooks have become. If your publisher issues the book on audio, expect to be paid a royalty based on the retail price of the tape — the standard audio royalty is 8 percent of retail to 25,000 copies sold and then 10 percent on copies sold in excess of 25,000. If the audio rights are licensed to a third party, the proceeds are divided equally between you and your publisher (50/50).

If you anticipate that your book will be published as an audiobook, or if you have a strong opinion about how the audio publication be accomplished, you should try to negotiate a few features of this contract. First, you need to stipulate whether the audiobook can be an abridged and/or unabridged edition of the book, or both. Second, if you hope to be chosen as the reader of the audiobook, you should work out a fee for this service. The going rate is low, usually under $5,000 and often as low as $3,000 or less.

- **Verbatim electronic:** This right refers to the right to reproduce all or part of the verbatim text of your book by electronic means, such as on a CD-ROM or on a Web site. This type of rights sale is going to become more and more prevalent as the e-world continues to explode. In a standard contract, the proceeds from the sale of verbatim electronic rights are divided equally between you and the publisher (50/50).
- **Multimedia:** Similar to verbatim electronic rights, this one is the right to adapt your book for use in databases and multimedia products. Multimedia rights are currently being treated like performance rights, being retained by the author and sold by a literary agent. However, if the publisher retains and sells these rights, the proceeds are split evenly between you and the publisher (50/50).
- **Public reading and rights for people with disabilities:** If someone requests the right to read from your book on radio or television, they must purchase that right from the publisher. Additionally, if a publisher of Braille or Large Print editions wants to purchase the right to produce these kinds of editions of your book, the proceeds from the sale of these rights are divided equally between you and the publisher (50/50).

Royalty advance and payout

The *royalty* is the rate at which you earn money from the sales of your book after it is published. The *royalty advance* is the amount of money that your publisher gives you as a nonreturnable loan that can be repaid from the book's earnings, derived from sales or from licensing fees. When the contract arrives, you have already negotiated not only the amount of your royalty advance, but also the size and date of each payment of the advance (see Chapter 14).

Accounting period and joint accounting

After your book is published, and at regular intervals during each year of your book's life, the publisher will issue a summary of the book's sales and subsidiary rights activity, called a *royalty statement.* If the royalty statement shows that you are owed money, you will receive a check about a month after the statement date. For most publishers, the standard interval between statements, referred to as an *accounting period*, is six months.

Joint accounting is a term that only has meaning if you sell more than one book to a single publisher. When two or more books are joint accounted, no royalty income is paid on any of the books until the combined royalty advance on all of them has been earned back. If your publisher buys a second and/or third book from you, they will try to persuade you to joint account your books. If you are unwilling to accept joint accounting, the publisher may ask you to accept a lower total advance, thereby reducing its risk.

Right to audit

Face it, mistakes can happen, and if you think an error has been made, you'll want to look into the publisher's records to either find the problem or ensure their accuracy. Most publishing contracts grant the author the right to hire an accountant to audit the publisher's records pertaining to your book. Make sure that your contract has such a clause.

Warranties and indemnities, legal reads, and libel insurance

In this section of the contract, you confirm that the book you are writing is original, that you are the owner of its content, and that it does not slander, libel, or otherwise infringe on anyone's rights. If it does, you will be held accountable under the law (you *indemnify* the publisher) and hold the publisher blameless in the event of a suit.

Most warranty and indemnification clauses include language about how you and the publisher will work together to defend against a lawsuit filed against both of you. The publisher takes the position that the author is solely liable in the event of a lawsuit, though most plaintiffs believe that the publisher shares liability with the author.

This clause includes a provision stating who pays in the event that a legal reading of the book is deemed necessary. It also tells you whether the publisher has paid for libel insurance — some do, some don't. So, read through this section carefully. If your publisher has a libel insurance policy, you will be covered by it. If they don't have a policy, they certainly won't obtain one to cover your book alone. Obviously, it's preferable for the publisher to pay for, or at least share, the cost of a legal read.

Noncompete clause

In most nonfiction contracts, noncompete language prevents you from writing a book in the future that will compete with this book. Sounds reasonable enough. But say that you're an expert on a certain subject, and you plan to write many books on this subject in the coming years. If that's the case, you better modify the noncompete language with the help of a professional. One good way to solve this problem — though it may not be acceptable to your publisher — is to place a time limit on the noncompete language — say, two or three years after publication of the present work.

Option

In the option clause, your publisher stakes a claim to your next book. In a perfect world, you would want your current publisher to publish your next book and every book after that. But no publisher is perfect, and editors move from publishing house to publishing house with alarming speed. If you agree to an ironclad option clause, your freedom is quite limited.

I recommend that you amend the option clause to allow the publisher a 30-day "first refusal option" based on an outline and sample chapter — not a full manuscript and not upon publication as is often stated in the contract (see Chapter 14). This amendment grants your publisher the sole right to see an outline and sample pages of your next book and gives it 30 days after it has accepted your first manuscript to come to terms with you on the new book. If the publisher doesn't make you a reasonable offer within 30 days, you are free to show the book to other publishers.

Know that the publisher won't want to decide on your next book until your first book has been published and they have some idea of how well it is selling.

The standard option clause "First refusal based on a full manuscript" may look innocent enough, but it isn't. It means that you have to write your entire second book — on spec! — before the publisher is obliged to make any decision whatsoever. And you can't even show it to another publisher until 30 days after your current publisher receives it and decides whether to bid or pass.

Another fairly standard option clause is, "First refusal with topping." What this means is that if you don't come to terms with your publisher, and other publishers bid for it in good faith, your first publisher is entitled to buy the book by bidding 10 percent more than the highest bid received from another publisher.

Additionally, you might see an option clause that grants "First refusal with matching." What this means is that the original publisher can buy your next book by simply matching the best bid received from another publisher.

Author's rights of termination

This clause protects you in the event that the publisher fails to perform. If you deliver your manuscript on time, the publisher must publish in a timely fashion. If your publisher fails to publish your book as required by contract — provided that a natural catastrophe or labor strike (a so-called "act of God") isn't the cause — you are entitled to keep your full advance and to recover the rights to your book.

Publisher's rights of termination

This clause protects the publisher if you don't deliver the manuscript at all, deliver the manuscript late, or deliver an unsatisfactory or unacceptable manuscript.

If you don't deliver a manuscript after the contractual grace period (usually 90 days after the due date), the publisher is entitled to a full repayment of the advance.

If the manuscript you deliver is unsatisfactory, even after the publisher works with you to improve it, the publisher also has the right to terminate your contract. Some publishers demand repayment of the monies paid you up to that point. Others allow you to keep the money paid so far, but they ask to be repaid out of *first proceeds,* or the initial earnings, from the book in the event that another publisher chooses to publish the book.

Signature

The time to sign the contract is when you are completely satisfied that every point is fully negotiated, and every agreed upon change has been made.

The standard signing procedure is for the author to sign each copy of the contract at the end of the document on the signature line and initial every clause that has been altered. Then make a copy of the entire contract and send all of the originals to your publisher. The publisher then countersigns the contracts and returns a copy of the countersigned contract to you along with a check for the initial payment due on signing.

The negotiation is complete. Congratulations!

How the contract can protect you

A well-written publishing contract, conscientiously negotiated, can protect authors in a number of ways — before, during, and after publication. Here are some of the benefits.

- Clearly defines each party's roles and responsibilities.
- Ensures that payments to you are based on sales of and earnings from the book.
- Protects the text of your book from being altered without your permission.
- Guarantees that the publisher will publish your book, in a certain format, prior to a certain date.
- Compels the publisher to keep the book in print or revert the rights to you.
- Obliges the publisher to provide accurate accounts to you and allows you to audit those accounts.
- Provides you with free copies of your book.
- Allows you to purchase books at a significant discount.
- Guarantees that your book will be formally registered for copyright.
- Enables you to recover the rights to your book if it goes out of print or if the publisher breaches the contract.

Sample Contract

Every publishing company has its own *boilerplate contract,* an all-purpose document that is modified in the course of every negotiation. Figure 16-1 is a rough boilerplate contract, issued by a fictional company, which features most of the clauses and the type of wording you will encounter in your publisher's contract.

AGREEMENT made this DD day of MM, 2000, between
First name Surname
Address
("the Author") and
AMERICAN PUBLISHERS, Inc. ("the Publisher")

This Agreement refers to a work tentatively titled __________(insert title) (hereinafter "the Work").

2-3 line Description of "the Work"

Under the terms of this Agreement, the Author and Publisher agree to the following:

1. GRANT AND TERRITORY
The Author grants to the Publisher during the term of copyright the exclusive right to publish, reproduce, and distribute the Work in all languages and to exercise and grant to third parties the rights to the Work described in Paragraph 6 throughout the world (the "Territory").

2. DELIVERY OF SATISFACTORY MANUSCRIPT
The Author shall deliver to the Publisher by ________(insert date) one copy of the complete manuscript of ______words in length acceptable to the Publisher in content and form and computer disk(s) on which the Work is stored, together with any necessary permissions, and all photographs, illustrations, drawings, and indexes necessary to the completion of the Work. If the complete Work is not acceptable to the Publisher, the Publisher shall ask the Author for changes and revisions. The Author shall have 60 days from the Author's receipt of such a request to deliver to the Publisher a revised manuscript and/or computer disk(s) for the Work that is acceptable to the Publisher.

If the Author fails to deliver any necessary permission or illustrations, the Publisher may obtain these materials and charge the resulting cost to the Authors royalty account.

If the Publisher deems that an index is necessary to the Work, Publisher may prepare such an index and charge resulting costs to the Authors royalty account.

3. PUBLISHERS RIGHTS OF TERMINATION
If the Author does not deliver the complete and satisfactory manuscript in a timely manner, per Clause 2, the Publisher may have the right to demand repayment of all moneys advanced hereunder. When such advances are fully repaid, this Agreement shall terminate.

If the complete manuscript and/or computer disk(s) as first submitted by the Author is unacceptable and the Author, after receiving the Publisher's request for changes and revisions, in good faith makes a timely delivery of a revised, complete manuscript and/or computer disk(s) for the Work that satisfies all the provisions of this Agreement except the requirement of being acceptable to the Publisher in content and form, the Publisher shall not be required to publish the Work and the Publisher shall give the Author notice of its decision not to publish. Thereafter, the Author may offer rights to the Work to other

1

publishers and shall repay the Publisher the sums paid to the author under this agreement from the first and all subsequent payments due the author from another publisher, up to the total amount paid hereunder.

4. NEXT WORK
The Work shall be the Author's next book. The Author shall not offer rights to another book to another publisher nor accept an offer for another book from another publisher until a complete manuscript for the Work has been delivered to the Publisher, and the Author has complied with the option provisions of Paragraph 13. This provision applies to future works whether by the author alone or in collaboration with others.

5. EDITING AND PROOFS
The Publisher may not effect any material change in the Work without the Author's approval. However, the Publisher may copyedit the Work in accordance with the Publishers house style for spelling, capitalization, punctuation and usage. The Publisher shall send the copyedited manuscript to the Author, who shall make any revisions and corrections and return it within two weeks of receipt.

The Author shall review and return within two weeks of receipt proofs or other production materials submitted by the Publisher.

6. PUBLICATION
Provided the Author delivers a manuscript, satisfactory to the Publisher in form and content, and in accordance with the delivery date stipulated above, the Publisher shall publish an edition of the Work. Such first publication is to occur no later than _________ (insert number) months from the date of the Publisher's acceptance of the manuscript. All publication details, including but not limited to format, design, price, marketing, and manufacture, are at the sole discretion of the Publisher.

The Author shall receive ten free copies of each edition of the Work from the Publisher. Additional copies for personal use only, and not for resale, may be purchased at a discount of 50%.

7. SUBSIDIARY RIGHTS
The Publisher shall have the right to license the following subsidiary rights to the Work, in the agreed Territory indicated above. Proceeds shall be divided between the Author and Publisher as stipulated below:

1) first serial publication of a newspaper or magazine excerpt prior to book publication; 90% to the Author

2) second serial publication of a newspaper or magazine excerpt following book publication, including syndication rights; 50% to the Author

3) permissions, including publication of an excerpt in an anthology; 50% to the Author

4) book club publication; 50% to the Author

5) foreign-language publication (including the right to sub-license the other rights granted in this Agreement to foreign-language publishers); 50% to the Author

2

6) English language publication outside the United States and Canada (including the right to sub-license the other rights granted in this Agreement to English-language publishers); 80% to the Author

7) condensations and abridgments; 50% to the Author

8) Premium or special sale publication of editions for direct sale to consumers; 50% to the Author

9) paperback reprint editions; 50% to the Author

10) hardcover reprint editions; 50% to the Author

11) Performance rights, including adaptations for use in song lyrics, motion picture, television, radio and live-stage dramatic production, commercial and merchandising. The Publisher will acts as exclusive agent on behalf of the author in the sale of such rights, subject to the Authors approval. 90% to the Author

12) Audio recordings or adaptations of the Work, either the whole work or an abridgment; 50% to the Author

13) the right to any recording or transmission of the verbatim text of the work, in whole or in part, in electronic form; 50% to the Author

14) the right to produce and distribute multimedia adaptations of the Work; 50% to the Author

15) the right to authorize public readings of the work, excepting such readings as those performed by the author without charge or payment for the purpose of promotion of the work; 50% to the Author

16) Braille, large-type and other editions for the handicapped; 50% to the Author

(b) Any of the above rights, for which a royalty has not be indicated, may be exercised by the Publisher itself upon negotiation with the Author of a mutually satisfactory royalty rate.

8. ACCOUNTING
After the Work has been published, the Publisher shall thereafter render to the Author a regular accounting of earnings, as well as payment of amounts due. Such accountings are to be provided twice annually, on April 1 and October 1 of each year, for the periods ending respectively December 31 and June 30.

The Publisher may deduct from each such payment of earnings a reserve against returned copies. The Publisher will provide a written explanation of any such reserve upon request.

Any overpayment of royalties received by the Author may be deducted by the Publisher.

9. ROYALTIES
The Publisher shall pay to the Author royalties on sales, less returns, of copies of the Publisher's editions of the Work as follows:

3

(1) on all hardcover copies sold through regular trade channels, and not otherwise credited as indicated below, the following percentages of the suggested customer's price: (A) 1 to 5,000 copies: 10% of the retail price(B) 5,001 to 10,000 copies: 12 1/2% of the retail price (C) in excess of 10,000 copies: 15% of the retail price.

(2) all copies sold in the United States at discounts above 50%, two thirds of the prevailing rate.

(3) on all hardcover copies sold outside the United States or for export to Canada or to other countries throughout the Territory, 10% of the amounts received by the Publisher;

(4) on all trade-size paperback copies sold through regular trade channels in the United States (except as otherwise provided below), 7 1/2% of the suggested customer's price;

(5) on all trade-size paperback copies sold in the United States at discounts above 50%, two thirds of the prevailing rate;

(6) on all trade-size paperback copies sold outside the United States or for export to Canada or to other countries throughout the Territory, 7 1/2% of the amounts received by the Publisher;

(7) on all rack-size paperback copies sold through regular trade channels in the United States (except as otherwise provided below), the following percentages of the suggested customer's price:

1 to 150,000 copies: 8%
in excess of 150,000 copies: 10%

(8) on all rack size paperback copies sold in the United States at discounts above 50%, 8% of the amounts received by the Publisher;

(9) on all rack size paperback copies sold outside the United States or for export to Canada or to other countries throughout the Territory, 8% of the amounts received by the Publisher;

(10) on all large print hardcover copies sold through regular trade channels in the United States (except as otherwise provided below), 10% of the suggested customer's price:

(11) on all large print hardcover copies sold in the United States at discounts above 50%, two thirds of the prevailing rate.

(12) on all large print hardcover copies sold outside the United States or for export to Canada or to other countries throughout the Territory, 10% of the amounts received by the Publisher;

(13) on all large print paperback copies sold through regular trade channels in the United States (except as otherwise provided below), 7.5% of the suggested customer's price;

(14) on all large print paperback copies sold in the United States at discounts above 50%,

4

two thirds of the prevailing rate;

(15) on all large print paperback copies sold outside the United States or for export to Canada or to other countries throughout the Territory, 7 1/2% of the amounts received by the Publisher;

(16) on all copies of the Publisher's editions of the Work sold directly by the Publisher to consumers in response to mail order or other direct-response solicitations sponsored by the Publisher, 5% of the price paid by the consumer, exclusive of shipping and handling charges;

(17) on all copies of the Publisher's editions of the Work sold as remainders at more than the cost of manufacture, 10% of the amounts received by the Publisher;

(18) on copies given to or sold to the Author, given away to promote sales or to charitable institutions, sold at or below the cost of manufacture or damaged or destroyed, no royalties shall be paid.

ROYALTY ADVANCE AND PAYOUT

The Author shall be paid an advance against all earnings, including royalties, subsidiary rights payments and other proceeds, derived under this Agreement as follows:

$_____________(insert amount) on signing and execution of this Agreement.

$_____________(insert amount) on acceptance by the Publisher of a manuscript, satisfactory in form and content to the Publisher ; and

$_____________(insert amount) on first publication of the Work.

11. RIGHT TO AUDIT
The Publisher will provide, upon written request from the author, the following information:

The number of copies of each edition of the Work printed by the Publisher; the date of each printing; the total number of copies sold, returned, distributed free of charge, remaindered, destroyed or lost; copies of any licenses made by the Publisher; and any other information the Author may reasonably request on the basis that it is required in order to ascertain the accuracy of accountings rendered.

The Author may upon written notice examine the Publisher's records relating to the Work during normal business hours under such conditions as the Publisher may reasonably prescribe. If an error is discovered as a result of any such examination, the party in whose favor the error was made shall promptly pay the other the amount of the error.

12. RESERVED RIGHTS
(a) The Author reserves all rights to the Work not granted to the Publisher in this Agreement.

13. NONCOMPETITION (b) During the term of this Agreement, the Author shall not

5

without the Publisher's consent publish any book on the same or similar subject matter as that of the Work hereunder.

OPTION

The Author grants to the Publisher an option on the Author's next book-length work (the "option book"), such option to be exercised as follows: The Author shall submit to the Publisher an sample chapter and outline for the Authors next work before offering rights to the option book to any other party. The Publisher shall have 30 days from its receipt of the option book to advise the Author whether it wishes to publish the option book and upon what financial terms, such 30-day period to commence no earlier than 60 days following the Publisher's first publication of the Work. If within such 30-day period the Publisher does not advise the Author that it wishes to publish the option book, the Author may offer the option book to other parties without further obligation to the Publisher.

If within such 30-day period the Publisher does advise the Author that it wishes to publish the option book but within 30 days of the Publisher so advising the Author, the Author and the Publisher have not agreed on financial terms for such publication, the Author may offer the option book to other publishers, and is not further obligated to the Publisher. This option provision shall apply to the next book co- authored by the Author as well as the next book solely authored by the Author.

15. COPYRIGHT

The Publisher shall print a copyright notice in conformity with the United States Copyright Act and the Universal Copyright Convention in the name of the Author in each copy of the Work printed by the Publisher and require its licensees to do the same. The Publisher shall register the copyright on the Work with the United States Copyright Office promptly after first publication and may record this Agreement with the United States Copyright Office.

16. WARRANTIES

The Author warrants to the Publisher that:

the Author is the sole author of the Work and sole owner of the rights granted in this Agreement, has not assigned, pledged or otherwise encumbered them and has the right to enter this Agreement;

The Work is an original work, has never before been published in whole or in part in any form in the Territory, is not in the public domain in any country in the Territory and does not infringe any copyright or any other proprietary or personal right; and

The Work contains no material that is libelous, in violation of any right of privacy or publicity, or harmful so as to subject the Publisher to liability to any third party or otherwise contrary to law.

17. INDENMITIES

The Author shall indemnify the Publisher from any loss, damage, expense (including reasonable attorneys' fees), recovery or judgment arising from any breach or alleged breach of any of the Author's warranties, subject to the limitations stated below.

Each party shall promptly inform the other of any claim made against either which, if sustained, would constitute a breach of any warranty made by the Author to the Publisher in this Agreement. The Publisher shall defend any such claim made against the Publisher with counsel of the Publisher's selection. The Author shall fully cooperate with the Publisher in such defense and may join in such defense with counsel of the Author's selection at the Author's expense.

If the Publisher wishes to settle on its own behalf any claim made against the Publisher, the Publisher shall consult with the Author and give serious consideration to any objections the Author may have, and the Author and the Publisher shall attempt in good faith to agree in writing on the percentage of any such settlement costs which each shall bear. Failing such Agreement, the Publisher may on its own behalf settle any such claim made against the Publisher on terms the Publisher deems advisable. In such event, the Publisher may recover from the Author amounts paid in settlement if settlement costs are incurred because of a breach of a warranty made by the Author to the Publisher in this Agreement. Alternatively, the Author may, at the Author's discretion, provide security reasonably acceptable to the Publisher for the further costs of defending the claim, in which event the Publisher shall not settle without the Author's written consent.

If any such claim is successfully defended, the Author's indemnity shall be limited to 50% of the costs (including reasonable attorneys' fees) incurred by the Publisher in the defense of the claim.

If any such claim is made, the Publisher may withhold a portion of payments due the Author under this Agreement to cover the Author's obligations stated above.

The Author shall be responsible for any claims made against any third party to which the Publisher grants subsidiary rights to the Work to the same extent as the Author is responsible to the Publisher under the indemnification provisions of this Agreement.

The warranties and indemnities made by the Author in this Agreement shall survive the termination of this Agreement.

Prior to the first publication of the Work, the Publisher may have the Work read by the Publisher's counsel at the Publisher's expense.

18. AUTHOR'S RIGHTS OF TERMINATION
If the Publisher fails to publish the work in the period stipulated in Clause 5 above, unless because of production delays caused by the Author, the Author may demand publication in writing. If the Publisher does not comply with such demand within 90 days, all rights in the work will revert to the Author, and the Author may keep any moneys advance to date hereunder.

(1) After the work is out of print, if the Author requests reversion of rights, the Publisher must revert print rights to author, or announce reissue of an edition of the Work under one of its imprints within six months of Authors request.

(2) The Work shall be considered out-of-print if no edition is available for sale through ordinary channels of the book trade in the United States from the order fulfillment department of the Publisher or a licensee of the Publisher and no license is in effect which provides for the distribution of an edition of the Work through regular trade channels in the United States within twelve (12) months from the date of the Author's

request for a reversion.

19. ADVERTISEMENTS
No advertisements (other than advertisements for other publications of the Publisher) shall be included in any edition of the Work published by the Publisher or under license from the Publisher without the Author's written consent.

20. USE OF AUTHOR NAME FOR PROMOTION
The Publisher may use the Author's name, likeness and biographical data on any editions of the Work published by the Publisher and in any advertising, publicity or promotion for the Work and may extend these rights in connection with grants of the subsidiary rights made by the Publisher.

21. THE MANUSCRIPT AND PRODUCTION MATERIALS
The Author shall keep at least one copy of the manuscript for the Work and any other materials submitted to the Publisher under this Agreement. The Publisher shall upon the Author's written request, made within a year after first publication by the Publisher, return to the Author the copy of the manuscript used for typesetting; the Publisher shall not be required to retain such manuscript for more than one year. However, if editing of the Work is done solely on disk, the Publisher shall not be required to return the edited manuscript to the Author.

22. BANKRUPTCY AND LIQUIDATION
In the event of the bankruptcy, insolvency or liquidation of the Publisher, this Agreement shall terminate and all rights granted to the Publisher shall revert to the Author automatically and without the necessity of any demand or notification.

23. PAYMENTS TO AUTHORS AGENT OR REPRESENTATIVE.
All payments due to the Author under this Agreement are to be paid to the Authors duly appointed representative, ______(insert agents name), whose receipt thereof shall be a valid discharge of the Publishers obligations. The Author irrevocably assigns to the Agent a sum equal to ____(agents commission percentage) of the income earned hereunder to the Authors account, and the Agent is empowered by the Author to act on his behalf in all matters arising from and pertaining to this Agreement.

24. HEIRS AND ASSIGNS
This Agreement shall be binding upon and inure to the benefit of the heirs, executors or administrators and assigns of the Author and the successors and assigns of the Publisher and may not be assigned by either without the written consent of the other, with the following exceptions. The Author may assign the Author's right to receive payment under this Agreement upon written notice to the Publisher. The Publisher may upon written notice to the Author assign this Agreement to any company that acquires or succeeds to all or a substantial portion of the assets of the Publisher.

25. COMPLETE AGREEMENT AND MODIFICATION
This Agreement constitutes the complete understanding of the parties; no modification of it shall be valid unless written and signed by both parties.

26. DISPUTE RESOLUTION
Any dispute arising from this Agreement shall be submitted in the State of New York to

American Mediation Council, LLC, under its Mediation Rules, before the parties resort to arbitration, litigation, or some other dispute-resolution procedure.

Unless signed and counter-signed within 60 days of issuance, this Agreement shall not be binding to either party. By signing below, the parties accept the terms of this Agreement, as of the date stated above.

AUTHOR

____

AMERICAN PUBLISHERS INC.

By:__________________________________

President and Publisher

Part VI
After the Deal Is Done

"Your new book, 'Help-My Head's Caught in a Pipe,' has been called by some to be semi-autobiographical. Can you comment on these rumors?"

In this part . . .

With contracts signed, the real work begins. In this part, I take you inside a publishing house to look at exactly how a book is created — from manuscript to the printed book on display in bookstores across the country. And while the publisher may help you promote your book for a few weeks, it's ultimately your job to interest readers in your book. So I look at many different ways that you can promote your book — in print, on radio, TV, online, and in person.

Chapter 17

Know the Players

In This Chapter

- Meeting your publishing team
- Knowing how to work with them
- Understanding your role in the process

Meet the other publishing insiders who have a role in the creation of your book. Get ready — you need a surprisingly large number of people to successfully publish a book. While your editor continues to be your main contact at the publishing house, many other people are also working on your book — the copy editor, proofreader, page designer, jacket designer, art director, managing editor, marketing director, publicity team, promotion and advertising folks, sales manager, subsidiary rights staff, and (should you need them) the royalty and finance departments, contract manager, legal team, and so on.

This chapter tells you who accomplishes exactly what task, and what you can do to help. Keep in mind that the easier you help make their job, the better able and more willing they are to give your book the support it needs. When all the team members get involved and excited about your book, their enthusiasm gets passed on to the bookseller, who in turn passes it on to the reading public, which translates into sales!

It Takes Team Work

No single individual can perform the myriad tasks of a full-service publishing company. That's why the jobs are divided up among specialists — each performing a specific role. You, the author, are expected to be ready with an answer or additional material when one of these individuals calls, yet no one introduces the specialists to you or alerts you to who is working on your manuscript at each step in the process. That's why I recommend that you ask your editor for both a detailed production schedule and an opportunity to meet at least some of the many people who will work on your book.

Be cooperative

Acting as a liaison between an author and a publishing insider is part of an editor's job, so chances are your editor may try to convince you that you don't need direct contact with the various players. An editor's reluctance to grant an author access is, unfortunately, based on experience. Authors are known to make unreasonable demands on the hard-working individuals who simply aren't used to dealing with the fears and insecurities inherent to writers.

Assure your editor that your purpose is to facilitate a spirit of cooperation and open communication. Explain that you understand, only too well, that they need to work without interruptions and that you have no intention of interfering. On the other hand, you also understand that it is your job to provide assistance when asked and the better informed you are about the process, the better prepared you can be to supply the most complete and up-to-date information at the appropriate time.

Assume that they haven't read your manuscript

Save yourself a lot of aggravation by assuming that whoever you speak to at the publishing house, other than your editor, has not read your complete manuscript. Most publishing companies publish so many books that expecting everyone to thoroughly read each book is unreasonable.

That said, be prepared to provide both basic and supplementary information to every person you speak to about the book. Don't put them on the spot by asking what they think about a certain point in your book — instead answer their specific questions as fully as possible and mention what's especially important and interesting about your book. Make it your job to make their job easier. Both you and your book benefit.

Be your editor's advocate

Your editor, the person who fought to publish your book in the first place, is your strongest advocate. She is responsible for coordinating the efforts of every employee at the publishing house who works on your book. While a system is in place to ensure a smooth transition for your book as it moves from one department to the next, you should be aware that problems can occur. That's why I recommend that you make it your responsibility to know where in the publishing process your book is at all times. Your editor, devoted as she is, has many books in the pipeline — you have only one.

No editor purposefully loses track of a book. Whatever problem occurs isn't usually her fault, but the editor takes responsibility for it. Let your editor know that you understand the pressure she's under due to such an immense volume of work. Tell her you'd like to relieve at least some of the pressure by taking a more hands-on role if possible. With your actions and attitude, show her how truly cooperative you are. This attitude can greatly enhance your relationship.

The Heart of Any Publishing House: Editorial

The editorial side of any publishing company is responsible for finding, acquiring, and perfecting the contents of books — the product a publishing house manufactures and sells. In most publishing houses, the editorial department consists of an editor in chief, several acquiring editors, editorial associates and assistants, a managing editor, and copy editors. While the editor in chief usually makes the ultimate decision on acquisitions, the acquiring editors themselves are responsible for finding and presenting myriad book projects to the editorial board. When the board decides to publish a particular book, it is the acquiring editor's job to prepare the manuscript for the production process, often with the help of an editorial associate or assistant. The managing editor then coordinates the entire production of the book including the proof reading and copy-editing stage where the text is read and reread for accuracy.

The editor: Your advocate and guide

The average editor at a general trade publisher, like Simon and Schuster or Hyperion or Chronicle Books, is responsible for acquiring and publishing between 10 and 20 new books each year. So, at any given time, your editor is likely juggling between 30 to 100 titles — bouncing from the books she is acquiring, to the ones she is editing, to the ones that are about to publish, to those already published yet needing attention.

In addition, your editor is attending weekly editorial, marketing, and sales meetings, writing catalogue and jacket copy, chasing after new book projects, commissioning others, helping and placating frustrated authors, as well as pursuing authors whose manuscripts are late. Meanwhile, your editor is fielding a steady stream of new submissions, negotiating contracts, and attending to the tasks associated with presenting and acquiring books for future publication.

In the midst of all this chaos, your editor is also focusing her attention on you, the editing of your manuscript, and the marketing of your book. In fact, she coordinates every phase of the publishing process, from start to finish. She attends meetings with each department when your book is discussed, where budgets are formulated, jackets designed and approved, and strategies developed.

The actual editing of your book, which most authors think is the biggest part of an editor's job, is usually accomplished at home after work hours. And this so-called editing of your book actually consists of an in-depth *content edit* where the editor looks at the book's overall organization, style, pacing, voice, and more. She is likely to ask you to restructure, clarify, add, and/or cut certain elements.

As a rule, book editors do not rewrite. They ask you to revise the manuscript based on their suggestions. Be prepared to engage in at least one round of revisions and possibly more. This edit is not meant as a personal slight. Nor is it intended to make your life miserable. It's simply the way an editor helps you create the best book possible.

Managing editor: A master mechanic

The managing editor acts as the liaison between the editorial department and the production process — some companies refer to this person as the *production editor*. It is the managing editor's responsibility to create a schedule for and keep each book moving smoothly through the production process, from copy-edited manuscript to final bound books. Staying on top of each book's production schedule is critical because once a publication date is announced and the book is promised to be on bookstore shelves, marketing plans are set in motion and promotional activities are secured for the author. If books don't arrive on time, these careful plans are in vain.

Additionally, the managing editor works with the marketing director to ensure that the company's books are scheduled to publish at the most advantageous time — either to coincide with the proper season and holiday or to avoid facing competition from a similar book. In other words, a spring gardening book needs to be in bookstores in plenty of time for readers to plan and plant their spring garden. Likewise, it's best to avoid having two pasta cookbooks publish in the same month.

Copy editor and proofreader: Dotting the "i's" and crossing the "t's"

Once your manuscript is revised and accepted by your editor, it's given to a copy editor. Copy editors are a writer's best friend — they work incredibly hard to make you look good. In fact, their meticulous eye checks every detail in your manuscript, from spelling, grammar, and punctuation to any noticeable contradictions or ambiguities, as well as the accuracy of all dates, locations, and so on. You can relax knowing that the copy editor is sure to catch and correct any little mistake you make.

In most publishing houses, the manuscript is read by the copy editor not once, but twice — before it is set into type and again after it's in typeset pages in order to catch any typesetting errors. Expect to receive the copyedited manuscript — full of flags and queries — four to six weeks after you've handed it in to your editor. You then have approximately ten days to answer all the copy editor's queries, make corrections, and return it. Then, about four to six weeks later, you'll receive typeset pages with flags and queries from the copy editor. Again you'll have approximately ten days to make corrections and return the typeset pages. You will not be shown corrected typeset pages unless you specifically ask. So, if you feel the work has been sloppy or you have a lot of corrections, ask to see the corrected pages before they're printed.

Production: Paper, Printing, Binding, and Magic

The actual production of the book includes all elements of the book's design and physical manufacturing. A production team turns manuscripts — usually on disk — into expertly designed pages and, finally, into printed and bound books, ready for sale.

The art director and designer: The perfect look for your book

The art department transforms your typed manuscript into an attractively designed package, all wrapped up in an alluring jacket. Two teams within the art department carry out the necessary design parts. The art director oversees both of these teams — deciding when to use on-staff designers and when to hire freelance designers. The first team consists of the layout specialist, who spends his or her days at the computer screen, carefully designing and laying out each page of your book. Secondly, the jacket designer specializes in designing the book's jacket. Because the overall effect of the book jacket's design can have an effect on sales, many publishing pros get involved in the final jacket design decision. And if you've secured approval or consultation in your contract, then the publisher is legally required to include you in the jacket design process.

It's not unusual to come up with more than one jacket design for a specific book. So if you feel the jacket design for your book is not right, speak up.

The production manager: Bringing it all together at the plant

The production manager oversees the complex task of bringing together the design and editorial components of a book. The production manager is responsible for many different pieces in the process — purchasing the printing supplies, such as paper, binding, and cardboard covers; negotiating press time at the printing plant to personally supervising the printing on complex books; and providing editors with informed estimates of what it will cost to manufacture different books with various specifications.

Marketing and Sales: From the Printing Press to the Customer

In order for books to sell effectively, the publishing company sales and marketing efforts need to mesh. The sales department arranges for the distribution of books to bookstores and other retail sales outlets. The marketing department works to make customers aware of the books and stimulate book sales as soon as they hit the marketplace.

The marketing director: Orchestrating the campaign

It's the marketing director's responsibility to formulate a marketing plan for each book, secure the money to execute the plan, and make sure that the plan is carried out. In a small publishing company, it's often the publisher or the promotion/publicity director who performs the role of marketing director. In a large conglomerate publishing company, marketing managers are often assigned to each imprint and are overseen by an overall marketing director who coordinates the company's entire marketing strategy, which consists of both publicity and promotion.

The publicist: Handling the media

Publishing companies are highly dependent on book publicity to promote the sales of their books. In fact, publishers think of publicity as "free" or nearly free because, compared to every other marketing effort, it's relatively inexpensive. It's through the tireless work of your publicist that your book gets press coverage. So help your publicist in any way possible to ensure plenty of hype for your book in the following ways:

- **Reviews:** A publicist sends your book to hundreds of reviewers and follows up to make sure that timely reviews appear in all the right newspapers and magazines.
- **National media:** The publicist maintains relationships with producers at all of the national television shows where authors are often featured. Of course, every author wants to be on "Oprah" — and hopefully your publicist can secure a half-hour spot for you. Publicists need to be creative to secure bookings on shows like "Oprah," "60 Minutes," or "Dateline." Help your publicist brainstorm a unique angle, format, or grouping of guests to pitch to the show's producer.
- **National print:** The publicist meets with magazine and newspaper editors to offer interviews with and profiles of the publishing company's authors. If an aspect about you is especially interesting, let your publicist know so that she can use it in her pitch.

- Do as much up-front work for your publicist as possible. If you can pull facts, distill points, or come up with a Question & Answer or True/False list relevant to your book, newspapers and radio producers are often willing to run with it. The point is to make it a no-brainer for someone to want to promote your book. Give him or her the lead or hook or handle.
- **Tours:** The publicist also organizes tours and press events across the country so authors can appear on local media — TV, radio, and print. Tours are a great way for writers to personally connect with their specific audience in cities all around the country.

The promotion manager: Attract eyeballs and make the book stand out

Promotion is the piece of the marketing effort that the company has to purchase or pay to create. So all the attention-grabbing techniques a publishing house pays for to get your book attention is the responsibility of the promotion manager. These techniques include such items as sales brochures, catalogs, posters, floor and counter displays, all advertising, postcards, bumper stickers, key rings, advance reader's editions of the book, and even special bookstore display space at the end of an aisle or on a tabletop. Some books are better suited than others for these efforts, and the Publisher will decide where to allocate funds. If you have any great promotion ideas that may interest him or her, speak up early in the planning process.

Distribution: Out into the World

Distribution refers to the way books get distributed to the various sales outlets throughout the country. The distribution of books is the responsibility of a publishing company's sales department.

Sales representatives: Your pitch person with the booksellers

Sales reps act as the liaison between the publishing company and the book retail market. Each sales reps is based in a different sales region in order to effectively service the more than 10,000 bookselling accounts spread out across the country.

Most publishing companies hold what is called a *sales conference* two or three times a year, where all of their sales reps come together with the company's editors to hear about the upcoming books. Armed with catalogs, sales brochures, and information direct from the editor, the reps return to their sales region, meet with each of their bookselling accounts, present the publishing company upcoming books, and secure advance orders.

Special sales representatives: Your pitch person with other customers

Most publishers have special sales representatives who sell books to nontraditional accounts such as corporations, government agencies, direct mail catalogs, and direct marketers like QVC, the Home Shopping Network, Publisher's ClearingHouse, and many others. Unlike regular sales, these special sales are often made at a deep discount and on a nonreturnable basis.

The sales manager: Commanding the troops

Once the sales representatives have met with all their accounts (bookstores) and secured orders, they send these orders to the sales manager who's based at the company's headquarters. By compiling these advance chapters and estimating orders still to come before publication, the sales manager determines the size of your book's *first printing,* or how many copies of your book the company will actually print.

The bookstore buyer: The key gatekeeper

Bookstore buyers are the people at the bookstore who decide, often in seconds, whether they will stock your book. They make this decision based on the catalog copy, the book's jacket, and any extra information the rep conveys.

The warehouse manager: Supervising the flow of books

While the larger orders are sometimes shipped directly from the printer, bypassing your publisher's warehouse entirely, the rest of your printed books go to the publishing company's warehouse where the warehouse manager oversees the order fulfillment process. The warehouse manager also keeps close tabs on the inventory of each title alerting the sales manager when stock is low and when it's time to order another print run of your book.

Many people don't realize that books are sold to almost all accounts on a fully returnable basis. What this means is that booksellers can stock their stores full of books, however, if the books don't sell, they just return them to the publisher's warehouse for a full credit.

Support Departments: Behind the Scenes

Several behind-the-scene departments in a publishing company can have a significant impact on your book.

Subsidiary rights director

The subsidiary rights director is responsible for licensing certain rights to third parties, including serial excerpts of your book to newspapers and magazines, translation rights to foreign publishers, book club editions, paperback reprints, and more.

You earn a percentage of each of these sales (see Chapter 16), so the more information you supply about your book and the markets you think it will interest, the more easily the subsidiary rights director can work on your behalf.

Your editor will provide the rights director leads you can suggest, such as whether your book is ideal for serialization in a new magazine with a full manuscript as early in the process as possible, and detail any information of interest, such as your company is conducting business in Italy. This sort of information could be of great use to your subsidiary rights director. Be responsive when someone in the rights department secures an offer, especially if your contract grants author approval on subsidiary rights sales. The subsidiary rights director works hard to give your book as much exposure as possible.

Contracts and legal

The contract department drafts each contract, based on information given to them by the acquiring editor. Whenever a specific contractual question arises, the contract manager consults with the legal department.

The legal department performs another especially important function that impacts authors. If an editor feels that your book contains something that could provoke a lawsuit, the editor will ask the legal department to *vet* the manuscript, which means to read it with an eye toward any potential legal issues that could result from the book's publication. Most publishing contracts explicitly assign the author full responsibility for any lawsuit that arises out of the book's publication. If your book is libelous, or defamatory, or plagiarized, the publisher's view is that this problem is yours and yours alone.

In truth, most lawsuits for libel or defamation or plagiarism are filed against both the publisher and the author. That's why publishers are strongly motivated to read every manuscript with an eye for potential lawsuits in order to satisfy themselves that the risk of an expensive legal battle is extremely unlikely.

In a manuscript where a lawsuit seems likely, a lawyer — either on the publisher's staff or hired by the publisher — is brought in to read the manuscript and highlight areas where legal alterations or substantiation may be necessary. Most publishers won't accept a manuscript for publication until this process has been completed to the publisher's attorney's satisfaction.

Royalty department

The royalty department keeps a detailed record of the earnings of each book that is in print with the publishing company. In addition to the amount of the original advance, the royalty department keeps tabs on all book sales, as well as other income from the book such as subsidiary rights sales, and provides a running tally. This tally is printed and sent to each author twice a year in the form of the royalty statement.

Authors have a right to hire an accountant to audit the publishing company's books if for any reason they believe an error has been made on their royalty statement.

Finance manager

The finance manager is responsible for ensuring that each editorial imprint at the publishing company makes a significant financial profit. The finance manager's goal can be at odds with the editor's goals of publishing the best books possible. Everyone knows that the best books don't always make the most money. However, the finance manager reminds editors that while it's okay to publish a few books that don't turn a substantial profit, the overall bottom line of their department must be profitable in order for the company to survive. Book publishing is, after all, a business.

Chapter 18

Creating the Actual Book

In This Chapter

- Demystifying the editorial process
- Overseeing your book's design
- Following your manuscript through production
- Getting the finished book that you want

In this chapter, I walk you through the steps that transform your manuscript — the one you deliver to your editor — into an actual printed and bound book. I let you know what kinds of changes your editor may ask for and how best to respond to her content edit. I also describe what's involved in each stage — from the moment you receive the copy-edited manuscript and first-pass pages to final mechanical, blueprint, right up to holding your actual book.

The Editor: Your Guide

Your editor is the glue that holds the publishing process of your book together. She acts as your guide throughout the entire manuscript preparation stages. She is also your advocate in any number of meetings where the fate of your book is being decided. Your editor is fully invested in the success of your book — not only because she believes in it, but also because her job survival depends on the success of the books she brings to the company.

Editors have a diverse range of talents. They're able to work well with writers, are experts at improving manuscripts, and have a gift for articulating the important benefits a particular book can offer. Because this combination of skills is rare, when you find a talented editor who appreciates your work, you have an opportunity to enjoy an extremely productive relationship.

In fact, the bonds that develop between writers and their editors can run deep. For example, F. Scott Fitzgerald and Ernest Hemingway produced their greatest books while working with their legendary editor, Maxwell Perkins, at Scribners. More recently, Robert Ludlum produced a string of international bestsellers in collaboration with Richard Marek, his editor at the Dial Press. Danielle Steele has enjoyed great success with her editor of over 15 years, Carole Baron, who recently moved from Delacorte to Dutton. John Grisham credits a measure of his success to David Gernert, his editor at Doubleday, who eventually left publishing to become an agent, taking Grisham on as his first client. Many of Stephen King's best-selling books have been edited by Charles Verrill, a former editor at Viking who, even after becoming an agent, continues to edit King's manuscripts on a freelance basis.

If you're writing your first book, the editor may ask to see the first chapter or two as soon as you complete them. This way, she can assess how your work is progressing and make sure that you're on the right track. No one wants to waste time and effort writing material that isn't moving the book in the right direction. Alternatively, if you find as you're writing that you want or need editorial feedback, talk to your editor about how this can best be accomplished. Each editor works differently, so you need to find out early in the process how your editor likes to proceed.

Delivering Your Manuscript

Once your manuscript is completely written, ask your editor for specific submission guidelines before sending it off. Most publisher's require one or two *hard* copies of the final version of the accepted, edited manuscript, meaning printed copies, as well as a computer disk containing the entire document using Microsoft Word for Windows software program. The formatting of the manuscript changes slightly from publisher to publisher. However, the following format requirements are fairly standard:

- 12-point standard type
- Double-spaced copy
- Single-line spacing between paragraphs — no indenting
- Unjustified text
- Page numbers
- One computer file per chapter
- Hard copy printed on a high-quality laser printer using white 8½ x 11-inch paper

Congratulations! Your manuscript is now ready to begin its journey to becoming a printed and bound book.

Manuscript Editing

Excellent as your manuscript no doubt is, be prepared for your editor to find areas that can benefit from a little more work. First, your editor reads the entire manuscript to get a sense for the whole book. Then she reads it a second time, making painstakingly detailed notes and recommendations right on the manuscript itself. (Look at the sidebars to get an idea of the types of editorial comments you can expect to see on your manuscript.)

Contrary to popular belief, editors don't rewrite. What they do is perform a content edit on your manuscript. During the second, more careful reading, the editor queries or flags problem areas and may offer suggestions for remedying the problem. However, it is always the author's responsibility to actually make any changes or revisions.

After annotating the manuscript, your editor puts together a detailed editorial letter presenting all the content issues that need addressing in the manuscript. This editorial letter usually includes an overview, stating what is especially successful in the manuscript and what can benefit from more work. The letter then itemizes specific problem areas, usually offering recommendations on how to remedy these issues.

Keep in mind that your editor's intent is not to make your life miserable, but to make your manuscript more accessible and enjoyable to read.

Nonfiction editorial comments and revision requests

Following are some of the types of editorial comments you may receive on a work of nonfiction.

Cut. Your editor may suggest specific cuts to reduce repetition, redundancy, and/or to reduce the book's length. Skillful cutting can improve the pace of the book and help sustain a reader's attention.

Repetition. Editors flag instances where you repeat yourself.

Clarity. Your editor may ask for clarification when your prose is unclear, unpersuasive, or just plain confusing.

Digression. If it's not relevant or you stray from your point, your editor makes a note of it.

Legal problem. Your editor flags statements that could get you in legal trouble.

Not believable. If an assertion rings false or an argument doesn't bear up, your editor lets you know.

Sourcing or verification. Passages that need proof, verification, or sources to be specifically identified are carefully marked.

Awkward. Awkward or clumsy writing is pointed out and rewrites requested.

Fiction editorial comments and revision requests

Following are some of the types of editorial comments you may receive on a work of fiction.

Character. If a character isn't developed well enough or acts inconsistently — for example, *out of character* — your editor brings it to your attention.

Setting. When a scene is not described or *set* well enough for the reader to see or imagine it, your editor marks it.

Plot. Your editor alerts you to plot development that is clumsy or diverges from the original outline.

Dialogue. Your editor marks any dialogue that doesn't ring true.

Pace. Passages where the pace of the writing lags or reader engagement declines are marked, and often your editor suggests solutions.

Show, don't tell. If you lapse into exposition and tell information rather than show it through dialogue and action, an editor immediately flags it.

Chronology. If the chronology is unclear or violated in some way, the editor notes it on the manuscript.

Confusing. An editor doesn't ever want to lose readers — if any part of the story becomes confusing, she'll tell you.

Awkward. Clumsy or awkward writing is always pointed out.

Transition. Editors like to see smooth transitions. If the transitions are a bit rough as you move from scene to scene, your editor will note them and suggest skillful fixes.

Responding to an Annotated Manuscript

For most writers, the editing process is an exciting time of discovery, when their work is studied and examined as never before. Your editor has likely been improving manuscripts her entire professional life and can offer advice you won't receive from a nonprofessional. Keep this fact in mind as you read through the entire annotated manuscript. Look carefully at each of your editor's comments and try to get a sense for what the recommended changes accomplish. Stay open-minded as you consider how these revisions will affect your overall work.

If you have questions about or strongly disagree with some of the editor's recommendations, make note of these on a separate piece of paper as you read through. Go ahead and make the simpler changes on this run-through. Then schedule a time to talk with your editor about the queries or comments you disagree with. Often, a full-blown discussion of what you mean to accomplish can help the editor come up with a solution that satisfies both of you. However, if you still disagree with your editor's recommendations, remember that a publisher cannot make a single change in the text of a book without the author's agreement and approval.

There are unfortunate cases of editors demanding offbeat, unreasonable changes complete with threats to cancel the contract if the changes aren't made. Likewise, there are writers who flatly refuse to make requested changes, and as a result, their manuscripts are deemed unacceptable for publication. Publishing contracts are clear on this issue: The manuscript won't be published, nor the full advance paid, until the finished manuscript satisfies the publisher "in form and content." Most editors and authors have strong opinions about the books they work on and because rethinking or reworking a manuscript is difficult, authors can find this stage particularly stressful. Try to remember that you and your editor are working toward a common goal — creating a wonderfully readable book for public consumption. For that reason, you need to address each content edit as realistically and fully as possible. Then, when all the changes are made, return the revised manuscript to your editor.

Production Scheduling

When the manuscript has been fully approved by your editor, it is given to the managing editor who ushers it through the production process. At this point, a complete production schedule for your book is issued. Study this schedule carefully because you'll need to be available at key times in the schedule to answer and approve copy-editing queries and edits and again to read and approve sample pages and first-pass pages.

Following is what a typical production schedule includes.

- Date manuscript is due by contract
- Date manuscript is actually delivered to editor
- Date manuscript delivered to copy editing
- Copy-edited manuscript sent to author
- Copy-edited manuscript due back to copy editor from author
- Date manuscript due to designer
- Sample pages completed
- Sample pages approved (by editor and author)
- First-pass pages due to copy editor
- First-pass pages sent to author
- First-pass pages back to copy editor from author
- First-pass pages back to production
- Bound galleys received from printer

- Index work begins. In some cases, the author is shown the index to correct for accuracy
- Second-pass pages to copy editor
- Second-pass pages back to production
- Disk to printer
- Blues from printer to publisher
- Jacket flap copy due to copy editor. At most publishing houses, the author is consulted on the jacket flap copy prior to this stage
- Mechanical due to printer
- Jackets ship from jacket printer to book printer
- Bound books due to warehouse
- Release date
- On sale date
- Publication date

The production schedule described in this chapter is the arrangement used at most major *trade houses,* meaning publishing houses that produce books to be sold primarily in retail bookstores. Publishing houses that are geared more toward the academic and professional markets are usually organized differently: The acquiring editor departs from the process once the book has been acquired, and the book itself is prepared for manufacturing by a production editor who serves the function of content editor as well as copy editor. These two steps are accomplished in one single phase of the production process, which is accomplished through one or more passes of query and correction between production editor and author.

Copy Editing

A copy editor is responsible for the final polishing of your manuscript. This highly trained professional is well versed in the company's grammatical style rules. The copy editor reads carefully through the manuscript several times, with an eye toward correct word usage, grammar, spelling, and punctuation, as well as overall clarity and coherence. The copy editor looks for factual errors or inconsistencies, noting each in the margin, flagged with a *query tag,* which is a colored slip of paper. If the copy editor is using an electronic copy-editing system, like the revision mode in Microsoft Word, editorial queries are written directly in the electronic version of the manuscript in a special revision font. The author's responses are also tracked electronically.

You can rest easy knowing that whatever inadvertent errors your editor misses, the copy editor will catch and correct.

Copy editors also check the following items as well:

- **Proper names:** What are they, and are they used and spelled consistently throughout the piece?
- **Chronology:** Is the chronology of events correct, and is it consistent throughout?
- **Coherence:** Do the ideas follow logically?
- **Offensive:** Is the manuscript potentially offensive to a sector of the audience?
- **Libel or plagiarism:** In some cases, the copy editor is expected to flag any passages in the book that may possibly be libelous or taken improperly from another work. Is a correctly cited source listed for all references?
- **Word usage:** Are words used correctly? Is another word more appropriate?
- **House style:** Many publishing houses have what they call a *house style* of accepted spellings, usages, and grammatical conventions. It's the copy editor's job to make sure the book conforms to the publishing company's house style.

Think of your copy editor as an objective consultant whose meticulous examination of your manuscript not only improves it, but gives it a professional shine. If you don't like some of the copy editor's suggestions, that's fine — just cross them off or stet them. (*Stet* is a mark that instructs the printer to reinstate a deleted item.) The copy editor's recommendations are not binding — they're intended to improve the overall book.

Authors are usually given two weeks to respond to the copy editor's queries so check the production schedule for your exact dates. Be sure to answer each query, even if it just requires a simple yes or no, so that the copy editor knows you saw her questions. When you're finished, return the manuscript to your editor so that it can be set into type.

Sample Pages

Be sure to ask your editor to see *sample pages,* which show you how the actual pages of your finished book will look. To produce sample pages, a designer in the art department comes up with a layout based on many different criteria. For example, trim size or physical size of the book as well as the length of your book influences the size of the type and the amount of white space that will appear on each page. A typestyle is selected, a page layout is designed, and the look of the title page, table of contents, and chapter heads are determined. All of these design elements come together on the sample pages that are printed out by the designer for you and your editor to approve.

First-Pass Pages

First-pass pages are the first set of pages produced from your manuscript, and they look exactly as they will appear in the final book. These pages are usually generated from a Mac-based computer in the art department. Once the copy-editing queries are incorporated, the text is transferred electronically from a Windows-based computer to a Mac computer that runs Quark Express or another layout software program. In Quark, each page of the book appears, exactly as it will appear in the final printed version, and any corrections made after this point are done right on the Quark pages.

These first-pass pages determine the final shape of the book. In fact, the paper, binding materials, press time, and printing schedules are ordered based on the specifications of these pages. Because the publisher has locked in a schedule, a paper purchase, and press time in advance of first-pass pages, keep in mind that changes made to the book after first-pass pages may upset the production schedule and the entire publishing plan for your book. Especially if you and your publisher are entering corrections on paper instead of a computer, changes in first-pass pages can also increase the likelihood of errors creeping in to your text.

Proofreading

One copy of the first-pass pages along with the copy-edited manuscript is sent to the author, and another copy goes to a proofreader. Both parties are asked to compare the final copy-edited manuscript to the first-pass pages in order to catch any errors missed in copy editing or generated during the computer software transfer.

A production editor at the publishing company incorporates all changes from the author and the proofreader onto one set of pages. This set is then used to make changes in the Quark Express version of the book. While editorial changes are still possible at this stage, be sure to discuss the extent of the revisions with your editor because you don't want to alter the number of pages in the book. Be aware that most publishers will charge you for any typesetting alteration that incurs charges in excess of 10 percent of the cost of setting the entire book. Also, extensive resetting can increase the risk of missing important production deadlines and possibly delay your publication. This may not sound so terrible, but it could cost you prescheduled publicity and bookstore promotion if the book was slotted and ends up being late.

Page count matters

You may be wondering why the length of your book — and the possibility that the book may emerge from the production process longer or shorter than you and your editor had originally planned — matters. Length is important for a number of reasons. When your book is originally envisioned by your editor, the factors of length and cost are taken into account quite carefully to determine the price that can be charged for the book and the number of copies that may be ordered by booksellers at that price. Before the book is printed, booksellers order copies of your book based on a specific price and specifications, including length. If your book then becomes longer or shorter, or cheaper or — as is more often the case — more expensive, booksellers may cut their order or fail to sell as many copies as they had hoped. For this reason, your publisher works hard to make sure that your book comes out at the length and price originally agreed upon at the start.

Dummy and Mechanical

If your book is heavily illustrated, it will require a production dummy and a production mechanical, which are created either on a draftboard or, more likely, on a computer in the production department.

The *dummy* is a schematic model of your book, using the first-pass page text, display type for headings and chapter numbers, captions for illustrations and charts, along with the illustrations in draft format pasted or scanned onto the pages for position. A designer and the copy editor, as well as the author and the editor, then carefully check each page of the dummy. Corrections are made, and a final version of the book is created using the final corrected second-pass pages, as well as final artwork, corrected captions, and display type. This final revised dummy, now called a *mechanical,* is sent to the printer. The mechanical is either made up of computer disks or cardboard pages with all the elements in final form.

Second-Pass Pages

Second-pass pages are usually for the publisher's eyes only unless extensive changes were made in the first-pass pages. Usually, a proofreader checks the second-pass pages to make sure that all the changes noted in first-pass pages are faithfully incorporated and that the result flows smoothly and correctly. Only glaring errors of fact and typography are altered at this stage.

Jacket Copy

The descriptive sales copy that appears on the jacket of your book is written by your editor — usually after the manuscript is fully edited — and sent to you for approval. Check it for accuracy, but don't be alarmed if it sounds too good to be true. It's meant to entice readers. Just make any necessary corrections and send the revised copy back to your editor.

The Blueprint

At the printer, each page of the mechanical is photographed on a giant camera, which produces sheets of film the exact size of the book pages. Each sheet of film is duplicated using blue-tinted photographic paper. The resulting *blues,* or blueprints, actually smell like the photographic development liquids they're soaked in. This set of blues is sent to the publisher for one final check, looking mainly for layout errors. At this late stage, any correction requires that the affected page of mechanical be sent back to the publisher, changed, returned to the printer, and then reshot on the printer's layout camera. Obviously, only the most vital corrections can be considered at this stage.

When the film is revised and ready, platemaking begins. Once again using a photographic process, the images from the film are transferred to the offset press's huge metal plates for actual printing.

Finished Books

The metal plates are fitted onto the lithographic press, and pages are printed on huge rolls of paper that are then folded, cut, and bound together into *signatures* — the technical term for each 16-page section of the text, which is folded but not yet glued, stapled, or sewn into the binding. The signatures are gathered together as folded and gathered sheets, *f&gs,* which are cut and glued into cardboard cases to form the finished book. The jacket (in the case of hardcover books) or cover (for paperbacks) is usually printed elsewhere, on a color press, and shipped to the bindery where it is attached to the finished books.

Your book has now taken on its physical appearance. Enjoy the vision!

Chapter 19

Selling Your Book

In This Chapter

- Understanding your role in the selling process
- Getting endorsements that sell
- Introducing the mediagenic you
- Advertising — what's effective and what's not

Many authors are so excited to see and hold their printed book that they overlook the sales and distribution process. Suddenly they wonder how copies of their book made it onto the shelves of bookstores and other retail outlets all across the country.

In this chapter, I discuss the selling process — from creating the positive *buzz* that persuades booksellers to order multiple copies of your book, right through to ways you can get out and promote your book directly to its target market. I reveal what marketing decisions are made behind your publisher's conference room door and how you can become part of that process.

The Crazy Way It Works

Exasperated Publishers often remark, "This business is so crazy, it's hardly a business at all." And maybe they're right. After all, what other business produces 60,000 brand-new products each and every year? What other business distributes these products to retailers on a consignment basis, pays an additional fee to have the products prominently displayed in stores, and then accepts all the unsold products for full refund three months after the original distribution?

This is exactly how American book publishing works, season after season, year in and year out. To a traditional businessperson, it must look insane. And yet, in its crazy way, the system works. Wonderful books are published each year, readers find them, and new writing careers are launched.

But the fact remains that it's a complex and highly inefficient system. In the vast array of fresh titles each season, an unwary newcomer can easily get lost. That's why you want to do everything in your power to ensure that your book makes a strong and lasting impression in the marketplace. The more active a role you take in marketing your book, the better the results — guaranteed.

In the Beginning: Acquisition

The marketing of a book begins during the acquisition process. In many publishing companies, the first conversation about a potential acquisition focuses on its marketability. Publishing is, after all, a business. For that reason, you want to present as detailed a marketing plan as possible in your original book proposal (see Chapter 8).

The editor uses this marketing information in the memo she attaches to your proposal to generate widespread interest at the editorial meeting. The perception gleaned about your book at this meeting is what lingers in the minds of key sales and marketing decision-makers. That's why it's important to carefully shape a succinct description of your book and its full market potential in your book proposal. This condensed selling description is what the editor uses to position your book in the minds of the company's in-house decision-makers. Be sure to keep your editor abreast of new developments or updated information pertaining to your book or the book's topic area and pass along all information about potential new sales avenues.

If you don't feel absolutely confident about how the marketing information is presented, consider hiring a professional marketer to help you create this one-page sales distillation of your book. It's the one document that will be used over and over again to position and market your book.

Preselling

Publishing companies market their books in groups called *lists,* which are separated into *selling seasons.* A publisher usually has two to three lists or selling seasons each year: houses that sell in two lists have fall and spring cycles; houses that have three lists usually have a fall, winter, and spring/summer list. For any selling season, the publisher creates marketing materials on each and every title to be used at sales conference and by the sales reps when they visit their accounts to solicit orders.

The preparation of these marketing materials usually begins three months before the list is formally presented to the sales reps. And the reps start selling each list four to five months before publication. For example, the reps begin selling the spring/summer list in January, the fall list in May, and the winter list in September. This means that if your book is going to be published in January, the in-house marketing discussions and plans begin in May. Your book is presented to the reps at the company's August sales conference and sold to stores in September. So preparations to sell your book usually begin just about the time you're handing in your finished manuscript.

The in-house preselling season at every publishing house is punctuated with meetings where the books are presented and marketing plans are formulated. Each publishing house is slightly different: What is called a *first look meeting* at one firm may be called a *launch meeting* at another. Publishers struggle to reduce the number of meetings on their calendars, and so meetings are blended together or omitted entirely from time to time. For the sake of simplicity, I have detailed the entire cycle of preselling meetings using the most common term to describe each meeting in the cycle.

Tip sheet

A *tip sheet* is the document used inside the publishing house to set the marketing plans for your book in motion. Your editor, who's busy editing manuscripts, acquiring new ones, and tending to ones just published, is responsible for writing this all-important document. Often, she's required to write it before editing the manuscript, so the more information you can provide for this document, the better. If you didn't include a one-page marketing description in your proposal, now is the time to create one and give it to your editor for her to use in writing the tip sheet. A tip sheet is a one-page document that includes a wide range of basic information about the book: the author's name, the book's title and subtitle, the season and publication date, and a one-sentence *handle* (or selling description) that can fix the book in the mind of the bookstore buyer. The tip sheet also summarizes the publicity opportunities, presents information about competing books, and lists celebrity endorsements, if there are any.

Keep in mind that the content of the tip sheet has a powerful impact on how your book is viewed within the publishing company and positioned in the marketplace. Believe me, it pays off to begin generating great word of mouth early on in the process.

Author questionnaire/biography form

When you deliver your manuscript, you'll be sent an author questionnaire to fill out and return. This three- to eight-page form asks for a great deal of biographical information about you as well as the vision you have for your book.

Devote time to answering these questions in depth. The information you provide helps your publisher design the most effective marketing strategy for your book. Be prepared to write a succinct biography to be used in all promotional materials and a 10- to 15-word description of your book. You'll also be asked to provide the names of organizations — local bookstores, religious societies, alumni clubs — that may be interested in having you speak, buying a bulk quantity of your book, or listing your book in their newsletter or on their Web site.

Some questionnaires ask who you think will actually buy your book and why. What benefits does your book offer this audience, and what makes it particularly relevant today? Be prepared to provide the names and contact information of influential people in your field from whom to solicit advance endorsements for the book, as well as the names of reviewers, columnists or opinion-makers who you think may be interested in reviewing your book.

Be as thorough in your answers as possible. This information, along with the one-page marketing description you write for the tip sheet, forms the basis for all your marketing efforts. If you do a superb job answering the author questionnaire, you'll be assured of a top-notch tip sheet.

Ten author questionnaire do's

Set aside plenty of time to complete the author questionnaire when it arrives from your editor. All those details may seem unnecessary, but believe me, each question is there for a reason. If you follow the ten author questionnaire do's listed here, both you and your book benefit.

Do fill in every item.

Do tell the truth.

Do list every media contact you know or think you know, complete with contact information. Be truthful about which reporters, journalists, and producers you actually know well and which ones you know only slightly. Also list each recent interview you've given: print, radio, TV, and online.

Do include a flattering, recent photograph of yourself.

Do brainstorm with friends for marketing ideas and clearly present each one.

Do take pains to describe your book, in a single page, as you would like to see it described. If it's nonfiction, provide a list of the book's key points, as well as any newsworthy items in the book.

Do provide a list of influential people whose endorsement can help sell the book. Make another list of people who can be counted on to provide an endorsement. Provide full names, titles, and contact information.

Do include a detailed resume of your life. Include your education, jobs, hobbies, family details, and any information that may be of interest to the media, your publisher, or potential customers.

Do supply a detailed explanation of your qualifications to write the book.

Do furnish detailed information about your writing career. Include articles written by or about you, editors you have worked with, and books you've had published including the sales figures for each edition.

Sample from your book

Because it's impossible for every publishing professional who works on your book to actually read it from cover to cover, the editor usually chooses a brief but telling excerpt from the book and circulates it along with the title information sheet to the in-house staff so that they can become familiar with your book. Your editor knows how to make this sample as compelling as possible. And in order to help the reader better understand the excerpt, she also prepares a cover sheet, which explains where, and how, the sample fits into the book. For your own information, ask which excerpt has been chosen and offer to write a contextualizing paragraph, if necessary.

Book people love to read. But they can't read every book their company publishes — there aren't enough hours in a day. You can help by pulling a tantalizing excerpt and creating a synopsis to help the marketing folks get to know your book. The more exciting you make your book, the better job they can do marketing it.

Launch meeting

The first formal marketing meeting where your book is discussed is called a *launch,* or *first look,* meeting. The editor, the publisher, the marketing director, and the sales director usually attend, and it is at this meeting that the company's vision of your book begins to gel.

This meeting is one of the most critical phases in the publication of your book. It's where significant aspects of your book's packaging and marketing efforts are thrashed out. For example, the editor and sales department discuss whether the book's working title is right and whether the sales handles are strong enough to secure the interest of booksellers. Marketing and sales reps describe the types of marketing materials they'll need to get the book across to booksellers. Additionally, an estimate of the dollar amount necessary to budget for marketing the book is debated.

Be aware that marketing budgets are not created equal. Publishers tend to apportion more marketing support for lead titles and less for books with smaller print runs. That said, runaway successes such as *Cold Mountain* by Charles Frazier (Grove-Atlantic, 1997) and *Tuesdays with Morrie* by Mitch Albom (Doubleday, 1987) are books that started with modest first printings and marketing budgets. So, no matter how modest the publisher's initial expectations may be, books can catch on and sell beyond anyone's expectations.

The marketing discussions that take place at the launch meeting usually result in questions and refining work for the editor and author. Say that it's decided that the title doesn't do the book justice. You'll be asked to brainstorm new titles. If problems are anticipated with the book's proposed format, such as the length or the illustrative content, you'll be asked to re-evaluate these with your editor. Likewise, if the sales reps feel that they need to give booksellers an advance reader's edition in order to show them the book's merits, this request, along with the cost, is evaluated.

The launch meeting is not the place where a detailed marketing strategy is developed. It's the place for discussion, formulation, and feedback.

Jacket meeting

Your editor meets with the art director around the time of the launch meeting to decide on a design approach for your book's jacket. If you have definite ideas about how the jacket of your book should look, put your ideas into a memo addressed to your editor. That way, she can include your memo in the package she sends to the art director, along with a synopsis of the book and the copy to appear on the book jacket.

Several weeks after this initial jacket meeting, the art director shows a sketch of the jacket to your editor. If your editor and the marketing folks approve it, the sketch is shown to you, either for approval — if you have contractual approval — or as a courtesy and as a check for accuracy. Most publishers retain the right of final approval over book jackets because they feel the jacket is an important element in the book's marketing. However, if you detest the jacket sketch, speak up and provide solid reasons why you feel it's inappropriate. Rarely does a publisher insist that your book be adorned with a jacket you loathe.

Planning meeting

A follow-up to the launch meeting, called a *planning meeting,* also occurs. At this meeting, the problems and issues raised in the launch meeting are ironed out, and a specific marketing plan is shaped and budgeted. Ideally, at the end of this meeting, a solid jacket design is in the works, and the marketing materials that need to be produced for the selling process are decided. These marketing materials can include book excerpts, sample art spreads if the book is heavily illustrated, representative ads and posters if these are part of the marketing mix, along with publicity events and tour information.

Catalog copy

Your editor writes the catalog copy for your book, using the title information sheet and the launch meeting discussions as a basis. Most editors show the catalog copy to the author for approval. If you haven't seen this copy, ask your editor. And once you read it, if you have suggestions for improving the copy, let your editor know.

Often promotion, marketing, and sometimes print run information is included in the catalog copy. It usually appears in a bulleted format, such as:

- National broadcast and print media campaign
- 25-city national radio campaign
- Author appearances in Boston and New York City
- Official author Web site
- Online promotion
- 50,000-copy first printing

While the catalog copy alerts you to what the publisher is planning for your book, keep in mind that publishing companies are notorious for inflating this information. Don't be disappointed if the actual sales advance is lower than the catalog promises and therefore fewer books are printed. Likewise, not all the announced marketing plans always pan out. But the more involved you become, the better your chances for widespread exposure.

Presales meeting

A presales meeting is held a month before the actual sales conference as a kind of dress rehearsal. It is attended by most of the sales, marketing, and subsidiary rights staff. At this meeting, the follow-up work from the launch meeting is evaluated. All of the advertising, publicity, and promotion plans are reviewed, book jackets are evaluated, catalog copy is approved, and audio recordings or video footage of authors to be used at sales conference are checked and evaluated.

By the end, detailed marketing plans for each book are finalized. Each attendee knows exactly what materials they need to prepare for sales conference, and work begins in earnest on the elaborate slide presentation meant to highlight the marketing plans for each book and create excitement among the sales reps.

The Selling Process

The sales force is responsible for getting books into bookstores. Large publishers maintain a full-time sales force — either salaried or commissioned — to call on independent booksellers, regional wholesalers, national wholesalers, and large national book-selling chains, like Barnes & Noble, Borders, and Amazon.com. Small publishers can't afford their own sales force, so they usually distribute their books through national wholesalers, like Ingram and Baker & Taylor, who feature their titles in a catalog but don't hand sell individual titles the way publisher-employed sales reps do.

National accounts

Publishers estimate that national chain booksellers, like Barnes & Noble, Borders, and Amazon.com, account for close to 80 percent of retail sales in the book business today. Most publishers designate a special sales team, called *national account reps,* to act as liaison between the publishing firms and the powerful retail entities. At smaller firms, the Publisher or the sales director (or both) services the national accounts.

Independent booksellers and regional wholesalers

The smaller independent stores and regional wholesalers are serviced by the company's sales reps. At larger firms, these reps are each assigned a specific regional territory. The territories are sized so that an industrious rep can meet with each area book buyer in the course of a four-month selling season.

Smaller firms, if they deal with the independent stores at all, use a telephone sales force or commissioned reps — who work for several small publishers at the same time — to cover the far-flung independent booksellers.

Sales conference

Publishers hold formal sales conferences two or three times a year — usually in a meeting hall somewhere near their main office or at an out-of-the way resort. At sales conference, the editorial and marketing staff come together with the company's entire sales force to present the house's upcoming list of books. These conferences usually operate as follows: The presenting editor stands at a lectern in the front of a hotel ballroom with the slide of a book jacket behind her. In under a minute, the editor describes the book to a roomful of sales reps, explaining in a few words what the book is, how its merits are best communicated to booksellers, and what the publisher plans to do to ensure that the copies displayed in stores will actually sell. Book after book is flashed on the screen, a description is given, and then the next slide appears. Some companies use slides, some use video footage of the author, and sometimes the editor appears on videotape instead of in person.

Once the presentations are delivered, the reps are given their *sales targets,* which are the quantity of each title they are expected to have their bookstore accounts order. With all of this information in hand, the reps then offer their professional feedback to the marketing and editorial staff. Based on the reps feedback, titles and jackets are sometimes changed, marketing plans are altered, and budgets revised.

As a general rule, authors are not invited to sales conferences nor are they welcome to just show up. Many authors believe that if they present their book to the reps, the reps would do a better job of representing it on the road. This hasn't proven to be the case. However, if you want the reps to have certain information about your book that will help them sell it more effectively, by all means prepare a memo to them stating the information as clearly and succinctly as possible. The marketing director will include it in the title information package each sales rep receives.

Sales solicitation

Sales calls are the actual prearranged meetings that reps make each selling season with individual bookstore buyers — whether they're independent booksellers or national chains. In either case, the rep arrives at the buyer's office or shop equipped with a catalog, a collection of tip sheets, sample book jackets, as well as other enticing sales materials. The rep then has about a minute to describe each book and sketch out the company's marketing efforts on its behalf, while the buyer reads along in the company's catalog. At the end of each one-minute spiel, the buyer gives an order quantity, which, based on the rep's presentation, is the number of copies he feels he can sell. Some buyers prefer to place their orders on a written form, which is sent to the rep sometime after the sales call.

Buyers do decline taking certain titles if they don't think they can sell enough to make it worth their while to stock. Extra assistance from you can really help the reps convince them to stock at least a few copies. Take the time to come up with specific selling handles and a succinct description of what's special about your book early on, to generate excitement among the reps about your book before they make their sales rounds.

Marketing meeting

Once the reps complete their selling rounds and all the orders for your book are in, the publisher schedules a *marketing meeting* to evaluate the book's status before publication. Have the sales targets been met? Are the marketing plans in place? Is the publicity schedule filling in with the kind of coverage anticipated? What reviews are expected? These types of questions get addressed, and, depending on the answers, adjustments are made.

Generally, the amount of money spent on marketing is based on the number of copies shipped. So the publisher takes a hard look at actual sales figures. If fewer copies are shipped than anticipated, the amount of money spent on advertising, promotion, and publicity for your book is lowered at this time. If, on the other hand, your book receives more interest than expected, promotion and publicity plans are added in an attempt to capitalize on this enthusiasm.

Surprisingly, authors are not usually told about this marketing meeting. It's considered an inside, behind-the-scenes update. However, the meeting's outcome has a great deal to do with how your book is treated when it hits the marketplace. For that reason, I can't urge you strongly enough to tell your editor that you'd like an update on the last-minute marketing review of your book.

Whether it's cause for celebration or means that you have more work to do, with this information in hand you know what your next move is. For example, if the reps distribute more copies of your book than expected, urge the publisher to add more publicity and promotion opportunities. Or if the distribution is low, you'll want to come up with some kind of creative promotional strategies to spur sales among the book's target market. Once consumers start asking for your book, bookstores start reordering.

Bound galleys

Bound galleys is the term publishers use to refer to the early edition of the book they create to solicit endorsements and book reviews and to acquaint TV and movie producers with the content of the book well before publication. This term is a holdover from the days when books were set in hot type and proof sheets were printed on long, narrow pages called *galleys*. These galley sheets were cut and bound together with colored paper jackets to form crude advance copies of the book.

Today, a bound galley is still a relatively crude, uncorrected early bound version of the book created before the publisher's official edition. Since first-pass pages are generally pretty clean, publishers now use these to create advance bound-galley copies of the book. If your book gets delayed in production, publishers will bind copies of the manuscript instead of typeset first-pass pages. Manuscript pages aren't as easy for reviewers to work with, so do everything in your power to keep the production process of your book on schedule.

Jacket copy

The text that appears on the outside of your book — hardcover or paperback — is called *jacket copy.* Your editor either writes or obtains the jacket copy for your book from the marketing department and sends it to you for review. Don't be surprised if it sounds especially enticing — it's promotional copy written to lure consumers into purchasing your book.

As you read it, ask yourself whether it conveys the appropriate feeling about your book. If you have an important point to add which improves the overall copy, by all means do so. If you — as most writers seem to — believe you can do a better job writing the jacket copy, take a stab at it. You'll be surprised how difficult this kind of writing can be. Editors and marketing writers are trained in creating concise, sales-oriented copy. They do it for a living, so don't be dismayed, after you've spent hours rewriting, to discover that the original version is actually better.

Endorsements

Endorsements from experts and celebrities sell books. A well-chosen endorsement received early in the process gets attention for your book and helps secure better distribution. It also looks great printed prominently on the book jacket. Endorsements received later in the process can't be used on the first edition jacket, but they can generate excitement in press releases and advertisements.

As soon as you hand in your manuscript, start putting together a list of potential endorsers. Include absolutely everyone who is even remotely appropriate: experts in your field; other authors who have written on your topic; television, radio, and movie celebrities who are interested in or somehow aligned with the book's topic; political figures; prominent professors; or writers whose opinions the public values. It's generally the editor's job to solicit endorsements, but be sure to review the list of potential endorsers and decide whether any of the names on the list might respond more quickly and easily to a contact directly from you. To receive early endorsements, you'll want to send either a complete bound manuscript or galley or, at the very least, sample chapters along with a brief synopsis of your book and an author bio. Take time to phrase these letters in a professional but friendly manner. You're asking people to lend their established name to an unknown quantity, so be sure to provide as much information about yourself and the book as you think will make them feel comfortable.

Here are the essentials to include in an endorsement request letter:

- Mention your connection to this person. "I admire your work. What you said in your recent "20-20" interview struck a chord in me. Our mutual friend Frank Smith encouraged me to write. I met you briefly at the Hawaii writers' conference. My brother tells me you have been fundamental in helping him," and so on.
- State your purpose along with your book's title, the publisher, and the pub date. Say why you think this person's endorsement would be especially valuable.
- Include any endorsements or words of praise you have already received.
- Thank them for considering your request.

Figure 19-1 shows you an example.

Dear Lotsa Willpower,

I so admire your steadfast ability to keep weight off. When I heard you speak four years ago at the worldwide Lose Weight Forever conference in Geneva, I was spellbound. In fact, your talk spurred me into action. I made it my business to study each and every published diet program in existence and have come up with a well-balanced, sensible, easy-to-incorporate lifestyle diet called The Down-to-Earth Diet. Because of your impact on my work, I'm writing to ask if you might consider giving an endorsement statement for my upcoming book *The Down-to-Earth Diet* to be published in November by Weight Loss Press.

I've included an overview of the diet along with some biographical information. I would be honored if you would like to see the manuscript, which I can send you immediately, or the galleys, which are due in mid-September, and consider providing a statement. (Or I've asked my editor to send you a galley of the book in the hope that you have the time and willingness to supply an endorsement if you find my work worthy.) Please feel free to contact me at (312) 488-5352 and thank you for considering my request. You have been such an inspiration to me.

Sincerely,

Flat Abs

Figure 19-1: A sample endorsement request letter.

If they agree to see a manuscript, send it promptly with a cover letter expressing your appreciation for the time and interest that they are bestowing on your work. If you hear nothing after two to three weeks, call to make sure that the person received your letter. Be polite and gracious.

When you receive an endorsement, be sure to write a personal and enthusiastic thank-you. And make sure to send the endorser a complimentary copy of your book as soon as it's published.

Subsidiary rights sales: First serial, foreign, book club

Once the manuscript is deemed acceptable, copies are made and distributed to the rights department. These copies are then sent to magazines and newspapers for serial consideration, book clubs for book club consideration, foreign publishers and their scouts to be sold overseas, as well as audio publishers, direct mail marketers, special edition marketers, book catalogs, movie and TV producers, and so on. Your agent or publisher — whichever retained the rights — makes an effort to place these rights as early in the process as possible. You can expedite this process by recommending excerpts that may be suitable for specific magazines. Each rights sale adds credibility to the book, and certain rights sales — especially first serial — can help spur awareness of the book at publication. A first serial sale is usually timed to appear in a magazine or newspaper about a month before the book appears in stores. Hopefully, this small portion of the book whets readers' appetites and makes them hunger to read the entire book.

Prepublication publicity

Several months before the book is printed and ready to go to stores, the publicity department begins to acquaint magazine editors and TV producers with the content of your book. Magazines commission stories about and interviews with authors well in advance of the publication date. Likewise, TV producers start planning shows months before their airdate. For this reason, the publicist sends bound manuscripts or bound galleys long before publication.

In the Marketplace

You and your publisher want to create the largest possible splash for your book as soon as it hits the market. Book sales are driven by word of mouth. Reviews, recommendations, media events, and articles about the book and the author all help stimulate word of mouth.

Great book promotion ideas

Here are 11 ways you can help boost sales of your book.

Sign books in a bookstore. Author-signed copies of a book are considered to be more valuable. Most booksellers welcome authors signing the copies they have in stock.

Solicit endorsements. Use every contact you can think of to solicit endorsements for your book. The right endorsements lend visibility and credibility to the book.

Give talks. Public speaking is critical to your success as an author. Sharpen your oratory skills and approach organizations that may be interested in hearing you speak. Fill your calendar with speaking engagements — even the smallest audience buys books.

Hire a freelance publicist. Most publishers' publicists begin booking author engagements and media attention for your book about a month before pub date and continue to focus on the book for a month or so afterwards. Then they move on to other titles in their lineup. If you want ongoing publicity support, you'll have to either provide it for yourself or hire a professional freelance publicist to help you. (See Chapter 20 for a list of ten great freelance publicists.)

Write an op-ed column for your local newspaper. To generate word of mouth for your book, write an op-ed piece for your newspaper. Carefully frame the piece around a timely news story that highlights or raises issues you discuss in the book. Share these points and offer your book as a place for readers to gain further insights.

Commission a survey and use the data to promote your book. Newspaper reporters and TV producers love data: Ever notice those little charts that run on the front page of *USA Today* every day of the week? Find or create data from your book to spin into a news story. Hundreds of market research firms can provide data or conduct a survey for you to mold into an enticing news story.

Send a copy to opinion makers nationwide. Create word of mouth by circulating copies of your book to people who can talk it up. If your book has social or political content, consider mailing copies to the members of Congress or religious leaders. If yours is a business book, Fortune 500 CEOs are great targets.

Post glowing reader reviews on Amazon.com and barnesandnoble.com. Encourage your friends and relatives to help get word out about your book by posting rave comments on the online sites. These online booksellers place these reader reviews up on line right next to the book's entry — no one's ever going to know if it's your best friend who writes it.

Use the Internet. Find all appropriate links and make sure that every Web site knows about your book. Offer to do online chats, workshops, and so on.

Create a Web site for your book. The key is to have valuable content to offer so that the Web site draws a lot of traffic and drives book sales. The sales part is easy. Just link your site to the book retailer of your choice — book retailers all post associate programs at their sites. Producing valuable content takes some effort. Many authors post a modified chapter from the book along with fresh content such as new findings in ongoing research. The more useful the information, the more active your Web site.

Offer workshops. Engage your book's audience by offering hands-on workshops. The relationship workshops John Gray offered certainly helped his book, *Men Are From Mars, Women Are From Venus* (HarperCollins,1992), climb the bestseller list.

Timing is vitally important. A book sells best while it is still perceived by the public and the media as "new." Bookstores' sales systems favor "new and noteworthy" books. In fact, 90 days after the bookseller receives your book, he can return it to the publisher for full credit. If your book isn't selling briskly, the copies that were originally displayed prominently — face out on the eye-level shelves — are moved to the back of the bookstore and shelved spine out far from the customer's line of sight.

Schedule coordination

The publisher carefully coordinates the production schedule of the book with the publicity and media schedule in order to place printed books into the hands of the media with enough lead time to allow for reviews to be written and interviews scheduled. Books must be available in bookstores immediately before the reviews and interviews appear so that when the buzz on the book begins, customers can find it immediately — displayed face out in the front of the store.

Your book arrival

Nothing is quite as exciting as the moment you hold the first printed copy of your book. This initial copy — hot off the press — is sent by your editor along with a note of congratulations. About a week later, your author copies arrive in a carton from the publisher. Place them proudly on your bookshelf. Express mail one to your mother and another to your best friend. Then curl up in a comfortable spot and savor the experience of reading your own published book.

Key dates

Just as a carton of your book arrives at your doorstep, similar cartons filled with your book are traveling all across the country. In fact, publishing companies have a unique system of coordinating bookstore and media book distribution, which hinges on several important dates. Most authors find the terminology of this system extremely confusing. Here's a quick explanation.

- **Bound book date:** The day printed copies of your book are shipped from the printer is called the *bound book date*. These shipments sent directly from the printer are called *bindery shipments*. Bindery shipments go immediately to a list of advance reviewers designated by your publicity department, as well as to the publicity department itself, with the remainder of the books being shipped in bulk to the publisher's warehouse.

Once the full print run of your book arrives in the publisher's warehouse, advance orders are boxed up and ready to ship.

- **Release date:** The day cartons filled with your book actually ship out from the warehouse is called the *release date*. On that day, the boxes are loaded onto trucks and dispatched to stores all across the country — the more remote locations leaving first. Once the boxes arrive at the bookseller or wholesaler, they must be unpacked, counted, and displayed in preparation for publication day. Publishers allow approximately three to four weeks for the shipping, unpacking, and display of books.
- **Onsale date:** This date is when booksellers are officially permitted to place the book on sale. It's usually set for three to four weeks after the release date.
- **Publication date:** Some publishers also announce a publication date roughly six weeks after the release date. This is when most reviews should appear, and author publicity is timed to begin.

A quick course in Web marketing

Web marketing is exploding. What follows is a snapshot of the state of the art, which is subject to constant update and innovation.

Your own Web site

For many authors, the first and most important step is to create a Web site dedicated to you and your book. The options for creating a Web site are vast. You can learn HTML, contract with an Internet Service Provider, or ISP, and hang out your shingle on the World Wide Web. Many authors do this, with varying degrees of success. The trick is to create a site that adds to the information contained in your book and/or engages readers in a dialogue. Some publishers are willing to construct Web sites for individual authors, housed either on the publisher's own ISP or the ISP of the author's choosing.

Attracting eyeballs

In order for your Web site to serve a purpose, it needs to be seen by Web surfers and incite these surfers to action — buying your book. To accomplish this, you need a strategy for attracting viewers to your site and driving sales from your site.

Register your site

Most Web site visitors find the sites via a search engine. They look up whatever interests them and then, if their interest matches a listing on a search engine, they'll click through to the listed site. So the first and most important step in attracting eyeballs to your site is to register your site with a search engine. Simply contact as many search engines as possible.

Here are some good ones to get you started:

- **AltaVista** `www.altavista.digital.com/av/content/addurl.htm`
- **Ask Jeeves** `www.askjeeves.com` (Then send an e-mail requesting that your Web site be listed.)
- **Excite** `www.excite.com/info/add_url`
- **HandiLinks** `www.handilinks.com/addform.htm`
- **Infoseek** `infoseek.go.com/addurl?pg=SumitUrl.html`

- **LinkCentre** linkcentre.com/addurl.html
- **Lycos** www.lycos.com/addasite.html
- **Webcrawler** www.webcrawler.com/WebCrawler/SubmitURLS.html
- **What's New** www.whatsnu.com/add.html
- **Yahoo** www.yahoo.com
- **Google** www.google.com

If you don't have the time or desire to personally register on each search engine, just sign up with Submitit! at www.submitit.com and for a $59 fee, they'll register you on dozens of search engines. Submitit! offers other Web marketing services as well. Visit its site for a full rundown of e-marketing options and fees.

Banner advertising

The most obvious method for attracting eyeballs is with banner advertising. Online ad agencies, like Doubleclick.com, sell programs that place banner ads on selected high-traffic sites for a fee. When a viewer clicks a banner ad, he goes directly back to your site or to the page at an online bookstore where your book is displayed.

Contact fan sites

Another way to attract viewers is to swap links with other sites, arranging to draw eyeballs to your site from, for example, a special-interest site, which attracts viewers who would be interested in your book. If you have a book about Marilyn Monroe, you want links to every Marilyn Monroe fan site.

Direct mail on the Web

There are two pieces to e-mail marketing: You need a list of customers who are likely to buy your book and a message that closes the sale with these customers. Consider working with a professional e-mail marketing firm if you are self-publishing. If you are working with a publishing house, your marketing team can help you develop an appropriate direct e-mail marketing strategy.

Live events

Live events and chats increase awareness of your book and drive potential customers to your Web site or to your book's page on an e-tailer's site. You or your publicist can arrange a live event or chat on one of several major sites that host chats, including AOL, Ivillage, Parent Soup, businessweek.com, and so on.

Bulletin boards

A related technique to live events is to post information about your book and your site at Internet bulletin boards where viewers with a special interest in your topic might frequently visit.

Be a Web expert

The Web is teeming with visible sites where experts dispense advice and information to specialized audiences: askjeeves.com, foreverything.com, and about.com are examples of expert sites. For example, Mary J. Shomon, the about.com expert on thyroid disease, scored a hit with her book, *Living Well with Hypothyroidism: What Your Doctor Doesn't Tell You . . . That You Need to Know* (Avon, 2000). When her book was published, she posted information about the book on all of the relevant bulletin boards, as well as on well-traveled sites dealing with thyroid disease. She also covered the book extensively on her own site at about.com and linked the about.com entry to a sale page for the book on borders.com. As a consequence, the book — in a category where sales generally move at a snail's pace — sold through three large printings within one month of publication.

Print runs

How many copies of your book does the publisher print? As a rule, most firms print enough copies to fill the orders secured by the sales reps, as well as a small overrun quantity. This overrun is used to fill reorders that come in during the first month or so after pub date.

There isn't an industry average print-run quantity. Large publishers that produce 200 to 300 new titles each year may have ten big books with first printings of 100,000 copies or more. These books are the ones you often hear about because they receive the most media attention. However, a 100,000-copy print run is by no means the norm. Most titles enjoy a first printing of between 5,000 and 20,000 copies. If your book is a first novel, expect the publisher to print between 5,000 and 7,500 copies at most. Rest assured, if the first print run sells out quickly, your publisher will go back to press for more copies.

Advertising and co-op

Publishers can advertise your book in two ways: by purchasing consumer ads or a cooperative marketing program.

- *Consumer advertising* is ad space, on radio, TV, or in print, that's paid for directly by the publisher. This kind of advertising is rare in the book industry because of the astronomically high price of ads and the relatively low cost of books. Even if the ad spurs sales, it's virtually impossible for the publisher to make enough money from these book sales to recoup the ad cost. Interestingly though, if your book starts to really sell, publishers do run ads to capitalize on the marketplace enthusiasm.
- *Co-op advertising* is money your publisher pays to a bookseller to perform a variety of marketing activities for your book, including ads, in-store placement, display, signage, and discounting. Most bookstores offer co-op programs, which combine in-store display and/or discounting such as the "new arrival" table at the front of the store and an ad placed by the store in a prominent newspaper or in the store's own catalog. Publishers prefer co-op to consumer advertising because it combines an in-store promotion component with print, radio, TV, and/or online advertising.

Reviews

Reviews announce the arrival of your book and help stimulate consumer recognition and interest. It's common knowledge within the industry that the tone of a review — whether positive or negative — doesn't matter as much as how prominent the review is and what publication it appears in.

Certainly a rave review on the cover of the *New York Times Book Review* or in *Time Magazine* can cause quite a stir and inspire sales. And the more reviews, the better. But less than glowing reviews aren't necessarily a catastrophe. In fact, most people don't read entire reviews: They catch the title and the author and read the first few paragraphs. If it's a topic that interests them, they may pick up the book the next time they're in a bookstore.

If you're wondering how books get selected for review, keep in mind that the process varies drastically from publication to publication. Major book review institutions, like the *New York Times Book Review,* for example, maintain a board of editors who constantly screen forthcoming books and painstakingly match appropriate reviewers to books. In contrast, the book review page at many daily newspapers is usually not as carefully orchestrated. This is due to both the high volume of books reviewed and the managing editor's wide range of responsiblities, which makes for a less systematic process of selection and reviewer assignment.

Be aware of the difference between reviews and "off the book page" coverage. A review treats a book as a type of cultural event, usually in the "arts" or "style" section of a newspaper or magazine. "Off the book page" coverage tends to treat book and author as "news" and can convey much more immediacy and urgency to a reader.

Author appearances

Nobody can sell your book better than you can. Author publicity is the single most effective means of gaining media attention and of stimulating the all-important word of mouth that entices people to buy books. Publicists arrange appearances for authors as soon as books appear in bookstores. Author appearances can take the form of TV, newspaper, or magazine interviews, news coverage, lectures, speeches, and bookstore signings. If your profession includes seminars and speeches, be sure to closely coordinate your schedule with your publicist — she may be able to book media or bookstore appearances in the cities where your business takes you.

Bestseller lists

All sorts of author appearances are known to drive book sales, but highly visible appearances on national televsion shows are more likely to actually stimulate the sort of sales that are detected by a national bestseller list. Booksellers report their sales on a weekly basis to several news organizations including the *New York Times Book Review*, *USA Today*, and *The Wall Street Journal*. Compilers at each news company use these sales reports to assemble and then publish the results in weekly bestseller lists. The bestseller lists show the relative standings of each book in the course of a prior week. What's striking is that these lists rarely agree about the order of the top-selling books.

National and local bestseller lists always reflect the relative sales of books over a specified week; the lists do not reflect cumulative sales of books over the long haul.

Say that after a TV appearance your book starts selling like crazy. Chances are good that it may appear at the bottom of the bestseller list. If this happens, many booksellers immediately reorder your book and place copies in the front of their store, at a discounted, bestseller price. This encourages more sales, which helps your book climb to a higher position on the bestseller list.

Remember that success begets success. So do everything in your power to get out in the marketplace and promote the sales of your book.

Oprah

No one has done more for books, authors, and publishers than Oprah Winfrey has. A book selected by the Oprah Book Club becomes an immediate runaway bestseller. Even a brief appearance on "Oprah" has launched hundreds of bestsellers. Certainly every book publicist in America knows Oprah's address by heart, and almost every new book is sent to her studio with the hope of interesting this powerful media diva.

If Oprah doesn't invite you on her show, don't despair. Publicists can get you on other shows both local and national. However, if Oprah does invite you to appear on her show — kick back and enjoy the surge in your book's sales.

Chapter 20

Publication and Beyond

In This Chapter

- Celebrating your publication
- Tracking sales
- Understanding a royalty statement
- Introducing a new, revised edition
- Planning your next book

Once your book is displayed in stores, you experience the thrill, and maybe the exasperation, of being a newly published author. You and your publisher continue to work toward making your book a success in the marketplace. Few authors realize that getting your book the recognition necessary to generate big sales can be a full-time job.

In this chapter, I explore some of the milestones and challenges of life as a published author. I explore such questions as how to know if your book is selling, is the publisher going back to press, will there be a paperback or revised edition, and do you want to repeat this whole experience again — with your next book.

Publication Day

Congratulations, your book is published! But what, exactly, does that mean? When all aspects of a book launch mesh perfectly, the scenario looks like this: Long in advance of pub date, reviewers and media producers are informed of your book's official publication date and asked to focus their media coverage as close to that date as possible. Book reviews, author interviews, and, if appropriate, articles about the book's newsworthy content should appear within the two weeks following publication. This media onslaught helps drive initial sales and, with luck, gets your book onto the bottom of the bestseller lists. In addition, second serial excerpts — portions of the book that appear in magazines or newspapers after publication — are usually scheduled to appear during this two-week window.

Be aware that all publication experiences aren't orchestrated quite this well. If you find there isn't much media attention surrounding your book's publication, you may need to get some going on your own. Take the initiative.

Sales of your book need to start immediately because booksellers are permitted to return slow-moving titles after only 90 days. That provides plenty of incentive for you to work closely with your publicist during the first few weeks the book is on sale to ensure brisk sales.

Publication parties

Most authors face publication day with excitement, anticipation, and trepidation. What will the reviewers think? Will people buy the book? Will they like it? Will they recommend it to friends? Will it be a bestseller?

Some writers deal with this anxiety by scheduling a wilderness vacation to coincide with pub date. But most writers commemorate publication day with a party — whether it's a gathering of intimates or a major media event complete with A-list celebrities, *People* magazine reporters, and camera crews from the three major networks.

Publication parties vary in scope enormously. Today, publishers are reluctant to throw even the most subdued publication party because of the high cost and low return in terms of book sales. For example, a dinner for 20 at an upscale New York restaurant commemorating the day can cost as much as the purchase of a modest co-op marketing program in one of the major bookselling chains or an ad in your local newspaper. In addition, planning a party can require the time and energy of a skilled publicist whose time could be better spent booking TV and radio interviews for you.

If your book is newsworthy, a publication party attended by national and local TV, radio, and print journalists may be a great way to create a major media event. But most books aren't especially newsworthy, and so it's no surprise that publication parties given by the publisher are on the decline.

Don't expect your publisher to give a party in your honor. But by all means commemorate the day in a way that's meaningful to you — you've worked hard, accomplished a lot, and deserve to celebrate.

Celebrate on the road

Publishers are finding other ways to celebrate a book's publication — ways that positively impact book sales, such as sending authors on the road to talk personally with their audience, offering readings from and insights on the ideas and themes contained within the book. No one's better than the author is at generating excitement around his or her own book. If you really want to be proactive, consider celebrating pub date in a far-flung city where you can reach an audience that may not otherwise know about your book. Call every bookstore in the city or cities you'll be visiting and let them know that you'll be in town and are available to sign copies of your book. Always ask to speak to the manager. Making yourself known to bookstore managers not only alerts booksellers to you and your book, but it may also ensure that they have a generous supply of your book on hand.

Post Publication

The weeks and months after publication is when your book's long-term success is determined. I introduce some of the decisions that you and your publisher may face.

The effects of publicity are cumulative

During the first three months after publication, promoting your book is a full-time job. Most authors don't realize what hard work it is. In fact, many authors assume it's the publicity department's job to promote their book. Luckily, you know this isn't so. A publicist is usually assigned to your book for the two to three weeks immediately following publication and then moves on to another book. Be sure to take full advantage of what the publicist is willing to do for your book and then build your own promotion campaign from there.

Don't get discouraged if, after the first few weeks of nonstop promoting, the results aren't what you hoped. Sometimes sales soar after a phenomenal TV appearance on "Good Morning America" or "Oprah." But more often, the effects of a publicity campaign are slow and cumulative. Reviews in local and national newspapers can help, but these alone may not sell many books. However, say that a woman sees a review and then a week later hears a radio interview with you. Following that, she happens to notice that you're giving a lecture at the downtown community center. She also hears a colleague at work recommending your book and just happens to catch the end of your three-minute spot on the evening news. If that woman walks into a bookstore and sees your book prominently displayed, chances are good she'll buy it.

You can't single out one particular promotional effort as responsible for that sale. So keep in mind that each opportunity to promote your book, no matter how small an audience, makes a difference — even if you don't feel its effects right away. The more exposure you and your book receive, the more people hear about it, and the more likely they are to purchase it.

Ten great freelance publicists

Here is a list of some of the most effective freelance book publicists in the business. Plan on spending between $10,000 to $30,000 plus expenses to hire one of these publicists to orchestrate a full-blown national publicity campaign for your book.

Lisa Ekus Public Relations, Co, LLC, 57 North St., Hatfield, MA 01038; phone 413-247-9325, fax 413-247-9873; e-mail Lisaekus@Lisaekus.com.

Full-service public relations firm, specializing nationally in cookbooks, food products, and chef representation; Media Training and Culinary Partnership programs. Recent campaigns: *Nick Stellino's Family Kitchen* (Putnam, 1999); *Moosewood Restaurant Daily Special* (Clarkson Potter, 1999); and *The Cook and the Gardener* by Amanda Hesser (W.W. Norton, 2000).

Personnel: Lisa Ekus.

Goldberg McDuffie Communications, Inc., 444 Madison Ave., Suite 3300, New York, NY 10022; phone 212-446-5100, fax 212-980-5228; e-mail bookpr@goldbergmcduffie.com.

Full-service public relations and pr firm, specialists in national media. Specializing in literary fiction, serious nonfiction, and business. Recent book campaigns: *Stiffed* by Susan Faludi (Morrow, 1999); *Galileo's Daughter* by Dava Sobel (Walker, 1999); *Africana* by Kwame Anthony Appiah (Editor) and Henry Louis Gates Jr. (editor); and *Ten Things I Wish I'd Known* by Maria Shriver (Warner, 2000).

Personnel: Lynn C. Goldberg (lgoldberg@goldbergmcduffie.com), Camille McDuffie, Grace McQuade, Mark Fortier, and Barbara Cave Henricks.

The Hendra Agency, Inc., 142 Sterling Pl. Brooklyn, NY 11217; phone 718-622-3232 or 212-947-9898, fax 718-622-3322.

Full-service public relations and pr firm, specialists in national media. Experts in business, management, and finance. Recent campaigns: *Global Literacies* by Robert Rosen (Simon & Schuster, 2000); *Reengineering the Corporation* by Michael Hammer and James Champy (HarperBusiness, 1994); *Arc of Ambition* by James Champy and Nitin Nohria (Perseus, 2000); and *Power Plays: Shakespeare's Lessons in Leadership and Management* by John O. Whitney and Tina Packer, (Simon & Schuster, 2000).

Personnel: Barbara J. Hendra, Linn Prentis, Jason Beardsley, Kathleen Crosby, and Jeanne Taylor.

Hilsinger Mendelson, Inc., 245 Fifth Ave., Suite 1401, New York, NY 10016; phone 212-725-7707, fax 212-725-7708; e-mail Hmieast@aol.com.

6100 Wilshire Blvd., Suite 1600, Los Angeles, CA 90048; phone 323-931-5335, fax 323-938-5335; e-mail Hmiwest@aol.com.

Full-service bicoastal public relations firm, specializing in national media, book tours, branding, and crisis management. Recent book campaigns: *The 9 Steps to Financial Freedom* (Crown, 1997) and *The Courage To Be Rich* (Riverhead, 1999) by Suze Orman; *The Horse Whisperer* (Delacorte, 1995; Dell, 1998) and *The Loop* (Delacorte, 1998; Dell, 1999) by Nicholas Evans; and *Until Now* and *Down in the Garden* by Anne Geddes (Cedco, 1999 and 1996).

Personnel: Judy Hilsinger and Sandi Mendelson.

Jericho Communications, Inc., 304 Hudson St., Suite 700, New York, NY 10013; phone 212-645-6900, fax 212-645-5800; e-mail: greg@jerichopr.com.

Full-service public relations and pr firm, specialists in national media. Also specialists for cookbooks, authors, food events, and celebrity chef TV public relations tie-ins. Recent campaigns: *Kitchen Suppers* by Alison Becker Hurt (Doubleday, 1999); *The Road Taken* by Rona Jaffe (Dutton, 2000); and *The Protein Power Life Plan* by Mary Dan Eades and Michael R. Eades (Warner, 2000).

Personnel: Gregory Mowery.

Maryann Palumbo Marketing Concepts, Inc., 304 Hudson St., Suite 700, New York, NY 10013; phone 212-645-8642, fax 212-645-5880; e-mail mpmarkcon@aol.com.

Full-service public relations and pr firm, specialists in national media. Recent book campaigns: *The Guinness Book of World Records* by The Guinness Editorial Staff (Guinness Media, 2000); *Direct From Dell* by Michael Dell with Catherine Fredman (HarperBusiness, 1999); and *The Green Mile* by Stephen King (Pocket Books, 1999).

Personnel: Maryann Palumbo.

Parkhurst Communications, Inc., 132 W. 22nd St., New York, NY 10011; phone 212-675-5650 or toll-free 800-49-BOOKS, fax 212-675-5053; e-mail parkhurstcom@mindspring.com; Web site www.parkhurstcom.com.

Specializes in electronic publicity: the production and syndication of author interviews through radio, TV, and cable outlets in all 50 states. Offers videotape production, media coaching for touring authors, AV presentations, and teleconferencing. Recent book campaigns: *The Girls' Guide to Hunting and Fishing* by Melissa Bank (Viking Press, 1999); *The Perfect Storm* by Sebastian Junger (W.W. Norton, 1997); *I Married A Communist* by Philip Roth (Houghton Mifflin, 1998); and *The Camino* by Shirley MacLaine (Pocket Books, 2000).

Personnel: William Parkhurst, Writer, and Laura Gilley, Producer.

Planned Television Arts, 1110 Second Ave., New York, NY 10022; phone 212-593-5820, fax 212-715-1667; e-mail lastnamefirstinitial@ruderfinn.com.

Full-service public relations and pr firm, specializing in electronic media. Recent book campaigns: *Bridget Jones Diary* by Helen Fielding (Viking Penguin, 1998); *Timeline* by Michael Crichton (Knopf, 1999); and *Pushing The Envelope* by Harvey MacKay (Random House, 1999).

Personnel: Richard Frishman (frishmanr@ruderfinn.com), David Hahn, Hillary Rivman, David Thalberg, and Margaret McAllister.

Selma Shapiro Public Relations, 250 W. 57 St., Suite 2315, New York, NY 10107; phone 212-867-7038, fax 212-315-2324.

Public relations and author pr, specializing in author publicity and public relations for cultural events and institutions. Recent campaigns: National Yiddish Book Center and Koret Jewish Book Awards.

Personnel: Selma Shapiro (selshapiro@aol.com).

Jane Wesman Public Relations, Inc. 928 Broadway, Suite 903, New York, NY 10010; phone 212-598-4440, fax 212-598-4590.

Full-service public relations firm, specializing in all aspects of book publicity. Recent book campaigns: *Murder in Brentwood* by Mark Fuhrman (Regnery, 1997); *Clicking* by Faith Popcorn (HarperBusiness, 1997); and *Who Moved My Cheese?* by Spencer Johnson, M.D. (Putnam, 1998).

Personnel: Jane Wesman, Lori Ames Stuart, and Andrea J. Stein.

Hire your own publicist

Once your publisher-assigned publicist disappears to work on the next book, you may want to consider hiring a freelance publicist. These talented professionals love what they do and can provide the necessary spark to keep you on track in your promotional efforts. They have lots of ideas and tons of enthusiasm. I provide ten especially good ones for you to choose from. Meet with any one of these professionals (see sidebar), and you'll see what I mean.

Sales reports

Once your book goes on sale, everyone you know asks, "How's your book selling?" You'll be astonished and frustrated to discover that it's almost impossible to get an answer to that question during the first few months after publication because even the publisher can't obtain complete sales information.

The publisher certainly knows how many copies of your book shipped out of the warehouse. But beyond that, he knows little. He doesn't know how many copies are selling at the many outlets. And he's aware that any number of copies out in the marketplace can be returned in the near future.

Still, in this age of computers, it's reasonable to expect booksellers to keep close track of sales. And most do. However, booksellers only provide publishers with weekly sales information on the top-selling titles at their stores. They don't provide sales figures on any of the other, lesser selling titles. So, if your book is one of the top 200 or so, your publisher can tell you how many copies are selling in the larger stores that provide reports such as Barnes & Noble, Borders, Amazon, and wholesalers such as Ingram and Baker & Taylor. However, your publisher still doesn't know how your book is selling at independent bookstores across the country.

Try to relax in the knowledge that you can only get a very rough idea of how your book is selling in the first few months. Nobody knows for certain until returns come in — which is usually around the time you receive your first royalty statement — how many copies of your book are sold. So, when people ask, just smile and say, "It's really selling — thanks for taking an interest."

Back to press

In the electronic age, it's easier than ever before to keep track of how your book is doing. Amazon.com tracks and constantly updates the relative sales level of every book displayed on the site. Many authors check their "amazon number" compulsively, tracking the relative popularity of their book 24 hours a day, seven days a week. You'll know for certain that your book is selling briskly when your editor tells you they've gone back to press for another print run. I was thrilled when my editor wrote to tell me, just a month after pub date, that they had ordered a 2,000-copy second printing of my last book, *Dress Your House For Success*. Take this kind of news as verification that your promotional efforts are paying off . . . and keep at it.

A paperback edition

If your book is a hardcover, you may see it enjoy another life as a paperback book. It used to be that most books published in hardcover were, about a year later, published in paperback. That's no longer true. The decision to bring out a paperback edition is based on your book's sales. The more you sell, the better your chance of having your book rejuvenated as either a mass-market or trade paperback. If there's a paperback, you'll have a chance to take part in your book's redesign and another opportunity to get out and promote!

Returns

Contrary to popular belief, the publishing industry's liberal returns policy exists for a very good reason. In fact, it was Simon & Schuster who initiated this policy during the Depression when book sales reached an all-time low. In order to encourage booksellers to take a risk and stock more titles — especially ones by new and unknown writers — Simon & Schuster began offering 100 percent cash back on any of the firm's books that booksellers didn't sell within 90 days. A year later, every publishing company followed suit, and returns have been a reality in the publishing industry ever since. Even today, the return policy encourages booksellers to stock books they may not otherwise order — often helping launch the careers of new and promising writers.

However, keep in mind that this returns policy — which allows booksellers to return any unsold books after 90 days on sale — means that your book isn't actually sold until a customer takes it home.

Royalty statements

Your royalty statement is the only document that provides complete and total sales information about your book. Royalty statements are issued twice a year by your publisher and give a detailed accounting of the sales of your book, the income from licenses sold by the publisher, and the money that's owed you once your advance is earned back. Royalty statements are usually issued in late March for sales and income received during the prior July through December and in late September for sales and income received during the prior January through June.

A royalty statement (see Figure 20-1) is an ongoing tally that begins with the amount of money the publisher advanced to you under the contract. Also shown on the statement are the various royalties negotiated in your contract that may be payable, itemized by category and royalty rate. The statement contains separate entries for hardcover and trade paperback bookstore sales, sales sold at a deep discount, special and premium sales, and so on. Additionally, it gives you an itemized list of income derived from other sources, such as subsidiary rights sales.

ROYALTY STATEMENT

Title:
Press:
ISBN:
List Price:
Pub Date:
Author:
Agent

Reporting Date 10/15/1999
For Sales Month Sep-99
Payment Date 03/31/2000

Reserve Rate: 25.00%
Participation: 100.00%

Channel Sales Type of Transaction	Quantity Shipped	Invoice Amount	Royalty Rate	Royalty Amount	Reserve for Returns	Net Royalty
US Book Sales	482	3,252.83	5.00%	162.64	40.66	121.98
US Book Sales at Discount Over 70%	251	1,224.00	2.50%	30.60	7.65	22.95
Mail Order	2	39.98	5.00%	2.00	0.50	1.50
English Export	835	4,475.28	5.00%	223.76	55.94	167.82
Subtotal				419.00	104.75	314.25

Sub-rights Type of Transaction	Invoice Amount	Royalty Rate	Royalty Amount	Net Royalty
Book Club	550.00	15.00%	82.50	82.50
SubRights	4,300.00	50.00%	2,150.00	2,150.00
Subtotal			2,232.50	2,232.50

Recap of Reserve for Returns

Balance of Reserve for Returns per prior statement	0.00
Plus: increase in Reserves this month	104.75
Less: actual returns this month	0.00
Balance of Reserve for Returns at end of this month	104.75

Recap of Payment to be Received

Royalties earned from channel distribution	314.25
Royalties earned from subsidiary rights	2,232.50
Less outstanding advance/unearned balance	(453.25)
Less: Indexing Fees	0.00
Payment to be received on 31-Mar-00	2,093.50

Figure 20-1: A royalty statement tells you more than just how much money you're making.

Royalty statements are not easy to understand — especially not at first. Publishers have tried to simplify these complicated statements by providing explanatory notes. However, don't be surprised if you can't make sense of your statement. You almost certainly will see columns or items you don't understand. Ask your editor to walk you through each line and explain how it all flows down to the bottom figure. If you still have questions, consult with your accountant. In consultation with your publisher's royalty department, a good accountant should be able to decipher the royalty statement tangle and explain to you what the numbers mean.

If, once you've received professional assistance, you find an error on the statement, you have the right, by contract, to hire an independent auditor to audit the publisher's books. Feel free to exercise this right, but do it in a non-threatening way. You certainly deserve to receive what's owed you, but you don't want to appear suspicious or grasping to your publisher or jeopardize your relationship in any way. Mistakes can happen.

Revised editions

How many times have you seen the words "totally revised," "expanded," or "updated to include . . ." in bold type across a book's jacket? If a paperback edition isn't in the works or your book is already a paperback, suggest creating a revised or updated version. As long as the book's topic is still of interest to readers and sales are strong enough, there's no reason not to continually update, improve, and expand on the success you've created. Whether it entails adding a new chapter, hiring a celebrity expert to write an introduction, or just updating and freshening the existing text, it translates into more income for you and your publisher.

Remainder

Over time, demand for your book may slow considerably — so much so that your publisher may feel it's no longer worthwhile to relegate precious warehousing space to its storage. When this happens, the publisher notifies you that they are *remaindering* your book or offering it for sale at a huge discount to a remainder house, which resells it at a bargain price. If you want to purchase some copies of your book before it's remaindered, let your editor know. The publisher is obliged, usually by contract, to offer you the same price it offers the remainder house.

Some writers wonder how many copies of their book to buy at a remainder sale. The answer depends on what you want to do with the books and how many are available. If the book is part of your business — say, for example, you're a decorator or consultant — you should purchase a large enough quantity to serve your business for the foreseeable future. If you want only enough to give to friends and family, a hundred copies is plenty. Remember, this is your last chance. It's a good idea to stockpile a reasonable number, as many as you can comfortably store, for future use.

If your book is remaindered or the publisher chooses not to reprint it once stock is gone, it is considered officially *out of print,* meaning that books are no longer available from the publisher.

Once your book goes out of print, ask the publisher to revert the rights to you. Your contract has a reversion-of-rights clause that stipulates when the book goes out of print or if the publisher fails to reprint the book within a certain amount of time, all rights revert to the author. It's best to ask for an official letter from the publisher stating that the rights to your work have been reverted to you on said date in order to avoid any problem. The book's contents are now fully owned by you, to exploit as you see fit. See Chapter 13 for publishing your own edition of the book either on the Web, in print, or as a print-on-demand book.

Moving On

For some writers, writing one book is more than enough. They've said what they wanted to say, spent plenty of time on the road getting their message out to the masses, and are ready to move on to other pursuits. If this is you, feel proud of your accomplishment. You have a lasting symbol of all your hard work and dedication — a published book.

If you want to continue your career as a writer, consider coming up with a sequel or perhaps building a series of books around the first. Chances are if your first book sells well (15,000 or more copies), your editor will suggest you do another, possibly similar, type of book. Of course, it's up to you to decide whether you want to continue in the same vein or break out in a new direction.

Either way, with a published book under your belt, it's much easier to get another one successfully published. You know exactly what publishers are looking for. Build on this specialized knowledge using all that you've learned. Refrain from blaming your publisher for ruining your shot at the bestseller list. Too many authors berate their publisher for low sales, claiming either that the jacket was all wrong, or there weren't enough books in stores, or the publicist didn't care about the book, or the editor left in the middle. Maybe that's all true. But sitting around complaining doesn't help matters. Dust yourself off and get back to work.

Check out some of the inspirational sources for book ideas I mention in Chapter 1. Open yourself up to what's going on around you: in your home, your neighborhood, and the world. Take classes, indulge a passion, collect fascinating pieces of information, identify a need, and most importantly of all, live life to its fullest. Readers are looking for a compelling voice, the voice of a person who has experienced many aspects of life and has something to say about it.

Enjoy your work. Hard and frustrating as it sometimes is, I can't imagine any other career choice. I wrote this book to share what I have learned about publishing books and getting my own books published. Getting published has nothing to do with luck, and everything to do with knowing how to present your book to a publishing company so that it feels certain that it can make some money with it. Publishing is, after all, a business. Congratulations. You've made it your business to learn the business of book publishing.

Part VII
The Part of Tens

"If you must know, the reason you're not in any of my novels is that you're not a believable character."

In this part . . .

Readers who are familiar with the *For Dummies* series know that near the end of every book, you find a bunch of top-ten lists. In this part, I've put together a list of the top ten best-selling books of all time, ten excuses publishers give for turning down book proposals and what you can do about them, ten clauses to watch in your contract, and ten common errors in dealing with an agent or author after your book has been accepted.

Chapter 21

Ten Excuses Publishers Give for Turning Down Book Proposals

In This Chapter

- Familiarizing yourself with major complaints
- Understanding what a rejection letter is actually saying
- Turning constructive criticism to your advantage

Rejection letters actually contain important clues as to how you can improve your submission materials before sending them to another publisher. Keep in mind that you should never resubmit your updated proposal or sample chapters to the same editor unless specifically asked to do so. Here are ten reasons publishers give for turning down your submission and what you can do to alleviate the problem and ensure a better outcome.

Your Subject Isn't Suitable

If a publisher says that the subject of the book isn't suitable for its list or for its firm's needs, you may not have done enough research or you sent your proposal to the wrong editor.

We Already Have a Book Like This One

If you hear this response, you have come across an important clue. Find out more about the other similar book. Chances are that other publishers also considered it, and when you submit your proposal to these other publishers, you want to be able to explain how your book is different from and better than the book that's somewhat similar to yours.

A Similar Book Didn't Do Well

The publisher may say that it, or one of its competitors, published a book similar to this last year, and there wasn't much of an audience. Again, get details on the similar book. When you submit elsewhere, you need to show why your book will succeed where that other one failed.

You Aren't Enough of an Authority

The publisher may not think you possess sufficient authority to be credible with readers. This problem may be a big one, but it can also mean that the section of the proposal describing your platform isn't doing you justice. Rewrite it, proving why you're the right writer/expert for the job.

You Don't Possess the Skills to Write This Book

If the publisher doesn't think that you possess the necessary ability to write this book, this feedback, especially if you've heard it before, may mean that the writing sample in your proposal needs more work. Schedule a consult with a professional proposal writer.

Your Proposal Is Not Well Written

Again, if you get this response, you may need help from a professional proposal writer.

The Audience Isn't Large Enough

This response means that the marketing section of your proposal needs work. Perhaps your conception of the book needs adjustment, or you need to target a different publisher.

The Book Doesn't Offer a Sufficient Promise to Readers

This feedback is very helpful. Certain kinds of nonfiction books must make a promise to readers, a kind of value proposition. With diet books, for example, the value proposition is to lose weight. Make sure that your book's promise or value proposition is presented clearly and invitingly.

Your Book Is Too Expensive

If the publisher says it's looking for books of this type, but the one you propose is too expensive to produce, you have a simple problem to solve: You just need to reconceive your book so that it's simpler and cheaper to produce.

The Format Isn't Appealing

If you're told that your book contains the right content but that the format isn't appealing to readers, you can solve this problem by scheduling a session with a professional editor and designer.

Chapter 22

Ten Clauses to Watch in Your Contract

In This Chapter

- Knowing what's important
- Understanding what the important clauses are saying
- Making the contract work for you

A publishing contract is a lengthy, technically worded document that can be difficult enough to understand, much less know, which clauses to focus your energies on. Here are ten especially important clauses that need special attention when you read and negotiate your contract.

The Payout: Time Is Money

Publishers try to hang on to their money as long as possible — they'd rather not pay out your advance until they start selling books. You, on the other hand, need money to live on while you're writing. Don't sign a deal that compromises your ability to do good work by causing undue hardship while you research and write your book.

Royalty Rate: It Adds Up

The royalty rate determines how much money you earn for as long as the book is in print. While the royalty rate may seem like an abstraction until after the book is published, it's important to make sure that you're receiving the industry standard rate (see Chapter 16).

Deep Discount: Don't Get Sunk

Publishers are compelled to accept deep discount terms from certain kinds of retail accounts, such as warehouse clubs, and they attempt to pass these discounts along to you. Be sure that the contract is explicit about exactly how your royalty rate is to be diminished by deep discounts.

Delivery: Know What You Can Do

It takes time to write a book — don't put yourself under impossible deadline pressure. Make sure that you can write the entire book by the delivery date.

Territory: It's a Big World

The territory specifies the countries where your publisher has the exclusive right to sell or license your book. If you are represented by a literary agent, your agent will advise you on which territories should be withheld from your publisher. If you don't have an agent, grant world rights to your publisher — you probably won't have the contacts to sell the foreign rights on your own.

Sub Rights Split: Know What's Fair

When your publisher licenses the right for your book's contents to appear in a magazine article, book club edition, or paperback reprint edition, the contract stipulates how the proceeds are to be divided. Study the industry standards for these splits and don't settle for less than the standard rate (see Chapter 16).

Permissions Cost: Let the Publisher Pay

If your book contains artwork, excerpts from other books, or song lyrics, permission fees may have to be paid for the right to reprint these materials. Most contracts require the author to pay all of these costs. If you anticipate a lot of permissions fees, try to persuade the publisher to pay this cost.

Right of Termination: Be Vigilant about First Proceeds

Carefully read the "right of termination" section in the contract. This language becomes especially important if you or your publisher decides not to go forward with the book (see Chapter 16). Be vigilant about what's called the *first proceeds* language because it determines whether you keep the money advanced to you or not.

For example, say that you write the book and deliver the manuscript on time. For whatever reason, the publisher decides that the book is not acceptable and, after working with you to revise the manuscript, decides to cancel your contract. If a first proceeds provision is in the contract, you get to keep whatever money has been advanced to you by the publisher. If no first proceeds language is present, you may be required to return to the publisher whatever money has been advanced to you so far. This language means that you have researched and written the whole manuscript gratis — not a very appealing prospect.

Option: Don't Be Tied and Bound

The option clause focuses on your next book. Ideally, you should have the choice of selling it to any publisher. But, in fact, most publishers require a clause in the contract that compels you to show the proposal for your new book to your old publisher before showing it to any other publisher. Option clauses vary, and you probably can't avoid the clause entirely, but you can limit it.

For example, the option clause should require the submission of only a proposal, not a complete manuscript. You shouldn't have to wait longer than 30 days after your present book has been accepted for publication before submitting your new proposal for consideration. If you and your current publisher don't come to terms, you should be free and clear to sell it elsewhere — no topping or matching language should bind you any further.

Electronic Rights: The Wave of the Future

Watch this clause carefully. Some publishers are treating income from e-books as a royalty, with the author receiving 15 percent of the list price; others are treating it as a licensing deal, with the publisher and author splitting the income 50/50. One increasingly common compromise is for the author to receive 25 percent of the retail e-book price.

Chapter 23

Ten Common Errors in Dealing with an Agent and/or Editor

In This Chapter

- Anticipating conflicts in the publication process
- Improving your working relationships
- Having realistic expectations

Once the contract is signed and your book is in progress, your agent and editor can be two vital allies on the road toward publication. If you anticipate some of the potential rough spots and successfully avert these common errors, you can be assured of a happier publishing experience.

Promise a Deadline and Fail to Meet It

Take care to work out your deadlines, in consultation with your editor and your agent, and then stick by them. Every deadline you miss erodes your overall credibility.

Drop in Unexpectedly without an Appointment

People in publishing live on carefully orchestrated schedules; their days are ruled by meetings and are planned. Unexpected visits can create havoc and undermine the very purpose you had in mind — to arrange a better outcome for your book and a better relationship with your editor or agent.

Get Defensive and Debate Editorial Suggestions

Feeling defensive when you get editorial feedback is natural. And in the end, you may decide that you cannot accept your editor's or your agent's advice uncritically. But most editorial feedback is professional and objective and meant to improve the quality of your work. If you get defensive, you may not benefit from some very sound advice.

Rewrite Your Manuscript in First-Pass Pages

Once your book is in first-pass pages, your publisher is committed on length, press time, and scheduling. Substantial editorial changes at this stage can imperil your schedule and potentially undermine the success of your book. Set aside time to make corrections in the copy-edited version of the manuscript before first-pass pages.

Wait to Fill Out Your Bio Form

Turn in your author bio form when you turn in your manuscript. Don't wait until the week before publication.

Disappear

Don't leave for a month-long vacation in Bali, shortly after delivering your manuscript, without inquiring about the delivery date of the copy-edited manuscript. Ask for a detailed production schedule when you hand in your edited manuscript, knowing you'll be needed to make corrections at fairly regular intervals in the months thereafter.

When Sales Conference Looms, Lie about Your Schedule

Don't commit to delivering your late manuscript on the eve of sales conference when it is going to be presented and then announce two weeks later that you will miss the deadline by six months, thereby forcing your editor to present the book at sales conference, and then announce a delay.

If your manuscript is presented at sales conference, your publisher's reps will begin to present it to booksellers within the following week. If the book is then delayed due to your late delivery, the booksellers will receive the unspoken message — perhaps inaccurate but still unavoidable — that your book is in trouble. If you are in danger of missing your deadline before sales conference, take the safe course and ask for an extension.

Speak at Sales Conference

Don't convince the publisher to let you speak at sales conference, unless you're a seasoned pro on the lecture circuit. If you're not an experienced speaker, sales conference is a dangerous place. For every author that improves his or her book's prospects with a sales conference speech, a dozen actually undermine their prospects.

Cancel a Promotional Appearance on Short Notice

Nothing undermines a publicity tour like an author canceling on short notice. Don't do it unless you're terribly, terribly ill.

Allow Conflicts with Your Publisher to Fester

Speak up and deal directly with issues as they arise. Often a simple explanation from your editor or agent can clear up any misunderstandings.

Chapter 24

Ten Top-Selling Books of All Time

In This Chapter

- Knowing what sells best
- Looking at the top selling books

The bestseller list is a good place for first-time writers to find inspiration; this bestseller list — the top sellers of all time — is perhaps the greatest inspiration of all. The range of topics is amazing, from spirituality, to politics, to education and reference, to sex and scandal. It's amazing that many of the biggest selling books of all time continue to sell well in today's market.

1. Holy Bible King James Version

First published in 1611 as the "First Edition of the Authorized Version," the *Holy Bible King James Version* (Viking Press, 1999) is the first translation of the Holy Scripture into modern English. It is still far and away the world's most widely distributed book with more than six billion copies sold.

2. Quotations from Chairman Mao Tse-Tung by Mao Tse-Tung

The book that shaped a generation of Chinese and changed the world is still in print with China books. Literally hundreds of millions of copies of Mao's famous *Little Red Book,* as it is widely described, have been distributed in dozens of languages. The current edition, available from China Books & Periodicals, 1990, is a facsimile of the 1972 edition (out of print in China for some time), containing the essence of Mao's philosophy, political thinking, and military strategy. More than 800 million copies have been distributed to date.

3. The American Spelling Book by Noah Webster

Originally published in 1788 and bound in a distinctive blue cover, *The American Spelling Book* by Noah Webster (Applewood Books, 1999) earned the nickname "the blue-backed speller." The Webster spelling primer, with 100 million in print, was used by American children as the standard spelling text for nearly a century.

4. Guinness 2000 Book of Records: Millennium Edition

In continuous publication for 35 years, this popular reference work has grown from 198 pages in the original 1955 edition to 580 pages today and is filled with amazing facts and figures from around the world. Having sold over 81 million copies, it's currently being published by Guinness Media Inc., 1999.

5. McGuffeys First Eclectic Reader, by J. E. Thompson, William Holmes McGuffey

McGuffeys First Eclectic Reader is the book that taught America to read. Originally published in 1879 and distributed in many editions to millions of school children, *McGuffeys First Eclectic Reader* has been called "the most influential book in the history of American education." Still in print with John Wiley & Sons, 1997, *McGuffey's First Eclectic Reader* has sold well over 60 million.

6. A Message to Garcia by Elbert Hubbard

This famous motivational story became an international phenomenon in the early 20th century. It describes a wartime incident of a young officer trusted to carry a message to a remote commander. Currently published by Peter Pauper Press, 1983, *A Message to Garcia* has sold approximately 50 million copies.

7. World Almanac and Book of Facts 2000

First published by the New York World-Telegram in 1947, the *World Almanac* became an American institution that has been the main resource for millions of student papers and has helped resolve untold arguments about the highest mountain, most populous state, and more. With sales of more than 40 million copies during its lifetime, the current *World Almanac and Book of Facts* is published by the World Almanac, 1999.

8. Dr. Spock's Baby and Child Care by Benjamin Spock, Steven Parker, Stephen Parker

Originally published in 1945, *Dr. Spock's Baby and Child Care* became the pocket bible for the postwar generation of American parents. Spock's book — still the most popular pediatric health reference in America — is a commonsense guide to the health and care of children. Currently published by Pocket Books, the book's cumulative sales figures have reached over 39 million.

9. Valley of the Dolls: A Novel by Jacqueline Susann

Originally published in 1966 by Bernard Geis Associates, *Valley of the Dolls,* by Jacqueline Susann, told the story of three women fighting to the top of showbiz. It's currently being published by Grove Press, 1997, and boasts sales of more than 30 million copies.

10. In His Steps "What Would Jesus Do?" by Charles Monroe Sheldon

Written by a Congregational minister in Topeka, Kansas, and first published in 1897, this classic novel, which depicts the members of a small town church who dare to live their lives for Christ, has inspired generations of believers. Currently published by Inspirational Press (1998), more than 28.5 million copies have been sold to date.

Index

• A •

• B •

• D •

• I •

• J •

• K •

• L •

• N •

• O •

• P •

• T •

• U •

• V •

• W •

• X •

• Y •

• Z •

Notes